CONTROLLING SOVIET LABOUR

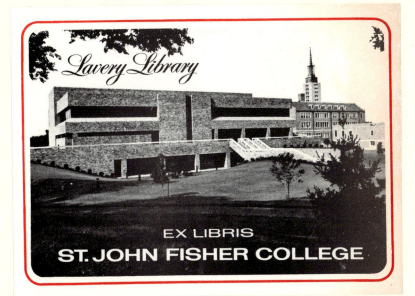

Controlling Soviet Labour

Experimental Change from Brezhnev to Gorbachev

Bob Arnot

M. E. SHARPE, INC.
ARMONK, NEW YORK

First published in the United States of
America in 1988 by M. E. Sharpe, Inc.

Printed and bound in Great Britain

Library of Congress Cataloging-in-Publication Data
Arnot, Robert.
Controlling Soviet labour.
Bibliography: p.
Includes index.
1. Labor supply—Soviet Union.   2. Soviet Union—
Economic conditions—1976–   3. Manpower policy—
Soviet Union.   I. Title.
HD5796.A76   1988   331.12′042′0947   87–32364
ISBN 0–87332–470–6

For Georgie and Julie

Contents

List of Figures and Tables

Preface

This book is a revised and updated version of work carried out at the Institute of Soviet and East European Studies, Glasgow University. I would like to acknowledge the practical assistance I have received. Firstly, from the SSRC, who provided a two year grant at the beginning of this work and secondly, from my colleagues in the Department of Economics at Glasgow College of Technology, who enabled me to have one term of study leave to complete the work.

I would like to thank Hillel Ticktin who supervised my work. It was a course of his lectures that originally stimulated my interest in this area and his continual assistance and support were invaluable in completing this book. Also I would like to acknowledge the assistance of everyone connected with the journal *Critique* who has provided both encouragement and criticism over the past ten years. Scott Meikle, Sandy Smith, Mick Cox, Bohdan Krawchenko, Michael Vale, Suzi Weissman and Don Filtzer have all participated in discussions that have directly or indirectly influenced this book. Clearly none of these named individuals are responsible for any errors that may remain.

My biggest debt is to those people who are closest to me. To Georgie and Julie I have to give the customary author's apology for lost weekends and late nights. Without their patience and support this book would never have been completed.

Glasgow   BOB ARNOT

Glossary

blat	Refers to the use of personal influence or favours to gain access to goods or services to which either the individual or enterprise is not legally entitled (see Berliner, 1957, p.182)
CMEA	Council for mutual economic assistance (COMECON)
Goskomsel'khoztekh-niki	The state committee for the production of agricultural equipment
Gosplan	The state planning committee of the USSR
Gossnab	The state committee for material and technical supply
ITR (inzhenerno-technicheskie rabotniki) staff	Engineers and other technical staff
khozraschet	Literally 'economic' or 'profit and loss' accounting. It implies the principle of being self-financing, and may be applied to an enterprise, brigade (or, indeed, any work unit)
Komsomol	The Young Communist League
KTU (koeffitsient trudovogo uchastiya)	Coefficient of labour participation used in the calculation of the individual brigade member's wage
NEP	The 'New Economic Policy' (1921–9) which contained an uneasy mixture of market and planned forms of allocation
nomenklatura	The party-controlled appointments list which determines all key jobs (for example, enterprise directors)
NOT (nauchnaya organizatsiya truda)	The scientific organisation of labour

Raion	Administrative district
Ratchet principle	Or 'planning from the achieved level': the idea that past plan performance provides the base line for uprating new plan targets
Storming	The completion of any planned tasks (either monthly or annual) at the last moment by intensive use of equipment and overtime working. Part of the general arrhythmic pattern of Soviet production
Techpromfinplan	The enterprise technical, industrial and financial plan

Introduction

This book is concerned with a series of issues that lie at the heart of contemporary Soviet economic problems and policy. According to western press assessments, since Mikhail Gorbachev has come to power his central concern has been the need to modernise and reform the Soviet economy. However, these concerns and the efforts they have engendered are not particularly new. The necessity for reform has been long recognised within the USSR and, furthermore, many of the initiatives that have been either implemented or discussed by Gorbachev have their roots in similar experimental initiatives undertaken by his predecessors from the late sixties onwards. This book seeks to explain why these experimental initiatives were necessary and will provide an assessment of a number of them, concentrating especially on the Shchekino experiment. The necessity for such experimentation and the longer-term experience of the experiments, will be utilised as an illustration of the distinctive nature of the political economy of the USSR. Furthermore, the impact of these older experiments indicates the possibilities of success for Gorbachev's reform initiatives and illustrates the potential problems which ultimately they will have to address.

The aims of Part I are to explain the interrelationship between the social relations of production in the USSR and current socio-economic problems, and to provide a theoretical underpinning to the later work on the experimental initiatives. These introductory chapters will illustrate the problems that made the experimental initiatives necessary and will highlight the features of the political economy of the USSR that made the Shchekino experiment so important. The adequacy of the political economy provided can be gauged by its ability to explain and evaluate the latter empirical sections that relate to the experiments.

It will be argued that the problems facing the ruling group in the USSR in the sixties necessitated, from their point of view, the implementation of a package of economic reforms and the Shchekino experiment, its variants and the later experimental initiatives, were part of that general movement.[1] From 1965 onwards the general thrust of the reforms has been interpreted by western commentators as economic. Berliner (1983, p.353) for example, points out that the 1965 Reform was the first reform in which economists, rather than planners and politicians, had a hand. The reforms were directed at specific

1

problems connected with the efficiency of the resource allocation mechanism. Indeed, from Liberman's articles onwards (Liberman, 1966), the belief, shared by both western pro-market reform economists (Nove, 1980, pp.325–7) and their Soviet counterparts, was that by resolving microeconomic inefficiencies a way could be found to resolve macroeconomic problems, specifically the deterioration of economic performance and declining rates of economic growth.

This was to be achieved by the technical manipulation of the 'mix' between planning and the role of market forces. The effort was directed particularly at the level of relationships between enterprises, ministries and the central planning agencies, and between enterprises themselves. This was seen to be particularly important in the face of growing consumer demands and discontent and the increasing resource needs of industrial, agricultural, space and military sectors. If a renewal of high growth rates could be achieved, then the ruling group would be able to assuage domestic discontent and maintain and reproduce their own social position.

However, this is a partial view of the problem which cannot be simply described as technical and economic, amenable to resolution by better systems of material supply or more elaborate incentive systems. The problems are more correctly identified as socio-economic and systemic. The cause of these problems should be located in the antagonistic nature of the social relations of production in the USSR and the specific effects these relationships have on the process of surplus extraction. This process, as will be argued in Part I, is not regulated and equilibriated in the same way as the labour process under the capitalist mode of production, but is subject to its own contradictory dynamics. The ruling group in the USSR is not able to utilise the same forms of control which are available to their counterparts under the capitalist mode of production. The specific nature of the Soviet economy, and the problems it faces, makes it necessary for the Soviet ruling group to adopt piecemeal, market-oriented reforms, in an attempt to gain some control and predictability over the magnitude and quality of the socially-produced surplus. This is the importance of the experimental initiatives, which will be explained as attempts by the Soviet ruling group to assert control over the labour process and the industrial labour force, with the intention of raising the rate of exploitation and thereby securing a growth in the relative surplus.

Part II deals with the experimental initiatives in more detail and concentrates particularly on the Shchekino experiment. The initial intention is to evaluate the specific reasons for its implementation, to outline the mechanisms adopted and the idealised form it was intended to take, and to detail its early apparent successes. Some consideration is also given to the variants of the experiment that emerged in this early period. An explanation is suggested for the initial successes that differs from both the usual western and Soviet interpretations. This explanation, based on the question of worker job security, is used to evaluate the longer term experience of the experiment, suggesting that after its initial implementation, significant problems exist in maintaining the momentum of the experiment.

Part II goes on to deal with the attempted generalisation of the experiment, with the aim of explaining why an apparently successful experiment, supported by both state and party, failed to achieve the expected radical transformation of Soviet industry. It is suggested that the reason for this is that the antagonisms and contradictions that made this experiment necessary for the ruling group in the first place also modify and undermine such attempted experimentation. Furthermore, the logic of the experiment is at odds with the principles of the planning mechanism, and the implementation of the experiment ultimately undermines individual enterprise performance.

The final chapter of Part II identifies other experimental initiatives which have been attempts to introduce complementary changes, concentrating particularly on the brigade form of labour organisation. The early period of this initiative is considered, along with other attempts to raise the level of work norms. From a survey of the experience of these initiatives, it is suggested that a similar range of problems and a similar pattern of growth and decline, evident in the case of the Shchekino experiment, can be identified.

The experience of all these experimental initiatives shows the difficulties of grafting piecemeal, market reforms onto the Soviet economic mechanism. This question is taken up in the concluding chapter, which considers Gorbachev's policy options. This chapter calls into question the possibility of a transition to a market socialist solution for the Soviet economy and, by extension, questions the prospects of any form of market socialism.

It is desirable at this point to say something about the approach and methodology adopted. The aim is to establish a conceptual framework that is based upon, rather than avoids, the contemporary socio-economic problems of the USSR. This conceptual framework can then be illustrated more clearly by its application to the empirical realities of the experimental initiatives.[2] This approach seeks to avoid the mechanical transposition of a particular theoretical viewpoint onto the Soviet

Union, so common within both western Marxist and more orthodox writings on the USSR, and recognises that it is insufficient to develop theoretical formulations in isolation from the empirical realities of the USSR.[3] Attitudes towards these fundamental questions of political economy colour all academic work, and whilst it is not my intention to tread the well-worn path of comparing, contrasting and criticising the various theoretical perspectives, it is necessary to outline clearly the theoretical origins of the book.

This book reflects two particular theoretical trends. Firstly, it reflects the work that has accompanied the resurgence of interest in the capitalist labour process evident over the last decade or so.[4] These debates have provided theoretical and conceptual insights in their analysis of capitalism that are far more convincing than the work of both neo-classical economists and their counterparts in sociology. Taking this focus of attention on the labour process as the starting point enables significant comparison to be made with the Soviet Union. However, writers in this tradition have had little to say on the Soviet Union, and when they have, it has been coloured by their limited empirical knowledge. For example Braverman (1974, p.14) argues, 'that the organisation of labour in the Soviet Union differs little from the organisation of labour in capitalist countries'.[5] Superficially, this viewpoint appears to be supportable because a number of features can be identified in the USSR that appear to replicate elements of the capitalist mode of production. For example the replication of the technical division of labour experienced under capitalism, the hierarchical nature of factory relations, similar forms of payment by time and by piece, and so on. However, this needs further consideration. It is not the appearance of the phenomena that is important but their social context, role and their interaction within the broader political economy of the USSR. Once this is identified, then the underlying differences emerge and invest a completely different meaning to the apparently similar features. This will be elaborated upon in Part I, particularly with regard to the nature of money and the role of wages, incentives, and so on.

Secondly, the perspective adopted rests heavily on the theoretical work connected with the journal *Critique* and particularly the work of H. H. Ticktin.[6] In its broadest sense, the argument developed is that the methodology of Marxist political economy can provide the basis for understanding non-capitalist, social formations. This differs from the view adopted by more orthodox western academics who argue, usually on the basis of an inadequate appreciation of the methodology of

Marxist political economy, that it has no explanatory value in the context of the USSR. This book takes the theoretical perspective developed by Ticktin as its starting point and applies it to the specific questions of the labour process, control over the workforce and the potentiality for reform involved in the experimental initiatives. In this sense, Part I is both a restatement and an extension of this theoretical perspective and Part II is an attempt to apply this to the concrete problems of experimental initiatives.

Not surprisingly, a number of features of the Soviet economy discussed in this book will be familiar from the work of other western writers.[7] However, their approach and explanation, often reflecting a background in western neo-classical economics, tends to remain at the level of 'economic relationships' and either ignores or minimises the importance of the underlying social relations of production. I believe that by shifting the focus of analysis to the labour process a more adequate understanding of the political economy of the USSR can be presented and the attempts at reform can be placed in context.

Finally, the view adopted throughout this book is that economic systems are impossible to comprehend within the watertight boundaries of academic disciplines. Consequently, I have sought to ignore the false divide between the economic, the political and the sociological, as much in evidence in Soviet academic work as it is in the west.

Part I

Social Relations of Production and Economic Problems in the USSR

1 The Surplus and Class Structure

The aim of political economy is to explain the predominant mode of production within the socio-economic system under consideration; to explain how it has developed, how it presently functions and how it may develop in the future. It is, therefore, an attempt to comprehend a dynamic process which is neither finished nor static, but is characterised by motion and change. Furthermore, the subject matter is often contradictory and complex, with superficial similarities to other periods of time and other social systems. It is for this reason that the mechanical transposition of categories from one social system to another, on the basis of little or one-sided empirical knowledge, as already noted, is doomed to failure. However, there are elements of methodology which are ahistorical and applicable to all epochs, and from a Marxist perspective these provide the starting point.

The key to understanding the nature of the social system and its mode of production is the socially produced surplus (Marx, 1983, p. 85). This is based upon the notion that purposive human activity, particularly when carried out in cooperation with others, acts upon nature and can produce more than is necessary to simply reproduce human life (Marx, 1977a, p. 315; 1977c, p. 818). Marx (1977a, pp. 208–9) identifies, as a consequence, a division within labour time between necessary labour (necessary labour time), that is, labour socially necessary to reproduce the direct producer, and surplus labour (surplus labour time), that is labour over and above necessary labour, when the direct producer produces not for himself but for another or others. This idea of a socially produced surplus, based upon surplus labour time, is therefore, according to Marx, a non-historical category (1977c, p. 819).

Capital has not invented surplus labour. Wherever a part of society possesses the monopoly of the means of production, the labourer, free or not free, must add to the working time necessary for his own maintenance an extra working time in order to produce the means of subsistence for the owners of the means of production (1977a, p. 226).

The basic antagonistic relationship, therefore, in any hierachically structured social system, is between the direct producers of the surplus and the controllers of the surplus once extracted. This relationship is fundamental to all hitherto known class societies. However, the actual form of surplus extraction will differ between different historical modes of production.

The essential difference between the various economic forms of society, between for instance, a society based upon slave labour, and one based upon wage labour, lies only in the mode in which this surplus labour is in each case extracted from the actual producer, the labourer (Marx, 1977a, p. 209).

The nature of the extraction of the surplus will provide the general contours of the social system, its class structure.

The specific economic form, in which unpaid surplus labour is pumped out of direct producers, determines the relationship of rulers and ruled, as it grows directly out of production itself, and in turn, reacts upon it as a determining element (Marx, 1977c, p. 791).

For example, in societies based upon slavery the extraction of the surplus is direct and unfetishised, because the direct producers are the property of the class owners and function simply as an instrument of production (Marx, 1977a, p. 191; 1983, p. 98). The surplus is extracted in a relationship ultimately based upon force and the class structure can be identified around this process, slave and non-slave. As Marx (1977a, p. 505) points out, it appears as if the whole of the slave's labour is unpaid work for the master and the onus is on the master to provide for the slave's reproduction. The relationship is one of complete dependency. In the end, any slave failing to fulfil his or her economic function can simply be disposed of and replaced, as well as being subject to barbarous conditions whilst working.

Under feudalism the nature of the surplus extraction process changes but is still direct and non-fetishised. As Marx (1977a, p. 81) suggests, under feudalism, 'we find everyone dependent, serfs and lords, vassals and suzerains, laymen and clergy. Personal dependence characterises the social relations of production'. Here the surplus is extracted via the medium of compulsory labour. The dependent labourer can clearly identify the magnitude of both surplus labour time, expended working for the owner of land (whether Lord or clergy), and the necessary labour time spent reproducing his own existence. There may develop a degree of independence within the surplus extraction process, which may even allow the labourer to generate a surplus of his own, but this is ultimately dependent upon his relationship with his master (Marx, 1977c, p. 790). This does differentiate the serf from the slave, but ultimately, both slave and serf labour can be viewed as 'an inorganic condition of production' (Marx, 1983, p. 489) and subject to the ultimate sanction of force to maintain their position in the surplus extraction process. It is only with the onset of the capitalist mode of production that these relationships are fundamentally changed.

Under the capitalist mode of production, the question of the surplus is more veiled than under previous modes of production. Capitalism relies not upon relationships of dependency but on particular forms of non-dependency, or freedoms: 'the economic structure of capitalist society has grown out of the economic structure of feudal society. The dissolution of the latter set free the elements of the former' (Marx, 1977a, p. 668). Free labourers, as Marx (1977a, p. 166) points out, are free in a double sense. They are no longer part of the means of production (as were slaves and serfs) but equally they do not own their own means of production. Their freedom from the fetters of feudalism also frees them from 'all the guarantees of existence afforded by the old feudal arrangements' (Marx, 1977a, p. 669). Consequently, capitalism ends dependency, custom and external extra-economic force as arbiters in the surplus extraction process, but it does not end that process itself, it simply transforms it, 'replacing feudal exploitation with capitalist exploitation' (Marx, 1977a, p. 669).

The free labourer, who is no longer an element of production, is, however, unable to make his labour concrete either in use-values to guarantee his own existence or in commodities to sell. As a consequence, to maintain his daily existence he is forced, (not by custom or direct force but by economic necessity), to sell the one commodity which he possesses, his capacity to work or labour power. This is sold to the owners of the means of production, for a specified period of time, in a freely contracted exchange.

The historical conditions of its [capital's] existence are by no means given with the mere circulation of money and commodities. It can spring to life only when the owner of the means of production and subsistence meets in the market with the free labourer selling his labour power (Marx, 1977a, p. 167).

Labour power, however, is a peculiar commodity. It has an exchange value, determined by the socially necessary labour-time needed for its production and reproduction, but its use-value to the capitalist is its capacity to produce a surplus:

> The value of labour power and the value that labour power creates in the labour process, are two entirely different magnitudes; and this difference of the two values was what the capitalist had in view, when he was purchasing the labour power (Marx, 1977a, p. 188).

In other words, the capitalist mode of production provides an economic motivation to both worker and capitalist. For one, necessity born out of freedom provides the impetus for alienated labour. For the other the desire to accumulate surplus value and capital is equally a necessity, because failure to do so threatens the individual capitalist's existence as an independent unit of capital (Marx, 1977a, p. 257 and p. 302). The capitalist labour process is not simply a process through which man acts upon nature to produce use-values, but a process of surplus extraction. Within the freely contradicted wage relationship between worker and capitalist (which ironically is an absolute necessity for both parties), an unpaid surplus is extracted; the major difference between this and previous forms of the surplus extraction process being that what was once open and obvious is now veiled in the apparent exchange of equivalents. As Rubin (1972, p. 5) points out, 'the theory of fetishism is, *per se*, the basis of Marx's entire economic system and in particular his theory of value'. And, as Perlman suggests, in his introduction to Rubin's book, the theory of value is essentially about 'the regulation of labour' (p. xxix).

Therefore, the mode of surplus extraction conditions the class structure of any social system. However, it should be recognised that at one and the same time class relations affect the nature and magnitude of the surplus. They are both determined and determining and interpenetrate one another. (This is just as much the case for feudal or slave-based societies as it is for capitalism.) The political economy of any mode of production is, therefore, the result of this process. The specific forms that develop reflect these fundamental relationships.

Analysis of the capitalist mode of production, therefore, begins at the level of the most basic economic relationship, within the labour process itself, identifying the manner in which the surplus is extracted from the direct producers. Under capitalism this would consist of analysis of the individual capitalist firm (Nichols and Beynon, 1977; Beynon, 1973). However, given that the productive capacities of capitalism have been so massively advanced by capitalism's necessary conquest of science and technology (Rose and Rose (eds), 1976; Braverman, 1974, pp. 157–67) why does the potential for production far outstrip actual production? (Baran, 1957, pp. 133–4).

Firstly, this is because production is social, but the surplus is appropriated individually by the owners of the means of production, and conflict is generated. This conflict manifests itself in the first instance in a reduction of production. It was precisely the aim of Taylor's scientific management (1947, p. 19) to break the 'systematic soldiering' of the workforce, through which workpace and output are deliberately reduced. This is supplemented by a lack of interest, on behalf of the workforce, in enhancing production capacities on the basis of their own initiative (Dubois, 1979, p. 51). Secondly, this form of resistance to the imperatives of surplus extraction necessitates the employment of a whole section of the employable population in activities of supervision and control, which, whilst they are functional to the class of owners, are not directly socially productive. Marx (1977a, p. 496), for example, points out that, because of the anarchic nature of capitalism, it generates 'a vast number of employments, at present indispensable but in themselves superfluous'. The purchase of labour power, after all, only gives the purchaser the possibility of extracting a surplus. Once purchased for the specific period of time, that potentiality has to be turned into a reality. As Braverman (1974, p. 67) suggests,

> Under the special and new relations of capitalism, which presuppose a free labour contract, they [capitalists] had to extract from their employees that daily conduct which would best serve their interests, to impose their will upon workers whilst operating a labour process on a voluntary contractual basis.

Consequently, 'the capitalist strives through management to control' (Braverman, 1974, p. 68). This necessitates the employment of foremen, overseers and layers of management responsible for control functions, whose job it is to see that an actual surplus is produced within the labour process.

Furthermore, the volume of the surplus will be affected by the ability of the direct producers to resist these attempts at control and to assert their own forms of control over the labour process. Dubois (1979), uses the term sabotage to describe a series of activities undertaken by workers as a response to their particular work circumstances under the capitalist mode of production. These activities range from active, illegal forms like vandalism, arson and theft to more subtle and less active elements, like go-slow, absenteeism, working without interest, enthusiasm or initiative. A wide range of examples of these activities can be found in Dubois (1979, pp. 21–59) and Friedman (1977, pp. 51–2).

Dubois's use of the term 'sabotage' for these activities does not appear to me to be particularly appropriate, as the term implies specific physical acts to halt the production process. It would be more appropriate to describe this resistance as forms of 'negative control' operated by the workforce over the labour process. This response either seeks to minimise the worker's participation in a necessary but alien system of surplus extraction, or is simply an attempt to make tolerable the conditions under which the surplus is extracted (Dubois, 1979, pp. 51–79; Marglin, 1976, p. 34). The forms negative control may take can be individualised or collective, consciously co-ordinated or spontaneous. However, the end result is the same. A reduction in the surplus extracted by the capitalist because some portion of the final output has been either destroyed or rendered useless, or because the potential for surplus extraction has not been achieved. This would arise if the workforce reduced the intensity of its labour, thus cutting the relative surplus extracted or if they reduced the time spent working, thus cutting the absolute surplus extracted. In other words, the class structure of capitalism generates conflict, which conditions the surplus extracted at the level of the individual firm and provides the objective basis of class struggle. This means the day-to-day struggle around production, and not just its periodic manifestation in strikes, occupations, sit-ins, and so on (Nichols and Beynon, 1977, pp. 133–46; Watson, 1971).

From the point of view of the individual capitalist, this necessitates a series of strategies which seek to limit the degree of negative control exerted by the working class. It seems futile to argue that any one strategy is the embodiment of capitalist rationality, as different strategies will predominate at different times and could well co-exist, both within different sectors of the economy or even within the same firm (Thompson, 1984, p. 151). It is more likely that the individual capitalist will adopt the strategy thought appropriate in differing circumstances. This will depend upon the nature of the production process, the level of technology, the level of worker organisation and the sophistication of worker responses, the degree of necessary autonomous initiative, the market conditions that the individual firm faces and so on. All these features will interact to produce the specific strategy. Presumably a firm operating in a market characterised by restricted competition, in a period of high unemployment, will adopt different strategies to a firm in a strongly competitive market, in a period of full employment. This needs qualification, as it cannot be assumed that the choice of strategy is always correct, nor does it assume that the range of choices is limitless. The reason for this latter point is that the struggle over the generation and control of the surplus manifests itself not only at the level of the individual capitalist's relationship with his own workforce, (that is, around the labour process) but also at the level of the class relationship between the capitalist class and the working class and within different fractions of the capitalist class itself. This critically revolves around the question of competition, labour productivity and the internal discipline of the capitalist mode of production (Nichols, 1980, p. 25). The form these categories take in the USSR is quite different to their form and function under capitalism. It is these relationships that are the key to understanding the particular socio-economic nature of the USSR.

In a capitalist economy, changes in the productiveness of social labour play an important role in the generation of the surplus. Obviously, increases in the amount of time spent at work or increases in the employed workforce will facilitate an increase in the absolute level of the surplus (Marx, 1977a, p. 477). The physical volume of goods produced will increase, but with a concomitant increase in expenditures of human labour time. However, increases in social labour productivity will lead to an increase in the generation of a relative surplus (Marx, 1977a, pp. 478–9). That is, the given amount of labour time expended now produces either a larger volume of products or results in more complex, higher quality products. The end result is that the necessary labour time decreases and the surplus labour time increases in the production of any specific product, and consequently the volume of surplus value extracted also increases. For the individual capitalist, increases in the productiveness of the labour power he purchases strengthens his position relative to his competitors. As the value of a commodity produced under capitalist conditions tends towards the average socially necessary labour time needed for its production, the capitalist experiences a temporary competitive advantage which, all other things remaining equal, results in increased profits. These profits may enable the individual capitalist to further revolutionise the productive process, hence gaining further competitive advantage as the more efficient producer expands at the expense of the less efficient competitor, or may allow for the takeover of the latter by the former. From the point of view of the individual capitalist, therefore, there are real advantages in attempting to raise labour productivity, even if the short term gains are eroded as competitors equal or surpass their example (Marx, 1953, pp. 92–3).

More generally, for the capitalist class as a whole, this process acts as an external compulsion upon all to keep up with the most advanced and seek to surpass them. This is because labour expanded over and above the average socially necessary in the production of any commodity is lost and creates no value (Marx, 1977a, pp. 190–1). Therefore, for the individual capitalist, his very existence as a capitalist may well be jeopardised if he fails to continually revolutionise production and continually raise the productivity of labour.

From the point of view of control over the surplus and over the labour process itself, the development of labour productivity has a number of ramifications. It leads to a cheapening of labour power, in value terms, since the socially determined necessities can now be produced with a smaller input of labour time and consequently at a lower value. As the value of labour power is determined by the average socially necessary labour time for its reproduction, this implies an increase in the surplus available for the capitalist. Furthermore, the continual necessity to increase labour productivity leads to an ever widening use of technology and science to improve constant capital and leads to the expulsion of labour from the labour process (Cooley, 1976, pp. 83–5). The creation of a reserve army of labour further depresses the value of labour power, as it acts to reduce the resistance of labour individually and weakens the organised response of labour collectively, thus improving the profitability of both the individual capitalist and the capitalist class (Marx, 1977a, 595–6; Yaffe and Bullocke, 1975, p. 17). Finally, the implementation of new technologies changes the nature of labour itself. For Braverman, this implies the deskilling and degradation of work under capitalism and the gradual erosion of control exercised by the skilled working class (Braverman, 1974, pp. 120–1). For his numerous critics, Braverman's notion is an overstatement, but all, nevertheless, recognise that the changing nature of the capitalist labour process under the influence of technological change has implications for the question of control. For a useful survey of this literature see Thompson (1984, pp. 118–21).

As Marx points out, this process is racked by its own internal contradictions which stem from the antagonistic relationships at its core and which precipitate wasteful expenditures, idle resources, unemployment and periodic crises. Nevertheless, capitalism's ability to increase the productiveness of labour and to accelerate its socialisation is seen as its great progressive function providing the motive force for the system's development and eventually creating the basis for its overthrow (Marx, 1977c, p. 250).

Under the capitalist mode of production, therefore, increases in labour productivity yield benefits that accrue to the individual capitalist firm and also to the class as a whole, hence both have an unambiguous interest in raising labour productivity. For the working class, the situation is more complex and contradictory. Undoubtedly the advances in living standards achieved over the last century and a half have been the result of the increasing productiveness of human labour. However, in a more immediate sense, as a class the working class can have little interest or incentive to improve labour productivity if it results in the cheapening of labour power and a rise in unemployment. The potential for resistance, however, can be reduced in so far as the working class can be segmented and groups and individuals within the class differentiated. Monetary inducements can lessen the degree of resistance to schemes designed to increase productivity at the level of the individual capitalist firm. The most obvious current form this takes can be seen with regard to redundancy payments which are used to reduce resistance to restructuring. The reason why these strategies, based on monetary inducement, can work is that under the capitalist mode of production money acts as the universal equivalent and will provide the individual with unambiguous access to consumption goods and services.

Ironically, the present phase of capitalist development is characterised by a contradictory dynamic that simultaneously fragments and homogenises the working class. The differences between segments of the working class, with regard to different industries, occupations, regions, work content, and so on, have been continuously reduced. This has stemmed in part from the use of similar technologies and work organisation in previously dissimilar industries. The interchangability of workers between different types of production is by no means complete, but is increasing. At the same time, fragmentation, for control purposes, along lines of gender, race, age, education and the most obvious line of cleavage between the employed and unemployed, is also increasing.

For the classical writers in the Marxist tradition, the contradictions inherent in the capitalist process of development act as fetters upon the further possibilities for revolutionising social productivity. They argue that this is only possible under socialism (Marx, 1977c, p. 250; Lenin, 1977, pp. 220–35). Before considering the USSR in detail, it is worth remembering the theoretical perspective that informed Lenin's view on the potentialities under socialism. A massive growth in labour productivity should be possible because advances no longer accrue to owners of capital, but to the direct producers, removing the central contradiction of the capitalist mode of production. As Lenin (1964, p. 420) argued,

> The communist organisation of social labour, the first step towards which is socialism, rests, and will do so more and more, as time goes on, on the free and conscious discipline of the working people who have thrown off the yoke of both the landowners and the capitalist.

The working class would now have a direct material stake in measures designed to improve productivity as these will potentially reduce the amount of labour time to be expended and not result in unemployment, increased rates of exploitation and fragmentation of the working class, but in increased leisure or increased material consumption or some combination of both. If this linkage is made and working class interests are directly stimulated, then the vast productive and creative potential of the direct producers can be released. Resistance to new technology would be irrational and disappear, as the gains of science and new technology will be available to all and their development encouraged. For Lenin (1964, p. 62) technological progress under socialism will, 'make working conditions more hygienic, will free millions of workers from smoke, dust and dirt and accelerate the transformation of dirty repulsive workshops into bright laboratories worthy of human beings'.

Lenin (1964, p. 427) was clear on the potential of this released force: 'Capitalism can be utterly vanquished by socialism creating a new much higher productivity of labour ... communism is the higher productivity of labour compared to that existing under capitalism. ...

of voluntary, class conscious and united workers employing advanced techniques'.

Once labour power is no longer sold as a commodity and the law of value no longer operates as the regulator of the socio-economic system, use values will be produced directly as the needs of the freely associated direct producers develop and not as profitability dictates. The replacement of the anarchy of capitalism will further destroy a whole host of socially useless functions and occupations, thus further resources can be drawn into social production. Classical Marxist writers saw the eventual outcome of this process, fuelled by the ever increasing productivity of human labour, as material abundance, where the division of labour could be overcome and class antagonisms eliminated.

The analysis provided in this section raises a series of questions with regard to the USSR: What form does the process of surplus extraction take? Who controls the socially generated surplus? What are the class relations that derive from this process? How do these relations condition the surplus and what form does the surplus take? What dynamic or laws of motion govern the operation of the Soviet economy? How do units (enterprises) within the surplus extraction process interrelate? To what extent is the process different from that operating under capitalism? To what extent has Lenin's analysis become a reality in the USSR? The second chapter begins to take up these questions.

2 The Political Economy of the USSR

SOVIET PERCEPTIONS OF CLASS STRUCTURE AND WORK

In order to begin to answer the questions posed at the end of the last chapter, it is necessary to consider the way in which Soviet political economists and their western counterparts regard the question of work and class structure. This is not an exhaustive treatment of the question, but is intended to point out common limitations in their work before developing an alternative analysis of work and labour in the USSR, linked specifically to the present performance of the Soviet economy. In this way, a more adequate political economy can be constructed which will provide the basis for explaining the motivation for the Shchekino experiment and the other experimental initiatives considered in later chapters.

The first general point to be made is that the analysis is couched in the terminology and categories of Marxist political economy. However, the same categories that can be used to such effect in the analysis of capitalism, seem hollow in the hands of Soviet theoreticians. The reason for this is that the present ruling group have inherited Marxism as their ideological foundation and it is not possible simply to cast it aside. The legitimating link between past and present makes it necessary to maintain the façade of Marxist categories, even if the content is neutered. As Yanowitch (1977) points out, 'Moshe Lewin has written that, "the vocation of Marxism is the analysis of class realities hiding behind various façades". One of the ironies of Soviet intellectual life is that Soviet scholars cannot apply this vocation to the analysis of their own society'. The class analysis adopted is a formalistic interpretation of Marxism which identifies classes in terms of legal forms of ownership. The analysis is rooted in the traditional Stalinist view of political economy. For Stalin, (1972, p. 5)

the province of political economy is production, the economic relations of men. It includes: (a) the forms of ownership of the means of production; (b) the status of the various social groups in production and their interrelations that follow from these

20

forms ... (c) the forms of distribution of products, which are determined by them.

As Ticktin (1986) has pointed out, in another context, this is an inversion of the usual Marxist methodology which normally proceeds from the socio-economic to the political and legal forms and not the reverse.

The working class and the peasantry are differentiated from one another as the two major classes, in respect to property relations. The working class are involved in production in the state sector, with state owned means of production, whilst the peasantry operate within the collective farm sector, where the means of production are owned by the collective (Kozlov, 1977, p. 33; Kudryavtsev, 1978, pp. 53–4). The utter formalism of this distinction is well illustrated by Stalin himself (1972, p. 15), as he points out, 'the land, which has been turned over to the collective farms in perpetual tenure, is used by them virtually as their own property, in spite of the fact that they cannot sell, buy, lease or mortgage it'.

As the collective farm peasantry could not determine the use to which the land was put, their position is in essence the same as that of the industrial worker. It is argued that these classes are overlaid by a stratum, the intelligentsia, who are not defined in terms of property but with respect to work function and education (Kozlov, 1977, p. 76; Blyakhman and Shkaratan, 1973, pp. 224–257). Both the classes and the stratum are defined as 'non-antagonistic' or 'friendly' (Kozlov, 1977, p. 75; Manevich, 1980, p. 11). As Manevich (1970, p. 16) states, 'It is characteristic of socialist production relations that the contradictions they are subject to, (with respect to the social organisation of production as well) are non-antagonistic'.

In relationship to Marxist political economy this characterisation is absurd. As already indicated, no class can be defined in isolation from its antagonistic opposite pole. The whole basis of class analysis around the question of the surplus extraction process, necessitates such a definition, unless what is being described is a classless society, then the concept of class disappears. The adjective 'friendly' has no analytical content whatsoever. The class relation, defined in a Marxist sense, is a relationship based upon contradiction which implies antagonistic forces and interests and it is this that provides the underlying dynamics of the socio-economic system and the mechanism for change. Interestingly, Manevich (1985, p. 254) talks of the elimination of 'non-antagonistic contradiction'. However, if contradictions are non-antagonistic why should they be eliminated and through what process would change come?

The Soviet formulation is undoubtedly desirable on political and ideological grounds for the ruling group, (who interestingly disappear by coalesence in this analysis). Stalin's vehement attack on central concepts of Marxist political economy confirms this desire to maintain the form of Marxist analysis whilst removing the content: 'we must also discard certain other concepts taken from Marx's capital. . . I am referring to such concepts, among others, as "necessary" and "surplus" labour, "necessary" and "surplus" product and "necessary" and "surplus" time' (1972, p. 17). Therefore, by starting from a legalistic definition of class and by declaring them 'non-antagonistic', Stalin and later writers in this tradition are able to conclude that all Soviet labour is 'necessary labour' (Kozlov, 1978, p. 64). The point of departure for Marx, the process of surplus extraction, disappears in Stalin's analysis and in the analysis of contemporary Soviet writers. However, if these formulations are inadequate to explain the political economy of the USSR, they are of equally little use with regard to the practical problems facing the present ruling group, particularly in relation to the management of the Soviet economy in a time of crisis. It was recognised by the ruling group, in the late sixties, that sociological research could play a part in identifying, understanding and eventually managing complex social processes, much like the role played by functionalist sociology in the west (*Sotsiologicheskie Issledovaniya*, No. 2, 1976, p. 8). The tasks of contemporary Soviet sociological work were clearly enumerated by Zdravomyslov (1983, pp. 2–3) as being: assisting in the formation of a socialist attitude to work, improving management processes, aiding economic science to improve productivity and efficiency and to assist in the scientific formulation of prices. More recently Ivanov (1984, p. 41) has argued that a principal aim must be working to improve the economic mechanism in a number of experimental forms. These attitudes in turn led to an easing of official proscriptions on sociological work and fuelled an internal debate, within Soviet academic circles, concerning the question of class structure (Mathews, 1978).

The consequence has been that over the last decade or so, traditional attitudes to class structure have been questioned and amended in concrete sociological studies. This revision, however, has not been in the direction suggested by Marxist political economy, but has involved the superimposition of a predominantly functionalist methodology over the traditional, Stalinist formulation of class structure. For example, Blyakhman and Shkaratan (1973, p. 200) argue that, 'the social structure of the present working class comprises an interlocking and interacting intra-class formation, the dominant ones being the socio-vocational strata that have arisen on the basis of the social division of labour'.

The revised approach is based particularly upon the intra-class occupational structure. For example, Shkaratan (1970, pp. 277–8) utilises an eightfold division into occupational groupings for 'management' to 'unskilled worker' in his work. This type of framework is then used to correlate questions like labour turnover, migration patterns and labour discipline and participation, to structural features like place in the hierarchy of skills, level of training, education, and so on. The end result is to provide policy responses to management problems (Podmarkov, Zaitsev, Novikov, 1977, pp. 163–4). The practical need for such work, in an increasingly complex and technologically based society, forced the political and ideological compromise embodied within this analysis. However, the two approaches co-exist and this has been further justified. It is claimed that this analysis is in full accord with the present stage of Soviet development, which is explained by Kozlov (1977, p. 53), within a two stage transition of 'socialism' and 'mature socialism' prior to 'full communism'. Socialist society, in the period when it is constructing the material preconditions for 'full communism', cannot overcome a necessary 'social division of labour'. This is seen as a function of both technology and the present stage of development: 'thus though there are no antagonistic classes under socialism, socio-economic distinctions and non-antagonistic contradictions between different kinds of labour nevertheless continue' (Manevich, 1970, p. 37). The remaining inequalities are seen as necessary, as distribution is based upon the quality and quantity of work performed: 'the economic law of distribution according to the amount and quality of work performed determines the entire system of wages and salaries' (Manevich, 1970, p. 52).

Work itself is described as being 'no longer an onerous duty' but 'a right and an objective necessity', whilst labour is no longer a commodity, but is 'hired along planned lines' (Manevich, 1970, p. 5). It is worth pointing out, in terms of the comparison Manevich is seeking to make, that work is not a duty under capitalism but an objective necessity and that the final statement conceals more than it reveals about the nature of Soviet labour.

The end result of this analysis is that the Soviet economy is described as being consciously regulated and not subordinate to the law of value. According to Kozlov (1977, p. 394), the absence of private ownership of the means of production and their control by the state excludes the possibility of exploitation. This is because the state is seen as the political expression of the working class. Consequently, it is argued, any socially produced surplus at the disposition of the state is consciously pre-determined by the planning process, which reflects the political wishes of the working class. Furthermore, this surplus is at the disposal of the direct producers via their control of the state (Kozlov, 1977, p. 397). The USSR is viewed as a society moving towards 'social homogeneity' (Oblomskaya, Starakhov, Umanets, 1983, pp. 28–34). As Table 2.1 illustrates, by defining the class structure in terms of only two classes, the appearance of homogeneity can be created and once again the ruling group disappears by amalgamation.

From this perspective, therefore, the whole question of the surplus and exploitation disappears. In the process of constructing the homogenous Soviet society, the leading role of the party and working class is continually emphasised, and the otherwise harmonious picture is only clouded by peripheral problems which, it is argued, will be overcome with better management of social processes (Blyakhman and Shkratan, 1973, pp. 245–53). The existence of a whole range of labour problems, which will be considered in more detail later, are explained predominantly as survivals from previous modes of production (Manevich, 1970, p.21).

A further element in this transition to homogeneity is the supposed destruction of the distinctions between mental and manual labour and the overcoming of disparities between urban and rural life (Blyakhman and Shkaratan, 1973, p. 149; pp. 167–8). Table 2.2 illustrates the shift in the USSR away from a predominantly rural to a predominantly urban population. However, the proportional size of the rural population, in relationship to other developed countries, is still large. Manevich suggests that the Soviet agricultural population is eight times that of the USA and in the USSR approximately twenty per cent of the economically active population are involved in agriculture in comparison with three per cent in the USA. Tables 2.3 and 2.4 show the increasing educational level of both agricultural and manual workers, but they are both still more likely to be less educated than their urban or non-manual worker counterparts. The low prestige afforded to manual work and the ever increasing pressure on working class children to obtain higher education, so that they need not become workers themselves, testifies to the gap between ideological claims and reality. Furthermore, the gulf between urban and rural

Table 2.1 The social structure of the Soviet population (%)

	1913	1924	1928	1939	1959	1970	1979	1982	1983	1984	1985
Whole population	100	100	100	100	100	100	100	100	100	100	100
Workers & employees	17	14.8	17.6	50.2	68	79.5	85.1	86.7	87.8	87.5	87.6
Workers only	—	10.4	12.4	33.7	50.2	57.4	60	60.9	61.2	61.5	61.6
Collective farm workers & handicraft workers in co-operatives	—	1.3	2.9	47.2	31.4	20.5	14.9	13.3	12.9	12.5	12.4
Independent peasantry & handicraft workers not organised in co-operatives	66.7	75.4	74.9	2.6	0.3	—	—	—	—	—	—
Bourgeoisie, landowners, merchants & kulaks	16.3	8.5	4.6	—	—	—	—	—	—	—	—

Sources: Narodnoe Khozyaistvo (1983), p. 7; *Narodnoe Khozyaistvo* (1984), p. 7; Manevich (ed.) (1971), p. 50; *Vestnik Statistiki* (1983), No. 4, p. 60; *Narodnoe Khozyaistvo* (1985), p. 7.

Table 2.2   Population structure in the USSR

	Total	Urban (m)	Rural (m)	Urban (%)	Rural (%)
1940	194.1	63.1	131.0	32.5	67.5
1961	216.3	107.9	108.4	49.9	50.1
1970	241.7	136.0	105.7	56.3	43.7
1979	262.4	163.6	98.8	62.3	37.7
1982	268.8	171.7	97.1	63.9	36.1
1983	271.2	174.6	96.6	64.4	35.6
1984	273.8	177.5	96.3	64.8	35.2
1985 (1st Jan.)	276.3	180.1	96.2	65.2	34.8
(1st July)	277.4	181.1	96.3	65.3	34.7

Sources: *Narodnoe Khozyaistvo* (1983), p. 5; *Narodnoe Khozyaistvo* (1984), p. 5; *Vestnik Statistiki* (1984), No. 4, p. 66; *Chislennost' i sostav* (1984), p. 6; *Narodnoe Khozayaistvo* (1985), p. 5

Table 2.3   Educational level of the employed population by social group
(No. with higher and secondary education per 1000)

	1939	1959	1970	1979	1983	1984
Workers	87	401	590	760	813	825
Employees	546	911	956	982	986	987
Collective farm workers	18	226	393	593	677	695

Source: *Narodnoe Khozyaistvo* (1983), p. 29; *Narodnoe Khozyaistvo* (1984), p. 30.

Table 2.4   Educational level of workers in manual and non-manual labour
(No. with higher and secondary education per 1000)

	1939	1959	1970	1979	1983	1984
Manual workers	45	325	543	732	801	815
Non-manual workers	515	896	953	981	985	986

Source: *Narodnoe Khozyaistvo* (1983), p. 29; *Narodnoe Khozyaistvo* (1984), p. 30.

workers is still large. As Table 2.5 illustrates, even though the average wage of collective farm workers has risen by 18.5 per cent in the last three years, it is still 22.5 per cent less than the average wage of their urban counterparts. The disparity appears even larger when it is realised that industrial workers work an average 231 days a year but this rises to 257 days for collective farm workers; 264 days for collective farm machine operators and tractor drivers; and between 309 and 315 days for collective farm workers involved in animal husbandry (Korupillo, 1983, p. 6).Therefore, the rural worker works longer hours for less. Of course the rural worker can supplement both his wage and living standards from the private plot, but this requires further expenditures of effort. It should also be noted that the allocation of consumer goods and social provision is worse in rural areas and this ensures that living and cultural standards in the rural areas are well below those in the urban centres.

Western, non-Marxist work on the Soviet working class and work has fallen into three distinct categories. Firstly, the American Cold War approach, which has sought to highlight the plight of Soviet workers, without applying similar criticisms to US or Western capitalism.[1] Secondly, collections of papers with a variety of theoretical perspectives.[2] Thirdly, sociological work which, whilst it may contain differences in nuance and detail, adopts a perspective which is functionalist like its Soviet counterparts. This is evident throughout the work of David Lane (1971, 1978, pp. 418–422; 1982, pp. 152–160; 1986, pp. 1–16) and his analysis is perhaps most explicitly expressed in his joint work with O'Dell (1978). Here they define the Soviet working class as, 'all manual and non-manual labour occupied in publicly owned institutions concerned with production, distribution and exchange' (p. 3). By pressing the formalism of Stalin's definition of classes to its logical conclusion, they argue that non-manual workers

Table 2.5 Average wages of workers, employees and collective farm workers

	1980	1981	1982	1983
Average wage of workers and employees	168.9	172.5	177.5	182
Average wage of collective farm workers	118.5	122.1	128.9	141

Source: *Vestnik Statistiki* (1984), No. 11, p. 37.

do not constitute a separate stratum but are an integral part of the working class, because 'in a Marxist sense their relationship to the means of production is the same as that of the manual workers: all are wage earners employed in state-owned enterprises' (p. 4).

They do not, however, define the class that stands in opposition to this working class. Logically, by applying this definition to the USSR it is impossible to leave anyone out of the working class and it would seem that Lane and O'Dell also reach this conclusion by their use of terms like 'a politically unitary class society'. The only conclusion that can be drawn from this is that they view the Soviet Union as a classless society. This is confirmed in the concluding chapter of their work, where they refer to the economic class structure as being 'unitary' (p. 132). In fact, what they do is simply reproduce the functionalism of their Soviet counterparts and state:

> It is certainly not the case that with the development of socialism the working class becomes a unitary and undifferentiated group. Social stratification arises from the division of labour, which gives rise to an occupational structure. The division of work activity involves specialised and different social functions and qualitative differences between groups playing specified roles (p. 6).

By the end of this paragraph the concept of class has disappeared. What is of importance is the occupational structure where 'groups' are differentiated by 'work activity'. The social division of labour they refer to is more correctly defined as a technical division of labour that stems from a particular stage of technological development. It is precisely the social division of labour that their analysis excludes by definition. For Lane and O'Dell, it is the level of technology and its rate of advance which influence and determine the occupational structure, and they conclude, 'in our view the occupational structure has evolved in a way not unlike that of capitalist societies' (p. 18).

In other words, we have confirmation of the 'logic of industrialism thesis' which is a form of technological determinism, suggesting that convergence is taking place between East and West, driven by the imperatives of a neutral technology. Lane and O'Dell then go on to conclude, like their Soviet counterparts, that problems like absenteeism (p. 49), drunkenness (p. 46), low productivity and poor quality production (p. 20), or the high proportion of unmechanised manual work (p. 15) are all either products of the recent peasant past of large sections of the workforce or simply attributable to the Soviet Union's late start on the road to industrial maturity. The argument would be more convincing if it could be shown that more industrially mature societies did not suffer from the same types of problems. It also raises the question of how long a peasant remains a peasant once removed from the countryside, employed in an industrial environment and living in an urban location. As the Soviet workforce becomes more of a hereditary class the idea of the peasant background becomes more tenuous. As a result the reasons for the types of behaviour cited have to be located in the present work situation of the Soviet population.

The general point is that this type of analysis assumes away the central question. By arguing that the class structure is 'non-antagonistic' or 'unitary' and that exploitation has disappeared, then by definition so, too, has the surplus. The question of control over the surplus (either direct, by the ruling group or negative, by the workforce) is also rendered irrelevant. The abandonment of Marxist political economy reduces the analysis of class to little more than a ritual for Soviet writers. For Lane and O'Dell, it is a term that is substituted in their analysis by the functionalism of occupational structures.

I would further argue that western writers in the Marxist tradition have fared little better in this debate. The analysis of class structure, the nature of the labour process and the mode of production has been hampered by a lack of empirical knowledge of the USSR, or the desire to force the reality of the USSR into an accommodation with a particular theoretical position.[3]

The problem is that some features of the contemporary USSR are superficially similar to forms existing under capitalism or under previous modes of production. Therefore, by magnifying these similarities and working them up into an all embracing theoretical perspective, the specificity of the USSR is either lost or reinterpreted to fit the theory. I would argue that the central question of surplus extraction and control has not been the starting point for any of these perspectives, and if it is mentioned at all it is deduced as a result of the analysis rather than forming its starting point.

All these analyses are indicative of a broader problem. They all divorce the concept of class from the operation and performance of the economy as a whole and from relationships both within and between enterprises, which condition that operation and performance. For example, the Soviet sociologists cited describe the society as socially harmonious. The theoretical political economy texts describe the development of the Soviet economy as planned and proportional. However, both sets of writers ignore the empirical realities of the Soviet economy. For example Berri (1977, p. 11) argues that 'planned management of the economy ensures its smooth, crisis free development at high stable growth rates, with full employment and increasingly efficient use of resources'. Likewise Lane and O'Dell, who make much of describing the Soviet working class in relationship to production, only mention the performance of the economy on the last page of their work (1978, p. 138). Class is treated as a sociological category, the main aim of which is the unambiguous classification of individuals into an occupational hierarchy, rather than a category of political economy. As previously suggested, class structure both reflects and affects the surplus extraction process and does not necessarily lead to such an unambiguous classification schema. It is irrelevant if one individual, or indeed group of individuals, cannot be fitted neatly into the 'class system' because it is not the intention of the theory to provide such a schema. Class analysis is not a labelling process, but is an attempt to grasp the central dynamic of the socio-economic formation.[4]

The degree of social harmony suggested by Soviet authors and their western acolytes, would tend to suggest that Soviet society should have little difficulty in motivating Soviet workers to produce more, more efficiently and with a higher regard for quality. If the Soviet Union is a 'non-antagonistic' social formation it raises the question of why it is plagued by a series of labour problems, leading to declining labour productivity growth and an overall slow-down in economic growth. It is only when these problems are placed in the context of the struggle around the generation and control over the surplus that they become explicable.

SOCIAL RELATIONS OF PRODUCTION IN THE USSR: AN ALTERNATIVE PERSPECTIVE

The perspective developed in this section rests upon the analysis outlined in Chapter 1. This would suggest that the ruling group in the USSR attempts, however imperfectly, to extract and control the distribution of a reliable, usable and growing surplus from the direct producers. From the viewpoint of the ruling group, this surplus is essential, not simply to maintain their own consumption privileges, but more importantly to legitimise their role and enable them to reproduce their socio-economic position. This has two related aspects.

Internally, a growing surplus is necessary to provide the ruling group with the ability to incorporate and control sections of the populace via gradations of consumption privileges, in the same way as the incorporation of the middle classes and the upper layers of the working class is achieved in the west. The intention is to deal with rising domestic expectations and the consequent discontent, noted by so many commentators (Haynes and Semyonova, 1979, pp. 109–110, 112–115; Holubenko, 1975; Teague, 1982, pp. 22–5). Their ability to do this is constrained by, amongst other things, the need to maintain artificially low food prices. As Nove (1978, pp. 10–11) points out, the USSR has, 'the most gigantic agricultural subsidy known in history'. This is the necessary price to be paid for dampening potential internal discontent and maintaining a minimal level of support. The examples of Poland in 1971, 1976 and later (MacDonald, 1977, pp. 93–9); Workers Under Communism, 1982, pp. 6–14), and the outbreaks of worker discontent in the USSR in the early sixties and more recently, serve as a reminder of the potential costs (Belotserkovsky, 1979, pp. 37–51; Boiter, 1964, pp. 33–43). Official concern over the availability and quality of consumer goods and agricultural products, evident from Stalin onwards, reflects this desire (Brezhnev, 1978, p. 1; Andropov, 1982, pp. 1–2). If this could be achieved, the incentive effects would strengthen the ruling group's control over the process of surplus extraction and guarantee their reproduction and coalescence as a ruling class. The pre-condition for this is a rising socially produced surplus. However, the proportion of national income utilised for consumption is growing very slowly, from 72.1 per cent in 1966–70 to 74.5 per cent in 1981–83 (Vestnik Statistiki, 1984, No. 11, p. 36).

Externally, it is necessary for the ruling group to maintain a sphere of influence on the world stage. This is achieved in a number of ways. Directly through arms and military expenditure, which guarantees the integrity of Soviet borders in regions like China or provides a buffer zone like the Eastern bloc countries. Indirectly through economic aid and trade with socialist bloc countries, friendly states or potentially friendly states (Marese and Vanous, 1983). The ultimate aim of this is to maintain the USSR outside the capitalist world economic orbit. The USSR is not driven towards external expansion by its own internal economic laws of motion, as with the imperialistic dynamic that operates within capitalism. It is almost the opposite, because the

USSR does not suffer from the overproduction of capital goods that need to find markets overseas; it is its economic backwardness that generates a need for a buffer zone between itself and capitalism. This is primarily a political and strategic question, although it does have potential economic advantages from an increasing division of labour, leading to specialisation and integration within COMECON and scale economies (Brada, 1983). The USSR cannot and could not compete on the world market with western capitalist countries, because of the nature of Soviet products. For example, only a little over four per cent of Soviet exports of machine tools go to developed capitalist countries, the main reason being poor quality and design (Smelyakov, 1981, p. 3). As Tselikov (1981, p. 2) complains, Soviet vehicles are inefficient and fail to compete with similar western models due to poor quality inputs which make Soviet vehicles 15–25 per cent heavier than their western equivalents. Hence economic contact with the west can only be carried out in a much modified form. The ultimate aim is to maintain the USSR outside the capitalist orbit, but again the pre-condition for this is a growing domestically produced surplus.

It should be pointed out that the surplus is not, as some writers maintain, simply the additional consumption privileges of the ruling group (Nove, 1983, p. 82). It comprises the whole socially produced surplus product, over and above that necessary to reproduce the direct producers, and control over the surplus implies control over decisions about present consumption, accumulation and distribution. Perhaps the most important result of control over the surplus is the determination of new investment in the economy which, as a consequence implies control over the future direction and proportions of the economy and the developments within the labour process.

As a consequence, the fundamental plane of antagonistic social relations lies between the direct producers and the economic administrators of the state, at both the central and local level and their management representatives within the enterprise. The role of management is particularly contradictory and this will be elaborated further. However, it should also be remembered that the antagonisms generated around the surplus extraction process also affect that process itself. The direct producers are able to exert negative control over both the quality and quantity of the surplus extracted via their indirect control of the labour process. This interaction gives rise to the particular economic performance of the system under examination. In order to explain this, it is necessary to outline the nature of the surplus extraction process in the USSR and the economic results that its specific form produces.

THE NATURE OF WORK AND REWARDS IN THE USSR

The starting point of this analysis is work and labour time, given that this is the pre-condition for the production of use-values necessary to satisfy human wants. The individual Soviet worker commits his labour-time to a pre-specified labour activity, at a particular enterprise or association, either for a specified period of time, no more than three years, or indefinitely, by signing a labour contract (Glazyrin, Nikitinsky, Maksimova, Yarko, 1978, p. 13; Labour Code of the RSFSR. Articles 15, 16, 17). The worker is compelled by economic necessity to enter this relationship because he is effectively divorced from the means of production which is necessary to turn his labour into the use-values necessary for his existence, at a given social and technological level. The means of production stands outside the direct control of the worker, much like the position described by Marx under capitalism where, 'dead labour dominates and pumps dry living labour power'. The access to use-values is conditioned by work, non-work is not an option. Once unemployment was eliminated in the USSR in 1931 (Manevich, 1985, pp. 28–9) the necessity for unemployment benefit also disappeared. As a consequence, it is difficult to live outside the world of work for two reasons. The distribution of consumption goods, services and particularly housing is often determined by the enterprise or workplace and, non-work inevitably means participation in illegal activities. Since the mid-sixties, Soviet writers have pressed for the reintroduction of some form of 'dole' (Manevich, 1969, p. 50). However, even though Soviet academics accept the principle, it has, as yet, not been reintroduced.

The worker has discretion over both the labour activity he undertakes and the location where he works, but this is constrained by three things. Primarily the labour activity is determined by previous education, training, skill level and experience, coupled with the available work opportunities and the demands for the skills of the individual worker. Complaints regularly occur in the Soviet press regarding the mismatch of skills (Khromakov, 1980, p. 2). As Manevich (1980, p. 57) points out, even though the USSR produces large numbers of engineers per annum, a considerable proportion work in jobs for which they are over-qualified. Moreover, the location, either geographically or between enterprises, is subject to control. For example, some cities have restricted access and the internal passport system can be used to control the freedom of movement of workers. Movement between enterprises and branches has and can be controlled. For example, movement out of the military production sector can be difficult. The record of the worker's performance in his work book can also be used for control purposes. There is also the obvious constraint that the choice of external emigration is absent. Finally, the labour laws in operation at any particular time will constrain the worker's freedom of choice.

In a sense, therefore, the Soviet worker is as free as his western counterpart and out of this freedom is born the economic necessity to expend labour time, in order to receive the means to attain the necessaries of life. However, this freedom needs to be qualified. Unlike his western counterpart, the Soviet worker is not only subject to the necessity to work, but also has the right to work (Simon (ed.), 1980, p. 16). This principle, enshrined in the Soviet constitution, is perhaps the major remaining gain from the October Revolution and creates a particular relationship of dependency, in so far as the individual enterprise cannot make superfluous workers redundant. If the enterprise wishes to remove workers, it can only do so in carefully defined circumstances and it must find them a similar job, with similar conditions, content and rewards. It is worth noting that the major criteria for deciding which workers should be retained during staff cuts are individual productivity and quality of work. After these two elements comes a whole series of personal and social questions, like size of family, length of service and so on (Simon (ed.), 1980). This is not to suggest that all enterprises stick to the letter of the labour law. As Lampert (1984) suggests, individual enterprises can avoid the formalities of the labour codes. In specific circumstances individual workers can be forced to leave their work, but even then the worker has recourse to the Trade Unions and the legal system for redress and reinstatement (Glazyrin *et al.*, 1978, pp. 169–75). The point is that even if individuals can be victimised by enterprise management, as the cases documented by the Klebanov group, amongst others, demonstrate (Labour Focus on E. Europe, vol. 2, No. 1, p. 2; Haynes and Semyonova, 1979, pp. 36–72; Feldbrugge and Simons (eds), 1982, pp. 62–3) the workforce as a whole, or even sections of it, defined by trade, skill, industry or region, is relatively secure. The Soviet worker is protected in a manner incompatible with and unseen under capitalism. There still remains a degree of dependency which is a function of the particular political economy of the USSR.

However, this relationship, between the worker and the ruling group, is both a product of, and a cause of, the ruling group's insecure position in Soviet society. As the social position of the ruling group rests upon state property and the historical legacy of Bolshevism, they cannot break this linkage without cutting the legitimating links with the October Revolution. Furthermore, it would remove the apparent validity of the claim that the Socialist bloc's superiority over capitalism is shown in the maintenance of full employment whilst large sections of the capitalist world experiences ever-increasing unemployment (Shishkov, 1983, pp. 41–3). The power of this ideological dimension should not be overlooked. However, the fact that this relationship cannot be severed is a partial cause of the insecure grip the ruling group has over the socially produced surplus and it in turn threatens their reproduction.

The consequence is that the dual freedom Marx referred to, with regard to the worker under capitalism, is not applicable in the Soviet context. Workers under capitalism are insecure individually and as a class and this insecurity is an important element of control at the level of both the individual capitalist firm and at the level of the whole society. However, while the Soviet worker may be individually insecure, if he transgresses politically, collectively Soviet workers are secure economically and cannot be controlled in the same manner as their counterparts in the West. The abolition of unemployment, clearly necessary for the legitimacy of the ruling group, undermines the ruling group's ability to extract a growing, usable surplus. This is the first element of the particular nature of the Soviet labour process; the second element refers to rewards.

In return for the labour time expended, the worker receives an individual return in the form of a money wage. This is predominantly administratively determined at the centre, but can be manipulated at the level of the enterprise by the use of premiums, bonuses and piece-rates. For example, currently on average, 80 per cent of the wage is accounted for by basic wages and the remaining 20 per cent by bonuses. However, there are two problems to be noted. There has been a general tendency for wage levelling and a reduction in wage differentials much bemoaned by Soviet sources. For example, in 1955 the relationship between the wages of ITR and workers was 1.68, but by 1977 it had fallen to 1.21 (Bunich, 1984, p. 13). Furthermore, as

Ticktin has pointed out, the wage in the USSR may be paid in a money form but money in the USSR does not function as the universal equivalent, hence the wage form is quite different from capitalism (Ticktin, 1973, pp. 36–7). Access to use-values is not determined on the basis of money alone. Access depends upon position in the hierarchy, access to privileged, closed supply channels, access to foreign currency, place of residence, influence and *blat*, chance or foreknowledge, corruption and the bartering of skills on the black market (Ticktin, 1973, p. 37). For the ordinary worker the holding of money may well be a necessary condition to gain access to use-values, but it need not be a sufficient condition. Evidence for this is the all-pervasive nature of the queue as an allocative mechanism and the continual rise in the level of personal savings. Therefore, the money wage is not the same as under capitalism, as money does not provide unambiguous access to use-values.

Furthermore, the worker receives a return for his expended labour in the form of part of the social wage which, it is estimated, accounts for 23.4 per cent of the family income of workers and employees and 19.1 per cent of the family income of collective farm workers. In fact, these payments are rising faster than individual wages; in the period 1971–81 average wages grew by 45 per cent for workers and employees and 72 per cent for collective farm workers, but per capita payments from the social wage rose 81 per cent in the same period (Peshekhonov, 1983, p. 15). This may take a number of forms. It can be state determined, like health, education, transport or subsidised food (again access will be a function of the elements noted previously, like place of residence, place in the hierachy and so on). It can be determined by the enterprise, for example housing, cultural and sporting amenities, holiday facilities, access to sanatoria and so on. Access to the first elements of the social wage are non-discriminatory and are unaffected by the individual work performance of the worker. The second category can be manipulated at the level of the enterprise, and some correspondence between work performance and access can be administratively arranged. Soviet sources, however, have expressed concern over the lack of correspondence between the social wage and work performed, particularly as throughout the period 1976–82, the per capita payments and benefits from public consumption funds have been growing faster than the growth in labour productivity (Peshekhonov, 1983, p. 15).

There are a number of ramifications that follow from this analysis. The particular nature of the wage form means that the relationship between work performed and use-values eventually received is tenuous, as the wage is mediated by a variety of other elements. This has two complementary aspects. By reducing work effort to a minimum, the consumption of use-values by the worker need hardly be affected. In the opposite respect, by increasing effort, even if wages rise marginally, there is no necessary impact on the volume of use-values at the disposal of the worker. The implication to be drawn from this is that in the USSR wages can neither be used as an incentive nor as a disciplining mechanism, except in the most limited form. Therefore, the Soviet workforce is controlled by neither the stick of unemployment nor the carrot of increased wages. Labour power cannot be considered a commodity because for this to be the case labour would have to be free in the dual sense referred to earlier. Economic regulation in the USSR can be seen in terms of overt and continual state intervention because the social relations of production are necessarily transparent (Ticktin, 1973, p. 41). The veil of commodity fetishism does not hide the political nature of economic decisions from the direct producers. This raises, therefore, the question of economic regulation and the nature of production itself.

During the labour time expended, the worker, operating with the means of production located in the enterprise and in cooperation with others, produces an output. The technological level, volume, rate of renewal and rate of innovation of the means of production are determined by the centre. So too is the flow of necessary inputs to produce the specified output. The general direction of output and its composition are determined by the political decisions of the ruling group and are turned into plan instructions in the iterative planning process between the enterprise and the centre. Here again the antagonistic nature of the social relations of production assert themselves. The reason for this is that planning is not solely a technical process, though it clearly has a technical dimension.

The argument associated with Ticktin (1978, pp. 44–8), and Smith (1975, pp. 27–32), is that effective planning is impossible in the USSR because socialist planning implies the conscious direction of the economy by the freely associated direct producers. In the absence of such participation, in conditions of scarcity and social antagonism, the supposed planning degenerates into over-centralised bureaucratic administration of the economy. In the Soviet context the plan is only amenable to control by the worker in the most formal sense. Participation, even to the maximum extent in the party, trade unions, production conferences at enterprise level and so on, gives the worker little direct control over the general direction of the economy, the assortment or quality of goods, or the particular output of his enterprise. The hierarchical nature of the society and of economic control, coupled with the principle of one-man management effectively excludes direct participation (Ellman, 1979, pp. 17–18). On top of this the very methodology of planning, on the 'ratchet principle' or 'planning from the achieved level', means that effective change is impossible, and the plan appears to take on a life of its own, outside the influence of the worker or even the manager (Birman, 1978, pp. 153–72).

The workforce is only able, in a negative and indirect sense, to maintain a degree of control over its own labour process and thereby affect the volume and nature of the surplus. As suggested in the first chapter, this type of control is implicit in any hierarchically ordered society where the direct producers are divorced from the means of production. It is, however, management's function to minimise this negative control and at an operational level extract the surplus which, under capitalism takes a value form. In the USSR this relationship is both qualitatively and quantitatively different.

Under capitalism, the role of rewards and discipline, via the media of money and unemployment respectively, reinforces management's task. However much the balance of class forces shift, ultimately these sanctions are at the disposal of management to discipline the workforce. The precise balance between reward and sanction will be determined by the broader features of the period. As already noted, with a significantly large reserve army of labour, management's concerns in recession will be different from their position during periods of boom when near to full employment exists and labour shortages develop. Coupled with this a particular feature of capital's control has developed during the current recession. That is the ability to shift productive capacity between locations and thereby discipline the workforce with the threat of such action. In the USSR the disciplining role of unemployment is absent, the role of money is ambiguous and the physical removal of productive capacity has no similar function in the USSR.

The role of management in the USSR is similar to that of its counterparts under capitalism, but it is more ambiguous and problematic. Under capitalism the performance of a manager or a management team relates directly to their economic results which are mediated through the impersonal market, and their rewards, either salary or more nebulous elements like prestige, are a function of this performance. Managerial remuneration packages under capitalism are increasingly composed of salary plus bonuses and so on, but, more importantly, commonly include shares in the company by whom they are employed. Consequently, any objective grounds for presuming that a divorce of ownership from control will lead to different patterns of behaviour, is being eroded. There is a unity of purpose between the eventual owners of the extracted surplus and those whose function it is to supervise the process of surplus extraction. Many radical writers have pointed out that the concept of a divorce of ownership from control need not lead to any fundamental change in the operation of capitalism, because ultimately managerial performance is subject to market disciplines (Blackburn, 1972, pp. 164–86). Even a more orthodox writer like Marris (1964) has pointed out that the divorce between ownership and control need not lead to a divergence of objectives. His argument that owners and managers may well have a single unified aim of maximising the 'balanced rate of growth', develops a concept not dissimilar to the Marxist notion of accumulation as the prime motivation of capital. Furthermore, the capitalist manager has, to varying degrees, depending upon the constraints placed upon him, control over the eventual disposition of the extracted surplus. He may determine the proportions of dividend paid, the level of retained profits and can determine the level and type of reinvestment in new capacity. This is a powerful motivating influence on the behaviour of the capitalist manager, because not only are current rewards dependent upon current performance, but so too are security and rewards into the future. There is, therefore, a correspondence between the interests of the owners of the surplus and the agents whose role it is to supervise the extraction of that surplus. Plus there is an unambiguous, objective medium through which managerial performance can be assessed.

In the USSR managers are also judged by their performance, and money rewards, prestige and advancement follow success. Money rewards may well be secondary, for the reasons already suggested above, to advancement up the *nomenklatura* or movement to a more prestigious enterprise or location, where access to consumer goods and cultural amenities may be easier or more certain. However, Soviet managers have little or no control over the surplus they are responsible for extracting and cannot guarantee that their success will lead to an enhancement of the productive capacity of their enterprise via reinvestment. Furthermore, the mechanism through which their performance is assessed, the plan, is amenable to manipulation by them.

Therefore, plan fulfilment does not necessarily reflect their ability to supervise the surplus extraction process, so much as it measures their ability in the bureaucratic process of plan compilation.

The fundamental antagonism between the ruling group and the direct producers is, therefore, supplemented by a further plane of antagonism between the economic administration at the centre, who control the disposition of the surplus once produced, and the immediate controllers of the means of production, whose task it is to put the plan into operation, enterprise management staff. The suggestion is that those who set the plan targets at the centre are continually thwarted by the self-interest of those whose task it is to supervise the process of production. The reason for this is that no Soviet plan, or indeed any plan, can be all-embracing and completely unambiguous. The complexity of the task can be illustrated by Gossnab's current responsibility for the compilation of 18 000 material balances and responsibility for the allocation of one million specific product lines (Fedorenko, 1984, p. 13). As a consequence this leaves a degree of discretion to enterprise management, who act in a manner most suitable to themselves. This disrupts the internal logic of the plan and instead of being a set of unified directives for the enterprise it degenerates into an ever-changing series of disjointed and often mutually contradictory administrative measures, as the centre attempts to keep up with the reality they are supposed to be directing. This is not to suggest that Soviet enterprise heads are deliberately corrupt or disruptive but is a recognition of a well-documented element of Soviet industrial life (Berliner, 1968, pp. 53–4). In fact some actions, even if they are illegal or semi-legal, are essential for the functioning of the system and even though their widespread existence is acknowledged and often criticised, they are nevertheless unchecked.

The ambiguous position of management has an impact upon the negative control exercised by the workforce. Managerial rewards are in the last analysis determined by plan fulfilment and their aim is to fulfil or marginally overfulfil the plan. This leads the enterprise director to courses of action directly in conflict with the aims of the centre.

Within the planning process, it is rational for enterprise management to underestimate the productive capacity of their plant, in this way the targets received will be achievable within present plant capacity, even if the enterprise is faced by the ever present supply problems that plague Soviet industry. This implies an underestimation of the potential surplus that could be extracted from the plant's workforce. Of course, ironically, this action exacerbates the supply difficulties.

Directly related to the above, if the enterprise anticipates supply difficulties, then it will be rational to overestimate the material supplies necessary for production. This is particularly true of labour supplies when the USSR is faced by an apparent labour shortage. It is irrelevant for the individual manager that his action actually creates the general difficulty he is trying to avoid. If he did not act in this manner it could not be guaranteed that other enterprises would follow his example and, therefore, no overall benefit, only individual harm, would result. As Berliner pointed out in the late fifties, labour will be hoarded to meet unexpected contingencies (Berliner, 1968, pp. 75–113). This situation has not changed and the continual changes in plan targets, changes in priorities, breakdowns due to poor quality machine tools coupled with inadequate maintenance and repair, staff being withdrawn for agriculture work at harvest time, late supply of essential inputs, all lead to arhythmic work patterns and confirm the rationality of labour hoarding for enterprise management seeking to fulfil plan targets. (These elements will be explored more systematically in the next chapter.) It is worth pointing out that this dynamic is the complete opposite of that which operates under capitalism, where the key to managerial success is the expulsion of living labour from the production process. The safety factor of hoarded labour in the USSR, leads to overmanning and underemployment which further reduces any correspondence between work and rewards. What effectively exists is a situation where the management recognise that they require at least the acquiescence of the workforce in order to be able to fulfil the plan. Hence a trade-off exists whereby the enterprise management quantify potential workforce resistance and underestimate capacity as a consequence, leading to a much lower intensity of labour than exists in the west. This in turn recreates the problem that the enterprise management is seeking to avoid.

It could be argued that the features of the labour process in the USSR so far identified are only different by degree to the capitalist labour process. However, whilst negative control exerted by workers exists under capitalism, it is nevertheless inimicable to that mode of production. At an abstract level it would be eradicated by the operation of the law of value. Consider a firm operating within a competitive market,[5] at a similar scale and technological level to its competitors, but where the workforce has been able to secure a degree of negative control. This may operate upon line speeds, manning levels or any other aspect of the labour process. The firm would find that the labour time necessary to produce the particular commodity would exceed the average socially necessary labour time. This expended labour power would not be reflected in the value of the commodity and the firm would find surplus labour-time, surplus value and profit all reduced. This decline of profitability, with respect to its more managerially aggressive competitors, would eventually lead to the firm being driven from the market, either by failure or takeover. The centralisation and concentration of capital that occurs as a consequence would mean that the control enjoyed by the workforce would be lost. This occurs either because the former employees will join the ranks of the reserve army of the unemployed, with all the effects that follow from that, or will be forced to work in the more aggressive environment without the negative control they once enjoyed.

The suggestion is that the operation of the law of value under the capitalist mode of production will undermine the objective basis of negative control and the form of control will tend towards the most efficient. This is not to deny that in reality this process may well be mediated by, for example, the operation of the social democratic state, which may well deflect the operation of the law of value under certain circumstances for some period of time.[6] Nor does it imply a unilinear movement towards the most efficient forms of control. The reality will be determined by the relationship between the antagonistic classes both globally and locally, but the inherent tendency will be as described above.

In the USSR, however, the forms of negative control are being reproduced continually as a feature of the political economy of the system and there is no inherent tendency for their elimination. They need not impair the enterprise's performance, if plan targets are deliberately manipulated to accommodate this behaviour, nor hinder the success and advancement of management, if this is dependent upon plan fulfilment, nor the worker's access to use-values, if this is only tenuously linked to the amount and quality of his work. Inefficient enterprises may well be criticised in the USSR, but they are not closed down, their means of production removed and their labour dispersed to more efficient enterprises. There is no real mechanism of managerial failure. Clearly there are managers who fail through corruption or incompetence, but an enterprise director who is well connected and adept at the process of planning will not be exposed by the economic mechanism. This is the point about the law of value under capitalism, it disciplines not only workers, but also capitalists and their managerial agents.

The outcome of production in the USSR is intended to comprise only use-values. However, as a result of the antagonistic relations of production, the result is an output comprised of two elements; firstly, a usable portion that has a use-value for the society as a whole, either as an intermediate product or as a finished product for consumption or investment purposes; secondly, an unusable portion that is waste and has no use-value (Ticktin, 1973, pp. 24–32). The determination of use-value and waste has both an objective and a subjective element. Objectively, an electronic switch that does not work is waste, but equally a pair of shoes that no one wants because they are of poor quality design, even though they could objectively function as shoes, are just as much waste as the switch. In the process of producing both waste and use-values, society utilises both living labour and labour embodied in the means of production. The end result is the same, some part of the socially expended labour time has resulted in no ultimate use-value for the society, even though the labour embodied in it has been recompensed as if it were socially necessary. This, therefore, limits the surplus available to the ruling group, extending apparently necessary labour time and reducing the surplus labour time of the workforce as a whole. This is not to suggest that only production under Soviet conditions is wasteful. Clearly under capitalism the antagonistic production relations lead to waste of a variety of forms. Again the discipline of the law of value will restrict the waste produced, from the point of view of the capitalist, and set into motion forces that will tend to eleminate wasteful production techniques and commodities. (This is essentially the same point as that concerning negative control outlined above.)

In the USSR this tendency does not exist in the realm of economic regulation as the automatic result of apparently impersonal forces. Wasteful production may reproduce itself, and administrative initiatives against it may succeed in specific instances, but only temporarily displacing the problem elsewhere, and such initiatives are continually necessary. The fundamental problem for the ruling group is that in the absence of the law of value, no unambiguous economic regulator exists that will simultaneously discipline the workforce and the enterprise management and provide the necessary correspondence and commensurability between labour time, use-values produced and rewards. The consequence is that individual enterprises effectively appear as autonomous elements in the surplus extraction process, representing localised trade-offs between enterprise management and workforce, yet continuously subject to necessary administrative interference from the centre. The next chapter considers the economic results produced by these antagonistic social relations of production.

3 The Vicious Circle of Soviet Economic Problems

SOVIET ECONOMIC PROBLEMS

So far, the antagonistic nature of the social relations of production in the USSR have been presented and developed in a theoretical sense only. The concrete expression of these relationships produces a series of interconnected problems. Figure 3.1 attempts to describe these interrelationships and present them in a circular flow diagram. The unbroken lines in the figure represent the direct links between particular problems, whilst the broken lines are an attempt to identify the way in which the problems feed back into other areas. This form of presentation, even though it understates the complexity and linkages involved, is useful for purposes of exposition and provides a framework which will be utilised over the next two chapters to analyse these questions.

The central element of this analysis is the failure of the ruling group to achieve planned levels of economic growth, through the extraction of the socially produced surplus. This can be viewed as both the culmination of the process and its starting point from one time period to the next. The slow down in economic growth has to be located within the operation of the Soviet socio-economic system and cannot be attributed to external or historically specific factors.[1] For example, commentators have sought to explain the decline of growth rates as a result of agricultural problems, demographic factors (this issue will be taken up more fully in Chapter 4), depletion of easily accessible natural resources, low elasticities of substitution of capital for labour and so on. Now, whilst it may be correct that these exogenous factors affect annual economic performance, they are unconvincing as explanations of the longer term trends with regard to economic growth.[2] This section will present a summary of the empirical evidence regarding these problems, will trace some of the linkages in the figure and will show that the problems are phenomena that have been reproduced over time.

The recent experience of the Soviet economy has been characterised

46

Figure 3.1   The vicious circle of Soviet labour productivity problems

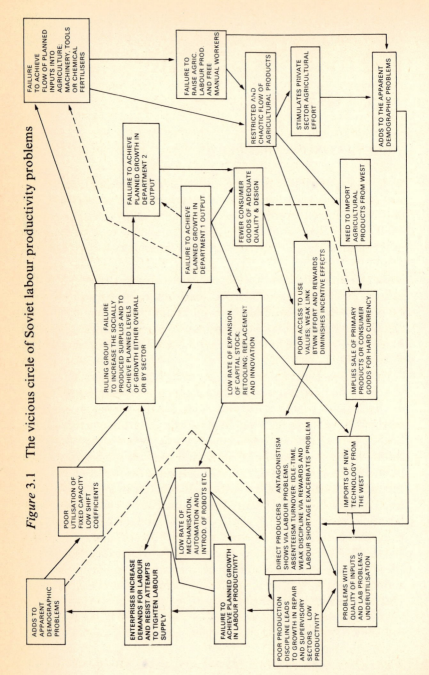

by a slow-down in overall rates of economic growth. The rapid growth rates of the 1930s and the post-war years of reconstruction have given way to much more modest and decelerating rates of growth in the present period. This, of course, ignores the question of the nature of growth itself. As Rakovsky (1981, pp. 16–21) pointed out in the early 1930s, quantitative growth may well be achieved at the cost of negative qualitative changes in production which may well cast doubt on the precise nature of the growth attained.

Table 3.1 indicates the general pattern of Soviet economic performance over the period since the Second World War. It should be noted that from this perspective Soviet growth appears impressive. The general indicators do, however, show a number of the distinctive features of Soviet development. Firstly, even though the gross social product and national income produced are still growing, this is appreciably slower than in previous periods. Secondly, there has been proportionally much higher growth in Department One than in Department Two, even though the ruling group has attempted to change this balance. Thirdly, growth in agricultural output is much more modest than growth in industrial output over this period. Fourthly, the stagnation in industrial output in the 1980s is mirrored in the output of both Departments. This generalised slow-down in growth can be confirmed from Table 3.2, where the annual average rates of growth of national income and gross industrial output are shown to have steadily deteriorated since the small rise from the Seventh to the Eighth Five Year Plan. Furthermore, the failure to meet plan targets in the Eleventh Plan is clearly indicated.

Failure to achieve planned levels of economic growth, either in the sense of failure to fulfill the overall plan or by failure to achieve individual sectoral targets, leads to three problems. The flow of inputs into agriculture will fail to reach planned levels, the output of Department One, investment goods, and Department Two, consumer goods, will also fail to reach planned levels. The actual proportions will be dependent upon the sectoral distribution of the failure and the priority accorded to the various sectors by the ruling group, during the particular production period.

The restricted flow of inputs into the agricultural sector, already plagued by geographical and climatic limitations and experiencing a situation where greater amounts of investment yield smaller increments in output (Smith, 1981, pp. 41–3; 46), will mean that the supply of agricultural products will either be reduced or made even more uncertain. As Soviet sources comment, large fluctuations in

Table 3.1 General economic indicators (1940–83) 1940 = 1

	1940	1960	1965	1970	1975	1980	1981	1982	1983	1984
Gross social product	1	4.2	5.7	8.1	11	13.6	14	14.5	15.1	15.6
National income	1	4.4	6.0	8.7	11.4	14.1	14.6	15.2	15.8	16.3
Basic funds for production in all branches of the economy	1	3.2	5.0	7.4	11.2	16	17	18.2	19.5	20.6
All industrial production	1	5.2	7.9	12	17	21	22	22	23	24
Production of means of production (Department 1)	1	6.6	11	16	23	29	30	31	32	33
Production of consumer goods (Department 2)	1	3.2	4.4	6.5	9	11	11	12	12	13
Gross agricultural production	1	1.6	1.8	2.2	2.3	2.5	2.4	2.6	2.7	2.7
Capital investment	1	6.4	8.7	12.5	17.5	20.8	21.6	22.3	23.6	23.3
No. of workers & office workers	1	1.8	2.3	2.7	3	3.3	3.4	3.4	3.4	3.4
Productivity of social labour	1	4	5.3	7.4	9.2	10.8	11.1	11.5	11.9	12.2
in industry	1	3	3.7	4.9	6.6	7.7	7.9	8.1	8.4	8.7
in agriculture	1	2	2.4	3.3	3.5	4	4	4.2	4.5	4.5
in rail transport	1	2.3	3	3.8	4.7	4.7	4.7	4.7	4.9	5.0
in construction	1	2.9	3.7	4.5	5.8	6.4	6.5	6.7	6.9	7.1
Real income per head	1	2.5	3	4	4.9	5.8	6	6	6.1	6.3

Sources: Narodnoe Khozyaistvo (1983), pp. 35–6; *Narodnoe Khozyaistvo* (1984), pp. 36–7; *Narodnoe Khozyaistvo* (1985), pp. 36–7.

Table 3.2   Average annual rates of growth (%)

Plan period		National income	Industrial output
1961–65	7th	5.6	6.5
1966–70	8th	7.1	7.4
1971–75	9th	5.1	6.4
1976–80	10th	3.9	4.4
1981–1985	Plan	3.4 to 3.7	
1981 (actual)		3.2	3.8
1982 (actual)		2	2.8
1983 (actual)		3.1	2.8

Sources: Khromov (1981), pp. 17–18; *Pravda* 24 January 1982; *Pravda* 20 November 1981; *Vestnik Statistiki* (1984), No. 3, p. 73; Fil'ev (1983), p. 13.

national income can often be attributed to agricultural problems (Zagaitov and Polovinkin, 1984, p. 75). This has a number of ramifications.

The ruling group will be forced to import agricultural products from the west in order to maintain the necessary supply of foodstuffs to the workforce, hoping, thereby, to reduce potential discontent and to maintain domestic stability. This will depend mainly upon external sales of primary products and limited sales of scarce consumer goods to earn the necessary hard currency to purchase the imports. The ability to do this is conditioned, particularly, by world market prices for primary products, especially oil. As a consequence it appears internally that the ruling group cannot resolve the agricultural supply question without western imports and externally it provides support for the argument that socialism has failed because the USSR cannot feed itself and has to rely on the west.

Furthermore, the uncertain supply of agricultural products stimulates private sector agricultural efforts (A. Lane, 1983, pp. 23–41). This may operate directly to the detriment of the socialised sector as collective farm workers spend increasing time on their private plot. It may also reduce the flow of labour to the socialised sector in general, as older people and women will tend to work on the private plot rather than attempt to get part-time work. The failure of socialised agriculture will bolster the private sector and legal and semi-legal markets. From the ruling group's viewpoint this will have a negative ideological effect. The practical impact is to add to the labour supply problems in the collective farm sector, as a result of this misdirection of effort. This is itself resolved in a particularly wasteful manner by drafting in industrial workers and students to assist in the agricultural sector particularly at harvest time. As Manevich (1981, p. 60) has pointed out, in 1970, collective farms called upon other branches of the economy to supply 1.4 times more workers for harvest work than in 1960, and by 1978, 2.4 times more workers than in 1970. Each worker stays on the collective farm for approximately one month and of the 15.6 million people involved, 7.8 million are drawn from branches of material production (Manevich, 1981, p. 60). This has a deleterious effect upon agricultural production, as the incoming labour is unfamiliar with the work and poorly motivated, and performs with half of the productivity of permanent agricultural workers. Moreover, as a basic production worker is four times more effective at his own work than at agricultural work, the loss to the economy is magnified (Manevich, 1981, p. 60). Also if 15.6 million people lose two days travelling to and from the collective farm, then that is equivalent to a year's work for 110 000 people (Manevich, 1981, p. 60). As previously noted, it also has a negative effect upon industrial production and encourages enterprise directors to overestimate their demand for labour to cover this eventuality. This is particularly the case if no mechanism exists to penalise this activity which in the circumstances is completely rational.

Failure to achieve planned growth in Department Two output leads directly to fewer consumer goods. This of course avoids the question about the desirability and quality of the output actually produced (Orlov, 1983, pp. 101, 103, 107; Ulybin, 1984, p. 22–31). Furthermore, if hard currency has to be obtained to purchase agricultural products, this places further constraints on domestic consumption. This is exacerbated by the fact that Soviet consumer goods destined for western markets have to be of higher quality and dependability than normal, if they are to be competitive. Soviet cars, for example, have even been rebuilt or refitted with appropriate accessories at special depots outside the USSR. This further reduces the flow of consumer goods internally, as a disproportionate amount of labour time will be expended upon commodities destined for western markets. As consumer goods include processed agricultural products, agricultural supply difficulties will further reduce the availability of consumer goods in general.

The failure to guarantee the supply of foodstuffs and consumer goods, taken together, implies a shortage of the necessary use-values to motivate the Soviet workforce and consequently diminishes the incentive effects of any attempted reforms. In the period 1976–80 wage funds and collective public consumption funds rose by 28 per cent and collective farm wages rose by about 30 per cent, but consumer goods production only rose by 21 per cent and retail trade turnover only rose 22 per cent (Belkin, 1982, p. 2. Boiko, 1982, pp. 131–8). Table 3.3 illustrates the diminishing planned rate of growth of retail trade turnover and also shows the continual actual shortfall. This, coupled with the problems of poor quality and unwanted goods, gives rise to the all-pervasive nature of the queue and the continuing difficulties in obtaining consumer goods.

Table 3.3   The annual average rate of growth of retail trade turnover

	1971–5	1976–80	1983–4
Planned	7.2	5.2	4.2
Actual	6.4	4.4	2.9

Source: Sverdlik (1985), p. 108.

Furthermore, personal saving now stands at its highest level ever. For example, in 1980 the level of savings equalled 156 billion roubles, two thirds of which was demand deposits (earning two per cent interest) and one third was time deposits (earning three per cent interest). Interest payments alone in 1980 totalled 3.5 billion roubles (Sverdlik, 1982, p. 120). This level of savings would be sufficient to allow all those employed in the national economy to take 209 days of unpaid leave. By comparison in 1960 the level of savings would only have allowed 50 days of unpaid leave (Sverdlik, 1982, pp. 121–2). To highlight the problems in consumer goods production it should be noted that the savings level in 1980 was equivalent to seven months' turnover in the retail trade sector (Sverdlik, 1982, p. 122). The problems of consumer goods production and the consequent increase in personal savings have a series of deleterious effects.

The trading network, faced by continual shortages, will tend to lower its standards for quality and accept anything the producers will supply and then will be left with unsold goods (Kondrashov, 1983, p. 3). Belkin (1982, p. 78) suggests that each year between three and four billion roubles' worth of unwanted goods are left in the trade network. Therefore, the distribution network does not and will not act to discipline the producers of shoddy goods. Moreover, the existence of considerable personal savings may explain the increase in the amount of time spent between jobs and the slowness with which youths are drawn into productive work. If people moving between jobs can afford to wait before returning to work and live off past savings, or if youths can live at their parents' expense before entering productive work, then there will be a negative effect on labour supply. Consequently, the failure in consumer goods production not only presents problems in providing adequate incentives for those in work, but also adds to labour productivity, labour discipline, and labour turnover problems.

Failure to achieve planned growth in Department One, investment goods, as already suggested, will constrain the future production of both agricultural and consumer goods. Soviet sources note that the share of capital investment in Department Two fell from 15.1 per cent in the Eighth Plan, to 13.8 per cent in the Ninth Plan, to 12.1 per cent in the Tenth Plan and in the first years of the Eleventh Plan reached only twelve per cent (Aleksandrova and Fedorovskaya, 1984). It may also restrict present consumption if resources are diverted to prioritised sectors. However, there is a further impact because if the flow of investment goods is inadequate this will lead to further potential problems (Rumer, 1982, pp. 53–68). The annual shortfall in the production of producer goods has been estimated at between 15 to 17 billion roubles per annum (Ryzhkov, 1982, p. 11).

Initially, there will be problems in expanding fixed productive capacity at the existing technological level and providing the correct mix of equipment, plant, instruments and tools. The lack of basic implements in some sectors is the result of priorities being placed elsewhere. For example, in construction 30–35 per cent of workers don't get the tools they require because they are not manufactured but have to be made by the workers themselves, and this is extremely wasteful (*Sotsialisticheskaya Industriya*, 31 October 1979, p. 4). In the trade sector, for example, only about 60 per cent of the demand for equipment is satisfied and much of this is obselete, and only 40 per cent of the required spares are produced (Shimanskii, 1983, p. 3).

Furthermore, the maintenance, replacement and re-tooling of present capacity will be jeopardised. Even though the USSR has the largest inventory of metal working equipment in the world, its annual rate of renovation generally is only two to 2.7 per cent and even if this is upgraded as planned to four per cent, it will take into the next century to renovate this critical sector (Kulagin, 1983, p. 102). In some crucial sectors of the economy this rate falls below two per cent. For example, it is 1.9 per cent in the petro-chemical industry, 1.4 per cent in ferrous metallurgy, one per cent in the pulp and paper industry and only 0.3 per cent in the electrical power industry (Kheiman, 1984). To put this into an international perspective, the comparable replacement rate in the USA is 5.5 to six per cent and in FRG eight to nine per cent (Kheiman, 1982, p. 34). As Soviet economists point out, only approximately 30 per cent of Soviet capital investment is channelled into reconstruction, whilst the comparable figure for the GDR is 60 per cent (Kostin, 1980, pp. 26–7; Chentemirov, 1980, p. 35). Furthermore, in the USSR, 50 per cent of the machine tool inventory is located in repair shops, which illustrates that the problems of inadequate production techniques and poor quality inputs lead to a growing repair sector which inefficiently absorbs not only capital equipment, but also labour on an increasing scale (Kulagin, 1983, p. 105). The rate of retirement of fixed equipment throughout the economy could be seen as a measure of the dynamism of the capital formation process and in the USSR this rate has been declining, from 1.8 per cent in 1970 to 1.3 per cent in 1981 (Smyshlyaeva, 1983, p. 26). This further reinforces the need for expenditure on repair, as approximately 30 to 40 per cent of equipment has been in use for fifteen to twenty years (Zotov, 1984, p. 19). As Abalkin (1982, pp. 6–7) suggests, functional but obsolete equipment represents wasteful production practices and it is no good to simply develop equipment extensively, but it is essential to raise the technological level.

Aganbegyan (1982, p. 2) suggests, machine building in general is declining in absolute output terms and he identifies the cause of this problem as difficulties in the metallurgical industry. He points out that in a five year period, between ten and twelve billion roubles were spent on repairs, whilst only five per cent of this amount was spent on developing this industry. Other Soviet sources have commented on the backwardness, the lack of innovation, the lack of specialisation and the disincentives to investment in this crucial sector (*Ekonomika i organizatsiya promyshlennogo proizvodstva*, No. 1, 1982, pp. 23–145). The outcome of these problems, as Pokrovskii (1984) notes, is that 30 per cent of machine building output is second quality, that is, either obsolete or sub-standard.

The failures also discourage innovation and process development.

In 1981, even though 205 000 machine tools were produced, only 10 000 of these were numerically controlled and only 830 sets of automatic and semi-automatic transfer lines were produced (Kulagin, 1983, p. 102). The production of new robotic forms of equipment are also proceeding more slowly than desired (Bachurin, 1981, p. 17). As Smirnov (1984, p. 14) points out, it is necessary to produce not just robotic equipment, but also the auxiliary equipment that can account for between 40 and 100 per cent of the basic cost. These difficulties are reinforced by a planning mechanism that often appears to penalise rather than reward innovation, and management will opt for proven techniques rather than adopt riskier newer methods, supplies for which may be dubious anyway. Planning from the achieved level reinforces these risk avoiding strategies on the part of plant management who have no direct personal interest other than plan fulfilment, achieved as easily as possible. This leads to a further set of problems.

Low rates of innovation and process development have led the ruling group to turn to the west and import technology, but this involves similar problems to those associated with agricultural imports, the need to earn hard currency. However, the problems are magnified with regard to technology imports. Agricultural imports are invariably utilised, but the technology imports are often inadequately utilised or even left idle. In 1973 there was 1.5 billion roubles of uninstalled foreign plant in the USSR and this rose by 500 per cent in the period 1974–9. In 1983 in the petro-chemical industry alone there was 845 million roubles of imported equipment lying unutilised (Selyunin, 1979, p. 2; Kuzmishchev and Odinets, 1983, p. 2). The long and troublesome history of technology imports can be explained, in the most general terms, as a result of western production processes being designed with western technology and inputs in mind. Consequently, the transplantation of processes into an alien environment will only be successful if the quality and flow of inputs is guaranteed.[3] Interestingly the importation of western technology demonstrates the point made earlier regarding comparable manning levels. Manevich (1969, p. 34) has pointed out that in the chemical industry, plant purchased from the west has led to the following manning levels; 1.5 times as many basic production workers; 3.5 times as many engineering, technical and administrative staff; eight times as many auxiliary workers. Recent Soviet criticisms of technology imports suggest that domestic innovation may well be more effective in the longer term. There is also a further dimension, in that for the USSR to appear technologically inferior, or worse, dependent upon the west, is undesirable for the ruling group on both strategic and propagandistic grounds. However, as Cooper (1985, p. 88 and p. 107) points out, the significance of technology imports should not be overstated.

Perhaps more importantly, failure to innovate exacerbates the impact of Department One failures on the rate of mechanisation and automation within the Soviet economy (Shimenkov, 1984, pp. 110–11; Baibakov, 1980, p. 109). This problem has a number of dimensions.

Firstly, even though the number of mechanised shops, workplaces and enterprises is growing (Rusanov, 1983, pp. 82–3) and the proportion of manual workers has been consistently reduced (See Table 3.4), falling by more than five per cent in the decade 1972-82, the absolute

Table 3.4   Percentage of industrial labour force employed in manual work (%)

1965	1972	1975	1979	1982
40.4	35.4	34.6	32.8	30.2

Sources: Kostin (1981), p. 32; Sonin (1977), p. 5; Kostin (1984), p. 25.

number of manual workers in material production at the beginning of the Eleventh Five Year Plan was still 40 million (Kostin, 1984, p. 25, and 1985, p. 8). This problem is distributed unevenly throughout the economy, but all Soviet sources are agreed that the volume of manual work must be reduced (Ivanova, 1984, pp. 31–41). As Danilov (1977) explains, the Central Statistical Agency classifies manual work in three forms:

manual labour where machines are utilised, for example loaders on conveyor belts
manual labour without machinery, for example assemblers, auxiliary workers, loaders and unloaders
manual adjustment and repair of machinery, for example, machine tool and equipment setters, repair mechanics (p. 42).

The bulk of manual work is of the second category and is concentrated in particular industries like machine building, food and light industry and mining (Danilov, 1977, p. 43). Whilst 70 per cent of basic production is mechanised, this falls to approximately 40 per cent in construction work (Ivanov, 1984, p. 37), 29 per cent for auxiliary production and 22 per cent for loading and unloading work (Tsvetkov, 1980, p. 73). In the metallurgical industry for example, over half of all heavy tasks are performed manually. Only twenty per cent of the work in the retail trade sector is mechanised, and in 1983, in the RSFSR, they only received 700 out of the required 3500 electrical loading devices necessary to reduce manual labour (Shimanskii, 1983, p. 3). There are over five million people alone employed in heavy manual work connected with loading and unloading work (Smirnova and Sabo, 1984, p. 252). As Aitov (1979, p. 2) pointed out in the late 1970s, 50 per cent more people were employed in loading and unloading work in trade organisations than there were employed in foundry and metallurgy work. In agriculture the proportion of manual work is highest of all.

This poses two pressing problems. Firstly, unnecessarily large numbers of people are employed in relatively unproductive, unskilled manual labour with a consequent effect on overall rates of labour productivity. (This is made worse by the low level of technically substantiated norms in the sectors where manual labour is predominant. This question is explored in more detail later.) Furthermore, while six to ten per cent of the basic workforce in production is unskilled, this rises to 60 per cent in the service sector (Aitov, 1979, p. 2). It should be noted that employment in the service sector has grown from 11.7 per cent of the workforce in 1940 to 25.1 per cent in the late 1970s (Kostin (ed.), 1979, p. 12). This trend has continued and in the period 1979–84 employment in the non-productive sector (auxiliary, service and repair work) has grown by 33.8 per cent, whilst employment in basic production has grown by only 12.7 per cent (Kostin, 1984, p. 33). Kostakov (1986, p. 3) suggests that at the end of 1984, 26.7 per cent of the employed population were employed in the service sector. The repair sector, as already noted, is a particular problem. At the beginning of the Eleventh Plan, 3.9 million people were employed in repair work, but only 400 000 of them were in specialist repair enterprises, which leads as a consequence to considerable duplication, inefficiency and idle-time (Kostin, 1984, p. 27). There is also a cost in terms of lost production as the following example suggests. In the late 1970s there were three times as many people and four times as much capacity engaged in making spares and repairing tractors as there were in basic production of new tractors (Manevich, 1977, p. 123). Furthermore, approximately 60 per cent of construction workers are engaged solely in repair work (Zotov, 1984, p. 19).

Secondly, as the majority of these workers are drawn from the older age groups, as they retire they will have to be replaced. Younger people are unlikely to want this type of work as their expectations have been raised by education. For example, 90 per cent of the migrants from the countryside now have secondary education and want more than unskilled loading work, hence there are problems of potential discontent. This will lead to the misplacement of trained cadres and the combination of their frustrated expectations and heavy manual work will exacerbate labour turnover problems. The only real possibility is to mechanise these tasks, but this process is itself contradictory.

Even though Soviet commentators call for increased production of robotic equipment it is highly uncertain that this would lead to any vast improvement in Soviet industrial performance. Even though the stock of robotic equipment is increasing, much of it is left unutilised for long periods of time (Vasil'eva, 1980, p. 2) and approximately 50 per cent is left completely uninstalled (Lebedev, 1981, p. 2). Furthermore, successful utilisation of robotic equipment demands a higher degree of production discipline than currently exists in the USSR (Vasin, 1981, p. 2). Robotic equipment requires reliable, standardised high quality inputs if it is to function efficiently (Vasin, 1981a, p. 2; Gerasimov and Petrov, 1983, p. 2). Constant breakdowns and inadequate spare parts simply add to costs and wastefulness. Furthermore, there is also evidence of worker hostility towards the introduction of robotic equipment and sabotage attempts against the devices have led, in some plants, to them being cordoned off from the workforce (Groys, 1984). It is likely that present Soviet robotic equipment is comparable to first generation simple manipulators which are technologically inferior to the third generation equipment now in increasing use in Western Europe, the USA and Japan.

A common complaint is that the design of Soviet robotics is not closely co-ordinated with industrial needs and that single isolated units are wasteful and irrational (Vasin, 1983, p. 2). Parasyuk (1983, p. 1) points out that the allocation of new technology is often undertaken in a formalistic sense, simply to fulfil the plan for new technology, without thinking out the implications for the whole work environment. As Aganbegyan (1985, p. 2) notes, it is not always sensible to replace a worker, with wage costs of 4000 roubles per annum, with robotic equipment costing 40 to 50 000 roubles.

There is also a problem with the disproportional mechanisation of basic production and auxiliary tasks. This occurs because 80 per cent of funds available to enterprises for mechanisation go on basic production and only 20 per cent on auxiliary production, and designers spend more time considering the mechanisation of basic production (Kostin (ed.), 1979, p. 129; Parfenov, 1979, p. 5; Tushinov, 1980, p. 3). However, measures to mechanise auxiliary production are 2.8–3.5 times more effective than similar measures affecting direct production. For example, it has been estimated that one million roubles spent on new technology will have the potential to release 137 people if spent on mechanising processing work; 170 people if spent on mechanising foundry work; but 476 people if spent on transport, loading and unloading operations (Baranenkova, 1980, p. 53). In machine building itself it takes ten thousand roubles to free one manual worker from basic production but only three thousand roubles to free one auxiliary worker (Kostin (ed.), 1979, pp. 15–16). Furthermore, whilst one million roubles spent on new technology in 1970 freed 80 industrial workers, by 1980 the same expenditure would only free 57 workers. This gives some indication of the rising costs of technology (Kostin (ed.), 1979, p. 26).

Enterprises tend to give a low priority to freeing auxiliary workers because it will not necessarily make plan fulfilment any easier and may even impinge on it if it reduces the pool of labour available for things like harvesting work or construction assignments for the local Soviet. Also, there is no guarantee that if one enterprise acts in a responsible manner that others will follow its example. Unless the plan specifically penalises the enterprise, there is no incentive to release auxiliary workers.

The low priority accorded to this problem at enterprise level is reproduced at the aggregate level. Organisationally, the machinery for auxiliary work is produced at 400 different enterprises which are the responsibility of 40 different ministries and only fifteen per cent of the output is centrally planned. Consequently, enterprises are forced to produce much of their own requirements of auxiliary equipment and tools. It has been estimated that approximately 75 per cent of requirements are produced in 'dwarf workshops' (Sonin, 1977, p. 13). This again is wasteful of capacity and reduces labour productivity, but from the point of view of the enterprise is rational if it gives access to otherwise unavailable equipment. Manevich (1980, p. 79) makes a similar point with regard to the production of specialised industrial instruments. In the machine building industry they are produced in

420 different plants, employing 460 000 workers. However, if the work was rationalised and specialised the same volume of output could be achieved by 175 000 workers.

The desired impact of increasing mechanisation, plus the introduction of industrial robots, is to increase labour productivity, labour discipline and release manual workers, but this is problematic. Mechanisation in itself does not necessarily automatically bring these advantages. The mechanisation of production takes place within the socio-economic context of the particular system and it is this which determines the eventual outcome of these processes. For example, as already noted, the importation of western technology does not necessarily raise labour productivity nor produce comparable manning levels. Likewise, as Dzokaeva (1982, p. 11) points out, the introduction of computers into accountancy sections does not necessarily lead to lower staff levels, less paperwork or more efficiency. An example cited by Khromov (1981, p. 20), illustrates the point that the re-tooling and re-equipping of Soviet enterprises need not diminish the workforce. In seventeen refurbished Moscow enterprises, ten envisaged an increase in the workforce of on average sixteen per cent; three had no plans for change; only four indicated a reduction in the workforce. Furthermore, once mechanised equipment is available, it too needs to be utilised efficiently. Balashov (1983, p. 2) notes that in the USSR machinery is often used unnecessarily for jobs that could be accomplished better manually and the net result is more waste.

Mechanisation will only lead to a tightening of labour utilisation, increasingly intensive exploitation and a growing extracted surplus if the socio-economic mechanism forces that conclusion. If it does not then mechanisation may well lead to the more wasteful utilisation of capacity. Modern automated equipment needs to be utilised on a three shift basis if it is to justify its costs of production. However, shift coefficients in many sectors of the Soviet economy are low and declining (See Appendix). An explanation for these problems can only be outlined after a consideration of the complementary problem of declining rates of growth of labour productivity.

LABOUR PRODUCTIVITY AND THE SURPLUS

It was argued in Chapter 1 that the socially produced surplus can be expanded in one of two ways. It can be expanded in the absolute sense by increasing the volume of labour inputs, either by employing more people in the socialised sector of the economy or by increasing the length of the working day or the working week. Or it can be expanded relatively by increasing the productivity of labour already employed, reducing necessary labour-time and extending surplus labour-time. During the course of economic development in the USSR, these processes have operated simultaneously and growth in output is a result of both an increasing absolute and relative surplus (*Narodnoe Khozyaisto SSSR*, 1983, p. 36). This is illustrated in Table 3.5.

Table 3.5   Growth in industrial production accounted for by productivity increases

1st Five Year Plan	51%	9th Five Year Plan	84%
2nd Five Year Plan	79%	10th Five Year Plan	75%
War Years and 4th	69%	11th Plan (planned)	90%
5th Five Year Plan	68%	1981 (actual)	62%
6th Five Year Plan	72%	1982 (actual)	61%
7th Five Year Plan	62%	1983 (actual)	80%
8th Five Year Plan	73%	1984 (actual)	93%

Sources: *Narodnoe Khozyaistvo* (1983), p. 36; Fil'ev (1983), p. 13; *Vestnik Statistiki* (1984), No. 4. p. 69; *Narodnoe Khozyaistvo* (1985), p. 37.

However, the possibilities of increasing the absolute surplus have been much restricted since the mid-sixties. This is a result of a series of factors. There has been a reduction in the natural growth rate of the population, even though the birth rate has risen recently, as indicated in Table 3.6. Furthermore, the average annual rate of growth of the number of workers in the economy as a whole has continued to decline, as shown in Table 3.7. When the industrial workforce alone is considered, the decline in growth is even more stark, as Table 3.8 indicates. The growth in the population of working age was approximately eighteen per cent for the decade 1971–80, but it is unlikely to exceed five per cent in the decade 1981–90 (Kostin (ed.), 1979, p. 12). Table 3.9 shows in more detail the expected growth in both absolute and percentage terms.

These demographic changes have been accompanied by an increase in average life expectancy which has led to a change in the age structure of the population and consequently a larger proportion of the population reaching a pensionable age (Novitskii, 1982, p. 2; Aper'yan, 1983, pp. 82–3). Pensioners now number 50 million in

Table 3.6   Birth rate, death rate and natural rate of
population growth (per 1000 population)

	Birth rate	Death rate	Natural growth
1940	31.2	18	13.2
1960	24.9	7.1	17.8
1965	18.4	7.3	11.1
1970	17.4	8.2	9.2
1975	18.1	9.3	8.8
1980	18.3	10.3	8
1981	18.5	10.2	8.3
1982	18.9	10.1	8.8
1983	19.8	10.8	9.4
1984	19.6	10.8	8.8

Sources: *Narodnoe Khozyaistvo* (1983), p. 30; *Vestnik
Statistiki* (1984), No. 4, p. 67; *Narodnoe Khozyaistvo*
(1985), p. 33.

Table 3.7   Average annual growth rate of
workers and employees employed in the
economy (%)

1929 to 1932	20.6	1956 to 1960	4.4
1933 to 1937	13.4	1961 to 1965	4.4
1938 to 1940	5.9	1966 to 1970	3.2
1946 to 1950	7.2	1971 to 1975	2.5
1951 to 1955	4.4	1976 to 1980	2

Source: Smirnova and Sabo (eds) (1974),
p. 246.

Table 3.8   Average annual rate of growth of
industrial workforce

1951 to 1955	4.2	1971 to 1975	1.1
1956 to 1960	2.9	1976 to 1980	1.1
1961 to 1965	2.5	'1982'	1.3
1966 to 1970	2	'1982'	1.1

Source: Fil'ev (1983), p. 15.

Table 3.9   Actual and projected growth in the
population of working age

1971–1975		8.5 million		7%
1976–1980		13.8 million		10.6%
1981–1985		7.7 million		5.4%
1986–1990	minus	1.0 million	minus	0.6%
1991–1995		4.2 million		2.8%
1996–2000		1.5 million		1.0%

Source: Perevedentsev (1982), p. 81.

comparison with four million in 1941, nineteen million in 1968 and 31 million in 1978 and account for almost 20 per cent of the population (*Vestnik Statistiki*, 1979, No. 2, p. 79; Dmitryev and Lopata, 1983, p. 3).

Added to this, the flow of the surplus population from the rural areas to the towns has slowed appreciably. In the period 1961–70 the agricultural labour force was reduced by a yearly average of 240 000 workers, but by the period 1971–80 this had fallen to 140 000 (Manevich, 1981, p. 56; Manevich 1985, p. 22). The only surplus rural population now identified by Soviet demographers is in the Central Asian regions (Smirnova and Sabo, 1984, p. 248; Perevedentsev, 1983, pp. 55–60; Rogovskii, 1982, pp. 7–8; Latifi and Usanov, 1984, p. 2). The question of surplus population is more complex and will be returned to later.

Little further addition to the workforce can be expected from increased participation of women, which is already high, see Table 3.10, without even larger social expenditures on nursery provision (Yanhova, 1980, p. 11).

A further possibility which has been discussed is an extension of out-work, but the opportunities for this are limited to the production of simple goods and this cannot provide a long term solution (Rad'ko, 1979, p. 13). Attempts have also been made to draw pensioners back into production and pressure has been exerted on enterprises to encourage them to provide more opportunities for part-time work, whilst allowing the retention of pension rights, particularly for specialists (TsK KPSS, 1980). Even though the pensions of workers and employees have more than doubled in the period 1965–80 and have risen by more than 230 per cent for collective farm workers, surveys suggest that over 50 per cent of pensioners would like to remain in social production. The vast majority of those questioned

Table 3.10   Average number of women workers
and employees in the economy

	(000s)	(%)		(000s)	(%)
1940	13 190	39	1970	45 800	51
1950	19 180	47	1980	57 569	51
1960	29 250	47	1983	59 350	51
			1984	59 699	51

Accounting for the following percentages –
Trade & Collective Food Provision 83%;
Education 75%; Cultural Work 74%; Public
Health, Sport & Social Services 82%.

Source:Vestnik Statistiki (1984), No. 1, p. 65;
Narodnoe Khozyaistvo (1985), p. 412.

suggest that this is for economic reasons (Slavina and Kogan, 1978, p. 136). Of those who want to work, 43 per cent want part-time work, while seven per cent would like to work at home but only seven million pensioners are actually employed (Novitskii, 1982, p. 4). The major difficulty is organisational because at the enterprise level it has proved difficult to provide the flexibility to arrange part-time work.

Increasingly increments to the workforce depend upon young people being drawn into production, to some extent before they have finished their formal schooling. Prokofiev (1982, p. 3) points out that in the early eighties there were over 2500 interschool production training complexes, but Soviet sources stress the need to strengthen these links (Rutkevich, 1983, p. 3; Dyachenko, 1983, p. 2). In the period 1961–65 young people accounted for only 30 per cent of new workers; by 1966–70 the proportion had risen to 57 per cent; by 1971–75 it had risen further to 92 per cent and the proportion is still rising (Smirnova and Sabo, 1984, p. 248). This has to be viewed against a background of increasing reluctance, on the part of young people, to enter the world of work, with higher education being the preferred post-school route. A number of Soviet sources have commented that the reluctance of young people to enter work is used extensively by parents as a threat to encourage good examination performance (Mitrofanov, 1979, p. 2; Kulagin, 1979, p. 10).

Attempts have also been made to increase the labour time expended in an absolute sense by the use of voluntary labour days, *subbotniks*, the results of which are ear-marked to improve social provision like health and educational facilities. For example, the *subbotnik* dedicated to the 60th anniversary of the October Revolution and the 107th anniversary of Lenin's birth involved 144 million workers who produced 767 million roubles of output. These funds were scheduled to provide pre-school facilities (*Pravda*, 30 April 1977, p. 2). However, this cannot be a lasting solution and is more symbolic than realistic. The real problem is not extensions of the absolute size of the workforce, extensions of the working day or year, nor is the problem demographic. The real problem is the inability of the ruling group to increase the relative surplus extracted from the direct producers already employed.

Labour productivity growth is the major method for attaining economic growth, and from a Marxist perspective the ability of a social system to enhance the productivity of human labour is some measure of its progressive nature. Once again, from a long term perspective Soviet achievements appear impressive and labour productivity has risen by a factor of 50 since the October Revolution (Kostin, 1980, p. 58). Since 1940, the level of labour productivity overall has risen more than eleven times, as illustrated inTable 3.1. It should be noted that overall levels of productivity have risen faster than the component parts, due to the structural change in employment that occurred in this period. This is demonstrated in Table 3.11, which shows a shift away from agriculture towards industry where productivity was higher (*Narodnoe Khozyaistvo*, 1983, p. 35). Again a number of elements are worthy of comment. Labour productivity has advanced more rapidly in industry than in agriculture and production of national income per worker is twice as high in industry as it is in

Table 3.11   The relationship between employment in industry, agriculture and construction (%)

	1940	1950	1960	1970	1975	1980	1981
Total employment	100	100	100	100	100	100	100
Industry and construction	35	40	52.5	63	65.5	69	68
Agriculture	65	60	47.5	37	34.5	31	32
For every 100 in industry number in agriculture	186	150	90	58	53	43	42

Source: A. D. Smirnova and K. Sabo (eds) (1984), p. 247.

agriculture (Kostin, 1980, p. 59). All the indices show a tendency towards stagnation. This needs to be placed in some comparative perspective. Soviet statisticians have calculated that by the mid-seventies the level of labour productivity in the USSR was approximately 40 per cent of the US level overall (*SSSR v Tsifrakh*, 1977, p. 62). However, Soviet industrial labour productivity as a percentage of the US level rose from 44 per cent in 1960 to 53 per cent in 1970 (Abalkin, 1985, p. 11). But in the decade 1970–80 the proportion only grew from 53 per cent to 55 per cent, indicating a significant slow-down in the catching up process. In the agricultural sector Soviet labour productivity is between twenty and 25 per cent of the US level. In comparison with the UK, where the average annual rate of labour productivity growth was 3.6 per cent over the period 1971–82, Soviet labour productivity growth, by a yearly average of 4.2 per cent, appears favourable.

The problem is, however, that now economic growth via increases in labour productivity is of prime importance, the rate of growth is slowing down. The pattern of declining annual labour productivity growth in industry is shown in Table 3.12. The same pattern emerges

Table 3.12   Rate of growth of industrial labour productivity

1967	6.7	1973	6.1	1979	2.4
1968	5.2	1974	6.3	1980	2.6
1969	4.8	1975	5.9	1981	2.7
1970	7.0	1976	3.3	1982	2.1
1971	6.3	1977	4.0	1983	3.5
1972	5.2	1978	3.6		

Sources: Khromov (1982), p. 13; Fil'ev (1983), p. 17; *Vestnik Statistiki* (1984), No. 3, p.73.

when labour productivity growth is considered alongside industrial production and workforce growth over the last five Plan periods, as in Table 3.13. As already pointed out, in Table 3.5, the planned increments to production to be achieved by productivity growth were not met in the Eleventh Five Year Plan period. Furthermore, the decline can also be demonstrated in relationship to the link between labour productivity and growth in the capital stock, as shown in Table 3.14. In comparison with other Comecon countries, the USSR

Table 3.13 Declining productivity, production and workforce growth

Year	Average annual rate of growth (%)		Proportion of growth due to labour productivity increases (%)	Average annual growth of industrial production personnel (000s)
	Industrial production	Industrial labour productivity		
1961–65	8.6	4.6	62	965
1966–70	8.5	5.8	73	829
1971–75	7.4	6.0	84	492
1976–80 (plan)	6.2–6.8	5.4–6.0	90	300
1976–80 (actual)	4.4	3.2	75	565
1981–85 (plan)	—	3.2–3.7	90	—

Sources: Rusanov (1983), p. 79; Khromov (1981), p.16.

Table 3.14   Growth in labour productivity for 1% growth in capital stock

Country	1961–1965	1966–70	1971–75	1976–80
Bulgaria	0.63	0.78	0.84	0.73
Hungary	0.82	1.33	0.94	0.49
GDR	0.54	1.08	0.91	0.67
Rumania	1.16	0.68	0.95	0.66
USSR	0.63	0.93	0.57	0.47
Czechoslovakia	0.33	1.76	1.04	0.58

Source: Aper'yan (1983), p. 189.

has a lower labour productivity growth for a one per cent growth in the capital stock and this has been declining consistently since the Eighth Five Year Plan.

When industry is considered alone, the average annual rate of growth of labour productivity was six per cent in the Ninth Five Year Plan (1971–75) but fell to 3.2 per cent during the Tenth Five Year Plan (1976–80) (Karpukhin, 1983, p. 87; Rusanov, 1983, p. 79). During the first two years of the Eleventh Plan (1981–85), labour productivity growth in industry was scheduled to rise by 6.3 per cent, but only actually grew by 2.7 per cent in 1981 and 2.1 per cent in 1982 (Rusanov, 1983, p. 87), and by 1983, although it had increased to 3.5 per cent it was still below planned levels (*Vestnik Statistiki*, 1984, No. 3, p. 73). Nevertheless, the significance placed upon labour productivity growth over the last ten years can be gauged from the following extracts from the Guidelines to the Tenth and Eleventh Five Year Plans.

> To concentrate special attention on the accelerated growth of the productivity of labour, an especially important condition for the further development of production and an increase in the people's well-being. To guarantee through higher labour productivity 85–90 per cent of the increment in industrial production, the entire increment in agricultural production and construction and at least 95 per cent of the increment in the volume of rail cargoes (*Pravda*, 7 March 1976, p. 1).

The Eleventh Plan reiterates these ambitious targets and aims, 'to raise the productivity of social labour by 17–20 per cent, obtaining at

least 85–90 per cent of the increment in National Income in this way'
(*Pravda*, 5 March 1981, p. 1). The Eleventh Plan called for higher
rates of productivity growth than those achieved in the Tenth Plan
but the results for the first two years showed that, just as the Tenth
Plan failed to reach the planned increase, the Eleventh Plan began in
the same way, see Table 3.5 (For details of the overall performance in
the Eleventh Plan see Table 10.1.) The individual indicators, shown in
Table 3.15, show the low rate of productivity growth. As Andropov
(1982, p. 1) pointed out at the Plenary of the CC CPSU in November
1982, labour productivity was still not growing quickly enough. It
should be remembered that a one per cent increase in labour productivity in the agricultural sector yields a one milliard rouble increase in
output and a one per cent increase in industrial labour productivity
yields a seven milliard rouble increase in National Income (Dymnov
and Dmitrichev, 1984, p. 68). By June 1983, Andropov (1983, p. 1–2)
was still arguing that, 'the key task in the economic sphere is an
increase in labour productivity'.

Table 3.15   Rate of growth of labour productivity – the Eleventh Five
Year Plan

	1981–82	1983–1984
Social labour productivity	102.9	103.4
Industrial labour productivity	102.4	103.7
Agricultural labour productivity	101	111
Rail transport labour productivity	Zero growth	102.9
Construction labour productivity	102.3	103.1

Sources: *Vestnik Statistiki* (1984), No. 4, p. 69; *Vestnik Statistiki* (1984),
No. 12, pp. 68–9; *Narodnoe Khozyaistvo* (1985), p. 53.

There is, however, a further dimension to this problem. The Plan
Guidelines for 1981–85 stipulate that productivity growth in the
economy must exceed wage rises (*Pravda*, 5/3/81, p. 1). In the Tenth
Plan the relationship between wage rises and labour productivity
growth did not maintain its planned proportions. As Karpukhin
points out, the increase in average wages per one per cent increase in
productivity was 0.69 per cent, rising to 0.84 per cent when sums
allocated to wage rises are included. In some sectors, coal mining for
example, productivity fell but wages continued to rise, and in a

number of branches average wages rose faster than productivity growth (Karpukhin, 1983, pp. 87–8; Volkov, 1983, p. 10). This situation has been replicated in the early years of the Eleventh Plan. In 1981 labour productivity in industry grew by 2.7 per cent and average wages rose by 2.3 per cent, in 1982 labour productivity grew 2.1 per cent and average wages rose by 3.5 per cent. As Kostin (1983, p. 2) has noted, the growth in the average wage has been 0.85 per cent for each one per cent increase in labour productivity in comparison with the planned growth of 0.63 per cent. A later source, reproduced in Table 3.16, adjusts these figures for 1981–2, but shows the clear tendency for labour productivity growth rates to decline and the increase in the average wage per one per cent increase in labour productivity to rise. As Andropov (1983a) pointed out, 'wage increases that are not closely linked to increases in labour productivity will ... ultimately have a negative effect on all economic life'.

Table 3.16 Relationship between increases in labour productivity and average wages

	Increase in labour productivity	Increase in the average wage	Increase in average wage per 1% increase in labour productivity
1951–55	49.0	11.3	0.23
1955–60	37.0	16.8	0.45
1961–65	25.7	13.4	0.52
1966–70	32.2	21.6	0.67
1971–75	34.0	25.6	0.76
1976–80	17.0	14.3	0.84
1981	2.7	2.54	0.94
1982	2.1	2.8	1.33

Source: Fil'ev (1983), p. 17.

The negative effects refer to the further erosion of the already limited incentive effects of money wages, because if they rise without attendant increases in production then they will not lead to access to use-values. Furthermore, this process will lead to a further erosion of the socially produced surplus if Soviet labour can continue to press average wages upwards and simultaneously retard productivity growth. Hence the pressure is on for increasing labour productivity

4 Labour Discipline and Labour Shortage

THE CONTINUING PROBLEMS OF LABOUR DISCIPLINE

The antagonistic social relations of production, which form around the surplus extraction process in the USSR, express themselves most directly through a variety of labour discipline problems. These are central to the explanation of the slow-down in economic growth provided in Figure 3.1 and they need to be placed in context.

Firstly, they cannot be treated as a peripheral problem, as has been suggested by Soviet political economists and their western counterparts. The Andropov discipline campaign, initiated only ten days after his election as General Secretary of the CPSU, indicated the centrality of these problems and his perception of their impact on economic performance. Andropov's analysis (1982, p. 1) locates the source of the problems within the present functioning of the socio-economic system.

> It is necessary to create the conditions, economic and organisational, that will stimulate good quality productive labour, initiative and enterprise. Conversely poor work, idleness and irresponsibility must have an immediate and inescapable impact upon the remuneration, job status and moral authority of personnel... We must wage a more resolute struggle against all violations of state, party and labour discipline.

The tenor of his comments indicates that those economic and organisational forms are absent and he continually stresses that the correspondence between work contribution and consumption is tenuous (Andropov, 1983, p. 2). Chernenko (1984, p. 1; 1985, pp. 1–2), during his brief period of power, in no way repudiated this analysis and when accepting his election as General Secretary stated,

> the question of organisation and order is a key fundamental question for us. Any disorderliness and irresponsibility is costly to society... it is quite natural that the measures the party has adopted with a view to improving labour, production, plan and state discipline... have received truly nationwide approval.

71

The current leadership also recognises that declining rates of growth of productivity, and the consequent poor economic performance, can only be reversed if workforce attitudes and practices are changed. This message has been forcefully articulated in the early speeches of Gorbachev since becoming general secretary (Gorbachev, 1985a, p. 2; 1985b, p. 3). His approach to these questions will be discussed in more detail in the final chapter.

Secondly, these problems are not transitory. The theme of maintaining and improving labour discipline, as already noted, features prominently in the writings and speeches of Andropov, Chernenko and Gorbachev, but it reflects a tradition going back to both the Brezhnev period and beyond (Brezhnev, 1976, p. 45). The Soviet literature places great importance on the continuity of this question from the time of Lenin, and most articles on labour productivity and discipline commence with justificatory quotations from Lenin (Nasach and Kotelenets, 1982). However, even though these problems have been long identified, they have been resilient to both administrative efforts designed to combat them and attempts at moral exhortation. They have as a consequence been reproduced over time and have to be explained within the political economy of the system and they cannot be treated as either exogenous factors or historical remnants. Furthermore, the view that these problems would be alleviated as the economy and the workforce became more sophisticated seems unproven. In fact, the impact and extent of the problems appears to be growing as a consequence of the increasingly technological nature of the economy. As Brezhnev pointed out, it is bad enough from a social point of view if a worker, provided with a shovel, does not work consistently and well, but the problem is magnified if the worker is operating sophisticated machinery (Brezhnev, 1976, p. 45). The social investment in the machinery represents previously expended labour time which has been embodied in the equipment, but which now fails to provide the expected increase in production. Hence, the same infraction of labour discipline now has a greater impact. As the previous section indicated, it is precisely over recent plan periods that the decline in productivity growth has taken place.

Thirdly, these problems are not unique to the USSR and it is difficult to sustain the argument that they are the result of a particular historical and cultural tradition. Similar problems are replicated elsewhere in Eastern Europe (Hethy and Mako, 1972; Harazsti, 1979; Burawoy, 1985), and in the capitalist west (Dubois, 1979, pp. 21–59); Taylor and Walton, 1971, pp. 219–46). It is, therefore, feasible to argue that these problems are common to social systems which are based upon exploitative social relations of production, and represent the common response of the direct producers. This is not to argue that the USSR (or the rest of Eastern Europe) is some variant of capitalism. As was pointed out in Chapter 1, exploitative relations of production occur in differing modes of production and take particular forms. The question is rather to understand the form the problems take, their impact upon the system, the methods by which the ruling group attempts to curb them and their degree of success in this endeavour. It is these relationships that determine the nature of the socio-economic system, not the simple existence of labour problems. In a specific sense, an understanding of these problems provides an explanation of the motives of the Soviet ruling group in initiating experimental forms of control like the Shchekino experiment, its later variants and the parallel experiments. An understanding of the political economy of these problems is essential if this experience and the likely future outcome of similar attempts at control is to be evaluated.

Labour problems in the USSR take a variety of forms, all of which, regardless of specific cause or motivation, result in a reduction of the socially produced surplus. According to a survey of enterprise directors, cited by Kolodizh (1980, p. 127) they see labour discipline problems as the major constraint on raising production. Sonin (1977, p. 5) identifies labour problems on two planes; the malutilisation of existing resources (due to supply breakdowns, poor repair work and so on) and failures in organisation and management of the labour process. However, he argues that ultimately both types of problem are reducible to the question of labour discipline, and Baranenkova (1986, p. 57) concurs, arguing that the major problem facing the USSR is the need to strengthen labour discipline.

There are a series of problems concerning the length of the working day, all of which reduce the volume of expended labour-time and hence reduce the volume of the absolute surplus. 'A major reserve for raising labour productivity is strengthening labour discipline, cutting losses in labour-time due to shirking and absenteeism, tardinesss and premature departure from work and inadequate organisation leading to overly long meal breaks' (Smirnova and Sabo, 1984, p. 194).

The statistical data available, according to idle-time records, suggests that this amounts to 0.1 per cent of the working day per worker or between one and two minutes per day (Sonin, 1981, p. 74). However, as Sonin points out, the true picture of intra-shift idle-time is not fully recorded and the recording of work-time losses generally is inadequate (Sonin, 1981, p. 75). Kolodizh (1980, p. 130) estimates that 30–40 per cent of the problem is unrecorded. The real losses only emerge from survey work and Soviet sources suggest that work time losses might, in reality, be as high as 15–20 per cent of the working day (Sonin, 1981, p. 74; Smirnova and Sabo, 1984, p. 195; Manevich, 1981, p. 59; Volgin and Sidyakin, 1985, pp. 41–7). Further estimates suggest that for every 100 Soviet workers, 30 are absent from their place of work for an average of 1.6 hours per day (*Trud*, 29 December 1982, p. 2) and at any time one million workers are idle at work (*Sotsialisticheskaya Industriya*, 17 May 1981, p. 4). Volgin (1982, p. 3), reporting surveys carried out at 245 Moscow enterprises, comments that some enterprises only have ten per cent of their staff at work for the last hour of the working day. Rusanov (1983, p. 89) points out that even if idle-time only accounts for two and a half to three days' loss per worker, per year, in industry this would amount to a loss of 91.5 million days. The significance of time losses is substantial and, according to Soviet estimates, saving one minute of labour time adds one million roubles to production or is equivalent to the loss of a day's work by 200 000 workers (Brezhnev, 1977, p. 11).

It is inadequate to ascribe these losses to human nature or to the 'non-industrial culture' of Soviet workers. The reasons have to be located within the work situation of the Soviet worker and the operation of the economic mechanism. As has already been suggested, labour discipline infractions need not necessarily affect the individual's access to use-values. Nor do they necessarily attract disciplinary sanctions from management, who can justifiably argue that it is better to have a worker who turns up late, takes over-long breaks within his shift and leaves early, than no worker at all (Sapov, 1982, p. 3).

One explanation that has been offered for these problems of attendance and time-keeping is the chaotic nature of the service sector. The necessity to queue and wait for repair services could provide an explanation for the time spent away from production and according to the survey cited by Volgin (1982, p. 3), 70 per cent of workers taking time off claimed it was because services were unavailable when needed. However, this avoids the question of why the service sector is chaotic. As the respondents to a questionnaire on labour discipline, circulated by the journal *EKO*, pointed out, the root of the problem is poor organisation and labour discipline in this sector as well (Kutryev, 1981, p. 36).

It is not only part-day losses that are important but also whole-day absenteeism which again reduces the volume of expended labour time and the absolute surplus. This has been a long-term problem in the USSR. For example, Sosin (1975, p. 66) estimated that in 1973 52 million man days were lost due to absenteeism, and Manevich (1976, p. 122) cites a figure of 59 million for the previous year. Contemporary sources suggest that presently absenteeism accounts for about twenty days per worker per year (Smirnova and Sabo, 1984, p. 195), three quarters of which is due to sickness and one quarter simply due to non-appearance (Manevich, 1981, p. 59). According to Manevich (1986, p. 68), the elimination of whole-day losses in work time could lead to the release of 7.5 million workers.

Sonin (1981, p. 69) notes that, as with work-time losses, absenteeism is underreported, and complains that time is often wasted on party, trade union, Komsomol or local Soviet functions, or rather that these are the excuses used for absenteeism. Varavka (1979, p. 3) suggests that there are few checks on workers leaving the enterprise for fire brigade or militia duties and this form of absence is often spurious. Furthermore, management may well give approval for absenteeism on spurious grounds to either maintain their workforce or to compensate workers for overtime necessary because of storming and poor work organisation (Sonin, 1981, p. 70). The combined result of absenteeism, idle-time within shifts and administratively authorised absence means that industry loses on average the labour of 170 000 workers per day (Baranenkova, 1980, p. 52).

Again the effects of the problems of absenteeism have to be viewed in the context of the economic mechanism. One of the results of idle-time and absenteeism is that arhythmic work patterns are established which necessitates storming and overtime at the end of the month (Kolodizh, 1984, pp. 43–44). The result of this, as one survey showed, is that conscientious workers ended the year with an average wage of 260 roubles per month, whilst discipline violators, because of overtime working, were able to supplement their wage and had an average wage of 226 roubles (Kolodizh, 1980, p. 129). Hence the link between work and rewards is further weakened.

The example of the construction industry illustrates another aspect of this problem. Between ten and 30 per cent of the losses in work-time are due to discipline infractions and, according to surveys, one third of these problems are related to alcohol abuse (*Ekonomicheskie Stroitel'stva*, 1980, p. 51).

Alcohol-related problems affect both the absolute surplus and the relative surplus, because they are a major influence upon both absenteeism and productivity. Sonin (1981, pp. 67–8), citing a survey in Magnitogorsk, points out that absenteeism is three to three and a half times greater after holidays and pay days and is usually drink-related. A review of the problem in *Molodoi Kommunist* points out that in 1925, eleven per cent of workers were chronic alcoholics, but suggests that currently 37 per cent of workers regularly drink to excess and that this has contributed to the increase in death rates and the high level of industrial accidents (*Molodoi Kommunist*, 1975, No. 9, p. 103; Lirman and Sheverdin, 1980, pp. 64–70). In the RSFSR, one half of all fatal accidents and one quarter of all industrial accidents are drink-related (Levin and Levin, 1979a, p. 6). Sosin (1975, p. 173) citing a survey in Krasnoyarsk, suggests that labour productivity in industry is 20–30 per cent reduced on Mondays, on days following holidays and on pay days, due to the effects of drink. Another source estimates that a generalised 15–30 per cent reduction in productivity occurs because of drink-related problems after pay day (Armeyev and Illarionov, 1984, p. 3). Alcoholism is strongly related to absenteeism problems and it has been estimated that one per cent of all industrial and construction workers are absent per day because of drink problems (Levin and Levin, 1979b, p. 13). A further study has suggested that nine out of ten cases of absenteeism are drink-related and that a ten per cent increase in productivity would be achieved if on-the-job drunkenness could be eliminated (Chernichenko, 1977, p. 4; Strumilin and Sonin, 1974, p. 38). Furthermore, 46 out of every 100 alcoholics begin their history of drink problems at work (Vychub, 1981, p. 3).

In the conditions of an apparent labour shortage, the unsolved problems of alcoholism result in problem workers simply moving from one plant to another. Again, enterprise management may adopt the view that workers with drink problems are better than no workers at all and there is considerable anecdotal evidence on managerial complicity with workers with drink problems (Yakushenko, 1983, p. 2; Panov, 1982, p. 2; Sapov, 1982, p. 2; Nikitinskii, 1980, p. 10). Zaigreev (1983, pp. 98–9) even goes so far as to suggest that alcoholism is the source of the labour shortage problem. This is a simplification of a complex problem that cannot be reduced to a single cause, but alcohol related problems are nevertheless an important contributory factor.

Labour turnover presents the ruling group with a considerable problem that has long been recognised by the Soviet leadership (Brezhnev, 1976, p. 12). This problem affects both the absolute surplus and the relative surplus, as it reduces both the absolute number of days worked but also reduces the intensity of that work for some period of time. The increasingly technological nature of the production process, and the fragmentation of labour tasks which arises as a consequence, necessitates constant co-operation between individuals in production. A stable workforce, as well as providing continuity in production, will enable an accumulation of technical and production skills on a collective basis. Furthermore, this will provide, according to Soviet writers, the correct psychological environment within the enterprise, generating a collective ethos of self-discipline and achievement which will be receptive to schemes aimed at increasing labour productivity, the quality of production or enhancing socialist competition (Kotlyar and Talalai, 1981, p. 34).

However, it has been estimated that in the late seventies and early eighties, labour turnover was in excess of 20 million persons per annum and this accounted for approximately one fifth of the employed workforce, excluding collective farm workers (Kostin (ed.), 1979, p. 237). More recently Kotlyar, (1984, p. 2) has suggested that the figure is 25 million out of 129 million. In some enterprises, labour turnover is as high as 25–30 per cent of the workforce per annum, in comparison with the esimated desirable level of necessary turnover, defined by Soviet writers to be between five and eight per cent (Baranenkova, 1983, p. 76). The average time between jobs ranges from 30 to 31 days for industrial workers, to 28 days for construction workers, with consequent losses in production (Silin and Sukhov, 1982, pp. 38–9; Maslova, 1982, p. 50). It has been estimated that this rises to two months when migration between cities is involved (Aitov, 1979, p. 2). This is exacerbated by the decline in productivity that occurs prior to moving between jobs, which has been estimated at 15–25 per cent for piece-rate workers and 50 per cent for time-rate workers (Baranenkova, 1983, p. 75). Also there are losses in productivity during the settling-in period in the new job which, it has been calculated, can take up to three months on average and results in a 10–20 per cent reduction in productivity (Sonin, 1977, p. 4). To these losses have to be added the costs of retraining, as over two fifths of those who change jobs also change occupation (Kotlyar and Talalai, 1981, p. 35). It has been estimated that those who change occupation take up to two to three times longer to achieve the average level of productivity at their new job (Baranenkova, 1983, p. 75). Even worse, as Kostin (1980, p. 67) notes, workers often do not master the skills of one job before moving on to another.

There are, however, further problems, as high levels of turnover undermine labour discipline in the enterprise. A shifting workforce will be more difficult to discipline and to motivate than a stable one, and if spontaneous turnover is easy, then disciplinary sanctions will be avoided by simply moving jobs. Management, faced by apparent labour shortages will be less inclined to press disciplinary measures if workers simply leave and will understate personnel turnover when it occurs (Kolodizh, 1980, p. 130; Kapelyushny, 1984, p. 2). There is also evidence that attempts at increasing the intensity of work by raising work norms leads to increased levels of labour turnover (*Pravda*, 30 July 1980, p. 2).

The problem is also acute in agriculture. One Soviet source provides an interesting example of the type of problems faced by agriculture, pointing out that in one decade ten million machine operators were trained, but by the end of the decade the actual number employed had only risen by one million (Kostakov, 1974, p. 75). Furthermore, by the late seventies Soviet agriculture had a shortfall of one million machine operators. Given the disparities between urban and rural work, wage payments and living standards, outlined briefly earlier, these phenomena may not be surprising. However, they do illustrate the problems of movement away from agriculture and the general irrationality of spontaneous labour turnover from the ruling group's viewpoint.

Labour turnover also presents a significant regional problem and it has been estimated that labour turnover in Siberia and the Far Eastern regions is between two and one and a half times higher than in the European regions of the USSR. Zaslavskaya (1986, p. 1) points out that whilst the Far Eastern regions required a million extra workers in 1983, not many more people went there than left. The problem has proved so intractable and impervious to material incentives as a solution that the Komsomol has suggested the formation of 'women's brigades' to encourage marriage and stability amongst the workforce (De Souza, 1983, p. 15).

The problems of labour turnover are accentuated by the fact that the USSR needs to encourage both inter-enterprise and inter-regional flows of labour. The apparent labour shortages, in both urban areas and Siberia, demand a degree of labour mobility, but this needs to be planned and controlled if it is to be viable. Kotlyar (1984, p. 2) for example, suggests that 40 per cent of the labour turnover that occurs is not in the social interest and studies have shown that twelve per cent on average (rising in some areas to 20 per cent) actually return to their initial place of work. The problem is that current labour turnover is largely unplanned and spontaneous. According to Maslova (1982, p. 50), the ratio of organised to spontaneous forms of manpower redistribution is about one to four and this rises to one to nine in the case of regional redistribution.

From the point of view of the individual worker, labour turnover may well be rational if workers can improve their working conditions, living conditions or rewards. Kotlyar and Talalai (1981, pp. 41–2) suggest that between 30 and 50 per cent of labour turnover may well be rational from this perspective. However, the meaning of these reactions cannot be understood in purely economic terms alone.

The labour problems identified so far, idle-time, absenteeism, alcoholism and spontaneous labour turnover, can all be explained as the individualised response of Soviet workers to their position in the process of surplus extraction. Soviet workers, like their counterparts in the west, lack any meaningful direct control over production decisions. However, unlike their western counterparts, they cannot organise independently in trade unions and cannot express discontent via a political process. Hence their dissatisfaction, in part, takes the form of spontaneous and individualised actions which result in significant negative control over their own labour process, as both the absolute level of labour time expended and its intensity is controlled by their actions. As Ticktin (1978) argues, this degree of atomised control over the labour process is a direct corollary of the political atomisation necessary for the maintenance of the Soviet ruling group and, in a sense, is the price they pay for the form of political control they enjoy.

Survey work in the USSR confirms this perspective and shows that labour turnover is the channel through which a series of discontents are expressed. For example, the reasons for labour turnover emerge clearly from the categories on the survey form issued by the State Statistical body in 1981 (Baranenkova, 1983, p. 76): dissatisfaction with occupation, poor work rhythm and organisation, heavy physical labour, monotonous work, poor work conditions, poor pay, poor or non-existent training, inadequate living, social and cultural conditions and so on. The reality of these problems are confirmed by the localised survey work reported in the Soviet literature (Shafronov,

1980, p. 67; Podorov, 1976, pp. 72–8; Skarupo, 1977, pp. 118–25; Kyuregyan, 1983, pp. 129–32). The characteristics of these problems tend to vary in relation to the worker's age, marital status, sex and length of service. For example, Soviet sources point out the disproportionate share of younger workers involved in labour turnover. The under-thirty age group account for 39 per cent of the workforce, but are responsible for 70 per cent of the turnover (Kuznetsov, 1979, pp. 98–107; Udovichenko, 1980, pp. 31–7).

The lack of correspondence between work and eventual rewards reinforces this tendency for workers to vote with their feet or work as little as possible. The culmination of this activity is to contribute to the creation of an apparent labour shortage, which further weakens management control and further exacerbates the vicious circle of problems. The irony of this is that the existence of an apparent labour shortage encourages enterprises to compete for workers and poach from each other which further deepens the problems associated with spontaneous turnover (Afanas'ev, 1981, p. 2). The political economy of the USSR is such that there is a tendency to reproduce continually the appearance of labour shortages. This is not an accidental, historically determined feature of the system, but an inherent tendency. However, before considering the question of labour shortages in more detail, it is necessary to consider the central controlling mechanism in the surplus extraction process itself.

WORK NORMS

As pointed out in Chapter 1, all social systems based upon hierarchical exploitative relations of production are faced by the problem of ensuring that the direct producers actually produce an increasingly large relative surplus. In the USSR this antagonistic relationship between the ruling group and the direct producers emerges most clearly around the question of work norms. Work norms have a special significance, as they are an attempt to control the pace and intensity of work and the level of remuneration. Thus they are central to the determination of the volume of the surplus. Furthermore, they are the only method through which different types of labour, of differing complexity and in different branches of production, can be evaluated. This complex problem can best be explained via a comparison with capitalism.

Under the capitalist mode of production concrete labour, either unskilled and simple labour or skilled and complex labour, is reduced to abstract labour by the operation of the law of value. As already suggested, the existence of the market acts as the eventual arbiter of whether or not the expended labour time embodied in particular commodities is the average socially necessary. This acts to regulate expenditures of concrete labour within capitalist firms. The efficient exploitation of human labour power will flourish whilst the inefficient will fail. Furthermore, it provides a means whereby different expenditures of concrete labour are reduced to their common essence and thereby made commensurable. The scope of this commensurability and the breadth of economic regulation is determined by the scope of the market and its freedom from external regulation, intervention and monopolisation. Consequently, for the individual capitalist, the regulation of labour time is not determined in an arbitrary manner but is consequent upon the externally generated compulsion to accumulate, which operates through the law of value. A similar point was made earlier with regard to both negative control and wasteful production techniques. This is not to argue that the capitalist labour process is free from its own contradictions and problems. Nor is it to suggest that the individual capitalist does not attempt to measure work or 'scientifically' control its pace. It is simply a recognition of the fact that his action corresponds to the underlying logic of capitalism and his success or failure will eventually be evaluated by the correspondence of his actions to this logic.

In the USSR, however, the problem is qualitatively different. Given the social relations of production outlined above, the law of value does not and cannot operate internally and the state monopoly of foreign trade precludes its generalised penetration from the capitalist west. As a consequence, concrete labour, complex or simple, is not automatically reduced to abstract labour. Therefore, no spontaneous commensurability arises between different labour times, intensities or skill levels or indeed in terms of the products produced, which can be derived from the operation of purely economic forces. It can be argued that labour is still the source of all value but the results of concrete labour are not expressed in a value form. This then raises two related questions. How is the commensurability necessary for economic calculation and control arrived at? How is the pace and intensity of labour regulated in the absence of the operation of the law of value?

The answer to both questions is via the medium of work norms which represent an attempt on the part of the ruling group to replace the spontaneous, unconscious regulation of the law of value with a different form of control which is essentially administrative. The intention is that the work norms should reflect the conscious regulation of the labour process and provide a basis for the payment of wages. As Kheifets (1982, p. 36) points out, the desired result of norming is to make wages and rewards correspond directly to the individual worker's expended labour and the end results of the collective's work. However, the setting of work norms are fraught with difficulties, as they reflect the antagonistic nature of the social relations of production.

As Manevich (1976, p. 117) suggests, there is a contradiction between the individual and social interests involved. On one hand, as a member of a collective, the individual worker has an interest in improving output by working more intensively and conscientiously. Manevich's explanation of this would refer back to the assumption that the Soviet worker controls the productive process through his control of the state. As a consequence, as the 'owner' of the means of production, the worker would increase the intensity of his own labour. Manevich does not appear to believe this explanation and this can be seen from his account of the other pole of the contradiction. On the other hand, for the individual, this would lead to more work for the same rewards.

Consequently, there is a tension between the ruling group's desire to extend and tighten the norming of labour and the direct producer's reluctance to accept this control. This problem is compounded by the composition of the norming committees (Mukhachev and Borovik, 1975, p. 34). For the norms to be in any way realistic they need to be based upon the expertise and knowledge of the direct producers and, therefore, over half of the members of the norming committee are workers. This leads to the underestimation of capacity as it is not in the worker's direct interests to work harder. Management will have no direct interest in undermining this underestimation. As already noted, from their point of view, slacker norms and the ensuing underutilisation of capacity will ensure, in the face of whatever problems, the fulfilment of the plan. These contradictions are inescapable in the context of the USSR.

Nevertheless, the necessity to increase the diffusion of work norms and extend the scientific organisation of labour (*NOT*) is agreed by all commentators. Manevich (1986, pp. 130–1) points out that since 1968 the *techpromfinplan* of each enterprise has included a section referring to *NOT* measures and in the years of the Tenth Plan for every expendi-

ture of one rouble on *NOT* measures, the economic return has been
1.5 to two roubles. However, there are a number of elements to this
question.

Firstly, whilst it is important to extend the diffusion of work norms
in industry, particularly to the 22.5 per cent of industrial personnel for
whom there are no norms (Manevich 1986, p. 135), there is also the
question of the nature of the norms. There is a need to replace
experimental-statistical (*opytno-statisticheskie*) norms by technically
validated (*tekhnicheski obosnovannie*) norms. As Manevich (1976,
p. 118) explains, the existence of the former accounts for the vast
overfulfilment of targets by piece-rate workers. This can be by as
much as 200 per cent in some instances, as the norms do not
accurately reflect productive capacities (Manevich, 1976, p. 118; Parfenov, 1980, p. 2). In 1981 a third of all piece-rate workers exceeded
their planned output by between 110 and 130 per cent and a further
third exceeded their targets by 130 per cent (Karpukhin, 1983, p. 91).
Sonin (1978, p. 7) suggests that the replacement of statistical-experi-
mental norms could lead to between a three and five per cent increase
in labour productivity. The diffusion of norms in general, and
technically validated norms in particular, throughout the 1970s are
shown in Tables 4.1, 4.2 and 4.3.

Table 4.1   Proportion of workers whose work is normed

	1974	1976	1978
All industrial workers	50%	70.3%	78.9%
Time-rate workers	33.2%	51.3%	65.2%
ITR & office workers	13.9%	36.2%	57.7%

Sources: Shkurko (1977), p. 44; E. Manevich (1980), p. 40

Table 4.2   Proportion of technically validated norms

	1974	1978
Piece-rate workers	72.1%	81.1%
Time-rate workers	33.2%	62.6%

Source: Kheifets (1980), p. 20

Table 4.3   Technically validated, branch and interbranch norms

	Proportion of workers working to technically validated norms as a % of the total number for whom norms have been set		Proportion of technically validated norms set from branch & interbranch norms as a %	
	1974	1976	1974	1976
All industrial production personnel	71.9	79.2	75.5	82.9
Workers	71.3	78.4	74.4	81.3
of the workers				
Piece-rate workers	71.5	78.8	72	78.3
of whom basic production	—	80.3	—	77.7
auxiliary production	—	71.3	—	81.3
Time-rate workers	67.9	77.4	83.8	88.1
ITR & office workers	87.8	87.6	98	98.2

Source: Shkurko (1977), p. 49

Secondly, there is the widely recognised need to extend norms throughout all branches of the economy and to all types of employee. The labour of piece-rate workers in basic production is, theoretically at least, easier to norm than those paid on time-rates. Yet it is this latter group who, it is believed, need to be controlled more closely. Furthermore, it is essential to extend norming into areas like auxiliary work, service and repair sections where the nature of the work makes the calculation of norms both more difficult and more necessary. Parfenov (1983, p. 2) points out that three and a half million workers and two million ITR have no norms whatsoever, particularly in the service sector and research. As previously noted, the high manning levels in these sectors has been explained by the problem of norming this type of labour. The potential results of introducing norms into these branches was indicated by Baranenkova (1980, p. 52), who stated that in the period 1971–75 the introduction of branch service norms into the auxiliary sector of the chemical industry resulted in 10 000 workers being released. There is also continuing pressure to norm the labour of ITR and employees whose work again can be difficult to quantify (Kostin, 1980, p. 71; Slezinger, 1979, pp. 81–4). There are, however, further problems that the establishment of norms, even technically validated norms, do not resolve. As Kheifets (1980, p. 20) argues, the quantity of norms may not be a reflection of their quality.

The first problem is that if work norms are to fulfil the functions of rationally controlling expenditures of live labour and providing a basis for remuneration and economic calculation, they need to be internally consistent and proportional. As Gavrilov, (1982, p. 31) suggests, work norms must approach, as close as possible, the socially necessary expenditure of live labour. This, however, presents a series of difficulties, not least of which is the sheer complexity of the task. According to Manevich (1980, p. 41), at the end of the Ninth Plan there were 217 million norms that had to be set administratively. In some engineering enterprises Manevich (1986, p. 136) suggests that there are tens or even hundreds of thousands of rates in operation. This poses an immense task of coordination to maintain proportionality and consistency.

For example, within a single enterprise all machinists operating the same equipment should have the same work norms and remuneration. So, too, should all other machinists in the same industry operating the same equipment. By extension, all other machinists in other industries involved with similar work should have similar work norms and rewards, then the consistency between labour expenditure and rewards would be maintained. This raises the problem of what is similar and what criteria for evaluation should be adopted, and how proportionality between more and less complex labour and its remuneration should be dealt with. In order to maintain consistency, there would appear to be a need for a centralised system of norm setting and this explains the pressure for norm setting from branch and inter-branch manuals, coordinated from the centre. However, by the mid-seventies, branch and inter-branch norms were only available for approximately 43 per cent of industrial workers (Chubanov, 1976, p. 61). Kulagin (1983, p. 105) points out that this is difficult as different enterprises have differing levels of technology, support services and organisation. He suggests, therefore, that a decentralised system of norm setting should be adopted to reflect these difficulties. However, if this is adopted, the whole regulatory role of work norms becomes questionable. What you are left with is a series of localised work norms that reflect localised patterns of production and past practices and investment decisions. This leads to different levels of rewards for the same objective expenditures of labour time. These disparities will lead to worker discontent if norms are perceived to be unfair and, as has been suggested, to increasing labour turnover as workers move to enterprises where the same type of work yields the greater reward or the same reward at a lower intensity (Kotlyar and Talalai, 1981, p. 40; Simakov, 1980, p. 2). It should, however, be noted that inconsistent labour norms or some disproportionalities are better than no labour norms.

The second problem is that labour norms cannot be static, but must be continuously subject to scrutiny and upgrading. The reason for this is that the increasing dexterity and skill of the direct producers, coupled with the improved co-ordination and organisation of the workforce, will increase the potentiality for production. If work norms are to reflect the average socially necessary labour time, they must change continually. As Kheifets (1980, p. 19) suggests, revision is often very slow or delayed completely and as Manevich (1986, p. 134) notes, many enterprises seldom review obsolete norms. Manevich (1976, p. 118) points out, for example, that between 1969 and 1975 only 3.65 per cent of output norms in the construction industry were revised or ruled to be obsolete. As Pogosyan (1977, p. 97) argues, the slow rate of norm revision, between one and three per cent per annum, explains why plan overfulfilment of 150–200 per cent can exist in some sectors, particularly when it is linked to non-technically validated norms. However, as Manevich (1981, p. 60) and Glyantsev (1981, p. 97) clearly demonstrate, the potential for increasing production and freeing workers exists. They suggest that improved norming in the years of the Tenth Plan released 1.7 million piece-rate workers. In the same period, improvements in norms contributed between 0.6 to 0.8 per cent to labour productivity growth and in some branches by as much as two to 2.5 per cent. (Smirnova and Sabo, 1984, p. 193).

The problem becomes even more acute when technological change is involved and the necessary revision of norms is not achieved fully or quickly enough (Kheifets, 1980, p. 20). As Bunich (1980, p. 9) has pointed out, the rapid revision of norms may well be irrational from the point of view of the individual enterprise. If some branches or enterprises revise norms more rapidly than others, they may well find they lose employees as a consequence. Low norms and higher pay for the same kinds of jobs makes hiring workers easier. Furthermore, it should be noted that conscientious norm revision throughout the economy as a whole would require an army of rate-fixers and time-study experts and further add to the paperwork pressures on enter-prises. This is presumably why the annual general review of norms was discontinued in 1957 (Manevich, 1985, p. 134). Bornstein (1985, p. 26) points out that many industrial ministries assign a very small number of staff to norm fixing and as a consequence fail to complete the necessary documentation and instructions for their enterprises.

The third problem is that, even if technically validated norms are introduced, they can be manipulated at the enterprise level by both managers and workers. Manevich has complained that managers operate a 'correction factor' which often nullifies the impact of the norms and it is rational for managers to manipulate norms in order to maintain their workforce at a suitable level. As Karpov pointed out, norms have more to do with the payment of wages than they have to do with the amount of work completed (cited by Kirsch, 1972, p. 168). Managers also manipulate norms in order to recompense workers for lay-offs which are management's fault, again in order to retain workers (*Ekonomicheskaya Gazeta*, 1982, No. 20, p. 6).

Furthermore, workers will work inside their real capacities even if the norms are set too low. Bunich (1980, p. 11) complains that workers will try normally not to surpass their targets by more than five per cent as any greater overfulfilment will lead to uprating. The tenuous link between work and rewards encourages and makes this behaviour rational. It leads to an underestimation of enterprise capacity, no improvement in labour productivity and increased demands for labour.

Finally, enterprises may claim to have introduced technically validated norms in order to avoid administrative sanction. Lisina and Krasnopol'skii (1984, p. 2) cite the example of an enterprise claiming that 65.2 per cent of its 5200 norms were technically validated, but an inspection of 1000 norms at the plant showed that only ten per cent were technically validated. This explains why individual norms at the plant were overfulfilled, whilst the plan was underfulfilled and why wages in the plant were rising faster than labour productivity.

Work norms are essential because of the antagonistic relationship between the worker and enterprise management, but this relationship in turn contradicts and distorts their operation. No norm can ever be scientifically valid unless the direct producer controls all aspects of the labour process and production decisions. This would have to include not just the pace and intensity of work but also fundamental decisions about what to produce, how to produce it and how to distribute the eventual use-values. Then the direct producer would have an unambiguous interest in directly validating every minute of his labour. Work norms would then be set by every producer/worker as a direct reflection of their own self-interest. Norms set by any external body, (whether it is a multi-national corporation or the Central Norming Bureau of the USSR) can never be scientific if the worker has no direct control over them. The whole notion of 'scientific', in this context, is a mystification of the social relationship between the worker and his work and the social group attempting to extract a surplus.

The labour problems identified contribute to the decline in the rates of growth of labour productivity and the stagnation of economic growth experienced in the USSR. These problems reflect the antagonistic nature of the social relations of production in the USSR and create the superficial appearance of an apparent labour shortage in the USSR. This is considered in the next section.

THE SOVIET LABOUR SHORTAGE

Soviet commentators and their western counterparts often refer to the Soviet labour shortage as a major contributory factor to the poor present performance of the economy and the slow-down in economic growth (Brus, Kende and Mylnar, 1984, p. 7). For Soviet writers, full employment is described as a basic law of the Socialist economy and is contrasted to the high and growing rates of unemployment in the western capitalist countries as proof of the superiority of the 'socialist mode of production' (*Vestnik Statistiki*, 1984, No. 11, pp. 52–3). The existence of significant labour shortages is usually overlooked in the theoretical material and is certainly not assigned a significant place in the political economy of the USSR. The extent and nature of the labour shortage can be gauged from Table 4.4. This indicates that in the years for which figures have been found, the number of workers and employees called for in enterprise plans consistently exceeded the actual numbers of workers. In fact during the Ninth Plan over two million workplaces were created that never reached their full complement of staff and in the Tenth Plan the figure was one million (Cherevan, 1982, p. 51).

The general problem of labour shortages can of course be exacerbated on a localised level by absurd planning decisions with regard to the location of new enterprises. For example, Chernichenko (1980,

Table 4.4   Difference between enterprise plans for
workers and actual numbers

1968	shortfall of	1	million
1971	,,	1.4	million
1975	,,	2.5	million
1976	,,	2	million +
1977	,,	2	million +
1978	,,	1.9	million
1979–80	,,	2–2.5	million
1980	,,	1.5–2	million

Sources: Novikov (1969), p. 102; Myasnikov (1979),
p. 2; Baranenkova (1980), p. 53; Baranenkova (1979),
p. 4; Manevich (1981), p. 57; Kostin (1981), p. 43;
Myasnikov (1980), p. 10.

p. 2) cites the case of a new diesel manufacturing enterprise, which
was built at a town with a total population of approximately half the
enterprise's manpower needs. This led to the necessity of transporting
workers in from the nearest large town (Yaroslavl) which already had
over 1000 vacancies, thus leading to unnecessary costs and further
disproportions.

It has been estimated, however, that the apparent labour shortage is
60 per cent greater in cities of over one million inhabitants than in
cities of less than half a million. As a consequence, this draws the
population towards the larger cities (Cherevan, 1980, p. 52; Korolev,
1981, pp. 20–45). During the Ninth and Tenth Plans the growth rate
of cities of over one million inhabitants was two and a half times
higher than the all-Union average. This obviously tends to place a
larger burden on the social infrastructure of the cities, putting
pressure on housing, health, education and transport facilities, as
people migrate in the belief that living standards will be better. The
labour shortage exacerbates the turnover problems, already referred
to above, as enterprises seek to attract workers to their plants to
overcome localised labour shortages but simply compounding the
problem. This poaching of workers is officially bemoaned, but in the
face of general labour shortages and specific skill shortages, is the
inevitable response of enterprise management seeking to fulfil plans.
Kostin (1979, p. 43) suggests that there are now more than two

million vacant jobs in the USSR and between 0.75 and 0.8 million new workers are required each year for new enterprises. In the crucial machine building sector for example, 200 000 machine tools stand idle because of manpower shortages and in agriculture approximately 50 per cent of trucks are unmanned for the same reason (Kotlyar, 1983, p. 108).

Recently labour economists, writing from a more critical perspective, have begun to argue that the labour shortages are non-existent and the problem is one of rational labour utilisation. Nevertheless, the notion of demographic problems underpinning economic problems still persists (Myasnikov, 1980, p. 10). The concepts of labour shortage and labour surplus have a dubious theoretical value unless carefully defined. They are not naturally occurring phenomena stemming from abstract, ahistorical laws of human reproduction. As Marx pointed out, during his comprehensive critique of Malthusian population theory, 'an abstract law of population exists for plants and animals only, and only in so far as man has not interfered with them' (Marx, 1977a, p. 592).

Consequently, the idea of a surplus population, which Malthus explains as a consequence of humanity reproducing itself on the basis of a geometric series and the reproduction of the means of subsistence on the basis of an arithmetric series, is for Marx, 'a historically determined relation, in no way determined by abstract numbers or by the absolute limit of the productivity of the necessaries of life, but by limits posited rather by specific conditions of production' (Marx, 1973, p. 606).

The total population is that which is developed upon a specific production basis, and surplus population changes in various historical conditions (p. 607). The surplus population, however, 'is purely relative: in no way related to the means of subsistence but rather to the mode of producing them' (p. 608).

Marx's argument is that within the process of surplus extraction, which is central to the laws of accumulation under capitalism, there is a mechanism operating that produces the appearance of a relative surplus population.

Since the necessary development of the productive forces as posited by capital consists in increasing the relation of surplus labour to necessary labour, or in decreasing the portion of necessary labour required for a given amount of surplus labour, then, if a definite amount of labour capacity is given, the relation of necessary labour needed by capital must necessarily, continuously decline, that is part of these capacities must become superfluous, since a portion of them suffice to perform the quantity of surplus labour for which the whole amount was previously required (p. 609).

The consequence is that the same external mechanism that forces the capitalist to accumulate, simultaneously through its operation, creates a relative surplus population. However, the relative surplus population is not simply the result of the accumulation process but it is also a precondition for its functioning and a necessary condition for the existence of the capitalist mode of production (Marx, 1977a, p. 592). The industrial reserve army, or relative surplus population, acts to discipline those in work and weaken their organisation but it is also necessary to allow the continual expansion of the mode of production. It provides literally a reserve from which the capitalist may draw hands as they are required. 'The course characteristic of modern industry . . . of periods of average activity, production at high pressure, crisis and stagnation, depends upon the constant formation, the greater or lesser absorption and the reformation of the industrial reserve army or surplus population' (p. 593).

Therefore, the concept of surplus labour is contingent upon the mode of production. Under capitalism the relative surplus population is a necessary condition for, and natural result of, the accumulation process. It can neither be reformed nor wished away. The logic of the process is such that at particular points in time the size of the surplus population may fluctuate but the tendency for its reappearance is ever present in the surplus extraction process . Consequently, a historically determined link exists between the production base, the technological level, and the phase in the cycle of accumulation that under capitalist social relations of production produces the working population and its constituent working and non-working parts. The actual relative surplus population at any time is a function of the interpenetration of these causes.

What are the implications of this analysis for the USSR? The first point to be made is that the appearance of labour shortages in the USSR and elsewhere in Eastern Europe cannot be considered as natural phenomena, but rather are also the result of the specific, historically determined social relations of production in that socio-economic system. As the USSR is not subject to the same laws of motion as capitalism, then consequently the accumulation process does not take the same form. The existence of a surplus extraction process, conditioned by external, unambiguous economic forces, acting upon formally free but contractually and economically tied individuals, is absent in the USSR. Consequently, the automatic pressures to economise necessary labour time and expand surplus labour time are absent. The contradictions inherent in capitalism which generate an industrial reserve army and create what Marx describes as 'the non-working worker', are absent in the USSR. However, a different set of contradictions exist and generate a tendency towards a relative labour shortage.

The Soviet ruling group's inability to control the surplus extraction process leads to the vicious circle of problems outlined in Figure 3.1 above. In terms of international comparison, their inability to revolutionise the means and methods of production across the agricultural, industrial and service sectors of the economy leads to highly labour intense activity, declining rates of growth of labour productivity and overmanning. The culmination of this process is the appearance of apparent labour shortages. For example, in machine building it has been estimated that Soviet enterprises employ between 30 and 50 per cent more staff than comparable capitalist firms (Myasnikov, 1979, p. 2). In engineering a comparison with comparable West German plants shows that while eleven per cent of the West German workforce is occupied in repair and transport work, this figure rises to 38 per cent in the USSR (*Pravda*, 8 December 1982, p. 2). In chemical plants in the USSR, three to four times as many design staff are employed in comparison with similar German and Japanese plants, and so on (Kulagin, 1980, p. 105). The planning process and success indicators have simply reinforced the problem as enterprise management have hoarded labour, underestimated plant capacity and inflated their demands for labour in order to be successful. Soviet estimates suggest that enterprise managers could free between 15 and 30 per cent of their staff with little or no effect upon the volume of production (Manevich, 1978, p. 77; Shimenkov, 1981, p. 109; Ponomarev, 1980, p. 7).

Furthermore, the wasteful nature of production reinforces these tendencies. If goods are produced that yield no use-value and if there is no mechanism to halt this inefficient production or reallocate the resources involved, then it will be necessary to hire more workers elsewhere to produce more, hopefully useful, goods. Wasteful production simply absorbs expended labour time with no social return and is a cause of labour shortage. As the problem is reproduced, the labour shortage deepens. Therefore, the overall economic mechanism exhibits a tendency to create conditions of labour hoarding, creating a relative labour shortage, rather than, as under capitalism, to shed labour, causing a relative labour surplus.

Subjectively, the ruling group has recognised the problem and has intervened administratively to attempt to gain control over the process of surplus extraction. However, the intervention, for example through the uprating of plan targets, simply heightens the uncertainty felt by management and exacerbates the problems the intervention is attempting to resolve. For example, the chaotic state of the material supply system coupled with delays and changes in plan targets contributes to the arhythmic nature of production and this makes labour hoarding rational. The arhythmic nature of production also indicates the degree of overmanning. Khromov (1981, p. 20) cites the example of a Moscow enterprise where in the first ten days 16.9 per cent of the month's work is completed; in the second ten days 21.9 per cent is completed; and in the last ten days 61.2 per cent is completed. This is not atypical and, as he points out, only where there are significant manpower reserves can between two thirds and three quarters of a month's work be completed in ten days. Furthermore, the bureaucratic nature of planning itself gives rise to large administrative burdens, which are often irrational, and this leads to a growing need for administrative workers, further exacerbating the labour shortage (Samartseva, 1980, p. 10).

The apparent labour shortage also feeds back upon labour discipline and turnover, as suggested above, and further weakens managerial control, reduces labour productivity and further negates the centre's intentions of increasing the surplus (Malmygin, 1982, p. 56). The apparent labour shortage, therefore, reproduces itself over time as a feature of the surplus extraction process. It is both the result and the cause of the ruling group's lack of control over the process and is a testimony to the degree of negative control operated by the Soviet workforce.

This raises a further question with regard to the nature of planning in the USSR. Soviet plans are intended to be rational, proportional and balanced. The plan for labour inputs is intended to reflect the size of the working population, its age and sex structure, the dynamic nature of changing education and skill levels and the law of growing labour productivity, and it is intended to be in harmony with the plan for output (Berri, 1977, p. 105; Breev, 1979, pp. 39–41). However, the appearance of labour shortages suggests that the plan is not harmoniously based upon the productive capacities of the economy, but is in fact a set of externally determined targets. If the plan is a set of arbitrarily-set targets, then the notion of a labour shortage makes some sense, but then the Soviet plan cannot be described in any meaningful sense as a plan. It is something reified and external to the direct producers and even to enterprise management. It is inadequate to suggest that the problem simply arises due to the complexity and size of the task, as it continually reproduces itself as part of the political economy of the system. The idea that the first 'planned' economy depends for its economic success or failure on the labour of old-age pensioners and the ability of Soviet women to produce more children shows the degree to which the concept of planning has to be stretched to accommodate current Soviet planning. The idea of planning, in the Marxist perception of the term, is not some technical exercise, although clearly it contains a technical dimension, but it is primarily a socio-economic regulator of a fundamentally different kind, reflecting directly the aspirations and needs of the direct producers. In this context it would be more accurate to describe the Soviet economy as bureaucratically administered, by a ruling group whose economic instability allows a hitherto unheard of degree of negative control to the direct producers, which in turn generates the apparent labour shortages.

A BRIEF DIGRESSION ON LABOUR SHORTAGE AND SURPLUS

The question of labour shortage or surplus can also be considered briefly on a more abstract level. If we consider some isolated individual in some habitable space, perhaps the desert island so popular in classical political economy, we can abstract from the specificities of both capitalism and the USSR. The individual we will assume is not a Robinson Crusoe figure, who has come from a developed mode of production to a more primitive world, but an individual with no prior knowledge of economic or productive potentialities. For our isolated individual, production occurs on the basis of his own expended labour time, acting upon the 'free gifts of nature' available to him. The individual will produce use-values to satisfy his own wants, which will be generated initially by physiological needs. His capacity to fulfil these needs will regulate his labour time in correspondence with the level of technique and available resources. In these conditions, both technique and needs will alter through experience. The individual's work activity will involve a learning process that will modify both needs and the means to satisfy them. However, in these circumstances there is no possibility of either a labour surplus or shortage developing, because the expenditure of human labour time will be directly regulated by the individual's needs. Surplus labour can have no meaning, because if the potential labour time expended is greater than that necessary to satisfy needs, then it can be curtailed and transformed into leisure time. The intensity of the individual's labour is, therefore, determined by his needs which change as the capacity to satisfy them changes. Equally there can be no possibility of a labour shortage because the individual will be unable to conceptualise production on any other basis than his own capacity for labour. These capacities may well change and develop over time but the notion of labour shortage need not emerge.

It is in this respect that this individual is different from the Robinson Crusoe figure, who was able to conceptualise production over and above his own labour capacities and could envisage the form of labour organisation that could provide it for him. Therefore, objectively he did experience a labour shortage as his perception of needs exceeded his ability, through his own labour, to satisfy them. Those needs, however, were generated in the context of a different social system and were never dependent upon his own expenditures of labour time for their satisfaction. They arose from a mode of production that relied upon a form of labour organisation that was exploitative and produced a surplus for the class of owners. For Robinson Crusoe, the eventual resolution of the problem was the relationship with Friday, through which an unearned surplus was extracted. Interestingly, this relationship was originally based upon direct force but was eventually replaced by a more suitable form of coercion as Friday was incorporated into Robinson's consumption patterns.

To generalise further, it is only when exploitative social relations of production exist that the possibility for labour shortages can begin to develop. Once the concept of utilising the surplus labour of the direct producers for the benefit of the surplus extractors develops, then the need for an increasing pool of direct producers becomes apparent. This is true in conditions of both feudalism and slavery. However, implicit in this relationship is the possibility of generating a relative surplus population.

It is the divorce of production, based upon the needs of the direct producers, from the individual control over labour time that creates this possibility. Objectively each individual has the capacity to be both producer and consumer, adding to both the productive potential of the society and to the claims made upon that production. Consequently, there cannot be a surplus population unless the social relations of production make the production of the means of subsistence (at whatever level of development) subordinate to some other law than necessity. This is indeed the case under the capitalist mode of production where profitable accumulation, achieved through the surplus extraction process, is that law. Furthermore, labour shortage can only come into being when the needs of the direct producers and their control over their own labour time is disrupted; if, for example, the planned results of production exceed the direct producers' ability or willingness to work. In the USSR the exploitative relations of production are not subject to the disciplines of the law of value but equally are not regulated by the needs of the direct producers. The plan, as already suggested, appears as an externally created phenomenon divorced from the immediate needs of the direct producers. Consequently, the indirect control of the direct producers over the surplus extraction process manifests itself as an apparent labour shortage which is reproduced over time as an inherent tendency of the system. Ultimately, only when harmony is restored between needs and control over labour time would it be possible to talk of full employment, individually regulated and controlled by the needs of the direct producer. This, however, implies the end of the exploitative social relations of production, something which is clearly not on the immediate agenda in either the capitalist world nor in the USSR.

THE CHANGING NATURE OF ECONOMIC
REGULATION IN THE USSR

This section draws together the major propositions developed in Part I, in order to place into context the need for the experimental initiatives, which will be outlined in Part II. The central proposition developed so far is that the antagonistic nature of the social relations of production in the USSR creates a vicious circle of problems, outlined in Figure 3.1, which explains the current decline in economic growth rates and poor economic performance. It was argued in Chapter 1 that the central question relates to the extraction, by the ruling group from the direct producers, of a socially produced surplus. The Soviet ruling group requires a growing, usable surplus to stabilise and reproduce its own socio-economic position.

However, the origins of the Soviet ruling group have produced a particular set of relationships around the surplus extraction process, which were outlined in Chapter 2. Unlike the ruling class under the capitalist mode of production, the ruling group in the USSR does not have its dominance stabilised in property relations. Nor is the Soviet workforce 'free' in the dual sense identified by Marx. Hence the relationship between the worker and the ruling group is one of semi-dependency. The absence of the controlling mechanisms of unemployment and meaningful wage differentiation and incentives means that there is little correspondence between work and rewards, and the law of value does not operate as the principal regulatory mechanism. Furthermore, the ruling group does not enjoy the unconstrained use of force that was available to the ruling group in both feudal and slave societies. The historical origins of this situation can be outlined briefly.

The October Revolution removed the law of value as the prime economic regulator in the USSR. Even during the period of NEP, the law of value only operated in an attentuated form, because the state monopoly of foreign trade removed any spontaneous equivalence with the world market and the state control of the commanding heights of the economy distorted the internal operation of the law of value (Preobrazhensky, 1965). During the early plan period the task facing the ruling group was the basic industrialisation of the economy and the creation of a military power capable of guaranteeing their survival in a hostile environment. The historical legacy of Stalinism was of an economy transformed, in the most brutal manner, from a largely agrarian, semi-industrial base to the second largest industrial force in the world. However, this transition was achieved on the basis of an economic mechanism reliant upon direct force and the atomisation of the workforce (Ticktin, 1978, pp. 52–5). The combination of highly repressive labour codes, the activity of the secret police, the forced labour of camp internees and the destruction of the party and labour movement, so well described by Schwarz (1953), combined to produce a workforce that was controlled and worked, however chaotic the eventual result (Krawchenko, 1947). This form of control was predicated upon the complete exclusion of direct producers from either economic or political decision-making, but in the process of de-politicising the workforce the ruling group ceded to them indirect negative control over their own labour process in the factories (Filtzer, 1986). This is the logical adjunct to the development of terror and atomisation as the prime means of economic regulation.

The basic tasks of this period was achieved primarily by the extensive expansion of the absolute surplus. That is by drawing into social production previously untapped material resources and mobilising a workforce which had been employed in the household, semi-subsistence sector of the economy or low productivity agriculture. The directly coercive forms of control that emerged were sufficient, even if extremely wasteful, for achieving the desired results, and the USSR, with limited, easily prioritised targets, was able to build up Department One industries and arm itself. Force and fear were the ultimate arbiters in the surplus extraction process, but as long as the surplus could be expanded absolutely, the appearance of growth could be maintained and the deterioration of control at the enterprise level could be tolerated.

However, in the post-war period the tasks facing the ruling group began to change and the objective basis of this form of control began to fracture. Both western and Soviet sources talk in terms of a change in growth strategy from extensive to intensive development (Berliner, 1976, pp. 431–3; Sorokin, 1982, p. 108; Abalkin, 1982, p. 3; Kulagin, 1983, p. 101). However, if labour activity is the only source for the production of use-values, then the change in Soviet growth strategy implies changes in the exploitative relationship between the ruling group and the direct producers. It would, therefore, be more precise to characterise this strategic change as a transition from the extensive expansion of the absolute surplus to attempts to increase intensively the relative surplus. The point is that this necessitates a change in the forms of control and economic regulation. What was once adequate for one set of tasks was no longer adequate. The expansion of the relative surplus depends upon a different species of control and regulation, which needs to be simultaneously more subtle, more all-pervasive, and more coercive. Belotserkovsky (1979, pp. 47–9) has argued that this transition was made more difficult because control was partially lost in the years immediately following Stalin's death as a result of Khrushchev's inept attempts to initiate some limited de-Stalinisation. However, more fundamental changes were taking place.

Firstly, the possibilities of further extending the growth of the absolute surplus had already begun to decline, as the system itself, because of its wastefulness and inefficiencies, posited the necessity for a large agricultural workforce relative to other developed countries. This curtailed the flow of population into the industrial sector where it had been absorbed, in increasingly large numbers into sectors of the economy like repair, maintenance and auxiliary production. The necessity for the growth of these sectors was based upon the poor quality of production and the loose control exercised by the centre over manning levels, but at the same time this reduced the possibilities for further expansion of the absolute surplus.

Secondly, technological change demanded changes in the form of economic regulation. Modern industry is based upon a complex technical division of labour which is simultaneously subject to two contradictory forces. On the one hand, it increasingly involves the fragmentation of tasks, thereby reducing the area of expertise and responsibility of the individual worker. However, it depends simultaneously upon an ever more complex integration and co-operation between these tasks. After all, the division of labour can integrate the activities of workers in separate plants, enterprises, regions and countries, both in the west and within the CMEA bloc.

Production is, therefore, becoming increasingly socialised. Furthermore, the vast outlays of social labour time necessary to construct the means of production and the R&D necessary for its continual upgrading, makes it essential that plant is correctly utilised. It is imperative that production takes place at the correct rhythm; that plant is utilised continuously and that shift coefficients rise; that the quality and timing of maintenance, service and repair are adequate; that factor inputs are of adequate quality and are used efficiently and economically, and so on.

This all implies the necessity for a discipline, within the ranks of both the direct producers and management, which is based on more rational grounds than that which existed in the thirties. Furthermore, the complex integrated nature of production gives individuals unprecedented potential for negative control and autonomy. As the economy becomes more complex, so the consequences of negative control become more far-reaching and the whole chain of linkages can be breached by the activities of small groups of workers, ITR or management. As a consequence, force and atomisation cannot be the basis of economic regulation and control over the modern industrial workforce, as it directly contradicts the logic of development of the productive forces.

Thirdly, the process of economic development and technological change also changes the nature of the direct producers and begins to present the possibility of destroying the atomisation characteristic of previous periods. The increasingly hereditary nature of the workforce, the distance from peasant individualist origins, the collective organisation and the integrated nature of modern work, the enhancement of educational and skill levels plus the rise in expectations all pose the possibility of undermining the old mechanisms of control.

Hence, the objective foundations for both sustained economic growth (the extension of the absolute surplus) and the methods of control (terror and atomisation) had diminished in the post-war period. Consequently, it can be argued that the social relations of production and the methods of economic regulation and control developed in the previous period, which at one time facilitated growth and the transformation of the social system, were now in decline and became a fetter upon the further development of the productive forces. This does not necessarily imply absolute decline, but the generation of an increasingly large gap between production potentialities and the actual level of production. This expresses itself in a twofold manner: in a decline in the rate of economic growth and labour productivity and in increased expectations and demands of the domestic populace.

This analysis calls into question the idea that the USSR represents a higher mode of production, in however a degenerated or distorted form. Marx after all identified capitalism's progressive function as its ability to revolutionise the material basis of production and consequently raise labour productivity. Therefore, a social system which is not capitalist but is technologically backward in comparison, that imports technology from capitalism, that is only able to raise labour productivity at a declining rate and is still seeking growth in the absolute surplus can hardly be described as a higher mode of production, however sophisticated the caveats.

The preceding argument suggests that the central problem for the ruling group, in the absence of the law of value, is that no unambiguous regulator of economic activity exists that can both provide discipline and maintain their privileged position. In their present form, control and regulation arise via the planning process, which is inherently conditioned and amenable to manipulation by the self-interest of the enterprise management and the negative pressure of the workforce. This mechanism is clearly inadequate for the task. It necessitates continual bureaucratic intervention from the centre, which in turn reinforces the problems that made the intervention necessary in the first place. Consequently, the Soviet ruling group's control over the labour process is more tenuous than that of its capitalist counterparts. The ruling group and its academic representatives recognise the locus of the problems in the process of surplus extraction. Many of the articles cited by Aganbegyan, Bunich, Sonin,

Manevich, Valavoi and Zaslavskaya will confirm this viewpoint; however, the terms and language they use are different. Obviously there can be no return to previous forms of control, which is not to say that force will not be used against recalcitrant individuals in the USSR, but it is widely acknowledged that it can no longer be the prime regulator of economic activity, if indeed it ever could. This is explicitly recognised by Zaslavskaya in the Novosibirsk Report (1983, pp. 83–108).

Nothing has been said thus far concerning the occurrence of direct worker activity in the form of strikes, co-ordinated go-slows, demonstrations and so on. The reason for this is that, although these activities occur because of the nature of the USSR, evidence of this type of activity is fragmentary and often disputed (Holubenko, 1975, pp. 14–18). More importantly, however, the existence or non-existence of these types of activity is not crucial to the general point being made. They represent powerful and concentrated evidence of the underlying antagonisms within the social system, (as they do under the capitalist mode of production) but they are not the only form of class struggle (this is also the case under capitalism). When strikes do occur, for example, they are usually localised and harshly repressed (Holubenko, 1975, pp. 14–18; Belotserkovsky, 1979, pp. 37–50; Haynes and Semyonova, 1979, p. 75). In present conditions, crude attempts to raise the rate of exploitation can be expected to produce the same results as those that occurred in the early sixties. For example, at Novocherkassk in 1962, attempts to impose simultaneous price increases for dairy and meat products, coupled with an increase in the length of shifts in the local enterprises, precipitated a workers' revolt and the seizure of the town. The struggle here and elsewhere in the same period was eventually harshly repressed. This, in itself, is a reflection of the nature of the system, because in the absence of independent trade unions or political parties, workers' resistance will either be individualised or spontaneously explosive. The events of the early sixties illustrate that the transparency of social relations in the USSR is such that any action by the ruling group to increase the rate of exploitation is seen as precisely that (Belotserkovsky, 1978, pp. 44–6). In the absence of the veil of commodity fetishism, economic discipline cannot be imposed, by reference to impersonal, immutable and apparently 'natural' forces, as it can in the west.

As a consequence, it has appeared necessary to the Soviet ruling group, since the mid-sixties, to attempt to shift away from the extra-economic, political control that had existed up to this time, to new economic forms of control which would not destabilise their position by provoking popular discontent, but which would simultaneously increase their control over a usable surplus and allow the incorporation of sections of the society and thus stabilise their political hegemony. The form of control would need to be less overtly coercive, but would need to be based upon a more subtle form of force. The attempts by the ruling group to reform the economic system, from the mid-sixties onwards, are part of this dynamic and represents their search for stability.

It is against this background that the experimental initiatives must be viewed. The experiments were essentially attempts to resolve the problems that have been identified in Part I, especially labour shortages, declining productivity and the forms of labour indiscipline. The aim was to deal with these problems of labour organisation at the level of the enterprise, simultaneously incorporate sections of the workforce by the stimulation of workers' self-interest and forge a link between effort and rewards. The following chapters assess the nature, results and meaning of some of these experiments.

Part II

The Experimental Initiatives

5 The Shchekino Experiment

INTRODUCTION

The aim of Chapters 5 and 6 is to reassess the nature and operation of the experiment initiated at the Shchekino chemical plant in Tula province, from its inception in 1967 until 1973. The reason for the delineation of this time period is twofold. It corresponds to the period considered by Soviet sources to represent the successful years of the experiment, both at Shchekino itself and in terms of its extension to other enterprises (Parfenov and Shvetsov, 1977a, p. 2). Furthermore, these are the years which concern the major western text on the experiment (Delamotte, 1973). The intention is to provide a reappraisal of the nature of the experiment and to provide an alternative explanation of these early, apparently successful, years.

Chapters 7 and 8 will consider the period from 1973, through the legislative changes of 1977, 1978 and 1979, until the present. The second period is characterised, at the outset, by diminishing interest in the experiment, but increasing pressure for its generalisation. The period 1977–79 represents another watershed in the history of the experiment, as considerable doubts arose about the performance of the Shchekino plant itself and the possibilities of fully generalising the experiment (Parfenov and Shvetsov, 1977b, p. 2). This resulted in a series of attempts to introduce new conditions for the implementation of the experiment, in 1977 (*Ekonomicheskaya Gazeta*, No. 7, 1977, pp. 17–18) and 1978 (*Sotsialisticheskii Trud*, No. 7, 1978, pp. 9–11) which finally culminated in the planning resolution of 1979 (*Resheniya partii . . .*, 1981, pp. 78–119). The success of these changes in the post-1979 period will also be considered.

A review of the early period of the experiment can be justified on a number of grounds. Firstly, the detailed empirical work published on the Shchekino plant, and the other enterprises that initiated the experiment in this early period, can be utilised to illustrate and verify the theoretical propositions advanced in the first part of this book. In this way, the continuity of the problems, which it was argued underpin the political economy of the USSR, can be illustrated. Secondly, with the aid of hindsight, the early period can be more clearly understood and the tendencies implicit in the early years of the experiment's operation can be more easily extracted. Thirdly, it is intended to evaluate the empirical evidence and present a counter argument to those which are commonly advanced, in both the Soviet and western academic literature, regarding the motivation for, and eventual impact of, the experiment.

THE NATURE OF THE EXPERIMENT

The introductory chapters of this book outlined a political economy of the USSR that was based upon, and sought to explain, the interrelationship between a series of contemporary Soviet problems that have given rise to declining economic performance. The continuity of these problems over time can be demonstrated by considering the reasons suggested by Soviet sources in the late sixties for the implementation of the Shchekino experiment.

Shilin (1969, p. 5), for example, catalogues a series of reasons. He cites insufficient growth in labour productivity and low intensity of resource utilisation, particularly in the auxiliary and service sectors of Soviet industry as a prime reason. It should be noted that labour productivity growth of five per cent in 1966, seven per cent in 1967 and five per cent in 1968 appears quite respectable by comparison with the current figures outlined in Tables 3.12 and 3.13.

As a consequence, this leads to an imbalance between the numbers involved in basic production and in auxiliary and service sectors, particularly by international comparison. Shilin (p. 6) points out that at this time the ratio between basic and auxiliary workers in the Soviet machine building industry stood at 1 to 1.2, in comparison with a ratio of 3.5 to 1 in the USA. A further example cited by Shilin (p. 8) compares staffing levels on imported plant. The foreign firm, from whom the plant was acquired, employed 1100 workers, whilst in the Soviet case the figure rose to 1860. When auxiliary workers were included, the figure rose further to 2450.

Shilin (p. 8) points to the decline in natural population growth, coupled with the exhaustion of the agricultural surplus population, implying the necessity to develop socio-economic mechanisms to speed the introduction of new technology and free previously under-employed labour as a further reason. He suggested that, by 1970, 92 per cent of the able-bodied populace would be employed in the socialised economy (p. 7) and that there was little possibility of further employment of second members of households.

The specific choice of the chemical industry as the initiator of the experiment is well explained by both Shilin (pp. 12–13) and Dela-motte (pp. 107–10). As Delamotte (p. 108) points out, the aim of the Seventh Five Year Plan had been to 'chemicalise' the economy, and to show the importance of this sector he quotes Khrushchev's addition to Lenin's famous dictum, 'if Lenin were alive he would certainly say Communism is the power of the Soviets plus the electrification of the country plus the chemicalisation of the economy'.

The continued development of the chemical industry was essential, as it provided intermediate inputs for many other sectors of the economy and finished products that were exported to other Eastern bloc countries. Perhaps more important, however, is the relationship between the output of the chemical industry and the agricultural sector. Reference has already been made to the problems of this sector and an increased output of chemical fertilisers could potentially increase crop yields, expand the cultivated and cultivable area, increase agricultural productivity and output, free labour for more productive sectors of the economy and provide more consumables to aid the operation of incentive systems, as suggested in Figure 3.1.[1]

Furthermore, the chemical industry was in receipt of significant amounts of imported plant, equipment and machinery, hence the desirability of rationalising labour organisation within the chemical industry to utilise more efficiently the scarce and costly foreign equipment, raising shift coefficients and not allowing this equipment to lie idle (Sobeslavsky and Beazley, 1980, Part II). The intention was presumably to attempt to replicate western manning levels with a hoped-for knock-on effect to other sectors. How successful this was will emerge later. Apart from these latter two points, which were perhaps more specific to the chemical industry, the problems facing the industry were broadly similar to other sectors of the economy; namely, labour shortages, lax labour discipline, high unplanned labour turnover and under-utilisation of capacity as a consequence.

The choice of the Shchekino plant is also explained by Shilin (pp. 11–12) and Delamotte (pp. 114–5), who both provide a brief history of the plant's performance. They cite as particular reasons the under-utilisation of fixed capital, which makes costs of production rise by as much as 50 per cent, levels of labour productivity below that planned, and over-manning in comparison with western plants. What they do not note is that in the Spring of 1967, six months prior to the implementation of the experiment, personnel chiefs from Shchekino went to their ministry in Moscow to ask for permission to hire an additional 400 workers (Tolstikov, 1968, p. 2). This was not to expand production capacity, but simply to keep the plant operational and attempt to increase the level of capacity utilisation. However, in less than a year the plant had effectively overcome the need for new labour and begun to shed existing labour resources (Tolstikov, 1968, p. 2). This dramatic turn-around effectively economised on 1000 workers in the first twelve months of the experiment's operation, the 400 additional workers that were requested plus those actually released in the first year. This can be explained by the nature of the experiment and its immediate results.

The overall aim of the experiment was to raise labour productivity (Shilin, p. 20) and although theoretically this could be achieved by a variety of means, the experiment adopted at the Shchekino enterprise marked a novel departure for the Soviet economy at this time. The aim of the experiment was to tie the remuneration of the Shchekino workforce more closely to the enterprise's performance, strengthening the weak link between work and rewards already noted.[2] This in itself was not novel, as all previous incentive schemes, introducing premiums, bonuses and so on, had had this as their ultimate objective. The novelty of the Shchekino experiment and its potential importance for the rest of the Soviet economy, facing supposed labour shortages, stemmed from the source of the material incentives. The experiment was based upon the internal rationalisation of the plant's labour organisation, the release of surplus personnel and the use of the economised wage fund for material stimulation (Sharov, 1975, p. 95). Tolstikov (1969, p. 2) summarises the experiment as 'keeping the total wage fund unchanged while reducing the number of employees, thus helping to increase the earnings of the remaining workforce and thus considerably increasing the collective's material stake in increasing output and labour productivity'.

Therefore, with a wage fund and plan targets stabilised until the end of the plan period, the Shchekino enterprise committed itself to release 1000 workers in the period from 1 October 1967 to the end of 1970 (*Izvestia*, 12 October 1969, p. 5). This is a significant contrast to the demand for additional workers in the Spring of 1967, already noted, and represented approximately 12–13.3 per cent of the Shchekino workforce.[3]

Delamotte (1973, p. 105) has argued that the experiment was based upon four essential elements. Firstly, the 'scientific' reorganisation of labour within the enterprise. Secondly, the stimulation of personal interests via financial incentives. Thirdly, the raising of workers' qualifications and skill levels by a programme of retraining, and finally, increased participation. Delamotte argues that these features explain the early successes of the experiment, but this needs to be re-examined and the contribution of each of these elements has to be re-appraised, if the longer term experience of the Shchekino enterprise and the fate of the experiment generally is to be understood. There are grounds to doubt two things; that all these elements contributed equally to the experiment's early performance and that these elements alone are sufficient to explain the experiment's progress in this initial period.

The basic source for raising labour productivity, in the first phase of the experiment, was to come through the freeing of surplus labour and the internal re-organisation of the workforce. As already noted, the contradictory internal dynamic of the Soviet economic system leads to labour hoarding at the enterprise level, which represents management's unpenalised response to uncertainty. Therefore, the first necessity was to identify the superfluous workers and it should be noted that over half the internal commissions established, identified in Table 5.1, had the rationalisation and tightening of internal labour organisation as their objective (Sharov, 1975, p. 96; Shilin, 1969, p. 19).

For each sub-division of the Shchekino plant and workforce, the commissions, aided by external scientific research institutes where necessary, calculated the optimal number of workers and produced 'technically substantiated' norms based upon that number of workers (Shilin, 1969, p. 24). In 1966, only 17.3 per cent of Shchekino workers worked according to 'technically substantiated' norms and by 1967 this figure had only risen to 20 per cent (Parfenov, 1973, p. 2). However, by 1969, 80 per cent of basic production workers and 55 per cent of auxiliary workers had switched to new norms, and by 1970 the figure reached 95 per cent (Karpenko, 1969a, p. 2; Parfenov, 1973, p. 2). Shkurko provides a more detailed breakdown for this early period which is reproduced in Table 5.2.

The introduction of technically validated norms and the work of the commissions was seen to be both the prime method for identifying surplus workers and also raising the intensity of the work of those who remained in the plant. All commentators agree that the greatest significance came in the norming of repair and maintenance work that

Table 5.1   Internal commissions established to implement the Shchekino experiment

1. Central All-Combine Commission – under the direction of the enterprise director with a membership including party, trade union, management, engineering and ITR representatives
2. Commission to Increase the Volume of Production and Improve the Utilisation of Production Funds – headed by the plant's Chief Engineer
3. Commission to Rationalise the Organisation of Energy Services and the Repair of Power Equipment – headed by the plant's Chief Power Engineer
4. Commission to Rationalise the Organisation of Maintenance and Repair Facilities for Control and Measuring Instrumentation and Automated Systems – headed by an engineer
5. Commission to Rationalise the Work of ITR Workers – headed by the Chief Combine Engineer
6. Commission to Rationalise the Organisation of Maintenance and Repair Facilities for All Technological Equipment – headed by the plant's Chief Mechanical Engineer
7. Commission to Rationalise the Organisation of Control of Production of Final Products – headed by the Central Factory Laboratory
8. Commission to Mechanise Manual and Heavy Labour
9. Commission to Evaluate and Introduce New More Progressive Wage Systems
10. Commission to Improve Working Conditions and Technical Safety
11. Commission to Redeploy Workers and ITR Freed During the Course of the Experiment
12. Commission to Verify the Introduction and Elaboration of Norms and to Calculate the Optimum Number of Workers

Source: Shilin (1969), pp. 18–19

Table 5.2   The diffusion of technically validated norms amongst Shchekino workers (as a % of the total number)

| Category of workers | % working to technically validated norms | | | | |
	1966	1967	1968	1969	1970 (plan)
Productive workers in technological shops	17.3	23.5	77.2	90	95
Repair workers	26.8	39.2	54.2	70	76

Source: Shkurko (1971a), p. 37.

had previously either had no norms or very lax norms (Sharov, 1969, p. 2). Karpenko (1973, p. 2) in particular, notes that the introduction of 'technically validated' norms had been impossible to achieve, either by moral exhortation or by direct orders, prior to the experiment, but now appeared to advance alongside the experiment's progress. Given the problems of introducing and raising norms, this is one of the experiment's most attractive features for the ruling group. However, one of the potential problems of this process was that the norms were developed within the plant and not set from branch or inter-branch manuals. Hence, even though norms were either raised or introduced for the first time, they still reflected the localised trade-off between management and the workforce. In this sense the experiment reflected previous practice, rather than changing it.

The process of internal re-organisation also included the rationalisation of production. For example, several shops producing the same products were amalgamated. The effect of this, apart from potential scale economies, was to free skilled workers, often with substantial training, skills and experience, who had previously been involved with lower-level supervisory duties, for more directly productive work (Tolstikov, 1969, p. 2). This type of transition was achieved fairly smoothly because, in the case of shop chiefs and foremen returning to the job of skilled machine operators, the portion of the economised wage fund they received compensated for any lost earnings, which, because of the previously existing small differentials, were not great anyway. It also had the added advantage for them of freeing them from the pressures of supervisory work.

Coupled with the combination of production facilities was the combination of jobs. For example, in both basic and auxiliary production rationalisation occurred; where previously ten operatives had tended ten machines, but with considerable idle-time, the labour process was re-organised so that six operatives tended the same ten machines and four could be released. Also, apparently disparate basic production work was combined. This process was, however, particularly pronounced in repair and maintenance sectors where, because of the nature of the work, considerable slack had developed. Here the number of workers was simply cut. The other alternative adopted was to combine what had been previously separate functions. For example, one repair worker would be responsible for both mechanical and electrical repair work or basic production workers would take on the repair work of their equipment. This produced a situation where two or three related occupations per worker was not unusual and in some sectors of the plant this even rose to four or five occupations per worker (Karpenko, 1969b, p. 3).

In this early phase of the experiment, some attempt was made to reduce heavy manual tasks, particularly in loading and unloading work, by introducing new technology and attempts were made to mechanise repetitive office tasks. In this early period, this did not contribute greatly to the overall numbers released, but the intention was that this should change in the second phase of the experiment (Cherednichenko and Gol'din, 1978, p. 14; Antonov, 1970, p. 1).

Rationalisation of repair and maintenance facilities was of particular importance to the Shchekino enterprise. The nature of the technology involved in the chemical industry demands regular service and maintenance, and given the record of Soviet plant and equipment this also needs efficient repair. Rather than having individual repair and maintenance staffs and equipment tied up in each shop, with the consequent problems of idle-time and under-utilised capacity, repair facilities were centralised. Furthermore, the zone of servicing was extended so that any section of service workers would be responsible for a wider area of plant and equipment. This leads to savings in terms of both staff and more efficient use of equipment. As Shilin (1969, p. 28) points out, repair functions can be best carried out in centralised specialist shops where particular repair skills and expertise can be developed. Given the large numbers employed in this sector, the high proportion of manual work and the consequently low productivity, this was not only important for Shchekino itself but also had great potential for the rest of Soviet industry.

Shilin cites the figure of three and a half million workers in the repair sector of Soviet industry in 1965. By the early seventies the figure quoted by Sonin (1977, p. 5) is two and a half million with a further two million loaders and one million quality control inspectors. In a comparative sense, Manevich (1969, p. 3) indicates the level of overmanning in one part of the auxiliary sector, internal enterprise transport. In the USA each transport worker in industry services 25 to 26 basic workers. In the USSR in the late sixties the comparable ratio was one to three.

A similar exercise was carried out with regard to laboratory services. Again, the nature of chemical production necessitates close scrutiny of product quality, both in terms of its final usage and in order to guarantee safety within production. Instead of a duplication of laboratory services in each shop or sub-division of the enterprise, these functions were centralised. Furthermore, the number of control

tests was dramatically reduced and parallel tests eliminated (Tolstikov, 1969, p. 2; Shilin, 1968, p. 29; Karpenko, 1969a, p. 2). For
example, the number of chemical analyses per shift in the production
of ammonia were reduced from five or six to two or three. This led to a
reduction in the number of control tests by around 4000. The wider
significance of this is explained by Sharov (1969, p. 2), who points out
that at this time 40 000 people were employed in control services at
enterprises under the control of the Ministry for the Chemical
Industry, and because of poor organisation it was estimated that 18
per cent of analyses were duplicated. Sharov also suggests that more
than 10 000 workers could be released simply by rationalising these
control services.

Overmanning was not just a shop-floor phenomenon. The contradictions of the Soviet system are such that an enterprise director will
also hoard managerial expertise. The experiment was also directed at
the management structure of the enterprise and sought to rationalise
where possible, thereby encouraging those who remained to broaden
the sphere of their responsibilities, combine previously disparate tasks
and improve their qualifications and skills as a consequence. In the
first phase of the experiment, the absolute numbers released from this
source were obviously not as large as from other sources, but this reorganisation should not be overlooked. As already noted economic
regulation and discipline, if it is to perform its essential functions, has
to apply to both management and workforce. Baranenkova (1971,
p. 243) goes as far as to argue that improved management was the
major single gain from the experiment.

Altogether the experiment tightened up the internal distribution of
labour resources within the enterprise. Furthermore, greater control
was placed upon the utilisation of time and the length of the working
day. Late arrival, early departure, over-long meal breaks and intra-
shift idle-time were all curtailed (*Izvestia*, 12 October 1969, p. 5). As a
result of this rationalisation and tighter organisation it was possible
to free workers from previous jobs (or perhaps more correctly, non-
jobs). If production levels could be maintained then labour productivity must necessarily rise. However, the aim was to go beyond this and
to stimulate an even greater increase in both output and productivity
via the use of the economised wage fund. It should be noted that in the
early phase of the experiment the improvement of the labour and
production organisation of the plant was the result of the close
scrutiny of the plant's work by the internal commissions and the
external bodies that assisted them.

The material incentives dimension to the experiment operated in the following manner. The economised portion of the wage fund, which arose as a consequence of the release of workers whilst the total wage fund remained constant, was split into two portions (Sharov, 1975, p. 95; Shilin, 1969, pp. 35–6).

One half of the amount was left at the disposal of the shop chief or foreman responsible for the shop where the saving was made and where the additional work was absorbed. This individual, after consultation with the relevant internal commission, comprising both management and trade union representatives, could use the economised funds to raise the wages of any worker by up to a maximum of 30 per cent of his basic wage rate (Shkurko, 1971a, pp. 44–5). This was only done if the worker had increased his work load, or if he had combined what were formally separate tasks or if he had developed a second (or third) skill or occupation, or if he had significantly increased the intensity of his work and thereby raised his individual productivity. On the shop floor, in basic and auxiliary production and in the repair and maintenance sectors, this operated in a direct manner. In the previous example cited, if the ten operatives were now reduced to six, half of the economised wages of the four workers released could be split amongst those who remained, providing the increment did not exceed 30 per cent of their basic wage. The idea was that those workers remaining could potentially see a direct link between the reorganisation of their shop, the increase in intensity of their work and heightened rewards, all stemming from the release of superfluous workers.

However, this needs some qualification as it should be remembered that the payments are discretionary and not automatic, and furthermore, the 30 per cent increment was the maximum and not the norm. As Karpenko (1969b, p. 1) points out, after attending a meeting of the commission that determined additional wage payments, the process was not over-generous. Each request for additional payments was closely scrutinised and no claim would be accepted if no economies to the wage fund had been made. The payment to the individual worker was only made if the commission was convinced that some real increase in productivity or responsibility had been achieved. The point is that the economised wage fund could not simply be used by shop chiefs to ingratiate themselves with their workforce. In a sense, this removes an area of discretion which used to be available to management alone, as it was now to be decided by the relevant internal commission (Andrle, 1976, pp. 80–1). If in any year the

economised portion of the wage fund was unutilised for wage increments, then, under the original terms of the experiment, the balance
could be transferred to the material stimulation fund and carried
forward to the next year for similar purposes (Tolstikov, 1969, p. 2).

The other half of the economised funds were passed to a centralised
fund that was controlled by the enterprise director. This could be used
by him to increase the basic wage rate, again by a maximum of 30 per
cent, for particular categories of personnel (Sharov, 1969, p. 2). This
related to managerial, technical or administrative staff who increased
their workload, productivity or responsibility under the terms of the
experiment. Extra payments could also be made to ITR whose ideas
led to an increase in productivity. Some portion of this economised
fund could also be used as special incentives for workers detailed to
particularly important tasks or in areas where norms are difficult to
apply and work difficult to measure. This relates mainly to the
maintenance and repair sectors where material incentives were
thought to be most desirable to encourage multiple jobs, skill and
qualification upgrading, and so on. As Shilin (1969, p. 139) points
out, of the first 636 workers who received payments from the
Director's centralised fund, 500 were maintenance workers. The fund
could also be used to increase the pay of lower grade management and
foremen who extended the scope of their responsibilities (Sharov,
1969, p. 2).

It was argued by Soviet sources, that the implementation of the
experiment would lead to benefits for everyone connected with the
enterprise. The workforce remaining at the plant would receive
additional payments and enhanced responsibilities; the enterprise
could rationalise its operations and increase output and productivity
for the same wage expenditure. For the ruling group, chemical output
would grow and superfluous workers could be released to be redeployed elsewhere. This begs the question of whether the interests of
those released were enhanced by the experiment. (This will be
considered after the initial results of the experiment are reviewed.)

In the Soviet Union the release of surplus workers poses the
immediate problem of what to do with the dismissed workers. As
previously noted, the Soviet consitution and labour codes guarantee
the worker the right to work and even if job security is not absolute on
an individual level, workers were nevertheless relatively secure as a
social group. However, the novelty of the Shchekino experiment was
that dismissals were no longer to be solely individual and particularly
political, but were to affect a sizeable proportion of the workforce

(12–13.3 per cent initially), potentially cutting across all sections of the enterprise's organisational, occupational and hierarchical structure. It was the case that these decisions would be influenced by the characteristics of the individual workers involved. For example, those workers chosen for release would be those the shop or enterprise viewed as least valuable. Consequently, in any shop an individual with a record of labour discipline infractions, (tardiness, absenteeism, drunkenness, a record as a 'rolling stone' and so on) would be most likely to be released. For the first time in their working lives, workers in the enterprises where the experiment was implemented saw a connection developed between common labour infractions and the implementation of an administrative sanction. Previously, even where sanctions existed, they were often unused by management, ignored by workers or ineffective. It could be expected that under these new circumstances a lesson would be learned by those who remained and those who were released, leading to a tightening of labour discipline in the plant and a modification of industrial behaviour.

The general intention of the experiment was that it should operate as a semi-impersonal force, reducing the accepted and usual levels of job security enjoyed by the Shchekino workers. The language of the experiment conveys this impression very clearly with talk of 'rational utilisation of labour resources' and the 'scientific organisation of labour', implying an irresistible force and logic of modern industrial production.

THE INITIAL RESULTS OF THE EXPERIMENT

The most obvious immediate results were the changes that took place in manning levels at the Shchekino plant. This was particularly the case in the first two years of the experiment, when the numbers released increased rapidly and by mid-1969, 870 workers had been released (*Pravda*, 9 October 1969, p. 1). Shilin (1969, p. 33) provides a detailed breakdown of the situation at the plant after fifteen months of the experiment, as at 1 January 1969, by which time 800 workers had been released. The distribution of these workers by general occupational category is shown in Table 5.3, and as would be expected, 75 per cent of those released are workers.

From the available evidence, it is difficult to calculate what proportion of each category of personnel these figures represent, but it is plausible to assume that in the initial phase they reflect the plant's

Table 5.3   Labour released at Shchekino up to 1 January 1969

	By 1 Oct 1968	By 1 Jan 1969
All personnel released	520	800
of whom,		
ITR	110 (21%)	159 (20%)
office employees	21 (4%)	32 (4%)
workers	389 (75%)	609 (76%)

Source: Shilin (1969), p. 33.

overall occupational structure, a point confirmed by Baranenkova (1970, p. 56). The fact that so many workers could be released so quickly is further evidence of the level of overmanning in Soviet enterprises. A closer examination of the occupations of those released, provided in Table 5.4, allows the basis of this overmanning to be identified.

Table 5.4   Workers released at Shchekino by occupation

	By 1 Oct 1968	By 1 Jan 1969
Machine operators	97	141
Machinists & pump operators	44	77
Laboratory assistants & control workers	32	68
Machine repair & maintenance	58	71
Electrical equipment, repair & maintenance	40	47
Instrument repair & maintenance	40	68
Others	38	137
of whom,		
dispatches loaders & unloaders	—	21
warehousemen & assistants	—	22
drivers of electrical cranes	—	10
other occupations	—	84
Total	389	609

Sources: Shilin (1969), p. 33; Delamotte (1973), p. 155

In the first phase, up to 1 October 1968, almost the same number of workers were released from the three repair categories as were released from basic production, and by 1 January 1969, only 27 per cent of the total number of personnel released were basic production workers. This, again, is a vivid example of the overmanning in particular areas of the occupational structure in Soviet enterprises concentrated in the repair and maintenance sectors, auxiliary production and service sectors, particularly warehouse work, internal transport and loading and unloading. An indication of this imbalance is the fact that, in the period 1968–69, because of increases in the plant's production it would normally have led, prior to the experiment, to an increase in repair staff of 20 per cent, rather than the reductions that were actually achieved (*Ekonomicheskaya Gazeta*, No. 28, 1971, p. 8).

The manner by which these savings in labour were achieved is summarised in Table 5.5. With the exception of the penultimate category and the unspecified last category, all the savings were achieved as a result of internal reorganisation of labour. This ac-Counts for 85 per cent of the labour released up until 1 October 1968; 81 per cent up until 1 January 1969; and 85 per cent by the end of 1969.

The initial impact of the experiment on production at Shchekino was impressive and Sharov (1969, p. 2) points out that in the first two complete years of the experiment output volume grew by 80 per cent and labour productivity rose by 87 per cent. By January 1970, in comparison with 1966, output had grown by 86.6 per cent and labour productivity had more than doubled and was the highest in the whole branch (Antonov, 1970, p. 1). Finally, taking the whole period from 1966 to the end of 1970, labour productivity rose by 140 per cent (Boldyrev, 1972, p. 2) and the volume of production doubled (Cherednichenko and Gol'din, 1978, p. 14). As Shilin (1969, p. 34) points out, the growth of labour productivity and average wages, resulting from the experiment's implementation, dramatically exceeded their planned levels. By the end of the plan period the Shchekino plant had achieved a growth in labour productivity more than double the planned level.

The economic results, therefore, were impressive at the Shchekino plant, but it should be noted that even though the experiment was initiated here, it was closely followed by eight other plants. These plants, which followed the Shchekino example in 1968, were not confined to the chemical industry, but included plants from the textile, petro-chemical and metallurgical sectors of the economy

Table 5.5   The source of personnel savings

	1 October 1968[1]	1 January 1969[1]	31 December 1969[2]
Uniting & consolidating shops	48	64	82
Uniting services with production	49	92	121
Combining occupations & widening the service zone	209	347	433
Strengthening the organisation of labour	97		
Revising the schedule of laboratory work	16	39	43
Introduction of time norms & technically substantiated norms	70	170	240
Mechanisation of manual labour	21	23	68
Other measures	10	65	—
Totals	520	800	987

Sources: (1) Shilin (1969), p. 33; (2) Shkurko (1971a), p.12.

(Shilin, 1969, p. 9; Shkurko, 1971a, pp. 8–11; Baranenkova, 1970, pp. 50–1). The results achieved at these plants are summarised in Table 5.6. Once again, the numbers released in such a short period of time indicate the level of overmanning (the average reduction being 13.275 per cent), and all the plants achieved impressive growth in labour productivity in comparison with previously planned levels. It is worth noting that in most instances the volume of sales did not increase by more than the previously planned level, but nevertheless this was achieved with a much reduced workforce. (This data will be returned to later.)

In the following year, 1969, the experiment was further extended and Shkurko (1971a, p. 5) cites two additional groups of enterprises; firstly, 25 enterprises in the petro-chemical sector (23 of which were part of three associations), which in less than three years shed 11.6 per cent of their workforce; the second group comprised five enterprises in the textiles sector which shed ten per cent of their workforce. The results achieved by these plants were also impressive, as labour productivity rose on average by 22 per cent, as opposed to the previously planned level of twelve per cent. Tables 5.7 and 5.8 illustrate how labour was economised at these two groups of enterprises. As at Shchekino itself, the majority were released as a result of tightening internal labour organisation and job combination, particularly in the area of service and repair work (Shkurko, 1971a, p. 13). For example, at Pyshminsk this took the form of metal workers in repair shops taking on electrical welding work (*Ekonomicheskaya Gazeta*, 1970, No. 17, p. 15).

By 1970, 60 enterprises were participating in the experiment and in the period 1968–69, 12 000 workers were released (*Ekonomicheskaya Gazeta*, 1970, No. 10, p. 11). By 1971 the number of enterprises operating on experimental lines had more than doubled to over 120 (Shkurko, 1971b, pp. 10–11). These enterprises employed 700 000 workers and raised their labour productivity on average by 22 per cent, ten per cent more than envisaged in the plan.

The intention of the experiment was to affect not only manning levels, production and productivity but also workers' remuneration. Tables 5.9, 5.10, and 5.11 indicate the volume of savings made and the uses to which these economised funds were put at Shchekino. A number of features emerge.

Firstly, the number of people receiving additional payments as a result of the experiment grew steadily over the early years, but by 1969 only a little over a third of the workforce remaining at the plant were

Table 5.6 Plants undertaking the Shchekino experiment
(For Production, the last year of the Experiment is expressed as a percentage of the first)
A = During the Experiment   B = Previous planned growth

		Increase in Sales Volume	Increase in Labour Productivity	Increase in Average Wage	Reduction in Personnel
Furmanov, Spinning & Weaving, No. 2.	A	7.6	29.2	27.5	15.1
	B	7.6	11.6	—	—
Severonikel' Combine	A	27.7	42.9	17.9	11.5
	B	27.7	34.2	15.3	—
Novomoskovsk Chemical Combine	A	41.3	36.9	18.6	17.1
	B	37.4	15.7	6.5	—
Kuibyshev Synthetic Rubber Enterprise	A	40.6	27	9.7	14.5
	B	40.6	13.5	1.7	—
Chelyabinsk Metallurgical Plant	A	7.1	61.3	12.6	7.0
	B	7.1	53.1	6.7	—
Pyshma Copper Plant	A	7.9	22.4	10.2	11.8
	B	7.9	8.6	4.2	—
Balakovo Chemical Fibre Plant	A	18.6	38.8	24.8	16.2
	B	18.6	23.2	11.5	—
V. V. Kuibyshev Synthetic Fibre Plant	A	12.2	23.7	14.8	13.0
	B	11.5	7.4	2.5	—

Source: Baranenkova (1970), p. 52.

Table 5.7   The reasons for labour released at 25 petro-chemical enterprises

	No. released	%
Combining skills	760	11
Widening the servicing zone	3200	46
Improving labour organisation	1400	20.8
Strengthening control over labour & reducing the ratio of transport services	735	10.7
Centralising repair & auxiliary services	291	4.2
Other measures	481	7.1
	6867	

Source: Shkurko (1971a), p. 12.

Table 5.8   The reasons for labour released at 5 textile enterprises

	No. released	%
Strengthening and widening the servicing zone, combining skills & other measures to improve labour organisation	490	40
Better management techniques	204	17
Introduction of automation	370	30
Other measures	160	13
	1224	

Source: Shkurko (1971a), p. 12.

in receipt of additional payments. Furthermore, by the beginning of 1969 only a little over 40 per cent of the economised wage funds were actually being redistributed. As a consequence of these two features, the average monthly increment per worker receiving additional payments was 10.1 roubles.

Secondly, it is clear from Table 5.10, that even though over half of the economised funds went to the centralised Director's Fund, this was distributed less than the Shop Chief's fund (22 per cent as opposed to 36 per cent). The bulk of the Director's Fund went to repair workers, as anticipated, but their average increment was below the plant average. The remaining funds from this source were distributed to ITR and employees who on average received above the plant

123

Table 5.9   Summary of wage savings and distribution up to 1 January 1969

	1 Jan 1968 343	1 Oct 1968 —	20 Nov 1968 689	1 Jan 1969 800
Numbers released				
Numbers receiving wage increments from economised funds	578	1 308	1 422	2 655
As a % of the workforce*	7.5%	—	19.4%	36.8%
Total monthly saving to the wage fund	R30 228	R45 800	R59 524	R67 900
Total additional monthly payments	R6 046	R15 226	R16 864	R26 600
Payments as a % of the total saving	20%	33%	28.3%	39.2%
Average increment per worker receiving additional payments	R10.46	R11.64	R11.85	R10.01

Source: Shilin (1969), p. 37.

Table 5.10   Distribution of the economised wage fund up to 20 November 1968

Composition of economised funds			
Directors' Fund	32 393	Roubles	(54.4%)
Shop Chiefs' Fund	27 131	Roubles	(45.6%)
Total	59 624	Roubles	
Total amount distributed	16 864	Roubles	
Total no. in receipt of additional payments	1 422		
Average amount received	11.85	Roubles	
Percentage of total economised wage fund distributed	28%		
From Directors' Fund			
Total no. receiving additional payments	636		
Total sum distributed	7 065	Roubles	
Average received	11.1	Roubles	
Percentage of fund distributed	22%		
Of 636 receiving additional payments repair workers constitute	500		
Total sum repair workers receive	4 723	Roubles	
Average received by repair workers	9.44	Roubles	
From Shop Chiefs' Fund			
Total no. receiving additional payments	786		
Total sum distributed	9 799	Roubles	
Average received	12.46	Roubles	
Percentage of funds distributed	36%		

Source: Shilin (1969), pp. 38–9.

Table 5.11   Distribution of additional payments by category of personnel up to 20 November 1968

Category	No. receiving additional payments	Total amount distributed (R)	Average payment (R)
ITR	125	2 202	17.6
Office employees	9	120	13.3
Workers	1 288	14 542	11.29
Total	1 422	16 864	11.85

Source: Shilin (1969), pp. 42–3.

average, see Table 5.11. The distribution of additional payments, and their average size at Schchekino, reflects the enterprise's pre-experiment employment and wage structure. Shkurko (1971a, p. 46) suggests that in the main, however, workers received a larger wage increment, in percentage terms, than their ITR counterparts. For example at the five textile plants cited, workers received on average a 14.6 per cent increment in comparison with ITR who received only 11.3 per cent. This effect would eventually distort the pattern of wage distribution and differentials within the plant and further level wages between ITR and workers. The problem of 'wage levelling' is closely related to the lack of correspondence between work and rewards and will be returned to later.

Thirdly, the average additional payment overall at Shchekino was 11.85 roubles and this needs to be placed in perspective. In 1968 the average wage at Shchekino was planned to be 1497 roubles per annum or 124.75 roubles per month. The actual wage was 1610 roubles per annum or 134.16 roubles per month. Therefore, the average increment represented approximately 9.5 per cent of the planned wage, or 8.8 per cent of the actual wage. The point is that even when allowing for the variations that existed between plants, this is a very small percentage increase.

The benefits accruing to the workforce were, however, not just received in the individualised wage. As previously noted, the remuneration of a Soviet worker, although primarily received in this way, also consists of social consumption determined at both the enterprise and societal level. During the early years of the experiment, part of the economised wage funds were directed towards social provision by the enterprise and this is outlined in Table 5.12. Clearly the provision of better nursery, hospital, clinic, recreational and holiday facilities is potentially desirable for all workers in the plant. In this way, even those workers not receiving any individualised wage increment from the direct operation of the experiment have some material interest in its success. Furthermore, if the enterprise workforce is reduced, then the facilities available will be allocated amongst a smaller number of workers, improving access for those who remain. The improved economic performance of the enterprise was, therefore, reflected in improved social provision for those who remained (Parfenov and Shvetsov, 1977a, p. 2; Shilin, 1969, pp. 52–3). In this sense, using economised wage funds to provide better facilities further reduces the welfare of those released who will no longer have access to these facilities, as this is determined via the worker's relationship to the

Table 5.12   Use of funds for socio-cultural purposes and housing construction (1000 Roubles)

	1967	First six months of 1968	1968
Financing nursery school provision	17	—	3
Reviewing the stock of the polyclinics, hospital and dispensary	18	40	74
Partial payment of the losses incurred in the upkeep of the cultural-sporting institute and pioneer camp	75	21	57
Maintenance of two tourist centres and purchasing equipment	65	53	107
Purchase of cultural and sporting equipment	18	17	17
Other expenses	7	6	60
Transferred to material stimulation fund	—	59	59
	200	196	377

Source: Shilin (1969), p. 52.

enterprise. Those released, therefore, provide the means to increase social provision and by their release are penalised and excluded from the use of that enhanced provision.

Within the plant, the experiment had a dual effect upon the skill structure. The choice of those workers to be released was such that the most skilled and experienced workers were retained. Hence the average skill level rose (Sharov, 1969, p. 2). Moreover, this was further enhanced by the impact of combining jobs, extending service zones and increasing individuals' work responsibilities, which made it necessary to retrain workers, raise educational levels and increase skill and expertise. In the first eighteen months of the experiment, 1000 employees mastered a second or related occupation and over 4000 raised their qualifications (*Problemy ispol'zovaniya . . .*, 1973, p. 110). The overall impact of this was that the average wage category rose from 4.6 in 1967 to 4.9 in 1969 (Sharov, 1969, p. 2).

A further result of the experiment, noted by all the commentators, was the increased level of labour discipline at the enterprise (Karpenko, 1969b, p. 2; Tolstikov, 1968, p. 2; Sharov, 1975, p. 94; Shkurko, 1971a, p. 13). This is illustrated on Table 5.13. The Soviet

Table 5.13   The state of labour discipline at the
Shchekino plant

	1966	1967	1968
Total punishments	409	489	330
Total failing to report	457	304	168
Man-days lost	1054	607	316

Source: Shilin (1969), p. 59.

sources cite the following changes occurring after the implementation
of the experiment: a better attitude towards work emerged; productive equipment was more fully and effectively utilised; the absentee
and idler became a rarity; the rhythm of work became more stringent;
even though there were fewer people in the enterprise, the number of
overtime hours was reduced by one third; idle-time both between
shifts and within shifts was reduced; a widespread acceptance of
technically validated norms emerged. Furthermore, the level of spontaneous labour turnover at the plant was significantly reduced by the
experiment (Baranenkova, 1970, p. 60). Within a year of the introduction of the experiment, labour turnover fell from 17.3 per cent to 10.4
per cent and idle-time was cut in half, in the same period (Shkurko,
1971a, p. 13). It should be noted that the pre-experiment level of
overtime working was 10 500 hours per annum. After the implementation of the experiment, reflecting its impact on labour discipline and
general production organisation, the volume of overtime hours fell to
340 hours per annum (Sharov, 1975, p. 99).

   A similar pattern emerges from the other plants cited who initiated
the experiment in this early period. Labour discipline generally
improved and, for example, at Furmanov No. 2, turnover fell from 22
per cent in 1967 to fifteen per cent in 1969 and the number of labour
discipline infractions was halved. At the Bashkir Petro-Chemical
Association (Bashkirneftekhimzavod), within nine months of the
experiment's introduction, labour turnover fell by 25 per cent and
idle-time was reduced by a similar proportion (Shkurko, 1971a,
p. 13).

   Shkurko (pp. 37–8) also notes that the acceptance of 'technically
validated' norms by the workforce also accompanied the introduction
of the experiment at other plants. At Omsk the proportion working to

these norms rose to 88 per cent of the workforce and at Kuibyshev to 85 per cent.

Finally, as a parallel to the experiment, internal *khozraschet* mechanisms were strengthened at Shchekino (Karpenko, 1969b, p. 3). This took the form of setting wholesale prices for output, on a shop by shop basis and the fulfilment of these value criteria become the basis for the payment of wages and bonuses. This led, according to Karpenko, to a steep rise in claims made by one shop against another. This economic sanction worked in the following manner: one shop suffering losses in production due to the actions of another could be reimbursed, with the full cost being met by the shop responsible. This economic discipline was intended to supplement the impact of increasing labour discipline within the plant, by disciplining management staff.

But what of the workers released? As pointed out by Sharov (1969, p. 2), the Shchekino plant, in the initial period, was in a fortunate position and was able to absorb a relatively high proportion of the workers released. As he explains, 'we did not have to worry about the released personnel being without work for a short period. A large plant to manufacture synthetic fibres is being built near our combine and several thousand workers were needed'. Therefore, the workers released could be absorbed into the immediate locale. This was of great significance for the introduction of the experiment as the majority of workers chose to change their occupations rather than to change their place of residence. If management could at least offer the possibility of staying in the same locality it would ease the uncertainty involved in the experiment's implementation and potentially reduce discontent and resistance. Delamotte provides a useful breakdown of the eventual destination of the workers released which is reproduced in Table 5.14. It should be noted that over 25 per cent of those released were not re-integrated into the plant and even if only 50 were made redundant, another 100 left of their own accord.

As Baranenkova (1970, p. 54) points out, the experiment was implemented primarily at enterprises which had undergone expansion and required new staff, hence this pattern of absorption of released labour in the immediate vicinity was replicated at the other plants cited. For example, at Novomoskovsk during the Ninth Five Year Plan, 2000 workers were scheduled to be released, but an additional 2034 were required over this same period for new shops (p. 55). In the initial year of the experiment at Novomoskovsk, of the 556 workers released, 450, almost 80 per cent, were placed at the plant; at

Table 5.14   The placement of the 800 workers initially affected by the experiment

	Absorbed at the enterprise	Placed in vicinity	Departed
Workers			
Transferred to vacant posts in plant	337		
Transferred to synthetic fibre plant		101	
Transferred to other organisations			5
Left of their own accord			76
Redundant			33
Entered the army			38
Left to continue studies			19
	337	101	171
ITR & office workers			
Transferred to vacant posts in plant	102		
Transferred to synthetic fibre plant		31	
Transferred to other organisations			20
Left of their own accord			20
Redundant			17
Retired			1
Total: 800 =	439	132	229

Total absorbed at enterprise & transferred in vicinity = 571
Total redundant   = 50
Total left of their own accord   = 96

Source: Delamotte (1973), p. 159.

Balakovo 70 per cent of those released were placed at the plant (Shkurko, 1971a, p. 15); at the Novokuibyshev oil processing plant, of the 1000 workers released in six months, over 60 per cent were reintegrated into the plant (*Ekonomicheskaya Gazeta*, 1970, No. 13, p. 8). This pattern was replicated at a wide range of other plants.

The overall experience of the Shchekino plant was broadly confirmed by the other enterprises which initiated the experiment in this early period. To summarise: a broadly similar proportion of workers was released from all the plants cited (in the range from seven per cent to seventeen per cent with the average around twelve per cent); the structure of the personnel released reflected the overall employment structure, with workers in the majority; the sources of released labour were similar (combining jobs, widening the service zone, improving labour organisation and strengthening norms); the workers released were predominantly auxiliary and repair sector workers; the results in terms of output and productivity were all positive; labour discipline increased and turnover and infractions decreased; average wages rose; social provision at the enterprise level improved; the majority of the workers released were re-absorbed in the same enterprise, association or locality.

This picture is confirmed by an analysis of 50 enterprises operating along Shchekino lines at the beginning of 1970 (*Problemy ispol'zovaniya*..., 1973, p. 111). Of the 23 800 workers released, 14 900 (62.5 per cent) were reintegrated at their old plants, 4700 to fill newly created vacancies and 10 200 to fill previously vacant places. Of the 8900 who left their enterprise, almost half chose this course of action themselves. Of the total numbers released, 79 per cent were workers, seventeen per cent ITR and four per cent office workers, administrators and management.

Generally speaking, the experiment was an economic success and the impressive results at Shchekino and elsewhere confirm that the problems of underemployment, low labour productivity, excess capacity are due to poor utilisation of existing resources, characteristic of Soviet industrial enterprises. If this could be achieved at the experimental plants, then the generalisation of the experiment to all industry would lead to significant advantages for the ruling group. A further indication of these possibilities emerged from a survey undertaken by the Chemical Industry's Bureau for the Scientific Organisation of Labour. After analysing 140 enterprises under their auspices, they concluded that if the experiment was generalised to all of them, then eighteen per cent of the existing workforce could be released and this would represent sufficient staff for all new planned projects for the following five years (Sharov, 1975, p. 99; Parfenov, 1973, p. 2). The actual successes and the future potential of the experiment led the CPSU and the Council of Ministers to support the experiment and press for its further extension (*Resheniya partii*..., 1970, pp. 539–41). However, before considering the attempted generalisation of the experiment, this early period of apparent success needs to be critically reassessed.

6 A Reappraisal of the Results of the Shchekino Experiment

AN IDEALISED VIEW OF THE OPERATION OF THE SHCHEKINO EXPERIMENT

The preceding chapter sought to outline the essential features of the Shchekino experiment and the short term results achieved. In economic terms the results appear most impressive but how were they achieved? It is possible to extract from the Soviet sources an idealised view of the operation of the experiment.

The assumption underlying the Soviet view of the experiment is that current output is a function of the plant's capital stock, the level of available technology, the size of the plant's labour force and the organisational efficiency with which these factors are utilised. The size of the labour force is assumed to be above the optimal level and the degree of overmanning at the plant in the original time period reflects the enterprise directorate's desire for a 'safety factor' of hoarded labour. This aspect will be reflected in the occupational structure of the plant, the preponderance of auxiliary, service, repair and maintenance workers and this will have a negative influence upon indicators like absenteeism, idle-time, and labour turnover. This is ultimately reflected in the average labour productivity of the plant, which is the total output divided by the number of workers, and this provides a measure of the intensity of work. It can be assumed that, because of labour hoarding, the plant is operating where the marginal productivity of labour is equal to zero or it may even be negative.

The underlying assumption of the experiment is that the optimal workforce is that which achieves the current output level with the minimum expenditure of labour. The freeing of workers will move the size of the workforce towards the optimum level and will simultaneously cause average labour productivity to rise. This initial achievement will be realised by reductions in the non-productive workforce, the activities of the internal commissions, the re-norming of labour, the general tightening up of the internal distribution of labour and so on.

It should be noted that the initial cuts in the workforce need not necessarily lead to the optimal size of workforce. Successive rounds of cuts may well move the plant nearer to its objective, but it should be clear that in the first instance these reductions will be based upon rule-of-thumb estimations coupled with management's desire not to completely destroy their safety factor.

It can also be assumed, in the initial period, that the planned level of output reflects the underestimation of capacity which the negative control, operated by the plant's workforce, forces upon both plant management and the ruling group in the process of plan formulation. A central part of the initial phase of the experiment was that planned output targets should remain constant. This was an attempt to remove one of the underlying reasons for labour hoarding. If plant management could be assured stability of plan targets, then they could safely expand output towards true capacity without fear of either short term plan instability or the operation of the ratchet principle, of planning from the achieved level.

The other important indicator to be held stable was the wage fund. With a fixed wage fund and the right to redistribute the economised portion of the wage fund that arises from the dismissal of some proportion of the workforce, average wages must rise. The eventual increase in wages will be determined by the cut in the workforce and any centrally imposed conditions, for example, the 30 per cent maximum increase, but as the reduction in numbers was approximately 12–14 per cent we may assume all the economised wage fund could be redistributed. The expectation was that raising individual wages would stimulate personal commitment to work and individual initiative. This, it was expected, would have an impact on average labour productivity.

Average labour productivity is a function of a number of elements. The capital stock available at the plant and the level of technology will determine the eventual outcome of particular expenditures of labour-time. The intention of the experiment, however, as the example of the Shchekino plant in the short run illustrates, was not predicated on changes in these two elements and they can be assumed to be constant in the short run.

Also, and more importantly for this experiment, changes in the average wage are intended to provide an incentive effect within the plant. If the average wage is rising, as the workforce is cut, then the expectation is that this will raise productivity. This was particularly the case at Shchekino as the wage increases were administered in such a way that only those who combined jobs, widened their zone of service, and so on, received the wage increment. The eventual impact of this incentive effect, however, will depend upon the availability of consumer goods and services. A great deal of stress is placed by Soviet sources on the importance of the material incentives effect of the experiment.

According to Soviet sources, the only other element that will determine average labour productivity is the level of labour organisation. As the efficiency of organisation is improved at any wage level, the level of average productivity will have improved. (I will argue later in this chapter that this is only a partial explanation.)

Therefore, the expectation is that reducing numbers, improving internal organisation and raising average wages will lead to an increase in average productivity (work intensity) and increasing output. The ultimate aim of the experiment is to encourage the plant to produce 'more with less'. The increase in average labour productivity, even with a reduction of numbers, will lead the plant to produce in excess of the previously planned level. This level of output, after all, accommodated and reflected the slack labour organisation and low intensity of work within the plant. For the ruling group the attainment of this, with a constant wage fund, has the effect of increasing the socially produced surplus and with the increase in plant discipline should guarantee this over time. If it is assumed that the wage fund represents a bundle of consumer goods, then the surplus will increase if output in the post-experiment period exceeds the pre-experiment output.

If the released workers are employed elsewhere and contribute to output so much the better. Even if they are released and simply paid the minimum wage and do not work, the surplus could still rise if the difference in output achieved by their release exceeds the amount of consumer goods they can purchase with the minimum wage. In the short term, therefore, Soviet commentators wholeheartedly supported the principle and the further implementation of the experiment.

NON-SOVIET PERCEPTIONS OF THE SHCHEKINO EXPERIMENT

Virtually all non-Soviet commentators adopted a similar initial reaction to the experiment and welcomed its introduction, although often for quite different underlying reasons. Advocates of economic reform in the USSR saw the experiment as a desirable and logical supplement to the other reforms of the mid-sixties (Nove, 1972, p. 31; Dyker, 1976, p. 117; Thalheim, 1975, p. 75). Advocates of a market socialist model of economic regulation, for example Brus (1972, pp. 71–5), have argued that the labour allocation mechanism is particularly amenable to the introduction of market forms. The experiment could be viewed as a step in this direction that would not only stimulate individual productivity, but would also potentially increase labour mobility and lead to the creation of a more flexible labour market. This is the reason why the eventual fate of the experiment should shed some light on the possibilities for market socialism as a viable form of economic regulation in the USSR. This question will be examined more fully in the final chapter, after the long term experience of the experiment has been examined.

For those commentators who believe, along with von Hayek (1969, pp. 237–43) and von Mises (1935, pp. 127–30; 1969, pp. 221–20), that it is only via market forms that rational resource allocation can be achieved, the experiment was also welcomed. Wiles (1977, p. 545, p. 560), for example, recognised the experiment's potential as a first stage towards the reintroduction of unemployment and a degree of rationality into economic affairs. He was sceptical, however, about the extent and scope of the experiment, believing that the party's influence in labour markets would eventually undermine the operation of the experiment.

For pro-Soviet, western commentators the experiment was not seen as a movement towards any form of market socialism. It was explained as an experiment that promoted the further technical refinement of the economic mechanism with little or no implication for the underlying political economy of the system.

The introduction of the experiment was criticised from some quarters and the most bitter condemnation came from Chinese sources, for whom the introduction of the experiment represented proof of the restoration of capitalism in the USSR (Wei Chi, 1978, pp. 7–8). The (then) standard Chinese textbook of political economy characterised the experiment as 'Taylorist', with a suitable quote from Lenin attacking the iniquities of the Taylorist logic, and described the experiment as suited to the 'demands of the Soviet, revisionist, bureaucratic, monopoly bourgeoisie' (Wang, 1977, pp. 205–7). For writers in the state capitalist tradition the experiment can be similarly explained in terms of the logic of capitalism in its state capitalist form (Haynes and Binns, 1980, pp. 43–4).

These two critical viewpoints are, however, inadequate. Neither of them address the problem that if the USSR is some variant of capitalism or simply restored capitalism, why it is then necessary to implement this type of reform? Given that the specific nature of capitalism implies the existence of the law of value as the mechanism of control, why should an initiative of the Shchekino-type be necessary? To pose the question slightly differently, what sort of capitalism is it that has no labour market, where labour is not free in the dual sense described by Marx and where labour power is not a commodity? Furthermore, they fail to examine the longer term experience of the individual enterprises that undertook the experiment and as a consequence, fail to see that this does not support the notion of any form of capitalism existing in the USSR.

Delamotte, however, has presented the most comprehensive description of the early years of the experiment. Her explanation of the motivation for the experiment is based upon a series of features of the Soviet economy and society during this period. She identifies correctly the combination of potential labour shortages, due to the demographic changes already evident in the mid to late sixties, with overmanning and low labour productivity, by international comparison, as the prime motives for the implementation of the experiment (pp. 110–14). What Delamotte does not do, however, is show the interrelationship of these elements nor provide a convincing explanation of their derivation and the pressures on the ruling group to implement Shchekino-like reforms. She locates the experiment within a theoretical framework which is based upon a view of convergence between the Soviet and western industrialised economies. The logic of industrialisation, determined by common technology and particular techniques of production (particularly production-line methods) is invoked to explain common problems that emerge with regard to worker satisfaction and its negative impact upon labour productivity, product quality, and so on. The Shchekino experiment is viewed by Delamotte as part of the wave of job-enrichment schemes that emerged in the late sixties and early seventies in the west (Storey, 1983, pp. 133–41), and it is the Soviet variant.

Superficially there are some similarities between the Shchekino experiment and the western examples cited by Delamotte. However, the problem with this analysis is that it fails to place the motivation for these experiments within the specific context of the respective social systems. Rather than identifying how the political economy of the respective systems provides differing motivations for perhaps similar experimentation, Delamotte takes the appearance of similarity to be sufficient. The Shchekino experiment, I would argue, was the result of very different pressures than for example, the scheme introduced at Volvo. Storey (p. 139) attributes part of the motivation for autonomous or quasi-autonomous work groups to the company's desire to either stave off or limit the impact of unionisation. Clearly, this type of explanation is inapplicable in the Soviet case. Furthermore, the experience of the enterprises over time, both in the USSR and the west, was refracted through totally different social contexts and led to quite different results. The introduction and success of innovatory changes in the labour process in the west are determined by a series of forces, like the level of unionisation and collective response, the overall state of the world economy (boom or slump), the level of competition in the particular industry and the state of local labour markets. In the USSR, as already suggested in Part I, a different series of criteria explain the introduction of experimentation and condition the eventual results.

In order to comment upon these interpretations and the Soviet view of the experiment, it is necessary to reassess the initial results and provide a different explanation for the apparent early successes of the experiment.

A REAPPRAISAL OF THE INITIAL RESULTS OF THE SHCHEKINO EXPERIMENT

The enthusiastic response to the initial results of the experiment and the pressure for its generalisation needs to be tempered by a closer look at the manner in which the results were achieved, the nature of the results themselves and the problems implicit in the logic of the experiment, even at this early stage. The problems that emerged in this initial period relate specifically to the implementation of the experiment at plant level and the relationship between different plants undertaking the experiment. The broader problems involving the generalisation of the experiment to all enterprises, and the maintenance of its impetus at the level of the individual plant, will be considered in the next chapter.

From the outset, the enterprise management and the CPSU were faced with the problem of explaining to workers, in a supposedly socialist society, that they were to be made redundant. Soviet commentators stress the initial 'psychological barriers' that had to be

overcome (Karpenko, 1969a, p. 2; Tolstikov, 1969, p. 2). These barriers are the inevitable result of more than 60 years of political
propaganda that contrasts the secure position of the Soviet worker,
the leading force in the planned socialist economy, with the insecure
position of his counterpart under capitalism, subject to the vagaries of
the market, with the possibilities of lay-offs, redundancies and long-
term unemployment. The experiment, therefore, demanded from the
outset a vast amount of preparatory work by the party cells in the
enterprise. In this early period party, trade union, Komsomol and
personnel department cadres carried out an extensive educational
campaign, delivering lectures and answering workers' questions to
alleviate their fears and to reduce these barriers (*Pravda*, 9 October
1968, p. 1). A. Mokin, the party secretary at Shchekino, points out
that it was necessary that workers should not evaluate their dismissal
negatively (Karpenko, 1969a, p. 2). The reason for this, apart from
alleviating the problems of any immediate discontent, was that these
same workers were to be redeployed elsewhere and a reduction in
their morale or self-image would presumably affect their attitude to
their new work and their productivity. Unlike a capitalist firm, which
can dismiss workers onto an anonymous market with little concern
about their ultimate fate or destination, the Shchekino management
had to re-integrate a considerable number of the workers dismissed
and ultimately all those released would need to be re-employed.
Therefore, instead of talk of 'dismissal' or 'redundancy' they spoke of
'releasing' or 'freeing' workers and a process of 'resource utilisation'
or 'the scientific evaluation of work', and so on.[1] The process, which
for a capitalist employer is veiled behind the cloak of commodity
fetishism, was, in the Soviet instance, shrouded in a spurious
in the branch (%)

As already noted in this first phase, at Shchekino and the other
plants cited, the problems of dislocation were limited by the absorption of surplus labour in the immediate locale. However, as Karpenko
(1969a, p. 2) points out, workers tended to evaluate the experiment in
a negative manner and workers in the plant talked of their comrades
who had 'fallen under the experiment', much in the same way as you
would describe someone falling under a train.

Nevertheless, at Shchekino, out of the 515 employees released in the
first year of the experiment, only seven appealed to the trade unions
and of these the trade unions accepted the dismissal of three workers.
Of these three, only one worker appealed to the courts and was
eventually reinstated (Tolstikov, 1969, p. 2).

To ease the problems of potential discontent at the level of the enterprise, the personnel department at the plant attempted to give great consideration to job placement of the workers released. The individual worker's skills, experience, education, length of service, family situation and so on, were all taken into account before he was offered a number of alternative jobs with similar work content, working conditions and comparable wages. However, as V. Polikarpov, the plant's personnel chief, admitted, not everyone was satisfied (Karpenko, 1969a, p. 2). It may be assumed that the figures for complaints, showing such a small number of claims for redress, minimise the actual level of discontent the experiment created. Furthermore, the personnel department's degree of success can be gauged from the fact that over 100 workers who were released chose to look for new jobs on their own and very few took the personnel department's advice and transferred to similar occupations in other towns. This is a grave potential problem, because if the ultimate aim is to utilise freed workers efficiently, particularly if they have scarce skills, then it is desirable that they do not change skills, with the attendant problems of re-training, but accept the advice of state or enterprise labour agencies. It can be inferred from the fact that these workers did not follow the advice given, that they were not wholly satisfied with the experiment nor the official options offered to them.

The second aspect of the 'psychological barrier' concerns the enterprise management staff who were wary of the experiment in the initial period (Karpenko, 1969b, p. 1). The experiment ran counter to their previous experience of the logic of the planning process and aimed to discourage them from hoarding labour. This generated fear of not being able to cope with existing plan targets with a reduced workforce, fear of taking on too much additional responsibility and fear of failure. This led the more conservative to resist the implementation of the experiment. After all, some of their number were also to be released and their work reorganised. To overcome this, significant retraining of management and supervisory staff took place at the plant and this stressed the role of economic, 'value' levers in plant management (Pravda, 9 October 1968). It is interesting to note that amidst all the staff reductions only one group of staff was expanded and that was the permanent department of economists, which had recently been established at the plant (Sharov, 1969, p. 2).

Management's initial negative response was rational, because there is a contradiction in the logic of the experiment. Even though the experiment could be viewed as an attempt to give them more decentralised control, through further plant level wage differentiation to reward hard work, it also simultaneously reduced their room for manœuvre vis-à-vis the economic administration at the centre. As already noted, the mechanisms of economic regulation also need to discipline management if they are to be successful and the Shchekino experiment sought to do that by reducing an important element of management's safety factor, hoarded labour. Karpenko (1969b, p. 1), however, points out that this initial negative response was only overcome in the medium term, when management saw the advantages of reduced absenteeism and tightened labour discipline, giving rise to a more stable, hard-working workforce along with stable plan targets. After all, if this can be achieved it partially obviates the need for hoarded labour. (Their longer term perception of the experiment will be considered in the next chapter.)

The successful implementation of the experiment can, therefore, only be achieved if correct attention is paid to overcoming potential resistance by careful preparation. The Soviet sources confirm this view. Volovich (1973, p. 2) cites the example of two plants in Irkutsk. One enterprise introduced the experiment in a formalistic manner with little preparation and failed to achieve significant results, whilst a nearby plant prepared carefully and received the anticipated favourable results.

Coupled with this is the necessity to mobilise resources to train staff remaining at the plant, particularly those combining occupations or changing jobs completely. For example, at Shchekino a number of laboratory workers, freed by the revised schedule of tests, retrained as lathe and machine operators (Tolstikov, 1969, p. 2). This all necessitated a huge training programme and at Shchekino alone, in the first eighteen months of the experiment, 700 specialists were involved in 'on-the-job' training (Sharov, 1969, p. 2; Karpenko, 1969a, p. 2).

The question of careful preparation and adequate training was confirmed at a seminar on the experiment at Tula in 1970 (Antonov, 1970b, p. 2). All the participants stressed the need for proper preparation and pointed out the great damage that could be done to the aims of the experiment if it were implemented by administrative pressure or if short cuts were attempted by bureaucratic bullying of either enterprises or workers (Karpenko, 1969b, p. 1). In other words, it was recognised that the experiment could only be implemented with at least the acquiescence of the workforce and the interest of enterprise management, and that attempts to impose it could only lead to failure.

The 'psychological barriers' to the implementation of the experiment, like the necessity for the experiment itself, stem from the peculiar political economy of the USSR. Workers, who can only be dismissed in special circumstances and who are ideologically supposed to be the leading force in the society, are able to exert their negative control even over reforms and experiments designed to control them. The ruling group needed the experiment to shake out surplus labour and to guarantee a usable, predictable and growing surplus, but even in the process of instituting this reform they cannot disregard the workforce's interests which act as a form of negative control. The experiment, rather than becoming an anonymous, impersonal, external constraint on the workforce, like the role played by unemployment under capitalism, is forced to partially accommodate workers' interests and this gives rise to the need for careful preparation, resettlement and training. Clearly if a ministry, let alone the whole economy, wished to convert all its enterprises to the Shchekino method, it would be unlikely to be able to achieve this simultaneously because of the resource needs for preparation and training at each plant. Therefore, the transition to the experiment is more likely to be piecemeal and relatively slowly accomplished, and will tend to concentrate on particular enterprises. Ministries will allocate resources, in the first instance, for enterprises to make the transition to the method if the enterprise is important to the ministry's overall performance; if it is in the process of expanding and is short of workers; if it is a large scale recipient of foreign technology or if it has particular problems. The blanket adoption of the experiment would be impossible for the ministry because it would not have sufficient resources to do the job properly, and the resulting discontent it would engender if it were forced through, from both workers and management, would negate its potential.

The implementation problems at enterprise level may well prove difficult. Their further significance will be examined in the next chapter, but they were obviously overcome at Shchekino and the other plants cited. Their successes, however, raise the further question, how were the impressive economic results achieved? As noted, Soviet commentators argue that the harmony of social and individual interests created through the material incentives offered by the experiment accounted for the success, and their western counterparts broadly concur (Shilin, 1969, pp. 35–9; Shkurko, 1971, p. 3, p. 20; Cherednichenko and Gol'din, 1978, pp. 11–12). It is difficult to support this argument for a number of reasons.

Firstly, as already seen in Chapter 5, the material incentives offered to individual workers were relatively small (Shilin, 1969, pp. 42–3). (See Tables 5.9, 5.10, 5.11.) From the very early years, Soviet sources complained that the wage increases were in the main a small proportion of basic wages for all categories of employees and could not be expected to fulfil their role as a stimulus for more conscientious work (Baranenkova, 1970, p. 54; Grigor'ev and Kheifets, 1970, p. 56). For the relatively poorly paid repair workers, the supplements may have been sufficient to narrow the gap between themselves and basic production workers, but even for them it was a relatively small proportion of their wage. Shilin (1969, p. 39) estimates the increase at between ten and 20 per cent for this category of workers and of the 2718 workers receiving wage supplements by 1970, 1740 were repair and maintenance workers.

Secondly, not everyone remaining in the enterprise received a wage supplement. At Shchekino only approximately 40 per cent of the workforce received any individualised increase in wages as a result of the experiment (Shilin, 1969, p. 35).

Thirdly, of this number only a small percentage received the maximum additional wage supplement of 30 per cent. At Shchekino, for example, only 1.4 per cent of the workforce received the maximum. This was replicated at other plants, at Severonikel' the figure was 2.2 per cent and at Furmanov No. 2, 3.8 per cent (Shkurko, 1971a, p. 45). As already suggested, none of this was automatic and had to be argued for in the relevant commission, so we may assume that a significant increase in effort was necessary to achieve the 30 per cent maximum.

Fourthly, the initial basis of the experiment assumed that the whole of the economised wage fund was redistributed. However, this was not the case in practice and, for example, at Shchekino throughout 1968, the percentage of the economised wage fund distributed grew slowly and had only reached 39 per cent by the beginning of 1969 (see Table 5.9). This obviously has a consequence for the potential increase in the average wage, which will rise less than possible. These retained funds still have an importance for the experiment's operation, particularly if it is used for collective provision of social services or housing at the plant, but not for the individualised reward. The fact that more than half of the economised wage funds were not distributed as individual wage supplements suggests that whatever effect financial changes had, they were at least as important on a collective basis.

Fifthly, during this period average wages were rising anyway as a result of state wage policies and the increment from the experiment was not the sole source of bonuses and premiums. Wages were also supplemented from the material incentives fund and the supplements from the experiment, for many categories of workers, were no more important.

Finally, and perhaps most importantly, even if wage increments were received, the perennial problem of consumer goods and services minimises the potential incentive effects of the experiment. If money does not function as the universal equivalent and cannot provide unambiguous access to the desired, good quality consumer goods and services, then its motivational impact will be limited. There is no evidence that any additional allocation of consumer goods occurred to ease the implementation of the experiment. One possible consequence of this situation is that prices in the private peasant market may rise, as the price of the commodities traded here will be sensitive to forces of supply and demand, but again it is impossible to provide any evidence one way or another regarding this.

Therefore, the wage increases were small, received by few and their impact weak. Nevertheless, productivity and output did rise impressively, so what else contributed to these impressive economic results?

I would argue that the initial success of the Shchekino experiment cannot be explained solely by the increased material incentives introduced. These new economic stimuli were subordinate in their effect to a heightened use of more traditional bureaucratic forms of control, coupled with the newly acquired ingredient of increasing worker insecurity. This is particularly true in the initial phase of the experiment when the workforce is at its largest and the possibility of being released is at its greatest. In this period, the internal reorganisation of the production and labour process was carried out by the internal commissions detailed in Table 5.1. Their role was to identify internal reserves and eliminate them, rationalise production, repair and services and press for the introduction of norms or raise existing norms. The internal institutes put the plant's labour practices under the microscope and eliminated slack by the administrative sanctions available to them, that is, by suggesting dismissals. Labour productivity, therefore, will rise in this initial period for a number of reasons.

Some of the jobs and individuals eliminated will be non-jobs and non-workers. They will not have contributed to production and simply by their presence will have reduced average labour productivity. If these individuals are freed, average labour productivity must rise. This will be the case particularly if these workers come from non-productive sectors like service, repair, maintenance and transport, as indeed they did.

Also, the emergence of the possibility of release will change both managerial control and the attitudes and performance of those workers remaining at the enterprise. This is clearly shown by the discipline indicators cited for Shchekino (see Table 5.13) and the reports from other plants cited by Soviet sources. The reason for this is that harder work at the plant, occupation and workplace that you know is preferable to the uncertainty engendered by change. The hierarchy of uncertainty rises from a change in occupation or workplace, through to a change in plant, to the worst possibility, a change in location. This uncertainty is clearly not identical with the insecurity associated with unemployment in the west, but nevertheless, in this initial period it performed a similar function.[2] Increasing worker insecurity provides an explanation of increasing work intensity and labour discipline, and accounts for the increase in production even with a smaller workforce.

Worker insecurity is increased not just by releasing surplus workers, but also by the reorganisation of production, the raising and introduction of norms and the combination of occupations, as all these elements operate against established labour practices and increase the pressure upon the individual worker. This will be further amplified by the use of some proportion of the economised funds for collectively provided social services, housing and so on. These funds will be growing and the benefits will only accrue to those remaining at the plant, and as they are distributed amongst a smaller workforce the possibilities for access or allocation will improve. This further pressurises the individual worker not to identify himself as an individual who should be released (that is an idler, absentee or drunk). Ironically, those released provide the means for increased collective provision, but because of the nature of dependency on the place of work for allocation and access to these services, they are excluded. For obvious ideological reasons, the notion that increasing worker insecurity contributed to the successes of the experiment has neither been investigated nor given explicit prominence by the Soviet sources.

However, this explanation can be substantiated on two further levels. The anecdotal evidence already cited, from Polikarpov and Karpenko, shows some evidence of worker hostility to the experiment in its earlier phase. Also, the evidence cited above from the personnel department at Shchekino, suggests that workers would rather change occupation than move even to nearby enterprises, which further supports the general point that the experiment increased worker insecurity.

Furthermore, there is evidence from Soviet statistical sources that also supports the general argument. This suggests that in other branches of the economy there is a strong correlation between increases in labour productivity and the dismissal of workers (*'Problemy ispol'zovaniya ...'* 1973, p. 105). It has been suggested, for example, that a one per cent increase in labour productivity can be achieved by releasing 0.8 per cent of the workforce. Table 6.1, based upon data from studies of the textile industry, suggests a series of bands linking changes in labour productivity to reductions in manning levels. The limited empirical evidence presented in Table 5.6, provides some further justification for this argument with productivity increases being more closely correlated to decreasing workforce size than to increases in wage levels.[3]

Table 6.1   Relationship between productivity increases and percentage of workers released

Rate of growth of labour productivity	% workers released
30% or more	20%
between 20 and 30%	18%
between 10 and 20%	14%
between 1 and 10%	9%

Source: *Problemy ispol'zovaniya ...* (1973), p. 106; Manevich (1980), p. 86.

Consequently, within the framework of the political economy of the USSR, the initial results were achieved by a partial change in the relationship between the worker and management and between the worker and his work, via the medium of increasing insecurity, and not solely through material stimuli.

The analysis so far has ignored the question of worker participation, which, it is suggested by both western and Soviet sources, contributed to the success of the experiment (*Pravda*, 9 October 1969, p. 1; Cherednichenko and Gol'din, 1978, pp. 18–19; Delamotte, 1973, pp. 106–7, 117–8). This argument is more complex than these authors suggest and demands a careful interpretation of the idea of participation.

Firstly, any participation could only occur after the decision to undertake the experiment had been made. Participation did not include discussions on the desirability of the experiment, with the enterprise workforce having the option of rejecting the experiment. The original guidelines for the experiment, and indeed the later revisions, specify that the enterprise can only be transferred to the experiment if the decision of either the ministry or enterprise management is ratified by the plant's trade union committee. Given the nature of Soviet trade unions, it can be assumed that once the management and party organs have decided to implement the experiment, the ratification of the decision is a formality. As would be expected, there is no mention in the literature of any enterprise rejecting management's decision.

Secondly, participation in the internal commissions leaves little scope for workforce influence, as the designation of the commissions and their remit are pre-determined by management. Furthermore, all the commissions were headed by management representatives and they simply mirror the hierarchical nature of the enterprise.

Thirdly, the participation in rationalising labour organisation can be viewed as participation in increasing and refining the worker's own exploitation. As has been shown above, the workforce itself did not control the economised portion of the wage fund at the level of the shop, nor did they decide how work was to be combined or redistributed. Their suggestions for rationalisation may have attracted wage supplements but the link was not direct and cannot be seriously viewed as participatory.

Fourthly, following from the above points, the logic of the experiment did not challenge the principle of one-man management, nor the hierarchy of relations within the enterprise. The thrust of the experiment was to do the opposite and strengthen this principle both for the foreman and shop chief at the level of the individual shop, and for enterprise management within the plant as a whole.

As argued already, the influence of the workforce on the experiment was primarily reactive and negative, which forced adaptation within the experiment and made necessary the extensive preparation outlined above. The workforce's acquiescence in the experiment may have been necessary but this can hardly be described as participation.

Soviet writers have also argued that multi-occupations, as a result of the job-combination promoted by the experiment, enhanced workers' interest and raised the level of work satisfaction. Karpenko (1969b, p. 1) claims that job combination, 'led to more interesting and meaningful work'. Cherednichenko and Gol'din (1978) support this general view and suggest that job combination will make workers more receptive to changing work conditions, an argument that closely parallels western arguments regarding the breakdown of 'restrictive working practices'. This whole approach is a repetition of a curious notion, that by increasing the number of boring, monotonous jobs a worker is forced to perform, this qualitatively enhances work experience. There is little reason to presume that the transition from one job to two, or three or indeed the rotation between jobs, does more than break monotony, rather than essentially enrich work experience.[4] There is no necessary transition from quantity to quality.

It has also been claimed that the raising of educational and skill levels, as a result of the experiment's implementation, leads to enhanced worker satisfaction (Cherednichenko and Gol'din, 1976, p. 54). These changes are a necessary by-product of the experiment. However, it should be noted that work content does not necessarily change, and therefore, its overall impact is open to doubt. There is little reason to presume that a worker who has enhanced his skills or qualifications and is employed at the same job as previously, or, more likely, is combining previously disparate tasks, is likely to be more satisfied with his work situation. This is particularly the case if the material incentives are less than anticipated and the new element of worker insecurity is introduced.

The general point is that for the workforce as a whole the experiment's benefits will be tempered by the nature of the work they perform, the new intensity with which it has to be performed and the nature of work in general in the USSR. The experiment did not fundamentally alter either the nature of the specific work nor the general nature of work, but simply attempted to raise its intensity. Claims, therefore, for its beneficial impact must be viewed sceptically.

So far, the success of the experiment has appeared self-evident from the results provided. However, this success has been viewed solely in Soviet terms and has to be qualified by international comparison. This is notoriously difficult to accomplish by means of considering finished product and trying to evaluate comparative values of output. However, in the case of Shchekino it can be illustrated in a different manner, as one year after the implementation of the experiment equipment was installed that was similar in design to that utilised by both Dutch and Italian chemical firms. The plans for the new processes stipulated that 278 operatives and technicians were necessary to operate them successfully. However, at Shchekino, even with the benficial impact of the experiment, the staff level was 806 (Manevich, 1969, p. 34). This again gives some idea of the level of overmanning and the degree of negative control exercised by the Soviet workforce, even after an experiment explicitly designed to reduce this. This does not deny that the experiment's success warranted its generalisation, but simply shows that its implementation does not guarantee even an approximation to western manning levels.

Furthermore, the release of workers from Shchekino and the other plants cited also illustrates another feature of the Soviet labour process and a further problem for the experiment's implementation. The percentage of the existing workforce released varied in the plants cited from seven per cent at Chelyabinsk to seventeen per cent at Novomosovsk. This can be interpreted in one of a number of ways.

It could be argued that this confirms the view advanced earlier, that the manning level of Soviet plants is the result of a localised trade-off between the wishes of enterprise management and the negative control of the workforce. Pre-experiment economic regulation provides no unambiguous measure of overmanning, therefore the introduction of a standardised experiment exposes the differing degrees of overmanning.

However, it could be argued that the level of overmanning at each plant is broadly similar, but the differences in the numbers released are explained by the more or less rigorous application of the experiment. This will be determined by the degree of worker resistance or management's risk aversion with regard to the experiment and will lead to differential results.

The point is that either, or a combination of both, of these explanations are equally plausible. There was no standardisation in terms of the rigour of the experiment, nor can the level of overmanning at Soviet enterprises be assumed to be standardised. This is exactly the problem as the experiment itself provided no mechanism for evaluating with any more precision than previously the level of overmanning. Nor did it provide a dynamic towards the equalisation or standardisation of manning levels in Soviet enterprises. For example, two similar plants could release the same proportion of their original workforce and one could be close to the optimum manning level, whilst the other well away from it, dependent upon the original level of overmanning. The implementation of the experiment will move the plants towards their optimum workforce size, but it is impossible to evaluate the precise position.

Furthermore, ironically, the logic of the experiment was to reward enterprises for their past negative practices and attitudes. Enterprises that had been most negligent and lax in their past control over manning levels could now implement the experiment, free apparently impressive percentages of their workforce and receive plaudits and rewards as a consequence. Yet these enterprises may still be no more efficient than their previously more stringent counterparts, who may not be able to introduce the experiment and would as a consequence receive no benefits but still might be operating more efficiently. The recognition of this contradiction in the logic of the experiment, coupled with a desire to adapt the experiment, led to the implementation of a number of attempted variants.

EARLY VARIANTS OF THE SHCHEKINO EXPERIMENT

It was recognised, soon after the inception of the Shchekino experiment, that while in principle it was generally applicable, in specific circumstances it would need adaptation. One such example is when the experiment is applied to an industrial association. The problem is that associations comprise previously separate industrial enterprises which were amalgamated as part of the organisational reform of industry (Gorlin, 1976, pp. 162–189). Within these enterprises, manning levels, labour organisation, labour productivity, work intensity and labour discipline are not necessarily uniform as they are the result of previously uncoordinated allocations, decisions and practices. As a result, the implementation of the basic Shchekino experiment will have a differentiated effect.

For enterprises that had previously been lax in controlling manning levels and so on, the experiment could be implemented with reasonable ease. An impressive percentage of the superfluous workforce could be shed, thus raising average productivity and from the economised portion of the wage fund, wage supplements could be paid and average wages would rise. The appearance of increased work intensity could be created while at the same time preserving a significant safety factor.

However, for enterprises which had previously been more disciplined the implementation of the experiment would be more difficult. It would be less easy to shed surplus labour, the economised funds available for material incentives would be smaller and the eventual safety factor retained would be smaller. Within this enterprise, work intensity will be greater but rewards smaller and the degree of managerial vulnerability to failure greater, even though it is more efficient than the former enterprise. No mechanism, automatic or otherwise, exists for equalising work intensity nor for providing a dynamic in this direction.

From the point of view of the association, at the end of this process labour will have been freed, to be relocated elsewhere, but there is no necessary correspondence between work and rewards across the enterprises in the association. Indeed, if workers are mobile between enterprises the net result may be even more harmful, as workers will tend to move from the more efficient, where labour discipline is tighter and rewards smaller, to the less efficient where discipline is more lax and rewards greater, thus undermining the association's performance and the logic of the experiment. In order to overcome these problems, a variant of the Shchekino experiment was implemented, in June 1969, at the Bashkirneftekhimzavody (Delamotte, 1973, pp. 194–202; Cherednichenko and Gol'din, 1978, pp. 22–3). The aim of the experiment was to recognise from the outset the differing levels of capacity utilisation and work intensity at the various enterprises in the association, and to reformulate the experiment to give comparable incentives to all enterprises to improve performance.

Prior to the experiment's introduction, the association had had a chequered history. From 1964, growth rates of labour productivity had declined sharply and failed to meet planned targets (Kudryashov, 1969, p. 3). The reasons for this, explained by the association's director, Petrov, are an interesting example of why Soviet management is wary of technological change that upgrades plant, product or processes, but that in the short term worsens economic performance.

In this period, the enterprise had introduced improved technology into auxiliary production and introduced new large-scale production lines. Much of this was being introduced into the USSR for the first time and had serious design shortcomings. The overall effect was that labour expenditures actually increased rather than decreased, and output failed to expand as the new plant underwent implementation problems that could only be resolved during production. It was against this background, not entirely dissimilar to that at Shchekino, that the experiment was introduced. As Petrov points out, the experiment's introduction disclosed enormous reserves for increasing labour productivity.

Once again this underlines the point made previously, that by simply introducing new technology either indigenous or imported, there is no automatic increment in labour productivity, no necessary movement to western manning levels nor increased output. New technology and technique is refracted through Soviet labour organisation and is subject to the negative control identified earlier.

The form of the experiment was essentially similar to the basic Shchekino model; the wage fund was frozen for a number of years (at Bashkir for three years only); manning levels were to be reduced by combining jobs and rationalising production and labour organisation; those taking on extra responsibilities received wage supplements up to 30 per cent of their basic wage or salary rate and so on.

The novelty came, however, in the system of material stimulation. This recognised the different levels of work intensity in existence across the association and the consequent differing abilities to free workers. For example, Khor'kov (1969, p. 36) cites the possibility of a 13.4 per cent cut in the workforce at the Ufa plant within the association compared with a potential four per cent cut at the Novo Ufa enterprise. Therefore, in order to go some way towards equalising the incentive effects of the experiment it was decided to centralise 30 per cent of all the economised wage funds, from each enterprise, under the control of the association director.

This was then utilised in the following manner. The individual enterprises would receive a seven per cent increase in their material incentive funds for each one per cent increment in their labour productivity plan. By the same token, if the labour productivity plan was underfulfilled by one per cent, then the material incentive fund was to be reduced by seven per cent. These allocations were then subject to a 'normalisation coefficient', that attempted to quantify differences in work intensity. For example, at the Novo Ufa plant, where work intensity was recognised to be higher than the average already in existence, it was harder to mobilise further reserves and the incentive fund rose by 7.5 per cent for each one per cent increase in productivity. As a result, this enterprise received 6300 roubles more from the centralised fund than it contributed through economised wages (Antonov, 1970, p. 1). Elsewhere the increment was below seven per cent. In this way it was intended to provide all enterprises in the association with an equalised incentive to free labour and raise productivity.

The original intention of the experiment was to raise output by 16.6 per cent and labour productivity by 16.4 per cent over the period 1968–71, thereby achieving indices almost double the average for the rest of the branch. This was to be achieved with 3224 less workers and with a thirteen per cent increase in average wages (Kudryashov, 1969, p. 3).

In the first six months of the experiment, over 1600 workers were released in the whole republic as a result of mechanising and automating production (Antonov, 1970, p. 1); the planned productivity increase of five per cent was exceeded and it actually rose by 9.4 per cent and output grew by 7.4 per cent (Kudryashov, 1970, p. 3). From this modest start the experiment accelerated and by 1971, the end of the first phase of the experiment, the volume of production had actually grown by 17.8 per cent, labour productivity had grown by 24.1 per cent and average wages had increased by 17.1 per cent (Gabidulin, 1975, pp. 6–7).

So the variant appears to have been as successful as the basic experiment, but its implementation was not without difficulty. As at Shchekino, not all the economised wage funds were utilised. This was due to difficulties experienced in dividing up the economised funds within the individual enterprises. The simple course of action would have been to divide the economised funds equally shop by shop, but this 'wage levelling' destroys the logic of the experiment, as more diligent workers would not be rewarded. However, if the funds are distributed on a differentiated basis, conflicts and resistance arise to the experiment from those who feel unfairly treated and ignored in the process.

Furthermore, Petrov cites the example of a shop where the reorganisation was scheduled to take three years, yet it was actually achieved in three months. As a consequence, the shop's chief should have received the 30 per cent wage supplement. However, if this had been initiated, then his wage would have exceeded the wage level of the enterprise's production chief. Therefore, the logic of the experiment can distort the internal wage structure of the plant and generate internal conflicts to the detriment of production effectiveness. For example, in the case cited, if the shop chief receives the supplement, then it is a clear message to the higher echelons of the plant's management that even if they are not recompensed for taking on additional responsibility, their subordinates will be. If he does not receive the supplement, it is a clear message to other shop chiefs that the experiment will be manipulated to maintain old wage structures and therefore, why bother to press its implementation. Petrov argues that the way around this is that enterprise directors should be given more autonomy in wage determination (Kudryashov, 1969, p. 3). However, this is also problematic.

There were also the usual problems with external factors. Even though the experiment was successful internally, it was constrained by the degree of interdependence between the individual plants and the rest of the economic system. For example, rapid increments in output were useless if the rail network could not provide sufficient tankers to transport the finished product away from the plant. This limited further possibilities for growth in output and productivity, as no enterprise is autarchic. Once again, the experiment, rather than altering its external environment, is constrained by the usual vagaries of Soviet industrial life. The initial successes of this variant do not of themselves prove its long-run viability. The long-run experience of this variant will be discussed in a later chapter.

A second variant of the Shchekino experiment was instituted at the Perm Electrical Machinery Plant (Shkurko, 1971a, pp. 28–31). This variant took the experiment in a different direction by recognising that stable wage funds and plan targets may not in themselves be desirable objectives, if the enterprise is producing a changing assortment of products with ever changing labour inputs (Boldyrev, 1969, p. 2). At Perm, therefore, the intention was to reduce the wage expenditures per rouble of finished output over a number of years. In 1969, planned wage outlays were 25.6 kopecks per rouble of output and this was to be reduced to 23.6 in 1970, 22.5 in 1971 and 21.3 in 1972. Over this same period, the plant pledged to increase output by 46 per cent, instead of the 33.7 per cent stipulated in the plan targets and to reduce the labour force by 1300, thereby increasing labour productivity by 53 per cent (Boldyrev, 1969, p. 2). As production increased with a decreasing workforce, even though wage outlays per rouble of output were declining, average wages would rise, thus stimulating output and efficiency. From the ruling group's perspective, this is desirable, as a declining wage cost with increasing output implies a growth in the surplus.

In the four years up until 1972, output actually rose by over 58 per cent, labour productivity increased by 53 per cent and average wages rose by almost 21 roubles per month. Inexplicably, the experiment was abandoned in 1972, with the explicit agreement of the State Committee on Labour and Wages (Selyunin, 1978, p. 2). The beneficial effects of the experiment were soon dissipated and whilst during the course of the four years of the experiment, managerial and supervisory staff had been cut by 60, in the next four years their number grew by over 400. Furthermore, without the controlling influence of the experiment, the wage outlays per rouble of output began to accelerate.

As well as the usual problems faced by Shchekino-like initiatives, there are two particular problems that may well explain the abandonment of the Perm variant. If the wage fund is to be determined in relationship to the value of finished output or the volume of goods sold, which is what is implied in the variant, then it is possible for the enterprise to manipulate its wage fund by changing the nature of the product. The intention was to raise productivity, but a similar effect can be achieved by embellishing the product, thereby raising the value of output even though in a physical sense output may not have expanded. Boldyrev (1969, p. 2) cites the example of an enterprise, previously making a simple glass, switching to produce a glass with a gold rim. The same impact could be achieved by manipulating the assortment of output away from low value towards higher value output. As the example below illustrates, the net effect would be to raise average wage levels simply by expending more raw materials but not necessarily raising labour productivity nor increasing the volume of use-values.

	Original situation
Workforce	100 workers
Wage outlay	10 k per R
Output	100 000 × 1R
Wage fund	10 000 R
Average wage	100 R

	Intended outcome
Cut workforce to	75 workers
Cut wage outlays to	5 k per R
Raise output to	200 000 × 1 R
Wage fund	10 000 R
Average wage	133.3 R

	Possible outcome
Cut workforce to	75 workers
Cut wage outlays to	5 k per R
Output	$100\,000 \times 2$ R
Wage fund	10 000 R
Average wage	133.3 R

There is also the familiar problem of how the wage normative is to be set. If it is developed on the basis of past production and wage levels, it simply legitimises past practices and provides no dynamic towards the equalisation of this relationship between different enterprises or different branches.

A further notable variant was undertaken at the Chelyabinsk metallurgical plant, where the experiment was introduced with the usual results and over 200 workers were released in the first few months. However, at this plant the nature of the previous production and labour organisation necessitated changes in the form of wage supplement payments. The experiment was introduced as a supplement to the brigade system of labour organisation and the wage supplements, rather than being individualised, were distributed via a 'collective piece rate' system. The idea behind this was to encourage a brigade to take on a specific integrated series of tasks and to encourage them to release workers, the net result being wage supplements for those who remained (*Izvestia*, 12 October 1970, p. 5).

Dramatic results were also recorded by an extended variant at the Polotsk chemical combine where labour productivity increased by over 42 per cent in one year (Latov and Gol'din, 1975, p. 10). Here the aim was not only to produce more output with fewer workers, but to increase the effectiveness of all aspects of production (Kostandov, 1975, p. 3). This was achieved by simultaneously renovating and reorganising production facilities and rethinking labour organisation. This included extensive use of work study techniques, photographing workers' activity, movements, and so on (Semin, 1976, p. 96). Coupled to this was the complete centralisation of the provision of services, and wages were tied directly to educational and skill attainments (Cherednichenko and Gol'din, 1976, p. 59). Semin (p. 96) refers to this as the 'complex–technical' method which eventually led to a 25–30 per cent reduction in service personnel, significantly improved labour discipline and productivity and eventually led to the release of 500 workers. The Polotsk variant really took the Shchekino experiment to its logical conclusion at the enterprise level, by effectively reorganising the plant from scratch. The obvious problem is that whilst this may be feasible at one plant, its generalisation is much more problematic because of the enormous resource requirements.

The Soviet press identifies a number of other variants, for example, the Groznenskii variant (*Trud*, 13 July 1973) and Kirovskii variant (*Pravda*, 19 March 1973). This however, raises a potential problem with the idea of variants. If the experiment is adapted to specific conditions and circumstances conscientiously, then it may well be the case, as at the Bashkir association cited above, that benefits follow. However, the adoption of a so-called variant may well be an attempt by plant management to create the impression that the experiment has been implemented whilst actually accommodating to the prevailing conditions. This is precisely the type of problem that makes it necessary to establish the experiment in the first instance. If there is no unambiguous mechanism of economic control, then all that can exist is administrative attempts to control the surplus extraction process. There is no mechanism for the evaluation of the variants which is not itself open to manipulation. Nevertheless, the variants implemented in this period and cited in this section were all seen as advances in the dissemination of the experiment. Their longer-term performance will be assessed briefly in the next chapter.

7 The Attempted Generalisation of the Shchekino Experiment

THE EXTENSION OF THE EXPERIMENT IN THE EARLY YEARS

The problems involved with the initial implementation of the experiment may well have proved difficult, but they were not insurmountable, as the experience at Shchekino and elsewhere indicates. This may be attributed partially to the fact that with any such experiment or prestige project, there is the potential for a great deal of kudos to be attached to the individuals involved with its successful implementation and, therefore, special efforts will be made by the relevant ministries, local party organs and especially plant management to guarantee its initial localised success. This is particularly true of plant management. For example, as a direct result of the implementation of the experiment, Sharov, the enterprise director at Shchekino, became a 'Hero of Socialist Labour' and was awarded the 'Order of Lenin' and the 'Hammer and Sickle Gold Medal' (*Pravda*, 13 January 1976). However, it must also be recognised that the experiment's initial successes, particularly at a range of enterprises in different Ministries and Regions, cannot be explained solely as the result of 'hot house' conditions. Soviet sources explicitly deny that the success of the experiment was created by the provision of an unusually favourable environment or the provision of special allocations of resources. At Shchekino, for example, prior to the implementation of the experiment it was found that the size of the enterprise work roster exceeded its currently planned ceiling by 200. The experiment was only authorised after these 200 jobs were removed from the roster (Parfenov and Shvetsov, 1977a, p. 2). However, the plants experiencing initial successes did have similar characteristics. They had a combination of existing labour shortages, reflected in considerable in-plant vacancies, coupled with the need for a growing workforce, either because basic capacity was under-utilised, or because it was in the process of expansion, or because new facilities were being completed nearby. Without this experiment, the new capacity would probably not have been banned because of the labour shortages cited earlier. Semin (1976, p. 4) points out that the numbers freed in the chemical industry alone up to 1975, were sufficient to staff an additional 350 shops. The combination of these circumstances made it possible to absorb the majority of released workers in the locality, hence reducing immediate discontent, whilst at the same time providing enterprises with the benefits of increased work intensity and discipline from the now more insecure workforce remaining at the plant.

Furthermore, even if the experiment did not lead to completely comparable manning levels at similar plants, nor to comparable norms for comparable jobs, it did, nevertheless, tighten the internal organisation of labour at the plants involved and free some surplus labour. The variants adopted in this early period were based upon a recognition of the contradictory logic of the experiment in some instances, or were adaptations to particular circumstances, and were attempts to stimulate the further dissemination and refinement of the experiment. This was essential for the ruling group because, however beneficial the impact on individual plants, if the vicious circle of labour productivity problems outlined in Figure 3.1 was to be broken, the experiment needed to be generalised to all enterprises. Quite clearly, the implementation problems would be exacerbated if all enterprises attempted to switch to the experiment overnight as preparation time, staff for retraining, and so on, would be under great pressure, as already noted. Nevertheless, generalisation of the experiment was the clear intention of the ruling group and this was consistent with the logic of the experiment. Furthermore, it was necessary to maintain the momentum of the experiment at the original enterprises, like Shchekino and the Bashkir association cited above, the aim being sustained change and not simply one-off success.

It could be argued that the results recorded by the Shchekino plant during the Ninth Five Year Plan indicated that the momentum was indeed maintained. As Sharov (1975, p. 89) points out,

> In the period 1967–74 the volume of production grew by two and a half times. In this same period the number of workers fell by 1500, the productivity of labour increased by 3.1 times, average wages rose by 44 per cent, significant gains were made in terms of returns on invested funds and profitability.

By 1975, the volume of production was 34 per cent up on 1970 and labour productivity had risen by 46.6 per cent, achieving the planned increase for the whole plan period in only four years ('Vospitanie...', 1975, p. 34; Cherednichenko and Gol'din, 1978, p. 14). Furthermore, by 1974, in comparison with 1966, losses in labour time due to absenteeism had fallen by fifteen times; absence with administrative authorisation had fallen by thirteen times; the hours of overtime had been reduced from 10 000 to 340 per annum and 4254 Shchekino workers had by this time raised their qualifications (Cherednichenko and Gol'din, 1978, p. 34; 'Vospitanie...', 1975, p. 34). The rise in educational qualifications was accompanied by a further increase in the average skill level. However, this general picture of continual advance will be qualified later, as it obscures a number of underlying problems.

An analysis of 326 industrial enterprises operating along Shchekino lines further confirms the picture of progress. By 1 November 1975 these enterprises had released 47 500 workers, 4.5 per cent of the total they employed, and between January and October 1975 alone they released almost 15 000 workers (Ivanov, 1977, p. 13; Shkurko, 1977, pp. 112–31). These enterprises raised their level of labour productivity by between fifteen and 20 per cent over this period (Cherednichenko and Gol'din, 1976, p. 52) and 91.7 per cent of their growth in output was achieved by labour productivity increases in comparison with 80.5 per cent of industry as a whole. In these enterprises 22.4 per cent of the released workers were employed in new shops or facilities at the same location, 52.4 per cent filled vacant places at the same plants and 25.2 per cent went to new enterprises (Ivanov, 1977, pp. 13–14).

Discipline indicators also improved, as was the norm with the experiment. For example, at an Artemovsk enterprise, labour turnover was reduced from seventeen per cent in 1973 to 8.7 per cent in 1975 and at the Angarskom petro-chemical plant losses in labour time were reduced to less than 40 per cent of their pre-experiment level (Ivanov, 1977, p. 14). Cherednichenko and Gol'din (1976, p. 58) point out that the increase in labour discipline, as well as having direct effects on production and productivity, has indirect effects. Supervisory staff, often skilled workers, can be freed for more socially productive labour. Another indicator of these benefits is cited by Mirgaleev (1977, p. 104) who points out that at plants in Perm and Minsk, overtime hours fell by seven and four times respectively.

Also similar changes occurred in the degree of work combination and, for example, at one plant cited, 250 people acquired four to five occupations, 550 acquired three occupations and 1518 acquired a second occupation (Golovin, Adamchuk and Savel'ev, 1974, p. 48). Alongside this the level of training also increased at a variety of plants. At the Angarskom petro-chemical plant for example, 10 000 workers received in-plant training in the period 1971–75 (Ivanov, 1977, p. 13).

Therefore, the general pattern of results from the experiment was being replicated in this period at a variety of plants. However, as the evidence cited above shows, the productivity increases were not as impressive as at the plants that had originally implemented the experiment and the numbers of workers released not so large. For example, the plant cited by Golovin et al. (1974, p. 47) only managed to increase its productivity by eight per cent and release 600 workers. The other feature of the experiment replicated in this period was the low level of additional payments resulting from the implementation of the experiment. These were estimated at a monthly average of thirteen roubles or 7.8 per cent of the monthly wage (Shkurko, 1975, p. 124; Cherednichenko and Gol'din, 1976, pp. 53–6 and 1977, pp. 134–5).

Nevertheless, even after its initial success, the immediate pressure to generalise the experiment and its extension during the Ninth Five Year Plan, Soviet commentators have continually complained about the slow generalisation of the experiment. Virtually every Soviet source referred to in this book, from 1970 onwards, is critical of the slow dissemination of the experiment (Semin, 1976, p. 93; Bunich, 1975, p. 67). The absolute spread of the experiment is detailed in Table 7.1, which has been compiled from the fragmentary sources available, and this shows the slow rate of dissemination up to 1977.

Table 7.1 The dissemination of the Shchekino experiment

1/1968	12/1968	1969	1970	1971	1972
8	22	30	60	120/121	300

1973	1974	1975		10/1977	12/1977
700	2%	3%		1 000	1 200

Sources: Baranenkova (1970), p. 51; Karpenko (1969), p. 3; Shkurko (1971a), p. 3; *Ekonomicheskaya Gazeta* (1970), No. 10, p. 11; *Planovoe Khozyaistvo* (1971), No. 8, p. 10; Boldyrev (1972), p. 2; Sonin & Zhiltsov (1974), p. 126; Khachaturov (1974), p. 12; Aganbegyan (1975), p. 2; Mirgaleev (1977), p. 105; *Pravda* 29 July 1978, p. 1.

To put these figures into perspective, the 300 enterprises operating on Shchekino lines in 1972 represented less than 0.5 per cent of the Soviet total (Boldyrev, 1972, p. 2). Consequently the figure of 1200 after ten years of the experiment is probably around three per cent of the total and represents a rate of transfer of 120 per year or ten per month (*Pravda*, 26 July 1978, p. 1). At this rate, assuming the number of enterprises remains fairly constant, it would take over 300 years for all Soviet enterprises to transfer to the experiment! In fact, the majority of the enterprises that initiated the experiment did so in the early years, even though they may have taken some time to become operational, and by the mid-seventies and the tenth anniversary of the experiment, the rate of transfer had slowed appreciably (Parfenov and Shvetsov, 1977a, p. 2).

The slow dissemination of the experiment has been accompanied by a differential diffusion of the experiment between ministries, branches and departments of the economy. For example, during the Ninth Five Year Plan, 150 enterprises in the chemical industry completed the transition to the experiment and freed 55 000 workers (Kostandov, 1975, p. 3), but in some branches, notably machine tools, civil engineering and road construction, no enterprises or work units had instituted the experiment. Table 7.2 illustrates the diffusion of the experiment in a number of selected ministries. As noted by Ivanov, the disparity between ministries in applying the experiment can be quite pronounced. Three of the ministries cited in Table 7.2 have over 40 per cent of their enterprises operating on Shchekino lines and in two ministries 70 per cent of the workforce are employed in Shchekino-like enterprises. At the other extreme, a number of ministries only have between two and six per cent of their enterprises on the experiment, accounting for at most six per cent of the workforce under their control (Ivanov, 1977, p. 12; Semin, 1976, p. 93). Furthermore, Ivanov (1977, p. 12) notes the disparity between machine building and light industry. For the former, Ivanov cites figures ranging from ten to 30 per cent of enterprises, whilst for the latter the figure falls to no more than two per cent on experimental lines. Bachurin (1978, p. 11) gives a further indication of the imbalance in the dissemination of the experiment. He points out that of 410 experimental enterprises for which he had information, as of 1 November 1975, 70 were in the petroleum and petro-chemicals sector, 150 in the chemicals industry, 100 in pulp and paper making, twelve in food processing and 28 in microbiology.

Furthermore, as can be seen from Table 7.3, different ministries had

Table 7.2   Enterprises transferring to the Shchekino experiment during the Ninth Five Year Plan

Ministry	Number of enterprises on Shchekino experiment	As a proportion of total enterprises in the branch (%)	Number of workers in these enterprises as a proportion of the total (%)
Petroleum & chemical machine building	70	30.1	43.1
Coal industry	6	1.9	0.4
Chemical industry	150	46.0	70.0
Heavy & transport machine building	7	6.8	6.4
Electrical equipment industry	7	2.4	2.8
Forestry & wood processing industry	29	3.2	2.6
Pulp & paper industry	100	54.3	70.3
Food industry	12	0.2	0.6
Microbiology industry	28	41.7	42.8

Source: Ivanov (1977), p. 11.

Table 7.3   Percentage of total workforce released by selected ministries

Ministry	Percentage of total workforce released
Non-ferrous metallurgy	15.3%
Chemical industry	10.3%
Energy industry	10.4%
Petroleum & chemical machine building	6.4%
Ferrous metallurgy	6.0%

Sources: Ivanov (1977), p. 11; Cherednichenko & Gol'din (1978), p. 15; Shkurko (1977), p. 119.

differing degrees of success with regard to the number of workers released. The figures in Table 7.3 should be compared to the percentage of workers freed by the chemical industry, probably the most advanced and successful proponent of the experiment, and its variants, where during the early years of the experiment an estimated eighteen per cent of the original workforce were released (Danilov and Korchagin, 1976, p. 25).

This differential diffusion of the experiment explains the substance of the comments about the experiment by V. Selyunin (1976, p. 2). He argued that it was desirable for the experiment to spread slowly during this period, because its implementation had been predominantly in Department One, producer goods industries. The increase in output and productivity, even though they are well in excess of wage rises and desirable in themselves, had, nevertheless, led to increased wages for workers in Department One industries without a comparable impact in Department Two, consumer goods output. Therefore, if the experiment continued to spread too quickly in this differentiated fashion, he saw the possibility of these disproportions generating destabilising pressures. His conclusion was that a cautious approach to the experiment was desirable if these problems were to be avoided and, therefore, it should be disseminated slowly. Manevich (1978, p. 82) refuted these criticisms and argued that whilst a slowing in the spread of the experiment would indeed reduce these pressures, it would not resolve the underlying problems and was, therefore, the wrong approach. What was necessary was a more rapid dissemination of the experiment and its beneficial effects in Department Two enterprises, and not to allow the scarcity of consumer goods to act as a constraint on the generalisation of the experiment. After all, as Abramov (1974, p. 22) suggests, the whole point of the experiment is eventually to link the work and rewards of all the workforce, irrespective of the sector of the economy where they work.

Nevertheless, there is an undoubted problem here. Increased production of consumer goods is necessary for the incentive effects of the experiment to work. Yet it would appear that the experiment is conforming to the traditional bias in Soviet economic development and further reinforcing the predominance of Department One enterprises. This can be explained in a preliminary manner, by the traditional pressure and attention on this sector and is another respect in which the experiment simply conformed to previous patterns of Soviet industrial experience without radically transforming them.

Although the usual argument regarding the experiment is that it is generally applicable (Radov, 1981, p. 2; Cherednichenko and Gol'din, 1978, p. 237), some Soviet authors, for example Kunel'sky and Kuz'mirov, (cited by Rutland, 1983, p. 351) have argued that the experiment is simply more suitable for some industries than others. However, it should be noted that this argument has little official support, as both party and state bodies have pressed continuously for the widest possible implementation of the principles of the experiment in all areas of economic life. It was never envisaged, for example, that the experiment should only be applied to basic production. It was thought that the problems experienced in the transport sector of the Soviet economy, both with regard to the transportation of raw materials and finished products, could be ameliorated if the experiment were to be introduced. Delays are a form of waste generally, but are most acutely felt in the agricultural sector where delay in transportation can lead to the physical loss of output. In industry, disruptions in the flow of production are often attributed to failures of the transport system to maintain the flow of inputs, and in some sectors, as already noted, production can be halted if the finished product is not transported away expeditiously from the plant. Consequently, the Shchekino experiment was implemented in a number of transport depots. As Kamzin (1973, p. 3) points out, the role of the experiment was not to release drivers, who tend to be in short supply, but to encourage job combination and to strengthen work discipline. At the depot cited, during 1972, 736 workers were released, primarily from auxiliary and repair work, the idle-time of trucks was reduced by eleven per cent and productivity rose by twelve per cent. The major remaining problem for this work unit was not caused by its internal labour organisation, but by equipment failures as a result of poor manufacture and the chronic absence of spare parts.

The experiment was also successfully extended to the work of researchers and designers working in research institutes (Drozdov, 1976, p. 2). From 1973, the State Chemical Design Institute introduced the experiment and over a three year period freed 92 members of staff. This reduced design costs, boosted productivity and raised average wages as the economised wage funds were redistributed among those remaining at the institute. The initial implementation of the experiment was a success showing the applicability of the principles of the experiment to the work of ITR and members of the intelligentsia. However, the experiment began to falter after three years, for reasons similar to those which will be outlined later in this chapter. The general point is that irrespective of the differential dissemination of the experiment, its wider applicability was deemed both possible and desirable.

It should be noted that during this period the experiment was 'exported' to a number of other East European countries facing similar problems. There are references to similar experiments taking place in both Hungary and Bulgaria. Furthermore, in Czechoslovakia, in 1972, 21 enterprises employing 116 000 workers implemented the experiment with similarly favourable results (Danilov and Kokhova, 1975, pp. 44–5). Great interest was also shown in the experiment by the chemical industries of the GDR and Poland (Cherednichenko and Gol'din, 1978, pp. 218–22). The experiment, with some adaptation, was also implemented in a number of plants with the same favourable results. In the GDR chemical industry for example, over a five year period, labour productivity grew by 140 per cent as a result of the more rational labour and production organisa- tion that the experiment introduced. At the 'Leina Verke' combine, production rose by 125 per cent and labour productivity grew by 128 per cent, as a result of reducing the workforce. In Poland the experiment, coupled with the introduction of the brigade form of labour organisation and *NOT* measures, has been further developed. Cherednichenko and Gol'din argue that the success of the Shchekino experiment, both in the USSR and elsewhere, shows graphically its utility in dealing with real socio-economic tasks, particularly in a time of rapid economic change when it is necessary to redeploy workers, and tighten labour organisation. This conclusion however, raises a number of questions.

PROBLEMS IN GENERALISING THE EXPERIMENT

Given the dramatic initial successes of the experiment, the success of the variants adopted, its partial extension to a variety of branches and regions and the virtual absence of any fundamental criticism of its underlying logic, why should the generalisation of the experiment have been so slow and uneven and why was not the whole of Soviet industry radically transformed?

I would argue that the answers to these questions shed light on the socio-economic nature of the USSR, allow an assessment of the viability of other market-orientated reform initiatives and illustrate the vacuity of considering the USSR as any variant of capitalism.

The slow dissemination of the experiment cannot be explained by indifference or reluctance on the part of the ruling group. The analysis outlined in Part I suggests that they, above all, had a vested interest in the successful generalisation of the experiment. The disciplining effects upon both management and workers, the shake-out of labour and enhanced productivity and output, would all contribute to a sustainable increase in the surplus and would eventually lead to a way out of the vicious circle of problems identified in Figure 3.1. In an immediate sense, the release of workers would ease manpower shortages. Brezhnev (*Materialy . . .*, 1976, p. 43), for example, noted at the 25th Congress of the CPSU that, 'the major problem is labour resources, there are no possible further additions to the workforce and growth can only come through raising labour productivity . . . increasing the efficiency of social production'. The Central Committee of the CPSU had earlier charged all party, trade union, republican and social organisations (for example, Komsomol) to search out all reserves for growth in labour productivity and to raise production with fewer numbers (*KPSS v . . .*, 1972, pp. 82–90). The impact of the Shchekino experiment in this endeavour was explicitly praised at the 24th Congress of the CPSU (*Materialy . . .*, 1971, p. 70) and the 25th Congress brought further pressure to bear for a strengthening and extension of the experiment, particularly to branches where it had not been implemented previously (*Materialy . . .*, 1976, pp. 172–3). Brezhnev (1976, p. 1; 1977, p. 1; Batkaev, 1978, p. 6) repeatedly expressed support for the experiment but complained about its slow generalisation.

The lack of control exercised by the ruling group over the process of surplus extraction made the experiment necessary, but this same lack of control resulted in a qualification of the experiment's expected impact. Its slow dissemination is evidence of the ruling group's inability to assert control over the labour process and is also evidence of the disjuncture between the interests of the ruling group and enterprise management. The failure of the ruling group to generalise the Shchekino experiment, almost immediately after calling for this, undermines the naïve view that sees the USSR as a completely totalitarian socio-economic system. The centralisation of economic decision-making is a function not of total control, but the reverse. It is the lack of a reliable unambiguous form of economic control that necessitates the centralisation of decisions and simultaneously undermines the possibility of those decisions being put into practice. Directives from the centre do not become immediate reality but are contested, both between enterprise management and the centre, and between workers and enterprise management. The end result reflects the balance of that conflict, not the immediate wishes of the ruling group, which are qualified in the process. Equally, the non-generalisation of the experiment undermines the idea that the USSR is socially homogeneous, harmoniously developing in a contradiction-free, planned manner.[1] How is this experience to be explained and what are the real forms of the contradictions it reflects?

SOVIET CRITICISMS OF THE SHCHEKINO EXPERIMENT

Perhaps the most appropriate starting point is to consider the Soviet criticisms, which largely, though not exclusively, concentrate on the failure to generalise the experiment. These criticisms emerge in the literature in the early 1970s and reach a peak in the period 1976–77. Although there was very little fundamental criticism of the experiment's methodology or intention, some misgivings did arise in the early years. Shkurko (1971, pp. 10–12) for example, whilst praising the achievements at Shchekino and elsewhere, noted that at a number of plants it was unfortunate that the productivity increases could only be achieved by displacing workers and producing the same level of output. He argued that it would be more desirable and efficient if Soviet industrial enterprises could stimulate their existing workforce to produce more. This would avoid the costly disruptions involved in retraining and movement of workers between plants. Implicit in this argument is the view that localised successes, or even the partial generalisation of the experiment, are inadequate. This is particularly the case if the released workers are simply reabsorbed in other enterprises and work as inefficiently as they had done previously. The net effect of the experiment could, in fact, be negative if the gains at the enterprise undertaking the experiment were offset by productivity losses elsewhere. In fact, as a large proportion of the released workers were simply re-integrated into their present workplace, this problem could be reduced. However, there is a complementary problem in that the experiment could degenerate into a formalistic exercise involving the shuffling of workers about the plant with little overall positive impact.

Further early criticisms that emerged pointed out the occasional contradictions between the terms of the experiment and the broader planning system. For example, as a number of authors pointed out (Sharov, 1969, p. 2; Baranenkova, 1970, p. 51; Babaikov, 1969, p. 2), the determination of the enterprise material incentive fund, on the basis of the absolute size of the workforce, is a clear contradiction of the basic Shchekino principles. Similarly, calculating managerial and administrative salaries on the basis of workforce size will militate against the adoption of the experiment and will prove counter-productive (Boldyrev, 1972, p. 2). Soviet sources point out that in the past it may well have been the case that extensive development of the economy led to a correspondence between a large workforce, the scale of output and managerial responsibilities, thus explaining the rationale for this form of wage calculation. However, in modern conditions this correspondence is broken as increasing mechanisation and automation (and the desire to extend their impact) ruptures the link between workforce size and managerial responsibility. This renders this form of salary calculation obsolete, particularly if the Shchekino experiment has been implemented successfully. The reduction in workforce size could lead to the downgrading of the enterprise and a consequent reduction in managerial salaries.

These problems are the inevitable consequence of grafting experimental initiatives onto the bureaucratic complexities of the Soviet planning process. Over time, administrative changes were made in a fragmentary manner which overcame these contradictions. However, the possibility of problems like these often arose as initiatives in one area set up principles which contradicted practices in another. An example of this is the wage reform, instituted in December 1972 (Sharov, 1975, p. 98), which will be dealt with later in this section.

Other early criticisms of the experiment centre on its operation and particularly the size of the material incentives offered. Baranenkova (1970, p. 54) argues that the incentive was too small and Khachaturov (1974, pp. 12–19) criticised the financial authorities for being too cautious. These criticisms, which are the opposite of the comments cited from Selyunin (1976, p. 2), are not criticisms of the experiment *per se*, but are a plea to strengthen its operation. The effect the commentators hoped for was that enhanced salaries and bonuses would ease the acceptance of the experiment, strengthen its operation and that, as a consequence, this would stimulate its dissemination.

It is the question of the generalisation of the experiment that attracted most comment and criticism. As early as January 1970, at a seminar on the experiment held in Tula involving state, ministry, party and enterprise officials, complaints were raised that the experiment was spreading too slowly (Antonov, 1970, p. 2; Suyumbaev, 1970, p. 3). Participants at the seminar agreed that the hasty administrative imposition of the experiment was counter-productive and stressed the need for proper preparation prior to implementation. The press reports also suggest that many enterprises were willing to implement the experiment, but the extension was not taking place. The reason for this was that even when the preparation was conscientiously undertaken, there was no guarantee that the enterprise would actually be allowed to implement the experiment (Karpenko, 1970, p. 3). Obviously, enterprises would be unwilling to undertake the expensive and time-consuming work involved if no such guarantee existed. The seminar participants called for closer co-ordination between the ministries and their enterprises and the State Committee on Labour and Wages to overcome this problem. This is the earliest manifestation of a recurrent problem that dogged the experiment. That is, who exactly is responsible for the decision to implement the experiment? At Shchekino itself, the decision was clearly taken by the enterprise at the behest of the ministry. The Central Committee resolution of 9 October 1969, is ambiguous on this issue. It charges ministries to draw up plans for the implementation of the experiment and calls for party organisations to propagandise for its generalisation, but it does not specify actual responsibility (*Pravda*, 9 October 1969). In the 1971 regulations governing the experiment's implementation, every enterprise is given the right to transfer to the experiment but only if it has the support of its ministry and the agreement of the Trade Union Committee (*Ekonomicheskaya Gazeta*, 1971, No. 1, p. 8).

What this means is that the experiment can only be implemented with conscious ministerial support, and enterprise autonomy is heavily circumscribed because without the specification of the stable plan and wage fund, the experiment will be undermined. Aganbegyan (1977, p. 4) is particularly critical of the failure to give enterprises real autonomy in implementing the experiment. However, this works both ways because any ministry wishing to see the experiment implemented in a particular enterprise would find it impossible to impose it and is, therefore, reliant upon enterprise acceptance of the experiment. For the experiment to be successful, both enterprise and ministry have to be actively supportive of each other. The possibility that one or the other may perceive the experiment not to be in their interest is a powerful reason for the slow generalisation. This will be taken up in more detail later in this chapter.

In Novozhilov's report to the Tula seminar (1970, p. 1) he argued that a contributory reason for the non-generalisation of the experiment was that the logic of its operation had been inadequately theorised. His argument was echoed by Boldyrev (1972, p. 2) who claimed that although Soviet economists were well able to collect empirical data for a number of years and then cautiously advance on the basis of this, they were unable to theorise and generalise the implications of the experiment. Parfenov (1973, p. 2) went even further and criticised not only economists but also sociologists, industrial psychologists and planning specialists who had failed to analyse the experiment and thereby aid its generalisation. Parfenov (1973, p. 2) suggested that one of the problems in extending the experiment was that some enterprises had oversimplified its methodology and saw it simply as a means to remove unwanted staff. As they had failed to implement all the elements of the experiment it had little overall impact on output or productivity as a consequence.

As a consequence of these failings, Novozhilov pointed out that perhaps the terms of the experiment were too static. For example, an enterprise, irrespective of its current state of labour organisation and production discipline, received all the economised wage fund to dispose of in the form of wage supplements or for collective consumption purposes. This led to the disparity already noted between 'advanced' and 'backward' collectives. The Bashkir variant addressed this problem when the enterprises were amalgamated in an industrial association, but in other cases this constituted a further blockage in the dissemination of the experiment. The advanced collective, by virtue of its past performance and by definition, would be the most likely to take up new initiatives, but would gain little from the implementation of the experiment. The backward collective, again by definition and past performance, would be unlikely to be innovatory, even though potentially it had most to gain. As one type of enterprise had little to gain and the other was unlikely to implement it, the experiment would falter.

Boldyrev (1972, p. 2) noted two further related problems. The implementation of the experiment in the early seventies was predicted upon pledges for increased production. This general principle reflects the 'resultism' common to many areas of Soviet planning (Rutland, 1984, p. 356) and disregarded whether increased production was either necessary or desirable. For example, it may generate disproportions if the product is an intermediate element in a complex chain of production. He suggested that perhaps enhanced quality or reliability would be a more useful basis for the experiment. Boldyrev also noted that the slow dissemination of the experiment may well be explained by the fact that its general thrust puts management into a potentially embarrassing position. During the process of plan compilation, management negotiate with the relevant ministry on the basis of scarcity of resources, particularly labour. Yet they are now supposed to shed labour and take on increased tasks. Management will be wary of exposing their hoarded reserves and laying themselves open to criticism, particularly as they will have been undoubtedly seeking additional resources shortly beforehand. The fact that management have discretion over the implementation of the experiment will slow the dissemination of the experiment.

A further general problem for many enterprises, noted by Parfenov (1973, p. 2), was the lack of clarity in the instructions for the implementation of the experiment. Contradictions in the instructions either stopped enterprises from adopting the experiment or simply dampened their enthusiasm, hence slowing its generalisation. Furthermore, Parfenov noted another contradiction in the instructions (1973a, p. 2). He pointed out that the instructions contain the warning that any wage supplements introduced can later be withdrawn if the work for which they are granted is changed by either technological improvements or renovation of existing capital stock. This implied that the benefits for the collective are potentially short term and may be removed later, as investment decisions are taken elsewhere, outside of their control. For Parfenov, this increased uncertainty hindered the broader acceptance of the experiment.

The overall impetus of the experiment was also undermined, as previously noted, by the 1973 wage reform. On the basis of the success of the experiment, all enterprises were to be allowed to introduce elements of the financial incentives operating at Shchekino without introducing the full experiment (Mirgaleev, 1977, p. 106). Therefore, with little preparation and no necessary commitment to either increase productivity or to reorganise labour, the incentive elements of the experiment could be introduced. From the point of view of the enterprise, this appears attractive because it avoids the necessity to tackle the workforce and at the same time holds out the prospect of some success, particularly if it is believed that it was the material incentives element that was crucial to the experiment's operation. The same is true for the ministries. Even those ministries which had been most supportive of the full experiment halted its systematic implementation, in the hope that they could achieve its intended effect without its full introduction.

The overall impact of this change can be seen from Table 7.1. In the years 1971–73 almost 600 enterprises initiated the experiment. However, in the following six years, only a further 500 enterprises joined the experiment. This decline, rather than acceleration in the rate of transfer, was accompanied by a continued decline in the rate of growth of labour productivity in the economy as a whole, as explained in Chapter 3. This suggests that the partial implementation of the experiment could not deliver the anticipated results and further supports my contention that the material incentives element of the experiment was not the critical factor.

All these criticisms emerged from the operation of the experiment or from the failure to generalise the experiment. For Soviet commentators, they do not undermine the idea of the experiment and all the authors cited are fundamentally supportive of the extension of the experiment. However, perhaps the best way to explain the failure to generalise the experiment is to consider the experience of the Shchekino plant itself.

THE EXPERIENCE OF THE SHCHEKINO ENTERPRISE IN THE SEVENTIES

After the initial period of dramatic success, the experience of the Shchekino plant throughout the seventies shows the specific problems of maintaining the momentum of the experiment. In two important articles, written around the tenth anniversary of the experiment, it was reported that the Shchekino plant was now one of Tula's lagging enterprises and was unlikely to fulfil its current plan targets (Parfenov and Shvetsov, 1977a, p. 2). The problems the enterprise faced cast further doubts on the coherence of its internal logic and are explicable only in terms of the contradiction between the underlying logic of the experiment and the nature of Soviet planning, which in turn reflects the particular political economy of the USSR. Furthermore, there is a direct link between the problems of maintaining the momentum of the experiment and the problems of extending its operation; and the specific experience at Shchekino explains the reluctance on the part of many Soviet enterprise managers to embark on the experiment.

In the first instance, the point of the experiment is to take up 'slack' within the enterprise by rationally utilising existing resources. In this sense, there will be an initial once-and-for-all impact, as surplus labour is shaken out.[2] But, as Soviet sources note, this cannot account for all the productivity increases achieved nor their continuation over time. It does however, explain the tendency for productivity increments to occur, but at a declining rate, and this is implicit in the logic of the experiment, whichever explanation of its functioning is accepted.

For example, if we accept the Soviet view that it is the incentive effect of the experiment which explains its success, then, as the workforce is trimmed, the potential for further wage increases or for extending the wage supplements to new groups of workers, from the economised wages of those released, is progressively reduced. Furthermore, if it is recognised that money does not function as a universal equivalent in the USSR, even if there is a short-term incentive effect, this will be dissipated as workers learn over time that increased money wages do not necessarily lead to increased access to use-values such as consumer goods, agricultural products, better housing and so on.

If, however, we accept the alternative argument presented in Chapter 6, which suggests that the success of the experiment was achieved by increasing workers' insecurity, then this too will have a diminishing effect over time. In the initial period, when the plant's labour surplus is at its highest, so too will be the possibility of release and consequently the level of insecurity will be at its highest. In this period, the salutary effect on labour discipline will be most pronounced and productivity gains will be at their highest. However, as surplus labour is shed, the possibility of release will diminish and the security of the individual worker will rise again, with a consequent negative impact on productivity gains, as further increments to work intensity will be progressively difficult to achieve. Therefore, whichever explanation is adopted, the result is the same: a tendency for the rate of growth of labour productivity increases to decline. Table 7.4 indicates the decline in growth rates that took place at Shchekino over this period. Most Soviet sources tend to obscure this question by calculating the growth of output or productivity over the whole time period of the experiment. The rapid increases in the early period provide the basis of the impressive figures this provides, but it hides the slow-down in growth that actually occurred.

Table 7.4   The declining impact of the experiment at Shchekino

Year	Increase in labour productivity	Increase in production
1966	100	100
1970	232	201
1975	341	270
1977	386	302

Source: *Sotsialisticheskaya Industriya*, 12 April 1978, p. 2.

Table 7.5, compiled from a number of sources, shows the time period over which labour was released from Shchekino. Clearly, the major impact was achieved in the initial 27 months of the experiment, when over 1000 workers were released, whilst over the next eight years only 500 more workers were released. For the period 1977–80, the anticipated release of workers was thought to be unlikely to exceed 300 (Cherednichenko and Gol'din, 1978, p. 14), and as Semin (1976, p. 94) suggests, inevitably in the second phase of the experiment there were fewer workers to release.

Table 7.5   Number of workers released from the Shchekino plant

1 January 1968	*1 July 1968*	*1 September 1968*
343	495	515
1 October 1968	*20 November 1968*	*1 January 1969*
520	689	800
1 June 1969	*1 July 1969*	*31 December 1969*
853	870	987
1 January 1970	*31 December 1970*	*1 July 1975*
1 039	1 175	1 300
31 December 1975	*1977*	*1978*
1 513	1 500 +	1 570

Sources: Shilin (1969), p. 37; Tolstikov (1968), p. 2; Karpenko (1969), p. 2; Slepykh (1969), p. 2; Sharov (1969), p. 2; Shkurko (1971b), p. 12; Boldyrev (1972), p. 2; Semin (1974), p. 31; Cherednichenko & Gol'din (1978), p. 14; Parfenov (1980), p. 2; Parfenov & Shvetsov (1977), p. 2; *Pravda* 26 July 1978, p. 1.

A similar argument, regarding diminishing effectiveness, could be applied to management. Their response to the experiment, once the original 'psychological barriers' were overcome, was enthusiastic and success, reflected in praise, public acknowledgement and rewards, will foster the experiment's extension. Their enthusiasm, however, will be tempered over time, as will be explained in detail below, and this diminishes the search for internal reserves and no management will willingly cut their safety factor to zero. The plant will settle into a new routine and implicit in this is a tendency for declining effectiveness, no matter how successful the initial implementation of the experiment.

The only way this tendency can be offset is if the plant's output and performance can be improved by the renewal of plant and equipment, the introduction of new technology, the mechanisation of what were previously manual tasks or expansion of plant capacity at the current technological level. The difficulties involved in this course of action for Soviet enterprises have already been noted. Nevertheless, this had been the intention for the second phase of the experiment in the period 1970–75 (Antonov, 1970a, p. 1) and prior to the Ninth Five Year Plan redevelopment of the Shchekino plant was agreed. On the basis of this, the Shchekino workforce agreed to increase labour productivity by 62 per cent, wages were to rise by 23 per cent and a further 9.6 per cent cut in the workforce was to take place (Parfenov and Shvetsov, 1977b, p. 2). However, the familiar problems of the supply and construction sectors of the Soviet economy were compounded by delays at the level of the Chemical Ministry, which took two years to approve the plans for the plant's redevelopment. Construction deadlines were consistently missed due to delays in deliveries or the complete non-appearance of essential materials. Even when work was carried out, it was poorly finished or was not completed at all.

Nevertheless, by even more intensive utilisation of the existing resources, the enterprise managed to slightly overfulfil its targets for the Ninth Five Year Plan but was now operating, in its own terms, very near to its full capacity (Parfenov and Shvetsov, 1977b, p. 2). The result of this was that in the first year of the Tenth Five Year Plan the enterprise failed to fulfil its planned targets. The specific reason for this was that newly completed plant failed; the modernisation of one key shop was further delayed and, finally, when it was opened it shut down after one month. This resulted in wage supplements being withdrawn and the thirteenth month bonus being reduced. This was coupled with another negative factor. As a result of freeing workers, the plant did not have sufficient workers to allocate to house building. The inability to provide housing had already been causing concern as it was resulting in spontaneous labour turnover (Slepykh, 1974, p. 3).

In other words, the dynamic of the experiment had now come into contact with the usual problems of Soviet industrial life. As long as the success of the experiment was dependent upon the internal search for reserves, its momentum could be maintained, but at a declining rate. However, it was now constrained by the external environment it was supposed to revolutionise and its further success was to be determined by the external support it received or, more correctly, was denied.

This had serious consequences for the Shchekino plant. The combination of declining success, with the consequent reductions in bonuses and wage supplements, coupled with the increasing pressure to achieve plan targets with a smaller workforce and the inability to provide adequate housing, led to skilled workers and technicians leaving the enterprise. The reduction in bonuses and wages, coupled with increased work intensity, could not be offset by wage supplements, drawn from economies in the wage fund as a result of workers being freed, because the spontaneous movement out of the plant simply generated labour shortages. Skilled workers could choose to move to nearby plants with better rewards, either wages or housing, and potentially less pressure, particularly if these plants were not part of the experiment. If this is the case, the initial effects on labour discipline and work intensity will begin to be nullified as the plant's management strive to retain necessary workers. Again, this is particularly the case if the experiment has not been adopted in all plants in a locality and ironically the experiment's previous positive effect on labour turnover may be reversed. The possible trade-off between increased work intensity and rewards will be broken as workers shift to plants with looser controls over work intensity. Therefore, for the individual plant, the duration of the experiment will be determined by the degree of under-utilised capacity at the outset and once this is taken up (as far as the enterprise management see this as desirable), the experiment will begin to falter. Once again, it is ironic to note that enterprises with the greatest amount of under-utilised capacity will be able to sustain the experiment the longest.

A further problem experienced at Shchekino resulted from the combination of the experiment with other central initiatives. For example, the Shchekino plant began to receive directives for the reduction of management personnel, over and above the changes that the experiment had engendered. This caused particular problems as the enterprise was left with insufficient staff, even to evaluate operational data. This problem reflects the administrative nature of the Soviet economic mechanism, where centralised instructions are often arbitrary and incompatible with other initiatives. This inevitably acts as a hindrance in the further dissemination of the experiment.

The experience at Shchekino during this period also highlights the contradictory relationship that exists between the ministry and enterprise management. It highlights the differences in their aims and the ambiguity that exists concerning the question of responsibility. This relates specifically to the central principles of the experiment.

An original cornerstone of the experiment was the provision of a stable wage fund and the right of the enterprise to utilise any economised funds to stimulate productivity growth, plus the right to transfer any unutilised balance from one year to the next. This last element was lost in the early seventies (Selyunin, 1976, p. 2). Furthermore, at Shchekino in the second phase of the experiment, 1970–75, four million roubles were lost from the wage fund (Parfenov and Shvetsov, 1977b, p. 2; Slepykh, 1975, p. 3). At another enterprise cited by Ivanov (1977, p. 17) the wage fund was 'corrected' on seventeen separate occasions. From as early as 1973 onwards, the Shchekino enterprise had to plead with the ministry for sufficient funds to pay the wage supplements (Parfenov and Shvetsov, 1977b, p. 2). The dynamic that this developed is clearly identified by Slepykh (1975, p. 2), who points out that up to 1974 labour productivity had grown by 34 per cent, but average wages had only increased by seven per cent. This is far less than the 23 per cent originally planned and is explained by the continual reductions in the wage fund. For Shchekino, this problem reached a peak in 1975, when, as a result of the introduction of new basic wage and salary rates, the enterprise had to cancel the payment of wage supplements for 1700 workers (Melent'ev, 1982, p. 3).

This occurred at a number of other plants. Mirgaleev (1977, p. 110) points out for example, that the Food Ministry had failed to budget the correct wage fund for a number of plants in the North Caucasus, even though they had reduced staff by 500 in two years. As a result of this, average wages fell rather than rose, as was planned. As he explains, some workers simply do not know their entitlement to wage supplements under the terms of the experiment. A further common phenomenon, cited by Mirgaleev (1977, p. 111), is the redirection of the economised portion of the wage fund away from the plant making the savings. This occurred because the ministry responsible has failed to budget for the wages of workers at newly opened facilities, either at the same site or elsewhere. According to Prokhvatilov (1975, p. 2), petro-chemical enterprises in the Dnepropetrovsk region suffered this fate and the implementation of the experiment led to no material benefit for the workforce.

No matter how sceptical one may be about the incentive effects of the experiment it is difficult to accept that anyone will be prepared to work with greater intensity for the same reward or less. However, the instability of the wage fund has an effect not only on the wages of the workforce, but also upon management. This type of instability increases uncertainty, reduces their room for manœuvre and will deter them from implementing the experiment.

This problem is similar to the non-distribution of economised wage funds noted earlier. However, in that case the economised wage fund was not utilised immediately, but held over or, perhaps more importantly, used for collective provision. However, at Shchekino and the other plants cited, these funds were taken out of the control of the enterprise. To compound these problems further, the savings made and subtracted from the wage fund now became the base figure for the next planning period and the wage fund moved downwards on this ratchet principle.

The second central element of the experiment's operation was the provision of stable plan targets for a specified time period after the implementation of the experiment. This, after all, was supposed to remove the management's motivation for labour hoarding. However, this principle was breached quickly. In the short run, the Shchekino plant had its production plans revised upwards as often as enterprises not operating on the experimental method (Sharov, 1969, p. 2). The same problem is reported from a number of other plants operating on the experiment (Dybtsyn, 1977, p. 2). Over the longer run, the transition from one plan period to the next, the traditional Soviet planning principle of 'planning from the achieved level' or 'ratchet planning' re-emerged and was widely criticised. Myasnikov (1979, p. 2) makes the familiar point that even if planning from the achieved level had had a purpose, it was now inappropriate for the experimental enterprises at least. For these enterprises, this form of instability poses a number of related problems, as well as acting as a deterrent to enterprises thinking about making the transition to the experiment.

Firstly, unstable plan targets will discourage management at enterprises already operating on experimental lines from identifying further spare capacity. At these enterprises, the whole point of the experiment was to reduce the safety factor of hoarded labour by improving labour organisation. However, the degree to which this has been achieved necessarily reduces the enterprises ability to respond to short-run plan changes, hence increasing the possibility of failure. If plan stability is not maintained, then the enterprise management will see no advantage in further extending the experiment and further reducing their room for manœuvre. Furthermore, non-participating enterprises will be deterred if the post-experiment situation is no better, and perhaps even worse, than the pre-experiment period.

This will also apply to ministries who will be reluctant to expose their reserves at the range of enterprises under their control (Mirgaleev, 1977, p. 109). If ministries are compelled repeatedly by planning agencies to increase their output or alter the assortment of production, this is easier to achieve if the plants they control are of the 'non-Shchekino' type. For those operating on the experiment, a change in a single plan indicator necessitates a complete revision of the commitments made in connection with the shift to the experiment and this makes the ministry's life even more complicated. Ministries will be unable to respond to future short-run plan changes if the experiment is extended to all the ministry's enterprises and all slack is eliminated. Therefore, if the ministry anticipates unstable plans, which is the norm, then they have a vested interest in retarding the spread of the experiment. It could be argued that if all ministries adopted a vigorous approach to the Shchekino experiment, then the vagaries of the planning system would disappear. The more conservative strategy, however, of maintaining spare capacity is self-fulfilling.

Secondly, even if short-run plans are stable and capacity utilisation is increased, there is still the broader problem of ratchet planning as targets are raised for subsequent plan periods. The major criticisms here are that the planning system fails to take adequate account of the changes the experiment brings and treats the enterprise in an arbitrary manner. The almost automatic uprating of plans in the pre-experiment period could only be accommodated (and justified) either because of the existence of the safety factor or because of the possibilities of attracting more workers. However, after the implementation of the experiment, by definition, these options do not exist. Therefore, the adoption of a ratchet planning mechanism will deter enterprise management and ministries from extending the experiment.

The reasons for 'ratchet planning' can be found in the analysis presented in Part I. If there is no way to unambiguously determine whether a plant is operating near capacity; if information is distorted by the self-interest of enterprise management; if there is a systematic tendency to underestimate capacity, then at the very least ratchet planning will reduce the degree of divergence between potential and actual output. In fact, the problem is more difficult when the situation is dynamic, that is, the potential for production is growing. Ratchet planning can be seen, therefore, as part of a further vicious circle, both the response to and cause of instabilities in enterprise behaviour.

Thirdly, if new plan targets are predicated upon extensions to existing capacity or upgraded, renovated plant capacity, which has not been undertaken or has broken down or is of poor quality and design, then the enterprise will fail as Shchekino did (Parfenov and Shvetsov, 1977b, p. 2).

The combination of the implementation of the experiment and the simultaneous erosion of its basic terms will ultimately lead to enterprise failure and the reassertion of old planning practices. Aganbegyan (1975, p. 2) cites the problem of shifting plan targets as the prime reason for the experiment's slow dissemination. In his view, enhanced enterprise autonomy is the only way simultaneously to free enterprises from this constraint and to make more rational use of manpower by extending the experiment. Ultimately, the failure to generalise the Shchekino experiment is explained by Aganbegyan, as a result of the principle that 'initiative is punishable' (1977, p. 4). He argues that eventually the internal search for reserves is hindered by the dependence upon outside agencies and even if a subjective desire for change exists, the necessary objective resources are absent. Aganbegyan points out that enthusiasm for reform initiatives is often drowned in a sea of paperwork, as increasingly complex instructions are set up to overcome each of a variety of inconsistencies.

It could be argued therefore, that the experience of the Shchekino plant could act as a disincentive to other plants contemplating following their initial example. Perhaps these problems could be overcome if the experiment could be established everywhere simultaneously and this may establish a dynamic that could sweep away the bottlenecks and blockages. As already noted, this is impractical, given the form of the experiment, and would cause massive implementational problems at the level of the enterprise, as the full benefits of the experiment only accrue if it is fully implemented after proper preparation and with adequate support.

The implicit logic of the Schchekino experiment, at enterprise level, is a tendency for initial success, which starts at a high point and then continuously declines and eventually leads to plan under-fulfilment[3]. The negative longer-term experience at Shchekino observed by other enterprise managers partially explains their reluctance to follow the Shchekino example and hence explains the slow generalisation of the experiment. This problem of generalisation raises a series of further questions that will be taken up in the next chapter.

8 The Shchekino Experiment and the Logic of Soviet Planning

THE SOVIET RESPONSE TO THE PROBLEMS OF GENERALISING THE EXPERIMENT

From the viewpoint of the ruling group, the slow dissemination of the experiment was undesirable and attempts were made to re-invigorate its extension (*Ekonomicheskaya Gazeta*, 1977, No. 6, pp. 17–18). In order to be able to do this, some idea of the blockage existing was necessary and it is interesting to note that the whole emphasis of their efforts was directed towards the regulations for the implementation of the experiment. This implies that in their view the failures were solely of an administrative or institutional nature. As already noted, ambiguities in the instructions had been a concern noted by a number of authors.

As a consequence, new instructions for the implementation of the experiment were introduced on 27 January 1977 (*Ekonomicheskaya Gazeta*, 1977, No. 7, pp. 17–18). As Cherednichenko and Gol'din (1978, pp. 119–22) point out, the instructions had undergone a series of changes already and they pick out nine essential elements of the operation of the experiment and show that each of these had been changed between two and four times up to 1977. Therefore, the aim in the 1977 proposals was to remove the impediments to the experiment's implementation and also to provide a stable and rational set of conditions.

The major problems needing to be remedied, according to the introduction to the new instructions, were the incomplete adoption of the experiment at enterprise level and the lack of support given to the experiment by ministries (*Ekonomicheskaya Gazeta*, 1977, No. 7, p. 17). The 1977 regulations reaffirmed that the decision to implement the experiment rested primarily with the enterprise, but at the same time charged ministries with the responsibility of compiling plans for the further introduction of the experiment. Nevertheless, enterprise autonomy was still constrained in so far as the responsibility for establishing output norms and the level of the wage fund remained

180

with the ministry. In order to stop the claw-back of economised wage funds, the instructions specified that 50 per cent of any unutilised economised wage funds may be retained by the enterprise. From the point of view of workers, the maximum bonus was retained at 30 per cent of the basic wage rate. Also major changes were made regarding the payment of bonuses and the evaluation of manning levels prior to and during the experiment, the implications of which will be considered below.

It was hoped that these new regulations would stimulate the extension of the experiment and they were seen as an advance in so far as they incorporated some of the previous criticisms made by practitioners of the experiment. However, there were still problems and the new instructions were strongly criticised by a series of Soviet writers, particularly those who had practical experience of the experiment. V. Slepykh (1977, p. 2) for example, pointed out that the new requirement set up in the 1977 regulations, that labour norms had to be set from branch or interbranch manuals as a necessary precondition for the implementation of the experiment, was theoretically correct. (This is desirable to overcome the problems already referred to with regard to differing initial manning levels in enterprises of the same type in the same ministry.) However, as these norms did not exist in many areas, insisting on their existence prior to the experiment could only slow down its implementation. By the end of 1976, for example, these norms only existed for 40 per cent of industrial workers (Chubarov, 1976, p. 61). By 1977, even though technically validated norms were available for 80 per cent of industrial workers, only 80 per cent of these were branch and inter-branch norms (Batkaev, 1978, p. 7; Shkurko, 1977, pp. 126–8). As Parfenov and Shvetsov (1977b, p. 2) point out, even in the chemical industry, the then current level of norms was only planned to extend to 70 per cent of the workforce by the end of the Tenth Five Year Plan. Therefore, the possibilities of further extension of the experiment were very limited even in this relatively advanced branch. As Selyunin (1978, p. 2) pointed out, this is almost a reversal of past experience. In the past the introduction of the experiment had prompted the acceptance of tighter labour norms. Now, however, one of the benefits of the experiment was stipulated as a precondition for its implementation. Slepykh argued that this undesirable state of affairs could be resolved if each enterprise was simply given a projected target size of workforce, without detailed norms. This may be attractive but it begs the question of equalising work intensity and raising the degree of labour utilisation.

Selyunin criticised the new instructions because they introduced a series of new restrictions. Unlike the previous situation, it was now impossible to raise the wage rate of piece-rate workers as a result of the implementation of the experiment. This represented an obvious impediment, particularly in industries, where piece-rate working predominated.

Kossoi (1977, p. 2) pointed out that the new regulations were excessively complex and in some instances contradictory. For example, the basic tenet that the enterprise makes the decision to implement the experiment was contradicted in almost every paragraph, as not one step, in either preparation or operation, could be undertaken without approval from ministry level. This was either a contradiction or the recipe for continual delays.

As an example of the complexity and possibilities for bureaucratic muddling slowing down the experiment's implementation, Parfenov and Shvetsov (1977b, p. 2) cite an interview with the then Minister for the Chemical Industry, Kostandov. It was pointed out to Kostandov that parts of a document produced by his ministry, which specified the conditions under which an enterprise might initiate the experiment, were contradictory. The minister admitted that he did not fully understand the document and that in order to do this it was necessary to consult resolutions from five different years. As the authors pointed out, at the enterprise level access to these resolutions would be difficult and the time necessary to comply with all the possible restrictions would hinder the experiment's implementation.

Basova (1977, p. 2) argued that the main intention of the new instructions was to encourage more plants to switch to the experiment. But for those enterprises well used to operating upon Shchekino lines, the new regulations failed to say anything on their future development. Basova goes as far as to state that the experiment was at a dead end for these enterprises. As a result of the ratchet planning principle all the best achievements of the experimental enterprises were now set as their base figures and at the same time the resources available to them were being reduced. This type of arbitrary decision undermined the momentum at enterprises already on the experiment and further discouraged those enterprises thinking of transferring to the experiment.

Mirgaleev (1978, p. 2) a senior member of the State Committee for Labour, responded to these criticisms, particularly that of Selyunin. He argued that the instructions themselves were not the problem, but it was the attitudes of both ministries and enterprise management that represented the major obstacle to the wider dissemination of the experiment. He particularly pointed to the reluctance of ministries to establish comprehensive plans for the introduction of the experiment as a key problem. The successful example of the petro-chemical industry was cited to show how close cooperation between the ministry, its research institutes and enterprises in the search for more rational labour and production organisation could ease the experiment's implementation. The reticence of other ministries to introduce such plans was explained as a result of the fact that it was easier to hide inadequacies in production if the ministry had surplus workers and capacity available. (Just in the same way as it was easier at enterprise level). Mirgaleev noted the need to keep to agreed wage funds, but pointed out that if wage funds were planned annually, based upon current results, there was little incentive for enterprises to reduce their workforce. What was necessary was a longer-term perspective which would provide both stability and incentive. What Mirgaleev was suggesting was that ultimately central planners cannot force ministries to implement the experiment, particularly if they do not perceive it to be in their interest.

Denisenko (1978, p. 2), a planning specialist at Gosplan, responded to both Selyunin and Mirgaleev's criticism. In a sense, his argument returned to earlier criticism, particularly that of Shkurko, and he pointed out that the Shchekino experiment was not applicable to all plants. Productivity could be raised by producing more with the existing workforce, but the enterprise would not be eligible for wage supplements under the terms of the existing Shchekino instructions, because no part of the labour force had been freed. He pointed out that in the Tenth Five Year Plan period, very few enterprises would be in a position to shed workers and he cited the Kharkov Tractor Association as a typical example. Here the plan provided for a 53 per cent increase in output and a 50 per cent increase in labour productivity, with no personnel reduction. This plant would clearly not be covered by the prevailing Shchekino instructions. Denisenko appeared to be arguing that the level of capacity utilisation at this and similar plants reflects adequate labour organisation and control with little opportunity to shed labour. All that was necessary was to make the established workforce work harder. As a consequence, he argued that the material stimulation of these workers has to be sponsored in a different way. He cited earlier experimental initiatives, at Perm for example, where over a longer time period norms for wage expenditures per rouble of output were established, as a possible way forward. The collapse of the Perm variant in the earlier period had been caused by the instability of wage norms set by higher bodies, yet Denisenko argued that the Shchekino instructions should be amended to accommodate this normative method. The source of the stimulation, at enterprise level, would then not only arise from the freeing of surplus workers, but also from enhanced output causing the enterprise wage fund to rise. As already noted, there is the possibility of a number of problems and inconsistencies arising with this approach.

The general point to be drawn from this debate was that the 1977 instructions were not likely to achieve their objective. As early as April 1977, only three months after their introduction, Lomonosov (1977, p. 2), the Vice-Chairman of the State Committee on Labour and Social Questions, instructed a wide reaching study of the logic, method and experience of the new instructions with a view to reviewing the experiment's dissemination at the end of 1977.

The result of the debate and criticisms, noted above, was further changes in the instructions for the implementation of the experiment, which were introduced in April 1978 (*Sotsialisticheskii Trud*, 1978, No. 7, pp. 9–11; *Ekonomicheskaya Gazeta*, 1978, No. 21, p. 2).

These new regulations explicitly recognised the problems associated with the experiment and sought to remove some of the instabilities associated with both the transition to the experiment and its operation. It was an attempt to restore the confidence of enterprises in the advantages of the experiment. This was to be achieved by retaining some elements of the 1977 regulations, restoring some elements that had been abolished in both the 1970 and the 1977 regulations plus the introduction of some new elements.

For example, the necessity, introduced in 1977, for ministries to provide comprehensive plans for the introduction of the experiment, was retained (Point 10). Furthermore, the responsibilities of ministries for the implementation of the experiment were extended. They were now obliged to establish, for every enterprise under their control, for the five year plan period, either normative levels for wage expenditures per rouble of output or fixed wage funds (Point 4). The intention was to remove the instabilities that, for example, the Shchekino plant had faced. To achieve a similar end, the ability to transfer the total unutilised wage fund economies to the material incentive fund, which had been lost in the early seventies, was restored. The intention was to provide confidence at enterprise level that the results of any savings would actually accrue to the enterprise workforce and not be clawed back by the ministry for other purposes.

The possibility of paying bonuses to piece-rate workers and special bonuses to repair workers, which was removed in the 1977 regulations, was reinstated (Point 2). These bonuses could be as high as 60 per cent of either the time rate for the job or the piece-rate earnings. Furthermore, the necessity for manpower reductions to be assessed in relation to branch and inter-branch norms was seen as unrealistic, even if it was theoretically desirable, and it was therefore abandoned. However, where workforce reductions were achieved not on the basis of these norms, then only 70 per cent of the economised wage fund could be retained (Point 4). This reflects an assumption, which is probably correct, that without the existence of these norms manning levels are even higher.

Ministries were also given the authority to grant premiums and bonuses directly to departmental administrators or association managers who successfully introduced the experiment into enterprises under their control.

The idea with these new instructions was to break the bottleneck in the implementation process (Kuznetsov, 1978, p. 30). If ministries were compelled to set stable wage funds, intermediate officials were to be rewarded for implementing the experiment and the level of incentives stabilised, then it was thought that the last impediments to the experiment's generalisation would be removed (*Pravda*, 26 July 1978). The 1978 instructions mark a shift in emphasis towards the recognition that the implementation of the experiment is mainly dependent upon the attitudes of ministries and association administrations (Podugol'nikov and Shcherbatykh, 1978, p. 22; Platonov and Shelyd'ko, 1978, p. 18). The Pulp and Paper Ministry is cited as an example of the desirable way forward, where the ministry had drawn up a special long-term programme linking the introduction of the experiment to measures to increase technological processes, retrain workers and reorganise production units (*Pravda*, 26 July 1978, p. 1).

However, the 1978 regulations for the implementation of the experiment operated for only a little over a year before they were in a sense superseded. In July 1979 a new planning resolution came into effect (*Resheniya partii . . .*, 1981, pp. 78–119). These regulations were an attempt on the part of the ruling group to reinvigorate the economic mechanism, and the regulations contain a series of measures that draw upon the experience of the experimental initiatives introduced in the period from the late sixties, including the Shchekino experiment. Consequently, the resolution includes provisions for the retention of economised wage funds, with any unutilised funds being transferred to the material incentives fund for use in the next year, plus a stipulation that they could only be used for their designated purpose and could not be clawed back by ministries and used for purposes like staffing new facilities (p. 105). The resolution stresses the necessity to link rewards to work performance, and increase labour productivity as a consequence, on the basis of long-term norms for wages per rouble or output (p. 113). The resolution gives all enterprises the right to pay bonuses to workers from savings in the wage fund, for enhanced productivity, widening their service zone or job combination (p. 114). A great deal of emphasis was placed on the future possibilities of job combination as a result of the introduction of the Shchekino experiment (Molchanov, 1979, p. 18; Bogomolov and Vanyarkin, 1979, p. 40).

Consequently, what were integrated measures designed for the implemetation of the Shchekino experiment have been made available to all enterprises, but in a fragmented form. This type of approach had been attempted once already, in the wage reform of the early seventies, with little appreciable success. It was argued then that the Shchekino experiment, in so far as it worked, achieved beneficial results because of the whole package of measures. The impact of the 1979 resolution, which appears to commit the same error, will be assessed in the next section. It should be noted that by 1980, the regulations for the implementation of the Shchekino experiment had been amended no less than seven times, (this does not include those other economic policy measures that have a tangential bearing on the experiment) and given the complexity and contradictions within the instructions anyway, these instabilities helped little to promote the experiment's generalisation (Cherednichenko and Gol'din, pp. 199–202).

THE SHCHEKINO EXPERIMENT IN THE AFTERMATH OF THE 1979 PLANNING RESOLUTION

After the introduction of the 1979 planning resolution, the pressure for the implementation of the Shchekino experiment remained. In the mineral fertiliser industry, for example, the importance of which has already been noted, the planned task was to increase output by over 48 per cent in the five year plan period (Borodin, 1983, p. 3). However, during the years of the Tenth Plan, the industry had seen its workforce grow by almost 24 per cent, but during the Eleventh Plan it could only expect the size of the workforce to grow by approximately six per cent, even though it had been estimated that it would require growth of at least 17.7 per cent to achieve the planned tasks (Fil'ev, 1983, p. 58). Hence the significance of the further implementation of the experiment, either to tighten internal labour organisation and release surplus workers in this industry or to do the same elsewhere and direct the freed workers into this industry. This situation was replicated in a host of other sectors and as Fil'ev (p. 58) notes what was needed was a 'socio–economic instrument to utilise labour rationally'.

At the Shchekino plant itself the experiment was still continuing and the summary of results for the period from 1967–81 still appears impressive, even after the difficulties the plant had experienced. The volume of production had risen 3.1 times since 1966, labour productivity was up 4.1 times and 1814 personnel had been released or 23 per cent of the initial total workforce (Fil'ev, p. 59). It is significant to note that there is hardly any alteration in the sources of labour saving over the whole period, as shown on Table 8.1. A further significant point is that such a small percentage of the workforce were released through automation and mechanising manual tasks, which illustrates both the problems at Shchekino and the more general problem of innovation and providing the fixed equipment to shed labour in this manner.

The 466 ITR released represented 37 per cent of the total ITR at the

Table 8.1   The sources of labour saving at the Shchekino
plant 1967–80

Reason for release	Number	(%)
Job combination, new norms, widening service zones	725	54
Mechanising manual work	71	5.3
Automating processes	67	5.0
Centralising and specialising auxiliary work	198	14.8
Rationalising laboratory work	154	11.5
Other measures	119	8.9
Total workers released	1 334	
Total ITR released	466	

Source: Fil'ev (1983), p. 59

start of the experiment and were released as a consequence of rationalising the management structure, condensing work and a variety of other similar measures. Likewise at the Bashkir Petro-Chemical Association, mentioned in Chapter 6, the experimental variant had been continued throughout the Tenth Five Year Plan and output had been increased by 22 per cent, whilst the workforce had been cut by 4600 (Mironov, 1981, p. 2). The experiment was still being introduced, at some Soviet enterprises for the first time, with good effect. For example, at an enterprise cited by Zharikov (1979, p. 47), the introduction of the experiment in 1978 led to a reduction of the workforce by 1500 and labour productivity growth of 38 per cent.

Furthermore, enterprises leaving the experiment fared badly. Aganbegyan (1982, p. 3) cites the example of an enterprise in Omsk, where in the early seventies labour productivity had been growing at four per cent per annum but after switching to the experiment this rose to eight per cent per annum. The plant, which previously had been 200 workers below full complement, was able, after the introduction of the experiment, to release 2000 workers and still raise output. However, in the mid-seventies at the behest of its ministry, the enterprise halted the experiment and as a consequence, over the whole of the Tenth Five Year Plan, was only able to raise labour productivity by twelve per cent. In the first two years of the Eleventh Plan this had fallen even lower and the enterprise had come a complete circle and is now experiencing labour shortages.

In a more general sense, during the years of the Tenth Five Year Plan, the experiment had released 968 000 workers, six per cent of the industrial workforce, and 433 000 of these workers had been re-integrated into vacant posts or new shops at the same enterprise (Batkaev and Semin, 1983, p. 44). Over the period from 1978, when the new regulations were introduced, a number of ministries increased the number of enterprises operating on the full experiment, as shown on Table 8.2.

However, the effect of the 1979 planning resolution on the dissemination of the experiment was to establish two types of enterprises. There were some enterprises that fully implemented the whole package of Shchekino measures and others that implemented some parts of the experiment. By early 1981, Fil'ev (p. 59) argued that 2003 enterprises were operating on the full Shchekino experiment and a further 7251 enterprises and associations had implemented elements of the experiment. Batkaev and Semin (p. 44), suggest that by the end of 1981 the figure had risen to 11 710 enterprises, employing more

Table 8.2   Number of enterprises operating on the
Shchekino experiment by ministry

	1978	1981
Food industry	57	311
Chemical & fertiliser industry	160	216
Light industry	36	161
Petro-chemical machine building	35	83

Source: Batkaev & Semin (1983), p. 44.

than 21 million workers. Radov (1981a, p. 2) notes that 216 000
people were released, 205 000 of whom were workers, and 40 per cent
of these were well qualified and filled posts at newly commissioned
production facilities that otherwise would have remained unmanned.
Clearly, the experiment remained an important mechanism for releasing workers.

Furthermore, the Shchekino experiment, as previously noted, was
not intended to be applied solely to the industrial labour force. By the
early eighties, it had also been introduced into a number of other
sectors of the economy, with similar beneficial short-run results,
although Soviet sources remain critical of its uneven distribution
(Batkaev, 1979, p. 33). For example, in 1980 the Shchekino experiment was extended to service workers in hotels, which are characterised by significant labour shortages. Pak (1980, p. 13), cites the
example of four Soviet hotels where the planned level of staffing is
4677 workers who are responsible for a maximum 7400 guests. In one
of the hotels, the planned staffing level actually exceeds the maximum
number of guests! Nevertheless, the hotels are unable to attract a
sufficient number of staff, hence the appeal of the Shchekino experiment, if it can tighten internal labour organisation and encourage job
combination.

Furthermore, the experiment was further extended in the transport
sector of the economy (Molchanov and Titskii, 1982, pp. 61–4). In
1981, it was introduced into both the maritime fleet and river
transport fleet where, as a result of job combination and widening
service zones, over 31 000 workers were released (Batkaev and Semin,
1983, p. 45). Also by 1981, the experiment was operating in 431
sovkhoz and 230 enterprises of the Goskomsel 'khoztekhniki (p. 45).
This resulted in enhanced output, productivity and increased average
wages. At one sovkhoz in the Crimea, for example, labour producti-

vity had increased 2.4 times over the eight years of the experiment's operation.

It would appear, because of the further implementation of the experiment in industrial branches, its extension to new areas and its continuation at plants like Shchekino and Bashkir, that the changes in regulations had been successful. However, closer inspection yields a series of problems that qualify the effectiveness of the experiment and still deter enterprises from making the transition to it. It should also be noted that the chemical industry, even though it was still one of the most advanced proponents of the experiment, was explicitly criticised in 1980 for lagging behind the needs of the economy (Brezhnev, 1980, p. 1). So the experiment was certainly no cure-all, even in industries where it was conscientiously applied.

In the 11 710 enterprises operating on the experiment in 1981, in comparison with 1980, labour productivity grew by an average of 3.4 per cent, whereas in non-Shchekino enterprises labour productivity grew by less than 1.5 per cent over the same period (Batkaev and Semin, 1983, p. 44). Obviously the Shchekino-like enterprises are doing better than their counterparts, but the fragmentation of the experiment has yielded much lower productivity gains than were achieved in the early days of the experiment.

Also the material incentive elements of the experiment were maintained at a similar level during this period. In 1982, as a result of the operation of the experiment, the total savings to the wages fund were approximately 400 million roubles and 1.4 million workers received wage supplements. But if 21 million workers are in enterprises operating on the experiment, this implies that only 6.6 per cent are receiving any direct material incentive from the experiment. The average wage supplement was a little over 20 roubles and, although for some skilled workers this might rise to as much as 35 to 40 roubles, for the vast majority of workers it is an unimpressive material incentive (Aperin, 1983, p. 6).

The scale of the dissemination of the experiment also has to be placed in context. Even though the percentage of workers employed in enterprises operating on either full or partial Shchekino lines has risen, (according to Aparin (p. 6) this figure reached 70 per cent by the end of 1982), only six per cent of the industrial enterprises in the RSFSR are utilising the full experiment and in the USSR as a whole the proportion is no higher (Valavoi, Nikitin and Shvetsov, 1982, p. 3). As Grotseskul (1982, p. 3) has commented, the real benefits of the Shchekino experiment are only achieved if it is implemented fully in stable conditions. The partial implementation of the system does little real good, but does serve as a cosmetic change and inflates the figures for the experiment's dissemination. This is a repetition of what occurred in the period after the wage reforms in the early seventies. As Mirgaleev (1982, p. 3) and Baranenkova (1980, p. 55) note, the opportunity to implement the experiment on a partial basis should not be seen as a substitute for full implementation where possible. In a study of RSFSR enterprises in the year after the 1979 planning resolution had been implemented, it was found that the full Shchekino system freed 50 per cent more workers than any partial Shchekino-like changes.

Even though the 1979 resolution demands wage fund and plan stability as the basis for the implementation of the experiment, this is still not being achieved and is bemoaned by virtually all commentators (Aganbegyan, 1982, p. 2; Nikitin, 1982, p. 2; Grotseskul, 1980, p. 2; Batkaev, 1979, p. 35). The Shchekino director, Melent'ev (1982, p. 3), points out that during the Tenth Five Year Plan, as in the Ninth, the wage fund at Shchekino was further reduced, this time by 1.3 million roubles. Even though this action is contrary to the resolution, unstable wage funds are still the norm. In an interview cited by Radov, (1981a, p. 2), he complains that a combination of small wage supplements and the claw-back of economised funds hinders the experiment's progress. Also during the Tenth Five Year Plan the Shchekino plant did not build one house or apartment for its workers because of the lack of funds. This represents a continuation and worsening of a problem noted earlier.

At the Bashkir Association, whilst productivity had increased by 24 per cent in five years, average wages had only risen by eight per cent because of wage fund instability (Mironov, 1981, p. 2). Ministries effectively ignore the advances made by these experimental enterprises. Furthermore, in the case of the mineral fertiliser industry cited above, its task of increasing productivity and overcoming the labour shortage was made more difficult by the fact that its overall wage fund was 280 million roubles less than it should have been (Borodin, 1983, p. 3). This makes it virtually impossible to implement the Shchekino experiment more widely, as the ministry is effectively asking for simultaneous increases in productivity and cuts in wage funds from its subordinate enterprises.

There still remains a degree of arbitrariness in the way the planners determine plans both for output and for subsidiary objectives, like the reduction of managerial and administrative staff. This is determined on a flat percentage basis and, as a consequence, discriminates against enterprises who have already reduced their administrative ranks by implementing the Shchekino experiment by giving them the same percentage target as enterprises which have not. Mironov points out that the Bashkir plant has labour costs equal to one third of the average engineering plant's costs, but receives similar targets for workforce reduction, which he argues is clearly unfair. Enterprise management can then reasonably argue that if the reduction is going to be administered from outside, why bother with the Shchekino initiative, because if you do implement the experiment you are at an immediate disadvantage when the targets are imposed. In both respects this further slows the introduction of the experiment. It has been argued that enterprises implementing the experiment should be excluded from the targets for staff reduction or, alternatively, that the size of the administrative staff should be assessed as a percentage of the total workforce and not as a simple flat rate reduction (Mironov, 1981, p. 2). This would require a greater degree of sophistication from planners, as differing production conditions would require a different ratio between managerial and administrative staff and the total workforce. The point is that in its present form the mechanism does not help the wider dissemination of the experiment.

Similar problems arise because statutes in one area still operate to negate initiatives in another. This results from the bureaucratic complexity of the Soviet economic mechanism. For example, until the early eighties, job combination could impair pension rights and, hence, when workers realised this they refused to combine jobs or reversed their previous decisions. This was only resolved by the new conditions for job combination (*Izvestia*, 9 January 1982, p. 2). It is interesting to note that the largest increments for job combination, up to 50 per cent of the basic wage, were for loading and unloading work, a problem area previously noted.

A further problem emerges from the experience of the Polimir Association (Novozhilov, 1980, p. 8). Here the introduction of the Shchekino experiment had encouraged the workers in a number of production shops to master all the skills in their shift and the consequence had been a reduction of workers per shift from thirteen to nine. The introduction of computerised control mechanisms had reduced the managerial staff, and the reorganisation of services like internal transport had led to further workforce reductions. The net effect had been to raise output by a factor of two, productivity by a factor of three and significant gains had been made in labour discipline. However, this successful enterprise is continually dogged by difficulties because the integrated technological nature of its production process makes it highly dependent upon good quality equipment. A breakdown in any section can bring the whole enterprise to a halt. Consequently, poor reliability and durability of equipment, coupled with a lack of spare parts reduces the effectiveness of the enterprise. This simple example shows that isolated success can easily be negated. This problem will remain unresolved unless all the enterprises in the supply chain switch to the experiment and product quality and availability change dramatically as a consequence.

All the points noted above refer to pressures operating against the implementation of the experiment at plant level and impeding its generalisation, but there is another dimension that requires consideration. When the experiment is introduced, it is implemented by an individual enterprise or by a series of enterprises at the behest of their ministry, but there is no necessary localised linkage between these plants. The potential localised problems this generates can be explained by considering the example of the Shchekino enterprise itself. In the early period, as already noted, a high proportion of the released labour was reabsorbed at the plant to fill existing vacancies or to man new production facilities. In this sense, the experiment is concerned with the internal reorganisation of one enterprise within one ministry. However, the ultimate aim is to bring about a freeing and redistribution of labour in a wider sense. One problem, noted previously, is that the labour released under the terms of the experiment is, by definition, likely to be absorbed into plants where the experiment is not in operation and where labour organisation is lax. As a consequence, no overall gains may arise. Furthermore, if the enterprise implementing the experiment runs into difficulties, as indeed the Shchekino plant did, workers may well leave the enterprise and avoid the experiment. In order to overcome this, attempts were made to disseminate the experiment to other enterprises within the locality. Given that the chain of economic and planning control is predominantly vertical, through the hierarchical structure of ministries, associations and enterprises, this horizontal co-ordination was primarily sponsored by the city party Soviet. The former director of Shchekino, Sharov, headed a city party committee, which spread the experiment to thirty eight collectives in both industrial and agricultural sectors in the area (Grotseskul, 1983, p. 2). By the early eighties, as Grotseskul (1982, p. 3) points out, nearly all the enterprises in

Shchekino, producing 90 per cent of the city's industrial output were operating on Shchekino lines. Furthermore, the experiment has been extended to the service and transport sectors. However, even in this context there is a long way to go to achieve real control over the utilisation of labour, because in the province of Tula as a whole there is an acute labour shortage which could only be resolved if the experiment was generalised even further into the countryside.

What is being suggested by the Soviet sources is that the Shchekino experiment should be extended in two directions. Firstly, the experiment should be comprehensively implemented in all the enterprises of one ministry. This is part of the inention of the economic experiment implemented by Andropov from January 1st 1984 (*Izvestia*, 2 January 1984, p. 2; *Ekonomicheskaya Gazeta*, 1984, No. 30, p. 2). The instructions for the ministries chosen for the experiment include all the major elements of the Shchekino experiment (Khadzhinov, 1983, p. 6; Simenenko, 1983, p. 7). For example, enterprises have a degree of freedom to reduce staff and use retained funds as bonuses. Enterprises have been given some discretion over the size and distribution of bonuses and are allowed to pay temporary bonuses. Special bonuses are available for job combination and in order to retain highly skilled workers.

Secondly, it has been suggested that the experiment should be extended not just vertically through a ministry but also horizontally through a particular region (Grotseskul, 1983, p. 3). This would have the advantage of coordinating the labour force across different boundaries of ministerial responsibility. Grotseskul points out that the Tula province would be ideal for such an experiment for a number of reasons. Not only was it the home of the original experiment, but also more than half of the province's industrial enterprises are already operating on the experiment and this is scheduled to rise even further during the Eleventh Five Year Plan. As the province has a severe labour resource problem, the implementation of a region-wide Shchekino initiative would allow greater coordination and direction of labour resources. Implicit in this is even further controls over the placement of workers released. As Dyker (1981, pp. 60–1) has pointed out, more Shchekino without more control is the recipe for greater turnover and wastage.

There are precedents for this type of initiative. An experiment in the agricultural sector was established at Abasha in Georgia in 1973 (Tchitanava, 1978, pp. 2–3). This was an attempt to group together, at a *raion* level, existing kolkhoz, sovkhoz and related organisations under one controlling body. This then provided a variety of material and financial incentives for workers and its success led to its adoption by other neighbouring *raions*, and from January 1st 1982, it was generalised throughout the republic. In March 1982 the wider dissemination of the experiment was pressed for throughout the whole of the USSR (*Pravda*, 11 March 83, p. 2).

Attempts were also made to transfer the experiment to an urban area at Poti in Georgia (Lebanidze, 1983, p. 2). This experiment illustrates the type of difficulties a horizontal Shchekino experiment could contribute towards. In Poti there were between 60 and 70 enterprises under the jurisdiction of 30 different ministries. This resulted in poor organisation of resources and little local coordination between enterprises. Overall, this resulted in a number of disparities in wages, housing and living conditions and levels of capacity utilisation. At the local level, the municipal authorities are powerless as enterprises relate upwards through the ministerial hierarchy. What the experiment instituted was a series of local linkages via a body known as the Territorial Inter-Branch Association, which was responsible for coordinating economic development in the municipal area. For example, a register of the various waste products from the different enterprises was set up and attempts were made to utilise these for the production of consumer goods needed locally. This is not unlike the attempts to set up 'networks' by local councils in the UK, as a localised response to job losses. Further initiatives involve setting up more enterprises to meet local needs and the possible linking of the town with nearby rural areas to extend the experiment.

It is an extension of this type of initiative that Sharov, Grotseskul and Melent'ev have called for in the Tula province. Nevertheless, it is instructive to note that almost eighteen years after the initial experiment was established, after no less than seven changes in the regulations for the implementation of the experiment plus changes in regulations referring to subsidiary elements, like job combination, work norms, labour turnover and so on, Soviet sources are still complaining about the slow dissemination of the experiment and citing similar reasons for this phenomenon. This suggests that the problems facing the experiment are much deeper than the administrative and institutional causes so far identified by Soviet sources. This question is taken up in the next section.

THE DISSEMINATION OF THE SHCHEKINO
EXPERIMENT AND THE LOGIC OF SOVIET PLANNING

As pointed out in the previous section, the Soviet response to the problem of the non-generalisation of the experiment was almost entirely administrative and sought to solve the problems by changing the instructions for its implementation. However, the non-generalisation is explicable by considering the underlying principles of the experiment in relation to the logic of Soviet planning and then relating this in turn to the political economy of the USSR. This latter task will be undertaken in the final chapter, after a number of other experimental initiatives have been considered.

The immediate paradox to be explained is that the Shchekino plant and the other experimental enterprises could successfully implement the experiment but still fail. For the individual enterprise, at Shchekino or elsewhere, the successful implementation of the experiment did not lead to an unambiguous strengthening of their position *vis-à-vis* their ministry, other enterprises, central planning bodies or their workforce.

The Shchekino plant, for example, was both successful and a well-known prestige project for the chemical industry. Nevertheless, this could not be translated by plant management into increased access to the necessary resources for investment and expansion; it gave the plant little or no advantage over other enterprises in the ministerial allocative process or in retaining or attracting skilled workers; it led to the eventual loss of sections of its workforce because of the removal of bonuses and the eventual poor provision of housing; and it weakened its position in relation to the chemical ministry, making it more dependent, as its safety factor had been removed. Overall it made the enterprise more vulnerable to plan underfulfilment and failure.

In comparison, consider a firm under the capitalist mode of production which had managed to introduce an innovatory form of work organisation that increased the productivity of the labour it employed. The benefits of increased exploitation would lead to an increase in the relative surplus value extracted and would be reflected in a higher than average rate of profit for the firm. This would yield direct advantages for the firm and would allow it to increase the level of investment, either through the use of retained profits or from its ability to attract external funds. In other words, success in the extraction of relative surplus value from the labour employed will be reflected in improved access to funds in the capital markets. Furthermore, other firms failing to follow the innovatory move will find their relative failure also reflected in their access to investment funds and the possibility of failure will emerge. In other words the dynamic of changes in the process of surplus extraction will be an external constraint upon all firms. A link exists between the efficiency of the surplus extraction process and the success and failure of the firm, not just as an isolated success, but as a dynamic process through time. This dynamic creates repercussions in both labour and capital markets. Labour organisation which is successful will be replicated elsewhere and resources will shift towards the innovatory firm and its imitators.

With regard to the Shchekino experiment in the USSR, the process almost worked in reverse. In so far as investment funds are still allocated by an administrative process from the centre, the successful implementation of the experiment gives no direct advantage. Remember that savings in the wage fund could not be translated into improved access to capital equipment or plant, only into increasing individual wages or collective consumption at the enterprise, and over time even this discretion was eroded. In so far as the individual plant's safety factor is reduced (and the problems that made it necessary in the first instance are not removed from the economy as a whole), the enterprise may well be in a worse position than previously and may well be more vulnerable to failure.

How is this vulnerability to be explained? I would argue that the ministries simply conform in this respect to the logic of the Soviet planning process. If an enterprise is successful from the point of view of the ministry, it could be viewed as a lesser priority than an unsuccessful enterprise. Hence it makes sense, in the short run, to transfer economised wage funds from a successful Shchekino-type enterprise to an enterprise which may be experiencing labour shortages, or to utilise these economised funds for hiring staff for new production capacity that may be otherwise unmanned. Given that the option of closing an enterprise down and transferring its resources from one location to another is limited both practically and politically, the ministry has to nurse along both innovatory and backward enterprises. The ministry is, after all, responsible for the entire output produced throughout the plants under its responsibility. Even though the Shchekino experiment introduced a method that was successful at some enterprises, it did not introduce a dynamic that unambiguously pressurised those enterprises which did not implement the experiment into adopting it. It introduced no mechanism to establish penalties for failure to introduce the experiment which could therefore be avoided. However salutary the impact of the experiment, its implementation remained at the discretion of ministries and enterprises, to whom it did not appear as an unavoidable necessity. As already noted, it is unlikely that any ministry could implement the experiment throughout all its enterprises simultaneously, given the negative control operated by the workforce even over experimental initiatives. Therefore, plants not operating on Shchekino lines would not necessarily have suffered and may indeed have benefited after the initial infatuation with the experimental plants. The experiment did not force enterprises to fail. This is clearly different from capitalism in general, where enterprises which fail to innovate go under.

Those who attempt to argue that the USSR is simply a giant statified 'capital' competing on the world market try to draw comparisons between the 'USSR Ltd' and multi-national corporations. However, the analogy is totally false. In a large multi-national, multi-plant firm there are no constraints of the sort identified above. The decision to close peripheral or branch plants is dictated by the same forces that determine whether competitive individual capitals survive. The law of value enforces its logic upon all firms, whether they are competitive, oligopolistic or monopolistic, multi-national or based in one country. However, that logic clearly does not penetrate the Soviet economy. If it did, experiments like Shchekino would either work or would be unnecessary in the first place.

A further question that needs to be considered is the differential diffusion of the experiment. Thus far, it has been explained as the result of the traditional bias in the Soviet planning system towards Department One industries but this needs further consideration.

It could be linked to the simple fact that some ministries are more innovative than others and, therefore, more supportive of the experimental initiatives. This explanation rests upon the chance element of staffing and personnel at ministry level. As staff changes it would be expected that the dissemination of the experiment would fluctuate. However, the uneven pattern of diffusion appears to remain over time. Therefore, this does not appear to be a particularly persuasive explanation.

Perhaps it is more convincing to argue that ministries adopt experimental initiatives if they are under particular pressure to improve their performance, within the overall economic performance. This was certainly the case with the chemical industry, which was, and still is, a high priority sector. Hence, state planning agency, ministry and enterprise attention will focus on specific problems and from this unity of purpose success will be achieved in particular sectors. However, as the focus moves away from these priority sectors no similar coincidence of interests exists and experimental initiatives will either not be introduced or if they are, only in a half-hearted manner. This, however, cannot be a complete explanation as there are problem sectors, like construction and agriculture, which in some senses appear tailor-made for the experiment, particularly given the labour-shedding potential of both sectors, yet it was not widely disseminated within either of them.

Finally, it could be argued that ministries resist the implementation of the experiment because it threatens their secure existence. As noted, ministries also have a vested interest in maintaining a degree of slack, *vis-à-vis* other ministries, as it allows room for manœuvre. Perhaps, therefore, low prestige and low priority ministries see the implementation of the experiment as undermining their already weak position and making them even more vulnerable. After all, there is no guarantee that the labour shed from one of their enterprises, in the course of tightening labour organisation, will be necessarily redeployed into other enterprises of the same ministry. In fact, the ultimate logic of the experiment could not provide such a guarantee, as radical redeployment of surplus workers is precisely its eventual aim. Furthermore, ministries may have perceived the experiment as an exercise in introducing greater enterprise autonomy and this could have increased their resistance to its dissemination. In reality, these arguments are difficult to sustain as the impact of the experiment, in those ministries most actively pressing for its generalisation, was to strengthen the ministry's position in relation to its subordinate enterprises, rather than the reverse. The enterprises became more dependent upon ministry level decisions, as their safety factor was cut, thus increasing their vulnerability and the possibilities of failure.

I would argue that there is a relationship between the dissemination of the experiment and the nature of work organisation and control in different branches of Soviet industry, both the actual forms of control prior to the implementation of the experiment and the possibilities of control after its implementation. Where direct producers had most control over the nature of their work and its intensity, in sectors like coal mining and construction, for example, the experiment was hardly implemented at all. However, in sectors with a higher degree of technologically based production and where work intensities were more amenable to technical control, the experiment was implemented

more successfully. For example, where line speeds are in part determined by automated or semi-automated production techniques, it
appears easier to implement the experiment. Again, the chemical
industry is a good example. From the point of view of enterprise
management in these sectors, the experiment could be viewed as a
method of breaching the traditional control exercised by the direct
producers and thereby allowing the introduction of further technically determined work patterns and intensities. This could also
explain the previously noted link between the introduction of the
experiment and the importation of foreign technology. The desire to
utilise this as efficiently as possible and to imitate manning levels in
the countries of origin would forge a link between the incidence of
imported technology and the introduction of the experiment. This
suggests, therefore, that the differential spread of the experiment
reflects the possibilities of partially modifying the degree of direct
producer control over their own labour process. This is another
example of the way in which the experiment accommodated to
existing Soviet industrial realities rather than radically transforming
them.

Ultimately, it is very difficult to provide an unambiguous answer to
the question why the experiment spread in a differentiated manner.
Similar difficulties are attached to the question of why different
ministries had different degrees of success when the experiment was
actually implemented. It could be that the experiment was applied
with varying degrees of intensity in different branches, or that initial
manning levels were very different or because of differing degrees of
ministry, enterprise management or worker resistance to the experiment. The point is, however, that the experiment introduced no new
dynamic to the Soviet planning system that would equalise manning
levels between disparate or even similar enterprises, pressurise ministries or enterprises into implementing the experiment or identify
unambiguously those enterprises which were failures.

There are limits to the potential achievements of the experiment
which will increase the possibility of failure for the individual enterprise. The rational enterprise manager will need to evaluate the costs
and benefits of implementing the experiment. Clearly many recognised the problems the experiment entailed, as increasing vulnerability was brought about by a combination of shifting plan targets,
reductions in the wage fund, failures to receive investment in either
new capacity or the renewal of plant and equipment, all against the

backdrop of reduced numbers of workers, the traditional way of dealing with such uncertainties.

Furthermore, if all enterprises did not simultaneously implement the experiment then, given the apparent labour shortages, workers would simply move to plants where work intensity was lower and rewards similar. The combination of these problems made the experiment a liability because, ultimately, enterprise management recognised that the success of the enterprise, still the key to their own success, would be constrained by the external environment which would not necessarily have changed. In other words, the operation of the planning system contradicts the logic of the experiment and will ultimately retard its dissemination. This is, therefore, an argument which suggests that neither enterprise management nor ministry personnel perceived the experiment to be unambiguously in their own interest; and as it set up no spontaneous dynamic that forced its implementation upon enterprises or ministries, it was avoided. This cannot be the final answer to the question, as it fails to explain why the planning system constrains the experiment and why the necessary dynamic is absent. This can only be explained after a consideration of other experimental initiatives which had similar intentions. The broader issue of the relationship between the political economy of the USSR and all of these experimental initiatives will be taken up in more detail in the final chapter.

9 Alternative Attempts to Assert Control Over the Labour Process

The Shchekino experiment and its variants were not the only attempts at reform that sought to alter the ruling group's control over the process of surplus extraction. Throughout the 1970s there were a series of experimental initiatives that ran parallel to the Shchekino experiment. These were partially derived from it and were either responses to the problems it encountered or were extensions of some of its elements. Some of the initiatives were more direct attempts to solve problems that the Shchekino experiment had only indirectly tackled. For example, the introduction of technically validated norms was an indirect consequence of the introduction of the Shchekino experiment but the major aim of the experiments initiated at the Aksai and Dinamo plants. All of these experiments can be viewed as alternative attempts to resolve the problems identified in Figure 3.1, by tackling the central question of control over the labour process.

This chapter cannot cover comprehensively all the experimental initiatives, but will consider a number of the most important that sought to bring about changes in the labour process.[1] The major portion of the chapter will consider the 'Brigade System' of labour organisation because of its importance and the close parallels between this initiative and the Shchekino experiment, both in intention and experience. The latter part of the chapter will consider the experimental initiatives concerned with work norms and wages introduced at the Aksai Plastics plant, the Dinamo plant and the Volga Automobile Plant.

THE INTRODUCTION OF THE ZLOBIN BRIGADE SYSTEM IN THE CONSTRUCTION INDUSTRY

The occurrence of labour discipline problems, as already suggested, is most acute where labour has greatest control over the nature and manner of its work. This is particularly the case in occupations which are difficult to physically supervise and where the pace of work is not determined to any great degree by technology. Perhaps the best example of this is the construction industry where in the early seventies two out of every three workers were manual workers (Novokshonov, 1975, p. 3). The USSR has a long history of problems in this sector, absenteeism and poor discipline and work quality being perennial problems. To supervise adequately the pace and quality of work of each worker would require even more supervisory staff and in conditions of apparent labour shortage, this is obviously not feasible. Therefore, it is not surprising that a major reform initiative was instituted in the construction sector in 1970 (Zelinchonok and Milyavskii, 1970, p. 2). This was originally known as the 'Zlobin Brigade System', named after the brigade leader of the first brigade to initiate the system, but later it became better known as the *khozraschet* or 'Contract Brigade System'. This experiment is an interesting attempt to change the process of surplus extraction in an industry where the Shchekino experiment appeared to have had little impact. The underlying principle of the experiment is a recognition that in the construction industry managerial control over the labour process is exceptionally difficult. Therefore, the experiment seeks to make the workforce, or small groups of workers, discipline each other. The basic operation of the experiment was that a definable sub-section of a particular building project was contracted out to a brigade of workers. For example, in the initial case of the Zlobin brigade, this was the work of constructing the shell of a building. The construction administration would contract to supply the workers with the necessary resources, tools and documentation and a contract would be set for the job and agreed with the brigade. Workers would not be paid any bonuses, but if, in the process of construction, they could economise in terms of time, labour expenditures or raw materials, 50 per cent of the savings made would accrue to them. Effectively the brigade can benefit from any savings it can make, but by the same token any losses incurred or delays would come out of the collective rewards of the brigade (Zelinchonok and Milyavskii, 1971, p. 2). This was an attempt to stimulate the self-interest of brigade members and use this as a mechanism of discipline. From the outset, Zlobin's brigade pledged to increase labour productivity by 25 per cent, reduce the time needed for their particular part of the construction process by 40 to 45 days and reduce overall costs by 25 000–30 000 roubles. In fact, the initial results were even more dramatic as the job was finished 80 days early and labour productivity rose by 36 per cent. The Zlobin brigade required only 2.34 man days per square metre of construction in comparison with 3.67 man days per square metre in a traditional brigade (Zelichonok and Milyavskii, 1970, p. 2). For workers in the Zlobin brigade, bonuses as a result were 50 per cent higher than in comparable brigades and as Zlobin himself points out, labour and production discipline improved dramatically (Agronovskii, 1971, p. 2). Absenteeism, drunkenness at work, overly long smoke breaks and general tardiness became a thing of the past in the Zlobin brigade, as workers perceived these activities to be detrimental to their own interests. Furthermore, when the brigade was over-allocated raw materials it refused to accept them as they would have to be paid for out of the brigade's contracted funds and would, therefore, have reduced their potential profitability. This economising attitude to raw materials is in direct comparison to the usual Soviet response to this type of situation. Normally, the response would be to accept the over-allocation, which would involve no financial penalties. The resource would then be stockpiled for later use as the enterprise or work team can confidently expect later supply problems. Alternatively, the resources could be utilised for barter purposes to obtain some other deficit resource. After their first successes, the Zlobin brigade went on to reduce building time even further on their next assignment. The apparent success of the experiment lead the Construction Ministry from early 1971 onwards to call for its wider dissemination within the industry (Zelichonok and Milyavskii, 1971, p. 2).

However, very early in the life of the experiment criticisms emerged, suggesting that the experience was atypical. For example, it was pointed out that the real originators of the experiment, Demestyev and Loholin, chose Zlobin deliberately because of his past excellent record of work organisation (Agronovskii, 1971, p. 2). Perhaps with lesser leadership the experiment would fare less well.

Furthermore, and more importantly, the leader of a rival brigade, which worked on the same construction project as the Zlobin brigade and which was used as a comparison to illustrate the advances made by Zlobin's brigade, pointed out that any comparison was unrealistic. He argued that although the Zlobin brigade did not necessarily receive 'special' conditions, they did, nevertheless, get first delivery of raw materials. Also when it was realised that one portion of the work could be accomplished better with a second crane, the Zlobin brigade were able, out of their allocated funds, to obtain one. They had to pay for it, but recognised the advantages in terms of cutting work time and making economies and therefore raising their bonuses. As Zlobin's rival commented, this kind of discretion was not unfair, even though this option was not available to them, but was simply what should be normal practice. However, the problem is that ease of supply and access to both specialist equipment and basic tools is not 'normal', not just for Soviet industry, but especially for the construction sector. Novokshonov (1975, p. 3) points out that even the provision of basic tools, costing twenty roubles, can double labour productivity, but only between a fifth and a seventh of the normed number of tools are actually supplied to construction workers. The point is that it may be possible to set up isolated brigades of workers who can achieve impressive results, but this is predicated upon the failures of other brigades to receive adequate support. Eventually this is irrelevant to the problems facing the Soviet ruling group, unless it is possible to generalise the experience and simultaneously change all work teams.

By early 1971 twenty work collectives in the Moscow area had initiated the experiment and the construction industry, convinced of its potential, pressed for its extension. By the end of 1972, approximately 800 brigades were operating on Zlobin lines, 83 of which were in Moscow alone, but this was a minute proportion of the possible total number (Agronovskii, 1972, p. 1). This slow dissemination can be explained by a number of further problems that emerged, which either undermined the logic of the experiment or made it unattractive to workers and management alike.

From the point of view of management there is a problem in setting the experiment up. It has to be a clearly defined section of work with the correct documentation, financing and tooling. A clear idea of the schedule of work and a reasonable completion date are also essential. So, too, is some idea of the brigade's capacity and in the absence of branch or interbranch norms, past performance is not necessarily a good indicator. Furthermore, the original conception envisaged the brigade not to be responsible for site preparation, although some management took the short cut of including this in the contract and allowed the brigade to commence from an unprepared site. Given the potential problems of site preparation and the necessity for specialist equipment, this deterred workers from switching to the system. All these pre-conditions were essential if the contract was to be concluded, and problems with any element destroys the acceptability of the experiment to the workforce. On the other hand, overlong and complex preparation destroys the attractiveness of the system for management.

There was also a problem about who was responsible and for how much? The logic of the experiment is that a brigade performing exceptionally badly could be left with 'negative bonuses'. However, this contradicts articles of Soviet labour law that stipulate the degree of financial responsibility working people have for their work. Whilst workers can be held responsible for losses incurred by their enterprise, there are limits linked to wages and salaries (Livshitz and Nikitinsky, pp. 187–9). The combination of this ambiguity and the experiment's voluntary form further delayed its extension as workers could see the potential financial problems.

The logic of the experiment is that if management fail to supply the brigades with the necessary materials or tools, then a penalty should be paid by management to the brigades. Given the general difficulties of the material–technical supply system, this obviously limits the enthusiasm of management for an experiment, the conditions of which they will almost certainly not be able to control and which, by its operation, may lead to automatic bonuses for the brigades.

Finally, the material incentives that emerged from the system are not that attractive. This is partially for the reasons already noted, that money does not have a strong incentive effect as it is not the universal equivalent in the USSR. Nevertheless, the wage supplements that were paid were relatively small. Consider, for example, the first two buildings constructed by the Zlobin brigade. The first was built in 155 days and resulted in average daily wages of 11.29 roubles; the second building was constructed in only 82 days but the average daily wage only rose to 11.85 roubles (Agronovskii, 1972, p. 1). This is hardly a worthwhile incentive as a major increase in work intensity, cutting work time by 47 per cent, led to an increment in wages of less than five per cent.

In this early period there was also some criticism of the underlying ethos of the experiment. It was thought that it would stimulate greed and poor quality work. Zlobin, however, rejected these arguments by pointing out that the underlying principles of payment by results would bring benefits to everyone concerned and was not necessarily 'anti-socialist' (Zlobin, 1972, p. 2). For the workforce, apart from any material benefit, there were the benefits of release from working under the petty tutelage of management, thereby increasing satisfaction. Payment by results would also resolve problems of labour discipline. Zlobin argued that what ultimately harms Soviet workers is indiscipline, idleness and the opportunity to act in a 'non-socialist' manner. For management, apart from the obvious benefits of enhanced production from a more disciplined workforce, there would be freedom from petty supervisory tasks, like checking time-keeping and daily production and quality supervision, thus freeing trained cadres for more productive work. For the state, production projects would be completed, in itself a desirable step forward, with economies in wages, labour outlays, materials and time.

In order to overcome the potential problems of slipshod work, it was decided that the eventual share of the economised funds received by the brigade should be dependent upon the quality of the work performed. This was evaluated on a sliding scale, so that excellent quality work received the full 50 per cent, good quality work 30 per cent and satisfactory work ten per cent of the potential bonus (Parfenov, 1972, p. 1).

In the Moscow brigades set up in this early period, construction time was reduced by an average of 23.8 days, labour outlays were reduced by 28 per cent, labour productivity rose by 21.9 per cent and wage fund savings averaged six per cent (Agronovskii, 1972, p. 1). The major attractions of this experiment, having the workforce discipline itself and saving funds and materials in the process, was clearly recognised by the decree generalising the experiment (*Izvestia*, 20 July 1972, p. 1).

Around the end of 1972, the brigades became more widely known as '*khozraschet* brigades' (Zlobin, 1972, p. 2) and by this time 564 trusts and construction combines had switched to the new system. At this time approximately 2000 brigade contracts were in operation, achieving an average reduction in construction time of between thirteen and sixteen per cent (*Izvestia*, 4 March 1973, p. 1). However, over the same time period, the rate of unfinished construction projects continued to rise, and pressure to resolve the problems of the construction industry via the further generalisation of the brigade system increased (Gavin and Chernetskii, 1972, p. 3). By early 1973, in the construction ministry, only 351 out of an approximate total of 20 000 brigades were operating on the Zlobin system. In the Ministry for the Construction of Heavy Industrial Enterprises, only 358 brigades, out of a comparable potential number, were operating on the system (*Izvestia*, 4 March 1973, p. 1). This represents a rate of transfer of less than two per cent. In the Ministry of Rural Construction the percentage was even lower at around 1.5 per cent. There was also a noted regional variation as most brigades making the transition to the experiment were either in, or close to, major urban centres, particularly Moscow and Leningrad.

This again raises the interesting question of why an experimental initiative, after initial successes and ministerial and state support, failed to be generalised. Part of the explanation for this failure is resistance to the experiment on the part of enterprise management and ministries. This is the result of the problems connected with its initial implementation, which have already been noted (Baiderin and Turbanov, 1973, p. 5). Resistance to change at all levels of management is perhaps a rational, if short term, view particularly if the change engenders the possibility of failure. However, more significant problems can also be identified.

PROBLEMS IN THE GENERALISATION OF THE ZLOBIN SYSTEM: THE KALUGA AND OREL VARIANTS

The major difficulty with the original conception of the brigade system is that no work unit or economic unit, whether as small as a brigade or as large as an industry, operates in isolation from everyone else. In integrated production processes, a wide variety of work units necessarily interrelate, and the performance of the individual unit is always constrained by other units and the performance of the economy as a whole. However, the brigade system rests upon the principle that the brigade is rewarded or sanctioned for its own work, the conditions of which they cannot totally control. This problem has two dimensions.

The first major problem is the question of supply. The contract entered into by brigade and management is predicated upon expected future supply. The job's specification, the order of work and completion date and the worker's acceptance of the contract is all undertaken on the assumption that the necessary supplies of raw materials, tools, energy, plans and blueprints and whatever else the job requires will actually be delivered and delivered on time. If any of these elements are breached, no matter how hard the brigade works, their efforts will be irrelevant, as completion dates will be missed and the share in economised funds will be foregone as a consequence. In Lvov, for example, out of eighteen brigades switching to the system, ten failed to meet their contracts and returned to the old way of working, not because of failings in their work, but because of supply difficulties (Agronovskii *et al.*, 1973, p. 2). In Kursk in 1975, only 32 out of 70 brigades successfully completed their contracts because of supply difficulties, and even in the best brigades supply conditions were described as chaotic (London, 1977, p. 1). Similar examples are cited

by a variety of sources (Gavin and Chernetskii, 1972, p. 3; Sevast'yanov, 1973, p. 2; Kucherenko, 1975, p. 2).

In the face of these supply difficulties, one other possibility is that
brigades will turn to their own production of intermediate products or
tools. This type of do-it-yourself activity is self-defeating as it is
wasteful of the brigade's time, leads to poor quality work and non-
standardised items which are eventually more costly to produce in this
individualised form (*Pravda*, 18 June 1975, p. 2). Non-delivery is not
the only problem, because late delivery can destroy work patterns and
lead to arhythmic work patterns, which then disrupt the brigade's
efforts. Without stability in supply, workers will be reluctant to accept
brigade contract working because it makes their wages/bonuses
dependent upon forces which ultimately they cannot control. Far
better to accept a slightly lower, yet guaranteed wage (particularly if
the material incentives are small and weak due to the nature of money
and the lack of consumer goods) and allow the headaches involved in
supply failures to pass to lower level management (Sevast'yanov,
1974, p. 2). There is really no incentive for workers to become
involved with responsibilities that have traditionally fallen on
someone else.

Secondly the original conception of the experiment identified one
section of an otherwise integrated construction project and set up a
contract for its completion. In the case of Zlobin's brigade, as noted,
they were responsible for the erection of the building's external shell
and then other work teams of plasterers, electricians and finishers
would complete the building. This sets up the obvious problem of
dislocations between the work teams. For example, Zlobin's brigade
constructed their portion of an apartment building 100 days early but
the building remained unoccupied for a similar length of time because
of shortages of finishing workers (Agronovskii et al., 1973, p. 2). This
again indicates that these experimental initiatives are irrelevant unless
generalised, in the first instance around a particular construction site
or in a particular region.

Just as problems in the operation of the Shchekino experiment
gave rise to variants, the same thing happened with the brigade
system. In order to overcome the difficulty of dislocations between
brigades, a variant of the Zlobin system was established at Kaluga
(Sevast'yanov, 1972, p. 2). The organisation of work here was different in that all the brigades within the combine simultaneously
transferred to the *khozraschet* system and individual brigade success
was now dependent upon the success of all brigades. This, inevitably,

produced greater demands for correct phasing and rhythm of work. In order to maintain cohesion and discipline, the brigades at Kaluga were coordinated by an elected council of brigade leaders (Sevast'ya-nov, 1973, p. 2). At Kaluga the initial experience was promising, with construction time falling from 105 to 75 days, costs per square metre were cut, the quality of work improved and average wages rose. Furthermore, the Kaluga collective weeded out drifters, loafers and drunks throughout all the brigades and substantially improved labour discipline and cut labour turnover. This new collective form of contract appeared very desirable, as it reduced the problems of integration, but it also generated different problems concerned with the size and co-ordination of brigades, which will be examined later in this chapter.

A further problem, concerning the time horizon over which plan-ning decisions are made, gave rise to both a further variant or addition to the Zlobin system and an attempt to reorganise construc-tion at a city or regional level. This was initiated at Orel in April 1973 and was known as the Orel Continuous Planning System (*Ekonomi-cheskaya Gazeta*, 1975, No. 13, p. 9). The basic principle behind the system was the recognition that at a local level construction projects were the responsibility of a large number of clients. In Krasnodar in the mid-seventies, for example, there were 98 separate construction clients (*Izvestia*, 17 July 1976, p. 1). This leads to the spreading of resources, needless duplication and little co-ordination between the different ministries, eventually contributing to the high levels of incomplete construction projects. Abalkin (1982, p. 10), points out that in the early eighties almost 90 per cent of capital investment was work in progress. Furthermore, long construction delays mean that new enterprises reach their capacity after between five and seven years (Tikidzhiev, 1981, p. 47).

Therefore, the intention at Orel was to reorganise the administra-tion of construction and place it under a unified body, in this instance the City Soviet Committee for Capital Construction. This would then provide continuous planning of the city's construction projects and continuous flow construction with unified design and construction responsibilities. The idea was to plan construction projects over a rolling or continuous period, in order to concentrate resources in the short term and actually complete projects and provide continuity into the future.

It was suggested that the introduction of this system would reduce the number of building sites by 33 to 40 per cent, with a consequent reduction in the labour shortage, and achieve cuts in construction time of between fifteen and twenty per cent (*Izvestia*, 17 August 1976, p. 1). Continuous planning would assist in the reduction of idle-time generally by cutting the period between projects, and it was estimated that a 50 per cent cut in this could result in an increase in the value of construction amounting to two and a half billion roubles per annum (Dmitriyev, 1976, p. 6).

Implicit in this scheme is better labour organisation provided by the brigade system. However, the intention was that the system of continuous planning should be applied directly to the brigades themselves. The reason for this is that it is counter-productive if brigades complete contracts with great speed only to find there is no further scheduled work for them. Therefore, the intention was to apply continuous planning to brigades and provide them with plans stretching into the future, perhaps two to five years (Sukhanov, 1975, p. 3).

In fact, attempts to generalise the Orel system, on both levels of operation, have proceeded very slowly for two major reasons. Firstly, the narrow departmentalism of ministries has led to reluctance on their part to surrender control over building projects to any unified body. Secondly, continuous planning has proved very difficult to implement at any level. This is due, in part, to the sheer complexity of the task, but this is compounded by the all-pervasive uncertainty brought about by plan instability from above. The problems involved with coordination and experiments across ministries will also be returned to later.

Further problems can be identified that affect both workers, who have to be encouraged to adopt this sytem, and management, who are responsible for establishing the conditions for transfer, and these retard the experiment's dissemination. Sevast'yanov (1973, p. 2) suggest that 30 to 40 per cent of the reluctance can be attributed to the workforce, who are dubious about the advantages for them. The balance is managerial reluctance due to the integrated nature of construction, the resulting difficulty in setting up and defining brigade contracts, plus their fear of failure (Kucherenko, 1975, p. 2).

There are problems regarding the status of the brigades themselves. Their initial status was both temporary and voluntary, and the choice of making the transition to the system would be determined by localised circumstances. This increased the instability of existing brigades and added no impetus to the establishment of new brigades and the generalisation of the system. Furthermore, as with other experimental initiatives, complaints were raised regarding the complexity of the paperwork necessary for the transition to the experiment. As Turbanov (1974, p. 3) points out, it could take an official up to 40 days to process the necessary papers to transfer a brigade onto a contract, and it was not inconceivable that the task assigned could be completed before the paperwork. Another source suggests that it could take two specialists up to a month filling in the 24 forms necessary to transfer to the *khozraschet* system (*Izvestia*, 17 August 1976, p. 1).

However, perhaps the major problem, as brigades actually transferring to the system have complained, is that the experiment was not carried out in sufficiently stable conditions, either for all the benefits to emerge or for other brigades to be encouraged to follow their example and transfer to the *khozraschet* system. This has a number of aspects.

Successful brigades were often not allowed to complete the project they were working on but were shifted, by management, from project to project and used as construction 'trouble-shooters'. This may make sense from management's point of view, using a cohesive, well disciplined brigade to cover problems, particularly as management are concerned with overall plan fulfilment and not just isolated success in one or two brigades. However, the effect is to destroy the logic of the experiment and it will deter brigades from changing to this form of working (Gavin and Chernetskii, 1972, p. 3).

Futhermore, even when a brigade is allowed to finish a particular project, there is no guarantee that the next project will be a contract of the same type. For example, Zlobin's brigade was switched from the construction of apartments to school building to house construction and so on, thereby losing any advantages to be gained from specialisation (Agronovskii *et al.*, 1973, p. 2).

Finally, there was no guarantee that norms would remain constant and for Zlobin's brigade they were continually revised upwards until eventually average wages began to fall as contract time periods became tighter. Once again, a contradiction emerges between the operation of an experiment and the logic of Soviet planning practice, and this requires some explanation.

The logic of this experiment, like the Shchekino experiment, is to expose slack labour organisation and indiscipline, but here the novelty is to pass the onus for controlling this onto the workforce itself. In the case of Zlobin's brigade the original contract was set up without technically validated branch or inter-branch norms (Agronovskii, 1972, p. 1). The original calculation was based upon past practice and 'rules of thumb'. The brigade's actual performance would allow management to evaluate the accuracy of the original contract because any time saving could only emerge on the basis of management's mis-estimation of the brigade's capacity. However, this sets management a considerable dilemma. Logically, once this slack is identified they should set the brigade a new contract for the same job which reflects the new tighter work organisation. This would have the dual attraction, from management's viewpoint, of encouraging specialisation and further moving the brigade towards its actual capacity by raising work intensity. From the brigade's point of view, as management's assessment of their capacity becomes more accurate the potentiality for easy bonuses and controlling their own work diminishes and only by increasing their work intensity even further can bonuses be earned. Clearly, workers will resist contracts for the same job which demand an ever increasing work intensity with diminishing possibilities for rewards. This may well explain why management shift successful brigades from one type of work to another. In this way, they can capitalise on the increased organisation and tighter labour discipline and, at the same time, disguise the increasing intensity of work they are demanding. The cost of this strategy for management is the loss of the advantages of specialisation. It should be remembered that both workers and management will learn from their experience and this will condition the bargaining over contracts. The net effect will be a growing reluctance on the part of the workforce to accept more restrictive contractual terms. As with the operation of the Shchekino experiment, eventually a ceiling will be reached and the possibility of further success will not come from internal factors, but from outside the immediate control of the brigade, for example, retooling, technological change and so on.

Whatever strategy management adopt, the overall result will be that the experiment will have diminishing success. Planning from the achieved level may well be necessary, but it will ultimately destroy the will to implement the *khozraschet* brigade form of organisation and the inbuilt slowing of its momentum will discourage those brigades that have transferred to the system. Once again, stable plans and norms are essential in order to maintain the momentum of the experiment and to encourage its generalisation. However, central planners and ministries can neither provide these conditions nor allow lower echelons of management the degree of autonomy necessary to allow them to establish them.

By the middle of 1973, 6000 brigades had transferred to the Zlobin method of working. These brigades were achieving labour productivity figures approximately twenty per cent above comparable brigades and had cut construction times by between thirteen and sixteen per cent (Sevast'yanov, 1973, p. 2). Although this appears an impressive number, it should be noted that they represented only 2.4 per cent of the 250 000 brigades operate in the construction industry. Furthermore, Soviet commentators have noted that these figures are misleading, as many of the brigades had transferred in name alone, and that in reality both the ministry and local management were resisting the implementation of the system (Baiderin and Turbanov, 1973, p. 5).

As a consequence of the problems that had emerged and the criticisms levelled at the experiment, new regulations for the transfer of brigades to the system were introduced (*Pravda*, 27 January 1974, p. 3). The major thrust of the new regulations was to introduce an extension of the Kaluga variant, which made it necessary for all brigades working on a particular project, to transfer to the *khozraschet* system. The intention of this was to stem the problems of dislocation between *khozraschet* and non-*khozraschet* brigades. The hope was that if all brigades were operating on the same system, then all wages and bonuses would be linked to the completion of the project and all-round economies in time, labour and materials would be achieved. It should, however, be noted that this condition raises a number of problems.

It increases the complexity of management's task in setting up the contracts. Secondly, the possibility of failure for both management and the individual brigades is increased as all the brigades are now dependent upon one another. Formerly local management could assist the *khozraschet* brigade by giving them priority and switching resources to them at the expense of the non-*khozraschet* brigades. Management would do this because the success of these brigades would reflect favourably on them. Also, the *khozraschet* brigades could be used for special projects and by keeping the workers in these brigades within the terms of the contract, management would be able to retain them. (Remember it is likely that the 'best' brigades would be transferred to the system first.) The remuneration of workers in non-*khozraschet* brigades would not necessarily be impaired by this action. This would no longer be possible however, if the new regulations were strictly adherred to, as all brigades would have to transfer to the *khozraschet* system and therefore, all brigades would find their rewards linked to performance. This raises a series of pressures on management from below. All brigades would now demand the opportunity to fulfill contracts and if any brigades were discriminated against, in terms of access to resources, then these workers would find their rewards reduced, even though their work intensity may well have increased (at least in periods when resources were available). These workers would then be encouraged to move to different enterprises where work intensity was not so high. Furthermore, the new instructions also increased the pressure on management from above, as ministries were now given the task of constructing plans for the conversion of all the brigades under their jurisdiction, onto a *khozraschet* basis. Management's response was to increase the introduction of the brigade form but in a formal and often empty manner.

For example, in 1976 at the North Caucasus Construction Administration Trust No. 5, local management, under pressure from above, introduced 21 *khozraschet* brigades out of a total of 69 brigades. Only two of these brigades fulfilled their plan and only then when their targets had been reduced (*Literaturnaya Gazeta*, 2 March 1977, p. 5). The reason for this is a good illustration of the problems. The trust's plan for 1976 was 51 per cent up on 1975, there was a labour shortage of 1000 workers and only 70 per cent of planned supplies were actually delivered during the year. By introducing brigades, but failing to undertake the necessary preparation, management were able to formally satisfy ministerial pressure but were unable to reap the benefits of the system. By the late seventies, over 30 per cent of brigade failures were attributed to failures in supply (Grinko, 1979, p. 2) and as Bunich (1975, p. 70) points out, in 1975 300 brigades reverted to the old form of working because of the lack of external support.

Table 9.1, indicates that the pressure from above led to a rapid increase in at least the nominal dissemination of the experiment.[2] Nevertheless, in 1976, Soviet authors assessing the six year period over which the experiment had operated, concluded that the experiment was a success and that in the *khozraschet* brigades, construction

Table 9.1 Brigades in the construction industry operating on the Zlobin system

1972	1973	1974	1975	1976
200	9 000	16 000	40 000	43 000

Source: Sevast'yanov (1977), pp. 37–46.

time had been reduced by seventeen to twenty per cent, overall costs were down by three to four per cent, and labour productivity had been increased by four per cent (Sevast'yanov, 1977, pp. 37–44). Clearly, the advantages of the system, notwithstanding the problems outlined above, had been maintained, but at a declining rate. Goncharov (1979, p. 2) points out that in Volgograd province, for example, the transition to the brigade *khozraschet* system is moving ahead rapidly, but only on paper as construction plans are still unfulfilled. Furthermore, many of the brigades are very small, leading to large numbers of brigades with complex coordination problems but very little positive economic effect.

From the point of view of workers, the transition to the *khozraschet* system was not necessarily reflected in material rewards. In 1978, Grinko (1979, p. 2) calculates that *khozraschet* brigades exceeded the average output of ordinary brigades by 30 per cent, but their average earnings were only 2.5 per cent above the rest. This is a good illustration of the degree to which work intensity could be raised and the potential impact upon the surplus.

Another significant feature that needs explanation was the differentiated diffusion of the system between different branches of construction. For example, over the course of the Tenth Five Year Plan it was expected that 70 to 80 per cent of all housing construction would be completed by brigades but only 20 to 30 per cent of industrial construction (Sevast'yanov, 1977, p. 46). This feature and the factors that gave rise to it, are an interesting precursor of problems that were to develop later, when attempts were made to generalise the experiment throughout industry. The different degrees of diffusion can be explained by the nature of work itself in the housing and industrial construction sectors.

In housing construction the work tasks are relatively simple and tend to involve small work groups. Even if the overall project is large, for example the construction of a number of apartment buildings on the same site, the total workforce can be easily separated into coherent, parallel work teams. This can be achieved either by grouping workers horizontally across a particular skill group, for example all plumbers, all electricians and so on; or it can be achieved, as in the Kaluga variant, by grouping workers laterally. For example, all the different skilled workers operating on a particular building would form one work brigade and this would comprise plasterers, plumbers, electricians and so on. In this way the introduction of brigade contracts and the coherent definition of brigades is made relatively easy for management and is easily identifiable for the workforce. (This, of course, is not to minimise the problems already noted in the operation of these brigades once established.)

However, on an industrial construction project, the absolute number of workers is liable to be relatively larger. Also the complexity and specialist nature of industrial construction, is likely to involve a wider variety of skilled workers and specialisms. This will lead to a high degree of integration and interdependence between workers on the whole project (Tokarev, 1975, p. 2). Identifiable tasks suitable for brigade contracts will be more difficult for management to define and workers will be reluctant to accept that their remuneration should be based upon tasks heavily dependent upon the performance of others. The only possible way forward for management is to incorporate into the brigade all the members of the construction project, but this then leads to problems regarding the size of the brigade that defeats its object of providing closer control over the activities of workers and linking their rewards to effort. These peculiarities of industrial construction explain the relatively slower dissemination of the experiment in this sector and provide a background for assessing the fate of the experiment when attempts were made to generalise it throughout the whole of Soviet industry.

THE EXTENSION OF THE BRIGADE SYSTEM TO INDUSTRY

In the early seventies, the apparent success of the brigade system in construction, coupled with the similar experience of brigades in agriculture (Wadekin, 1975), encouraged the ruling group to extend the initiative to industry. Even if the experiment had its own problems and had not been, as yet, fully generalised within construction, it nevertheless offered the possibility of improving industrial labour discipline and as a consequence, labour productivity. As early as 1973 the brigade form was introduced mainly into machine building enterprises (Baranenkova, 1980, p. 59). By the mid-seventies the system had been introduced into a variety of industries. For example, it was introduced into the Timber industry in August 1974, where it was used specifically to encourage workers to be less wasteful, by giving bonuses for good quality work completed on time (Kostin, 1976, p. 13). The result was that labour discipline indicators improved and wastage fell from an average ten per cent to 1.2 per cent per shift.

However, in some respects, this industrial example is atypical. As well as the more general problems already noted in this chapter, the transfer of the brigade system to industry posed a series of specific problems, which were similar to the problems experienced in industrial construction. These problems, however, were more pronounced because of the nature of the Soviet industrial labour process.

The degree of integration of work activities, both within a particular enterprise and between enterprises, exceeds that in the construction sector. The production of almost any industrial product is the culmination of an integrated and mutually interdependent chain of work processes involving a large number of people. In flow production plants, the integrated activities of hundreds of people produce the final product and it is almost impossible to separate out specific work tasks that can then form the basis of the brigade contract. Even if this is possible, the success or failure of a particular brigade will be totally dependent upon the success or failure of the brigade performing the immediately preceding task. In these conditions, we may expect the workforce to be reluctant to transfer to the brigade system. Management will find it very difficult to identify and set up coherent contracts, which will act as a disincentive to the introduction of he system. The transition to the system may well be eased if the work team perpetually carry out a standardised section of the production process. However, if their work is contingent on the needs of other sectors and changes, perhaps on a daily basis, either because of small batch production or because of the uncertainties of repair work and so on, then it will be very difficult to implement the system.

Linked to the first problem, industrial production in the USSR takes place in enterprises and plants, which are large. They are bigger for example, than their western counterparts. For example, the average-sized engineering works in the USSR employs 1600 workers, whilst in West Germany the comparable figure is 250 (*Pravda*, 8 December 1982, p. 2). The sheer size of the workforce can militate against the implementation of the brigade system, because a choice has to be made between setting up a large number of brigades, with consequent problems of coordination and contract specification, and forming very large brigades with consequent sacrifice of the self-disciplining benefits of the system.

Furthermore, industrial production, unlike construction work, takes place in a physical environment that is more amenable to control, hence shift working is the norm. This raises a further problem of coordination of brigades over time. Should separate shifts, operating with the same plant and equipment, constitute separate brigades with separate contracts or should the brigade and its contract be defined across shifts, making them part of the same brigade? The former option heightens the degree of dependence between the two shifts, whilst the latter option raises again the question of coordination.

Finally, the industrial workforce is composed of not only basic production workers, but also significant numbers of auxiliary and repair and service workers, as noted earlier. The question then arises, how are these workers to be integrated into the system? Should they be part of basic production brigades, as they contribute, however indirectly, to the finished product or should separate brigades be established for them? Is the composition of brigades to be vertical through occupations or horizontal through production?

Given the integrated nature of industrial production, a formal structure of brigade organisation has emerged that reflects plant and association structures. In the first instance, the decision to change to the brigade system comes from a shop floor workers meeting and has to be ratified by the shop's chief and trade union committee (Baranenkova, 1980, p. 60; Pashuta and Kulikov, 1983, pp. 5–12). The brigade is eventually established by the enterprise director and the enterprise trade union committee. The brigade leader (*brigadir*) is appointed by the shop chief on the recommendation of the shop foreman. Hence the brigade leader, although not a member of management, is indirectly their appointee. Each brigade then elects a council (*sovet brigady*) which must be composed of a production foreman and party and trade union representatives, with the brigade leader as chairman (Chernov, 1980, p. 8). The balance of the membership comprises top production workers. The role of this council is to review output norms, to enforce labour discipline, to supervise product quality and to ensure the fulfilment of output and productivity plans. The Brigade Council is also responsible for the calculation of the 'coefficient of labour participation' (*koeffitsient trudovogo uchastiya*) or 'KTU' which is used to calculate the individual worker's bonuses and is explained in more detail below[3]. The Brigade Council is also responsible for coordination with other brigades, organising socialist competition and the appointment of mentors for young workers (Barbashov, 1983, pp. 81–5). The collective control exercised by the brigade is viewed as a particularly appropriate way to inculcate good working practices into young workers (Kogan and Merenkov, 1983, p. 89). Furthermore, the Brigade Council is responsible for the allocation of labour within the brigade and has the right to accept or dismiss workers and to regrade them as they either upgrade their skills or undertake multiple functions (Levikov, 1978, p. 11).

Above the individual Brigade Council is a council of brigade leaders (*sovet brigadirov*) that is responsible for the coordination of brigades within a particular shop or plant (Chernov, 1980, p. 8). The responsibilities of this layer is to oversee the work within the whole shop or plant and to coordinate the brigades accordingly. It also considers plans for future production and re-tooling or renovation of the shop.

Where brigades are operating in Associations then two higher level bodies are established. The Association's Brigade Leaders Council comprises the chairmen of all the shop or plant Brigade Leaders Councils and this elects a presidium that deals with daily matters. The chairmen of both the highest body and the presidium have to be approved by the enterprise director. These higher bodies are responsible for the overall coordination of the brigades and deal with any inter-brigade conflicts. Meetings at this level are closely integrated with plant management and the enterprise director participates directly in their deliberations, and once decisions are made they become applied to the whole Association (Chernov, 1980, p. 8). This integration of brigades into enterprise management is claimed to represent a democratisation of the planning and production process (Kogan and Merenkov, 1983, p. 86). However, the claims for this are an exaggeration given that all the participants are either directly or indirectly management appointees and the range of their deliberations is strictly delineated.

What was the impact of this new form of organisation in industry? According to Ille and Sinov (1984, p. 63) the introduction of brigades operates on a number of levels affecting not only the production and output of a group of workers, but also their social cohesion and their individual social psychology. Burenkov, describing the 80 or more brigades established in machine building plants in the Sumy region in the period 1974–76, points out that they were originally based upon single occupations (*spetsializirovannaya brigada*) (Burenkov, 1976, pp. 1–2). However, over time it was found necessary to merge these brigades into all-purpose or integrated brigades (*kompleksnaya brigada*), the average size of which rose as a consequence, from approximately fifteen to 75 workers. At the Kaluga Turbine Plant over a broadly similar period, contract brigades were also introduced to replace the individual piece-work system that had operated previously (Levikov, 1979, p. 11). The contract system, in both examples, operated in much the same way as it had in construction. A contract was defined with management that specified the total value of the work, a completion date and targets for economising on materials and tools. Management committed itself to provide the necessary raw materials and tools and 50 per cent of any savings accrue to the brigade as bonuses, with higher bonuses for high quality work.

Consequently the brigade was paid on the basis of the final results it achieved collectively, but this should not be seen as an egalitarian experiment designed to level wages, even within the individual brigade. The overall intention of the brigade system is to link work performance more closely with rewards, and the collective discipline of the brigade is seen as the mechanism to achieve this. Centrally determined wage normatives, however 'scientifically' derived, are viewed by Soviet economists as being too inflexible and too far removed from actual work performance, to act as either an incentive or as a disciplining mechanism (Bunich, 1980; Kheifets, 1982). Consequently, the brigade form of organisation provides a desirable intermediate administrative link that provides a discipline mechanism over production, absenteeism and so on, but also a potential means of establishing a closer linkage between work and rewards.

The way this was to be achieved was that workers in brigades would find their wages calculated on the basis of three elements; their skill grading or wage category; the number of hours they worked; finally, their coefficient of labour participation, the *KTU* mentioned above (Sekachev, pp. 58–62).

For each brigade working on a contracted task, a collective bonus fund is established and the *KTU* is used to distribute these funds amongst the brigade members (Rzhevuskii, 1980, p. 8). The *KTU* for each worker is established by the Brigade Council and is a reflection of the individual's contribution to the work of the brigade over the month. The minimum value of the *KTU* is zero, which means the worker receives nothing but the base wage. Any value above zero, up to a maximum of two, reflects the worker's contribution either through job combination or high quality work. The intention is, therefore, that centrally determined wage categories will determine the basic wage, but over and above that, work performance evaluated by those most able and closest to the work, the brigade, will determine wage supplements. As Parfenov (1980, p. 2) points out, without the use of the *KTU*, the loafer will be paid the same as the diligent brigade member and the incentive and disciplining effects of the brigade system will be lost.

As Mokin (1977, p. 2) suggests, with regard to a machine building plant in Yurga which transferred to the brigade form of organisation, the operation of the system will lead to the number of workers in the brigade being adjusted downwards. Once the overall wage is calculated and the job specified, it is in the self-interest of the brigade to reduce their numbers and thereby increase their average wage. The brigade system operates in this respect as a shop-floor level, Shchekino-like, initiative but with the onus being passed directly to the workforce itself to reduce the numbers involved in any contracted task. For example, Baranenkova's analysis of ten contract brigades at the Gomesel'mash Production Association (1980, p. 61) showed that in the first quarter of 1979, compared with the same period in 1978, the size of the workforce had been reduced by 9.1 per cent, but output per worker had risen by 13.2 per cent. Gavrilov (1980, p. 2), calculated that if the engineering industry could increase the proportion of workers on the brigade system from 39 per cent in 1979 to 75 per cent in 1985, then 100 000 workers could be released in engineering alone. Furthermore, if the system allowed a streamlining or removal of some managerial functions, like norming, quality control and so on, then even more management staff could be released. This confirms the point often made by Soviet sources, that the reorganisation of labour within industry is a cheaper and more effective way of releasing workers than the more costly introduction of new technology (Sarno *et al.*, 1983, p. 97).

The brigade system, like the Shchekino experiment, also encouraged workers within the brigade to master second or third occupations (Ille and Sinov, 1984, p. 63). At the Yurga plant, for example, over 300 workers acquired second or third skills which enabled them to cover potential gaps in the brigade's labour supply and assist in the completion of contracts on time (Mokin, 1977, p. 2).

The operation of the experiment over this early period, in the three examples cited, led to favourable increases in output and labour productivity and labour discipline indicators showed similar improvements. At the Kaluga plant, the introduction of the brigade system led to annual labour productivity increases of ten per cent, labour turnover was reduced to a quarter of its former level and in the period 1976–80 the number of counter-plans generated in the plant rose from 186 to 300 (Levikov, 1978, p. 11). At the Frunze bicycle plant, after the implementation of the brigade system, labour turnover was reduced and labour discipline infractions fell from 30 to 40 a day in 1975, to three to four a day in 1980 (Chernov, 1980a, p. 9). One of the ways this was achieved was that the Brigade Council closely vets job applications, particularly from former employees, and they are only started if they are accepted by a specific brigade. The consequence is that at the Yurga plant in 1970, it took 850 norm hours to produce one loader/excavator, yet by 1976, as a result of the tightened labour organisation, this had been reduced to 108 norm hours.

The beneficial impact of the brigade system on labour discipline, and consequently on labour productivity and output, is confirmed by all the factory studies by a number of Soviet sources. (For example, Sarno et al., 1983, pp. 97–8; Ille and Sinov, 1984, p. 63). Kogan and Merenkov (1983, pp. 87–8) in their research point to reductions in labour turnover, absenteeism and increased labour discipline leading to increases in labour productivity of 20 to 25 per cent. Baranenkova (1986, p. 65) citing evidence from 25 machine building enterprises, shows whole day losses and late arrivals being reduced by six times, intershift losses reduced by four times, turnover down by a factor of 1.5 and productivity growth of 7.4 per cent. However, a question which cannot be adequately answered is, do brigades make good workers *or* do good workers form successful brigades? (Sarno et al., 1983, p. 98). The experiment was not only introduced to basic production but also, for example, at the ship repair yards at Astrakhan (Sobgaide, 1977, p. 4). Here the brigade system was specifically introduced in an attempt to increase work capacity, as the yard's planned output was increased from the repair of four tankers to the repair of seven tankers with no increment to manpower. The workforce was split into two portions. The first, comprising 23 workers organised into two brigades, completed 41 per cent of the work. The second portion of the workforce, comprising 47 workers, completed 59 per cent of the work. The positive results of the brigade system can be seen in the comparison and are attributed particularly to multiple jobs in the brigades. Eventually the whole task was completed in less than five months rather than the planned five and a half months.

These examples of the successful implementation of the experiment in the period up to 1977–78 led to approximately 160 industrial enterprises organising on the basis of the brigade system (Levikov, 1978, p. 11). However, these early successes need to be qualified. The usual problems of supply disruptions, plan instability and poor preparation for the experiment are bemoaned even in these successful instances. However, new problems also emerged. For piece-rate workers, the introduction of the experiment marked a transition away from the old system of 'profitable' and 'unprofitable' work (Haraszti, 1977, pp. 48–52). In the new circumstances, all work became necessary and equally important because bonuses would only be paid if the whole brigade fulfilled its collective obligations within the contracted time period. For some experienced piece-rate workers, this represented a levelling down of wages and they resisted the implementation of the scheme. As a consequence of these difficulties, the system was spreading slowly. For example, a survey of 200 industrial enterprises in Minsk and Vitebsk showed that in 1975, 28 per cent of the workforce was organised in brigades but by 1977 this figure had only risen to 33 per cent (Palitsyn, 1979, p. 93). Furthermore, at a fifth of these enterprises there were no brigades at all.

Nevertheless, the desirability of the *khozraschet* brigade system and the intention of the ruling group to speed up its extension, was confirmed by the planning resolution of July 29th, 1979 (*Ob uluchshenii . . .*, 1981, p. 114). As already noted, this resolution formally drew together a number of measures, drawn from the experience of a number of experimental initiatives. In this resolution, ministries, departments, associations and enterprises were all instructed to develop and implement the brigade form of labour organisation and it was intended that this would become the basic form of labour organisation during the period of the Eleventh Five Year Plan.

The resolution also formalised the role of the Brigade Council, giving them the right to determine wages and bonuses on the basis of the brigade's collective work results and an evaluation of the individual worker's contribution. They were also given the right to upgrade or change the wages of any worker who undertook a combination of previously separate jobs, improved, or learned additional, skills or consistently produced high quality work. The overall aim was to encourage the wider introduction of the system and thereby reap the benefits of improved labour discipline and productivity. It was also hoped that the new form of organisation would stimulate workers' initiative and reduce what Klimentov (1984) calls the 'hired worker' mentality.

Parfenov (1981, p. 2) reports that by the end of 1980, eighteen months after the implementation of the planning resolution, 1.2 million brigades had been formed, encompassing twelve million workers and it was hoped that the number of brigades would have risen to one and half million by the end of 1982. However, as Table 9.2 and Table 9.3 illustrates, the rate of dissemination has not been as

Table 9.2   Total number of brigades in Soviet industry

		1980	1981	1982	1983	1984
(1)	Total number of brigades (000s) of which	1 068	1 257	1 377	1 480	1 519
(2)	Integrated brigades	430	538	604	676	732
	of these *skvoznaya brigada*	67	95	113	133	158
	as a % of (2)	15.6%	17.6%	18.7%	19.7%	21.6%
(3)	Specialised brigades	638	719	773	804	787
	of these *skvoznaya brigada*	98	122	141	157	170
	as a % of (3)	15.4%	17%	18.2%	19.5%	21.6%
	of the total no. of brigades					
	Those operating on *khozraschet*	—	92	137	218	336
	as a % of (1)	—	7.3%	9.9%	14.7%	22.1%
	Those paid on basis of normed tasks	551	919	1 062	1 173	1 219
	of these					
	Those utilising KTU for payment	—	330	496	661	802
	as a % of (1)	—	26%	36%	44.6%	52.8%

Source: Svirchevskii & Nikol'skii (1984), p. 16; *Vestnik Statistiki* (1985) No. 7, p. 73.

Table 9.3   Number of industrial production workers encompassed by the brigade form of organisation*

	1980		1981		1982		1983		1984	
	(000s)	(%)†	(000s)	(%)	(000s)	(%)	(000s)	(%)	(000s)	(%)
Total no. of workers in brigades of whom	10 765	100	13 562	100	15 404	100	17 024	100	18 429	100
In integrated brigades	5 168	48	7 064	52.1	8 221	53.4	9 399	55.2	10 673	57.9
of these *skvoznaya brigada*	1 194	11.1	1 749	12.9	2 097	13.6	2 483	14.6	3 111	16.9
In specialised brigades	5 597	52	6 498	47.9	7 183	46.6	7 625	44.8	7 756	42.1
of these *skvoznaya brigada*	994	9.2	1 245	9.2	1 473	9.6	1 658	9.7	1 870	10.1
Of the total no. of workers										
Those in *khozraschet* brigades	—	—	1 252	9.2	1 949	12.7	3 074	18.1	5 268	28.6
Those in brigades paid on basis of normed tasks	5 191	48.2	9 813	72.4	11 876	77.1	13 609	79.9	15 026	81.5
Those paid on basis of 'end results'	—	—	6 927	51.1	9 053	58.8	10 859	63.8	12 098	65.6
Those paid on basis of KTU	—	—	4 155	30.6	6 420	41.7	8 670	50.9	10 966	59.5

*All figures year ending except 1980, as of August 1st.
†As a percentage of the total organised in Brigades.

Source: Svirchevskii & Nikol'skii (1984), p. 16; *Vestnik Statistiki* (1985), No. 7, p. 74

rapid as was hoped. By 1982, the total number of brigades operating in industry was 1.37 million and more than fifteen million workers were organised in brigades. Furthermore, the rate of dissemination of brigades and the growth of the number of workers in brigades were slowing down and the target number of brigades for 1982 was only just exceeded by the end of 1984. Nevertheless, according to Table 9.4, by the end of 1984 over 70 per cent of all industrial workers were organised in brigades. However, these statistics on the growth and extent of the brigade system are misleading and need considerable qualification.

Table 9.4   Number of industrial workers organised in brigades as a percentage of the total

1980	42.9%
1981	52.5%
1982	59.0%
1983	64.7%
1984	71.7%

Source: *Vestnik Statistiki* (1985), No. 7, p. 74.

Although the number of brigades in operation is a useful index of the dissemination of the system, there are also qualitative aspects to be considered. The experience gathered throughout the period of operation of the system can be used to develop a profile of the ideal brigade. If the maximum benefits are to be attained, the optimum brigade form is that of a complex integrated brigade, where workers of differing specialisms work together (Khrishchev, 1984, p. 53). The ideal brigade would not be a single shift brigade (*smennaya brigada*) but should be organised across a number of shifts (*skvoznaya brigada*) to complete from start to finish some section of the manufacturing process (Kozlov, 1980, p. 6; Kogan and Merenkov, 1983, p. 86). The brigade should be big enough to accomplish this end, without being over-large. Ideally, the brigade should be working solely on a single identifiable task, on a *khozraschet* basis, and the whole brigade's performance should be linked to final results (Gavrilov, 1980, p. 7; Tsarev, 1983, pp. 53–7). Individual remuneration should be based upon the individual's work performance reflected in the *KTU* (Milukov, 1980, p. 10; Pashuta and Kulikov, 1983, pp. 125–9; Klivets 1983, p. 102). In this way, the brigade is both encouraged and able to reduce both inter-shift and intra-shift idle-time and this leads, as a consequence, to the full utilisation of the plant and equipment at their disposition. Furthermore, it will encourage workers to master and combine additional skills and the brigade need never experience disruptions because of shortages of the necessary skills. The net result should be increased labour discipline, output and productivity.

However, in reality the 'actually existing' brigades fall short of this ideal type. As Parfenov (1983, p. 2) complains, in the first two years of the Eleventh Plan, even though 300 000 new brigades were created, qualitatively many of them were inadequate and were unable to raise their labour productivity. The brigade system has been introduced with a great deal of unevenness. Firstly, the size of brigades has varied widely and there has been concern expressed that 32 per cent of brigades have five or fewer members (Gavrilov, 1980, p. 7) and 70 per cent have ten or fewer members (Parfenov, 1981, p. 2). At the other extreme there are plants where the average brigade size is 100 or more workers and where the brigade is simply all the members of a shop or a shift. Gavrilov (1980, p. 7) cites the example of the Porshen plant at Alma Ata where the average brigade size is 120 workers. Whilst it is recognised that specific production conditions will determine the precise size of the brigades, Soviet sources agree that these extremes are undesirable. The small brigades fail to obtain any of the advantages from increased machine utilisation or job combination, and because of their necessarily large number, cause coordination problems, which increase the likelihood of failure. The large brigades are unwieldy and are not cohesive internally, and therefore they represent hardly any change from the previous situation. Estimates have suggested that the optimum size is somewhere between 40 and 60 workers (Stolyanov, 1982, p. 2; Lanshin, 1982, p. 6). However, as the figures in Table 9.2 and 9.3 indicate, the average size of brigades is much smaller and only rising slowly from ten workers in 1980, to 11.18 workers in 1982, to 12.13 workers in 1984.

The balance between specialised brigades and complex integrated brigades has also been changing slowly. In 1980, specialist brigades predominated in industry as a whole (Kozlov, 1980, p. 6), accounting for almost 60 per cent of the total number of brigades and for 52 per cent of the workforce organised in brigades. Over the period to 1984, the number of specialised brigades at first rose and then after 1983 has begun to fall. However, the numbers employed in integrated brigades has risen steadily and by 1984 accounted for almost 60 per cent of the workforce organised in brigades. It should be noted, however, that whilst the average size of the integrated brigades is larger than the specialist brigades, it is only rising slowly from twelve workers in 1980 to 14.6 workers in 1984.

Also the development of brigades operating over a number of shifts (*skvoznaya brigada*) has to be considered. In terms of the absolute numbers of brigades, over a fifth of both specialised and integrated brigades are multi-shift, but it has taken five years for the percentage to rise by only six points. In terms of workforce, numbers only 16.9 per cent of integrated brigade workers and 10.1 per cent of specialised brigade workers are in multi-shift brigades.

Furthermore, there have been continual complaints in the Soviet literature that many of the brigades that have been created are brigades in name only (Kozlov, 1980, p. 6; Sokolov, 1980, p. 2; Antropov and Lyakutkin, 1983, p. 2). For example, one study of the brigade system in enterprises of a variety of ministries showed that they had overfulfilled their plans for the creation of new brigades, but labour productivity had only risen by between 0.5 per cent and 1.2 per cent as a consequence (Glyantsev, 1983, p. 65). Klimentov (1983) points out that in 1981 the output of newly created brigades rose by a mere 1.7 per cent, and in 30 per cent of the brigades surveyed in one plant output had actually declined. This seems to cast considerable doubt on the efficacy of the brigade system, but the real reason for this type of result emerges from a further study of brigades in the machine building ministries, where only a third of the brigades were actually paid according to final results (Kozlov, 1980, p. 6). In ship building and repair, the figure is slightly higher at 50 per cent (Milukov, 1980, p. 10). Consequently, the introduction of brigades in these two sectors, in the majority of instances, has brought about no significant change. According to the information in Tables 9.2 and 9.3, the number of brigades operating on *khozraschet* principles has still to reach one third. As Soviet sources argue, this pro-forma adoption is inadequate.

This has a further dimension that is amply illustrated by the situation in Magnitogorsk. Out of the 2272 brigades operating there, which account for 62 per cent of the workforce, only 900 brigades are paid on the basis of final results, but more significantly, only 238 brigades utilise the *KTU* to calculate the inividual worker's bonuses (Glyantsev, 1983, p. 65). If all the brigades are approximately the same size, this implies that the full system only operates in Magnitogorsk for a little over ten per cent of the workforce. Furthermore, at enterprises of the machine building ministries, the collective bonus is distributed to brigade members by use of the *KTU* for only sixteen per cent of workers (Gavrilov, 1980, p. 6). Even more extreme is the example of the Lipetsk tractor plant, where there are 600 brigades in operation but not one is operating on *khozraschet* principles and in fact all workers are paid individually, on exactly the same basis as previously (Chernov, 1980, p. 9).

To generalise, the maximum percentage of brigades that fulfil the criteria of the ideal brigade form (that is a multi-shift, integrated brigade operating on *khozraschet* and paying on the basis of the *KTU*) can be no more than 10.4 per cent of the total and could indeed be less. In terms of the workforce as a whole, no more than seventeen per cent could possibly have been working in this ideal form of brigade by 1984. This places the statistics presented in Table 9.4 for the percentage of workers working in brigades into perspective. The figure of over 70 per cent is misleading and in fact the adoption of the brigade system may well mean little more than cosmetic changes to plant labour organisation. This, then, explains the limited impact on productivity and output figures over this period, when apparently significant changes were taking place in labour organisation.

There are further problems, because the experiment has been disseminated disproportionally between basic production work and auxiliary work. As Svirchevskii and Nikol'skii (1984, p. 16) point out, whilst there were over a million brigades in basic production employing approximately 11.5 million workers, there were only about a third of this number of brigades in auxiliary production employing under four million workers. It is to be expected that the brigade system will be easier to introduce to basic production work than to auxiliary, service and repair work. The reason for this is that basic production tasks are more amenable to coherent definition into brigade tasks, unlike repair work, which by its nature, is more uncertain. Nevertheless, it is in the auxiliary sector that the brigade system is most needed to resolve the problems noted earlier. Specialist auxiliary, service and repair brigades have been set up at a number of plants. The Togliatti car plant and the Volga Automotive Plants are the best known examples, where the centralisation of repair and service facilities has led to dramatic improvements in productivity and so on. In the shipbuilding industry, the introduction of multi-purpose auxiliary brigades has led to a 20 to 30 per cent increase in the productivity of auxiliary workers and the downtime of malfunctioning equipment has been reduced by 30 to 35 per cent (Egorov, 1980, p. 7). It is interesting to note that, while the shipbuilding industry intends to have 88 per cent of its basic production workers organised in the brigade system by the end of the Eleventh Five Year Plan, the comparable figure for auxiliary workers is only 60 per cent. However, generally even where specialist auxiliary brigades have been set up, the proportion operating on *khozraschet* is much lower than the overall industrial average. Furthermore, the introduction of the brigade system, in the same way as the Shchekino experiment, has not been uniform across all industrial branches, reflecting differing degrees of support and planning at ministry level (Svirchevskii and Nikol'skii, 1984, p. 17).

More significantly, even where brigades are operating fully on the *khozraschet* system, concern has been expressed regarding the preparations for implementing the system, the manner in which contracts are established and the internal organisation and management of the brigades. This has a number of aspects.

As already noted, to obtain the optimum results, the brigade requires a stable plan of assignments over a period of time, ideally five years, but at least two years. Apart from the operational desirability of this, in cutting idle-time, it also contributes to the cohesion and stability of the brigade. However, approximately two thirds of the brigades do not even have an annual plan (Lanshin, 1982, p. 6). As a consequence, it is unsurprising to find that brigades only work on contract work for an average of 60 per cent of the time; the balance is either idle-time or due to management redirecting them to other tasks.

Moreover, short term planning and organisation is also a problem. Kogan and Merenkov (1983, p. 90) point out that brigades are very conscious of the need for correct planning and the maintenance of the correct work rhythm; after all, their remuneration depends upon these factors. However, as Lanshin (1982, p. 6) notes, the internal organisation of brigades is often chaotic and during time spent on contracted work, no work schedules exist. This has two repurcussions. If the brigade is inadequately organised internally, the *KTU* becomes meaningless, because without adequate records and work schedules it is impossible to measure or record individual participation in the brigade's tasks. Also, if the *KTU* is non-operable, the remuneration of the brigade will be based upon allocation of the collective bonus on egalitarian grounds or it will be allocated on the basis of some other indicator; for example, the wage category or skill grouping used for basic wages will be applied to the collective bonus as well. Maksimova (1985, p. 192) reports that in some brigades in Central Asian republics the highest *KTU* is assigned to workers with the largest families. This may be socially progressive, but of course defeats the whole object of the *KTU*, and the intention of tying work and rewards through the brigade system is undermined (Gavrilov, 1980, p. 7).

There is a further problem in that the brigade system may degenerate into a form of perpetual storming by the brigade's conscientious workers, where workers will take on additional tasks simply to complete work and achieve bonuses. This may involve the brigade in fulfilling tasks in the easiest possible manner, as Maksimova (1985) suggests, raising productivity by muscle power alone and ignoring mechanisation and the technological requirements of the task. This may be rational for the brigade in the short run, but is wasteful in the long run. Furthermore, there is often haphazard coordination between brigade members and the work assignments, with skilled workers carrying out manual tasks simply to get them done. This represents a familiar misuse of skilled labour. This situation cannot be sustained over time and the brigade will disband and revert to the old form of working.

Furthermore, the establishment of contracts is often carried out in considerable ignorance and uncertainty, which leads to meaningless contracts and almost certain failure for the brigade. The resultant demoralisation often leads to a return to the old system of working and enhances resistance to change (Antropov and Lyakutkin, 1983, p. 2). This action amounts to little more than management attempting to shift responsibility onto the workforce. Lanshin points out that out of 40 enterprises investigated, 30 to 50 per cent of the necessary documentation, blueprints, designs and so on were absent and the delivery schedules for 30 to 40 per cent of the necessary equipment was unknown. Nevertheless, contracts had been established and failure to fulfil them, which in most instances was ascribed to supply failures or plan instabilities after the contract was determined, undermines brigade confidence and slows down the dissemination of the system.

Problems can be identified within the leadership of brigades themselves. Initially brigades were headed by exceptional production workers, but if the experiment is to be generalised, then the necessity arises for many more brigade leaders. At some plants, particularly where a whole shift or shop has been turned, in a formalistic manner, into a brigade, it has been suggested that foremen should become brigade leaders (Kozlov, 1980, p. 6). This has the disadvantage of destroying the foreman's function as managerial representative on the shop-floor, and in fact the precise relationship between line management, foreman and brigade leaders is somewhat muddled (Sarno et al., 1983, p. 100). The responsibilities of the brigade leader function involve technical, economic and engineering skills and the calibre of brigade leaders has caused concern. Lanshin points out that the proportion of brigade leaders with secondary education has risen from 27 to 37 per cent, over the period from the mid-seventies, but only approximately ten per cent of the rest are studying to upgrade their qualifications. Kalandrov (1982, p. 2) points out that it was difficult to recruit the right kind of worker for the brigade leadership function because the rights and duties were ill-defined and, particularly in *khozraschet* brigades, the rewards are inadequate for the additional responsibilities. This is a critical problem because the brigade leader in this system has a pivotal role in terms of both the plant's overall organisation and in controlling production (Antip'ev, 1985, pp. 83–7). According to Maksimova (1985), brigade leaders are often chosen by management not because they are best qualified or have superior technical skills, but because they are tough individuals. Furthermore, as brigade leaders point out, whilst they are subject to discipline from above and complaint from below, they have very little sanction over the actions of their superiors (Okhozin, 1983, p. 2). Therefore, it is a role with considerable responsibility, but little power and minimal rewards.

A further related problem is the relationship between managements and the brigade leader, the Brigade Council and the Brigade Leaders' Council. In the plants that have successfully implemented the system there is a degree of overlap between managerial and Brigade Council functions (Klivets 1983, p. 102), and also between trade union and Brigade Council functions. Furthermore, the addition of the Brigade Councils and the Brigade Leaders' Council, although it is claimed to streamline some aspects of production administration and decision making, does add another tier of bureaucracy alongside the management, party and trade union hierarchies within the plant (*Proizvodstvennaya brigada . . .*, 1982, pp. 28–30). There have also been criticisms that the Councils are little more than talking shops with effective decisions being taken elsewhere. Nevertheless, as some Soviet sources have noted, the implementation of the system begins a process of reorganisation of the relationship between management and the workforce. Management now have to negotiate with the brigades, rather than simply giving them orders (Stolyanov, 1982, p. 2). How far this has brought real change is dubious because, as noted above, few brigades operate on the full system.

Overall, management tend to resist the full implementation of the system, because in the last analysis, it increases both their workload and its complexity. It increases the possibilities of failure and potentially disrupts their relationship with the workforce by setting up, in a formal manner, a countervailing body at the level of the shop floor. As Kogan and Merenkov (1983, p. 90) note, the introduction of brigades places great demands upon both planners and management to provide the necessary conditions for success. However, for management there are few guaranteed benefits. Far better to formally fulfil the plan for creating brigades, whilst actually continuing to work in the same manner; after all, supply difficulties will continue to frustrate the operation of the system. Ratchet planning and the inability to transform productivity gains into additional investment funds operate to counter this experiment in the same way as they were seen to undermine the Shchekino experiment. In conditions of labour shortage, the disciplinary power of the Brigade Council is little stronger than that of the management, and while consumer goods are in short supply the incentive effects are dubious. From the worker's point of view, the brigade system is recognised as an attempt to further discipline and control their activities.[4] Soviet sources have reported that, in some instances, when workers are transferred to a *khozraschet* brigade, they have left the factory to work elsewhere (Morozov, 1982, p. 6). In other instances, for example at a works meeting at the Vladimir tractor plant, no one voted for the transition to the system because of uncertainty about the nature of the system (Gonzal'ez, 1982, p. 2). The basis of workers' antipathy to the brigade system emerges from a survey of readers letters to *Literaturnaya Gazeta* (Dzokaeva, 1982, p. 11). This article shows that, whilst correspondents are opposed to wage-levelling, which they argue is unfair to conscientious workers, they also see wage levelling as being in management's interest. This is because it gives management a quiet life and saves them actually identifying good and bad workers. However, correspondents were also dubious about the impact of the brigade system. Some argue that the implementation of the system will cause an irrational redistribution of workers towards plants with the most modern equipment, because here the possibilities of bonus are enhanced. Others suggest that the major problem with the system is that it replaces objectively-set centralised norms (based on skill, experience and so on) by localised subjectively-based norms. They fear the localised power of managerial favouritism, which could provide the circumstances of success for some but not for others. In fact, this fear captures exactly the eventual aim of the system, the

introduction of greater wage differentiation. Klimentov (1984) argues
that wage determination should in the future be solely dependent
upon the *KTU*, with no centralised wage setting. However, Maksimova (1985) reports that the use of the *KTU* causes friction within
brigades and, as noted already, it is often avoided. Ultimately
workers' opposition to the brigade system is grounded on the knowledge that the benefits that may accrue to them (and remember that
given endemic supply problems and plan instability these benefits are
not guaranteed) will be small.

Brezhnev (1982, pp. 1–2), speaking at the Seventeenth Trade Union
Congress in March 1982, was critical of the slow dissemination of the
full brigade system and the disbanding of brigades. Brezhnev argued
that the disbanding of brigades was caused by management failing to
accept their responsibilities and provide them with the necessary
conditions for success. As already pointed out, this is not necessarily
within management's power. It would seem that at this time the
impetus for the extension of the brigade system within industry was
beginning to flag. Furthermore, even within those plants that had
established the full system, the enhancement of productivity occurred
at a declining rate. The initial results of the implementation of the
system may well provide spectacular success, but after the first year or
two, the productivity increments begin to decline to around five per
cent per annum (Stolyanov, 1982, p. 2).

Even though the brigade system continued to expand in the
construction sector, as illustrated in Table 9.5, the original successes
of the system proved difficult to sustain and it was certainly not the
solution to all that sector's problems. In the early 1980s, Soviet
sources were still identifying the potential benefits of the brigade
system for construction. Gonzal'ez (1981, p. 6) cites the advantages of
the system in terms of a twenty per cent cut in construction time and
productivity increases up to 25 per cent. From Table 9.5 it can be seen
that even though the percentage of workers organised in *khozraschet*
brigades was under 40 per cent of the total, they nevertheless
accounted for almost 50 per cent of the work completed by the
construction sector. However, as Zotov (1983, p. 1) points out, by
1982 all the major construction ministries failed to fulfil their production targets and the level of machine idle-time had begun to rise. This
is precisely the opposite performance to that expected of a sector
where the brigade system had become widely implemented. In the
early 1980s over 40 per cent of the brigades working in construction
were supposed to be operating on *khozraschet*, almost three times the

Table 9.5   Number of brigades and number of workers organised in
brigades, in Soviet construction organisations (year end)

	1975	1980	1981	1982	1983	1984
Number of *khozraschet* brigades (000s)	34	81	85.7	88	93.22	98.5
As a percentage of the total number of brigades	16.5	39.6	41.8	42.7	43.8	44.9
Number of workers in *khozraschet* brigades (000s)	352	1 072	1 156	1 226	1 335	1 454
As a percentage of the general number of workers in construction work	9.5	27.8	30	31.9	34.3	37.3
Volume of work fulfilled by *khozraschet* brigades as a percentage of the general volume of work completed by construction organisations	12.1	37.2	39.6	42.1	45	48.8

Source: *SSSR v Tsifrakh v 1984 godu* (1985), p. 190.

percentage in industry at that time, but in reality the number was far
fewer (Zlobin, 1981, p. 6).

As Nikitin (1980, p. 10) points out, even apparently successful
brigades can run into difficulties. He cites the example of a Murmansk
Industrial Building Trust which had over the period 1974–79, raised
its production by 72 per cent, reduced its workforce by 33 per cent,
had a reputation for good quality work and had always completed
projects either on time or ahead of time, as a result of introducing the
brigade system. However, this Trust had overspent its wage allocations as a result of the reduction of the wage fund on a ratchet basis
and, therefore, any further extension of the brigade system was
halted. Once again, planning from the achieved level and the claw-
back of economised wage funds retard the momentum of an experimental initiative.

The example of the Orel Construction Administration illustrates
the problems that still arose in the construction sector (Kalakin, 1980,
p. 2). In 1979 more than 12 000 man days were lost through absenteeism, which usually occurred on Mondays and, as noted previously,
this is usually drink-related. The net effect of this was to severely
disrupt the rhythm of work. The aim of the brigade system had been
to overcome precisely this type of problem and the reasons why it did

not are instructive of the broader problems, even when the experiment is introduced.

The Brigade Council, charged with resolving these problems, fared little better than management had done previously. When punishment was meted out to labour discipline violators, they simply left the collective. As the Administration was already 1500 workers below the planned complement, it could ill-afford to lose workers. The usual problems of supply difficulties and plan instability, coupled with poor supervision of poorly motivated young workers compounded the difficulties and showed that, in these circumstances, the brigade system offers no more of a constraint upon labour indiscipline than previous modes of organisation.

The Soviet response to these problems was to seek administrative change and the adoption of a new resolution on the implementation of brigades (TsK KPSS, *Pravda*, 4 December 1983). This sought to deal with a number of the problems enumerated in this chapter; attempts were made to improve the preparation for, and the transition to, the brigade system; to provide longer term and more stable plans for brigades; pressure was brought to extend integrated complex brigades working on *khozraschet*; improvements were called for in both the training and remuneration of brigade leaders; calls were made for the increase of party activity within brigades, and so on. From the figures in Tables 9.2, 9.3 and 9.4 it can be seen that the brigade system has been further disseminated, but the problems of declining productivity growth remain. The arguments developed in this chapter suggest that such administrative changes will have a minimal effect on the dissemination of the full brigade system.

EXPERIMENTAL ATTEMPTS TO SOLVE THE PROBLEM OF WORK NORMS

This section will briefly review a number of other experimental initiatives concerned with the vexed question of work norms. The necessity for work norms in the USSR has already been explained as the result of the absence of the operation of the law of value, in a social system still characterised by exploitative social relations of production. As concrete labour in the USSR is not reduced to abstract labour and equilibriated through the mechanism of competition and the market, this process is achieved by administrative mechanisms. However, the contradictions inherent in the process of setting, upgrading and operating work norms make this highly imperfect. Given the centrality of this problem, it is not surprising that experimental initiatives were introduced in an attempt to resolve these problems. Specifically, it had been long recognised that Soviet workers would not strive to overfulfil their individual assignments, because overfulfilment would mean the uprating of work norms. This would leave the worker with no material advantage, only increased work intensity for the same return. Planning from the achieved level has a similar result for the individual as it does for the enterprise. This means that the operation of the economic mechanism posits a ceiling on potential labour productivity advances and leads to perpetual hidden reserves, and it is in the interests of both the worker and the management to evade their uprating.

In order to break this rational response to the logic of the planning process, an experiment was introduced at the Aksai Plastics Factory in Rostov (Smirnova and Sabo, 1984, pp. 186–7; Shkurko, 1977, 132–50; Kheifets, 1980, p. 20). The aim of the experiment was to give piece-rate workers an incentive to raise their work intensity by upgrading their work norms. If a worker, on his own initiative, increased his work norm by ten per cent, half of the savings obtained over the next three months as a result would be paid to him as a lump sum bonus. If the norm was raised by fifteen to twenty per cent, then the worker would receive a lump-sum bonus equivalent to half of the resulting savings over a six month period (Alekseev, 1973, p. 2). These payments were to be made prior to the impementation of the new norms and prior to the results being achieved. Furthermore, if the norms to be upgraded referred to the work of a brigade or work team of any size, this could only be undertaken if everyone in the brigade agreed. In any case, all changes in norms could only be carried out if they were ratified by the plant's trade union committee.

As an example, Alekseev (p. 2) cites a brigade that agreed to increase its production from 50 to 64 units per shift. The economic effect of this would have been a saving of 1030 roubles in the six month period, hence the brigade received an immediate bonus of 515 roubles. Under the terms of the experiment, the balance of any savings made were divided into two halves. The first portion was transferred to a centralised fund that could be used to pay further bonuses for high quality work or to recompense foremen responsible for raising or introducing norms. The other half was amalgamated into the income of the enterprise and transferred to the state.

Furthermore, it was agreed that the Aksai plant management

would only have the right to increase work norms independently of worker initiatives if the conditions of production were changed. For example, it was recognised that if plant or equipment was renovated or if new technology was introduced, this would affect the productive capacity of the workforce, and therefore norms would have to be raised. In all other cases, the initiative must come from below.

The initial results from the experiment were impressive. In each of the first five years of the system's operation at the Aksai plant, half of the plant's piece-rate workers filed requests to upgrade their norms. Over this period, 733 people actually raised their norms, saving 200 000 norm hours, or the equivalent of 400 additional workers. This saved 220 000 roubles, half of which was paid to workers, who as a consequence produced an additional two million roubles worth of output. In the period 1968–72 the plant achieved average labour productivity growth of 29.5 per cent per annum and wage outlays fell from 27 to seventeen kopecks per rouble of finished output (Alekseev, 1973, p. 2). These positive results were maintained over the first decade, but at a diminishing rate, as labour productivity growth by 1978 was averaging fourteen per cent per annum, three times the industry average (Nagibin, 1983, p. 13). Over the whole period, labour productivity grew by a factor of six and average wages by a factor of three. The plant also made significant gains as labour discipline was improved. Labour turnover for example, fell from 30 per cent in 1968 to only six per cent in 1978.

The obvious attraction of this experiment, from the viewpoint of the ruling group, is that norm setting and revision is no longer decided from above and then either manipulated or resisted by the workforce. If the experiment functions properly, norms would be determined either by the individual piece-rate worker or by the primary work unit, the brigade. This represents an attempt to get the Soviet workforce to heighten its own work intensity and take up the slack in production and labour organisation by introducing some degree of self-interest (Nagibin and Ryazhokikh, 1975, p. 3). As previously argued, the worker at the point of production is the only person who can really regulate and maintain the intensity of his own labour at the optimum level and see the potentialities for savings in time, materials and labour. From the viewpoint of the ruling group, the payment of lump sum bonuses will be recouped many times over into the indefinite future from the enhanced production, thus enhancing the extracted surplus. Consequently, it was decided to generalise the experiment.

By 1980 the Aksai model had been adopted by 365 enterprises in the Rostov region. Over the period 1974–79, over a quarter of a million piece-workers increased their norms, increasing labour productivity by 10.3% and adding over five million roubles worth of output to annual production (Manevich, 1986, p. 138). However, as Aganbegyan (1982, p. 3) complains, beyond this the experiment was not widely disseminated, even though the experiment appears applicable to any plant where piece-rates are in operation or collective brigade norms operate. The reasons for the failure to generalise the experiment comprise a catalogue of familiar problems.

Enterprises were lukewarm in their acceptance of the experiment and approached it in a formalistic and superficial manner. Often complaints were raised that enterprise management failed to abide by the terms of the experiment and arbitrarily disregarded time periods or attempted to uprate norms independently. They tended to treat the experiment as 'just another campaign' to be formally adhered to as long as it was topical and then dropped as soon as convenient or when pressure from above necessitated a hike in work norms. Furthermore, from management's point of view, the instructions for the adoption of the system were vague and the ambiguities caused reluctance to adopt the experiment.

Management's lack of enthusiasm was reinforced in some instances when there were no surplus funds to pay the initial lump-sum bonuses (Nagibin and Ryazhokikh, 1975, p. 3). This potentially meant withdrawing funds from elsewhere, which could cause immediate problems even if the experiment delivered the enhanced production in the future. Given the relatively short time horizons over which Soviet managerial decision making operates, it is likely that Soviet managers would be averse to such a potentially risky manœuvre. Furthermore, the 'profitability' of such a scheme does not necessarily yield specific advantage for plant management, as the enhanced profitability is dissolved in the enterprise's overall performance and, therefore, they do not perceive it to be in their direct self-interest.

Also, if workers accept tighter norms and agree to produce more, this is predicated upon the provision of conditions to enable them to meet their commitment (Nagibin, 1983, p. 13). There has to be a stable supply of raw materials, tools and energy supplies. Workers under the conditions of this experiment require the correct rhythm of production with little idle-time, either between or within shifts, if the higher norms are to be achieved. However, the chaotic nature of material and technical supply is outside the control of the workforce and management of the experimental plants. Furthermore, the enhanced performance of these enterprises does not translate into improved access to either raw materials or equipment. This instability deters workers from adopting the experiment and, furthermore, adds to management's scepticism over the benefits of the experiment, particularly if the lump sum bonuses have been paid and the enhanced production is not forthcoming in the short run. Once again, it should be noted that the poor frequency of supply leads to arhythmic production cycles, with a consequent effect upon both the quality and quantity of output. It leads to the abuse and, therefore, accelerated depreciation of fixed capacity and poor attention to maintenance and repair. The emergence of this destabilised pattern of production sets up the need for low norms and labour surpluses in order to accommodate supply difficulties and still fulfil the plan. Consequently, the vicious circle, which it was hoped the Aksai system would breach, reasserts itself.

The Aksai experiment as noted, refers primarily to the work of piece-rate workers but, this is obviously inappropriate for time paid workers. In modern industrial plants, particularly those based on flow production, time rates prevail. Nevertheless, the desire to increase labour intensity is no less pressing. This is achieved by maintaining a correct rhythm of work and gradually increasing the technically validated normed output. Another experimental initiative, begun at the Volga Automotive Factory (*VAZ*), is based upon the recognition that, in order to raise the degree of intensity of work, workers need to be recompensed (Kheifets, 1980, p. 17). The basic intention was to pay time-rate workers bonuses, up to 40 per cent of their base wage, for the fulfilment of a targeted output level which had been based upon technically substantiated norms for a particular brigade (Bunich, 1980, p. 8). Furthermore, as the plant had more staff than specified in the plan, further bonuses, up to twenty per cent of the base wage, were payable if the brigades moved towards the technically validated complement. These bonuses were implemented for a period of time, but when the regular reviews of base wages took place, they were integrated into the basic wage. In a sense they were temporary bonuses to tighten labour organisation. Bonuses were also payable for workers who upgraded their skills and qualifications and these elements of the experiment were integrated into the 1979 planning resolution. Even though the VAZ experiment received official support by mid-1980 it had only been implemented at just over 50 enterprises (Kostin, 1980, p. 68).

Another initiative to increase the level of workers' norms was implemented at the Dinamo plant in Moscow (Bunich, 1980, p. 7). The experiment implemented here, was based upon the recognition that norms are set as a basis for work intensity, but do not necessarily reflect the productive potential of each individual worker. Therefore, rather than paying bonuses to workers for overfulfilling unrealistically low norms, the Dinamo plant introduced bonuses for the fulfilment of workers' personal plans. The idea is that using the present overfulfilment as the base, the worker adopts a personal plan to increase his output and is paid according to this index.

The obvious problem with both these experimental initiatives is, why should workers cooperate? If there is a labour shortage, the option of movement would allow workers to avoid these administrative schemes for increasing work intensity. Furthermore, the material incentives are small and, as repeatedly noted, ineffective. The disappointing rate of success in generalising these two initiatives suggests that both worker resistance and managerial reluctance combine to frustrate the experiments.

The alternative attempts to change the Soviet labour process, outlined in this chapter, could be extended to include a number of other experimental initiatives both in industry and agriculture. However, I would argue that, irrespective of the detail of the experiments, their fate has been remarkably similar. The explanation and implications of this are taken up in the final chapter.

10 Conclusions

GORBACHEV'S INHERITANCE AND POLICY OPTIONS

Gorbachev's early speeches and writings on the problems of the Soviet economy provide a litany of familiar complaints and in many respects are a repetition of much that had been said before by his three immediate predecessors (*Pravda*, 12 March 1985, p. 3 and 17 March 1985, p. 1). Nevertheless, the western press response to his accession to power has been to stress continually both the necessity for reform and the possibilities for reform presented by a new leader (*Economist*, 26 July–1 August 1986, pp. 9–10; 6 September–12 September 1986, p. 10). Given that Gorbachev is neither a geriatric nor seriously ill, in stark contrast to Brezhnev, Andropov and Chernenko before him, a longer tenure of the post of General Secretary may well be envisaged, with a longer-term perspective on the problems and potential solutions. However, the possibilities for reform must be tempered by a realistic appraisal of past attempts at reform. I would argue that past leaders have been just as intent on change, and to ascribe the failure of previous reform to the character or personality of past leaders is obviously misleading. This concluding chapter will first provide an outline of Gorbachev's emerging economic programme before attempting some general conclusions.

As with the period immediately after the ousting of Khrushchev, the incoming General Secretary has acted to replace the old guard in several key political and economic positions within the ruling group, with a series of knock-on effects throughout the system. However, whilst this may have short-term superficial effects, the replacement of the old guard should not be confused with real change; neither should Gorbachev's sponsorship of the anti-alcohol campaign. (TsK KPSS, 1985, p. 1; Ovrutskii, 1985, pp. 35–41.) Like the Andropov discipline campaign before it,[1] whilst the problem it attempts to deal with is real and serious, it is something that cannot be solved in isolation. Past experience has shown that isolated legislative attempts to reduce labour turnover in 1980 achieved short-term results that were lost by 1981–2 and although Andropov's discipline campaign was successful for a time in 1983, with reductions being noted in work-time losses in a number of regions, by 1984 the effects were beginning to be dissipated (Aganbegyan, 1985a, p. 7). Personnel changes, single issue campaigns and moral exhortation may provide a short-lived impetus to the failing economy, as the plan results for the first quarter of 1986 seem to suggest (*Pravda*, 20 April 1986, p. 1); but what is more important is the analysis of the underlying problems, the policy prescriptions that flow from that analysis and the long-term potential for change.

In order to evaluate this, it is necessary to consider briefly the economic situation inherited by Gorbachev. The final outcome of the Eleventh Five Year Plan, illustrated on Table 10.1, shows that all the major growth indicators were underfulfilled. As previously noted, growth may actually have come to a complete standstill; and, according to Ryzhkov, (1986, p. 2) the major reasons for these failures were the inadequate preparation of the economy for intensive growth, coupled with outdated management techniques and lax discipline. Hence, the whole thrust of Gorbachev's intentions has been towards rectifying the slow-down in growth, which is hardly a new theme. The desire for growth is easily identified from the Twelfth Plan Guidelines, which envisage substantial increases in all the major growth indi-

Table 10.1 Comparison of Eleventh Plan results and Twelfth Plan targets Average annual increases (%)

| | Eleventh Plan | | Twelfth Plan |
	Planned	Actual	Planned
National income	3.4	3.1	3.5–4.0
Industrial output	4.7	3.7	3.9–4.4
Agricultural output	2.5	1.1	2.7–3.0
Industrial labour productivity	3.6	3.2	4.2–4.6
Per capita real income	3.1	2.3	2.5–2.8

Increase over plan period (%)

| | Eleventh Plan | Twelfth Plan |
	Actual	Planned
National income	17	19–22
Industrial output	20	21–24
Agricultural output	6	14–16
Numbers in material production	2.3	0.5
Labour productivity	16.5	20–23

Source: *Pravda*, 4 March 1986, pp. 2–5.

cators. Table 10.1 provides a comparison between the actual outcome of the Eleventh Plan and the planned figures for the Twelfth Plan, and the intention is not simply to arrest the decline in growth but to positively reverse it.

Gorbachev has argued throughout his period in power that his overall objective for the Soviet economy is to achieve increases in both the rate and efficiency of economic growth through the intensification of production (Breev, 1986, pp. 56–7). A major element of this aim is to economise on the use of all inputs, in particular labour, existing plant capacity, natural resources and energy, with the ultimate objective of raising both the quantity and quality of output (*Pravda*, 21 September 1985, pp. 1–2). Gorbachev (*Pravda*, 26 February 1986, pp. 2-10) has argued, for example, that there is no labour shortage, only poor labour organisation and much has been made of the malutilisation of existing plant, machinery and equipment (Aganbegyan, 1985c, p. 2). The overall aim is to raise growth in National Income from a 3.1 per cent yearly average in the Eleventh Plan, to a five per cent yearly average by the Fourteenth Plan. Virtually the entire increment in industrial output is to be obtained by labour productivity increases, without which 22 million more workers would be required to achieve these targets (Ryzhkov, 1986, pp. 2–5).

Gorbachev's overall objectives are to be achieved via broad improvements in the economic system which were perhaps most comprehensively set out by Ryzhkov (1986, pp. 2–5) and which have been underpinned in particular, by the work of Aganbegyan (1985a, 1985b) and Zaslavskaya (1986a, 1986b). The strategy has three major dimensions, the first of which may be described as broadly technical and has as its aim the modernisation of Soviet industry. It is intended to accelerate the rate of scientific and technical progress and integrate this more rapidly with production (Aganbegyan 1985b, pp. 15–19; Kostin, 1985, p. 3). It is hoped that this will lead to better products as well as assisting with the re-tooling and re-equipping of Soviet industry. For example, it is planned that the inventory of robotic equipment should rise by 200 per cent and the output of computing equipment by 130 per cent, over the plan period. Linked to this the priority in investment policy is towards the machine building sector with the aim of increasing the re-construction and re-tooling of existing facilities and allowing an increase in the annual rate of withdrawal of obsolete equipment to five or six per cent. As was pointed out in Chapter 3, if successful, this would eventually allow a reduction in the burgeoning repair sector and would facilitate the intended reduction in heavy monotonous work by 50 per cent, releasing 20 million workers as a consequence (Ryzhkov, 1986, pp. 2–5). Technological progress, integrated into production would, it is hoped, not only improve production processes, but also improve the quality and reliability of products. It is also intended to limit the extent of new construction in order to cut the scattering of new projects and thereby reduce construction lead times, which have in the past often resulted in plant becoming obsolete before it is finished.

The second dimension is directed towards improving the 'economic mechanism' and is concerned primarily with improving the organisational control and efficiency of the centre, as well as improving managerial control at the level of the individual enterprise. The problem identified by a number of Soviet sources (Aganbegyan, 1985a, pp. 20–22; Zaslavskaya, 1986a and 1986b) is that the middle layers in the planning process, at the ministry level, do not provide a smooth transmission of plan instructions from the centre to the enterprise, but impede centralised control because they promote their own narrow sectional interests. It is also argued that they stifle enterprise initiative by their over-cautious approach and conservative attitudes. The resistance of ministries to the implementation of the Shchekino experiment would be a good example. Zaslavskaya (1986a, p. 1) argues that the brigade form of labour organisation has been implemented more slowly than is desirable because of over-detailed regulation. The aim, therefore, is to strengthen centralised planning and couple this with more autonomy at the level of the enterprise. However, this does not mean that the centre wishes to relinquish control over enterprises; rather that the form of control should be changed. The overall intention would be to free enterprise decision-making from detailed bureaucratic supervision by the ministry and to replace this by more complete forms of economic accountability. This would have as its eventual aim the creation of an unambiguous link between management's material self-interest and enterprise performance, and this would inevitably have further effects on the functions performed by management.

If the analysis presented in Part I is correct, the elements discussed so far are all subsidiary to the relationship between the ruling group, enterprise management and the workforce. However much the planning system is refined or technological processes improved, ultimately it is in the process of surplus extraction that the success or failure of Gorbachev's approach will be determined. The technical changes referred to above will eventually be refracted through the social relations of production.

The third dimension of Gorbachev's approach is referred to in the Soviet literature as concern regarding the 'human factor' (Khachaturov, 1986, p. 16; Aganbegyan, 1985b, p. 7). As Baranenkova (1986, p. 64) points out, the major role for the economic mechanism must be to solve the labour discipline problem. It has already been noted that the aim is to dramatically increase labour productivity and Gorbachev sees this being achieved by developing what he refers to as 'the initiative and self-activity of labour collectives' (*Pravda*, 12 April 1986, pp. 1–2).

This has two aspects. Much has been made of the possibilities for workforce participation. The law on labour collectives introduced in 1983 (*Pravda*, 19 June 1983, p. 1) was seen as the mechanism through which this self activity could be mobilised.[2] (The extent to which the possibilities for participation are realistic will be considered in the final section.) However, in Gorbachev's view (*Pravda*, 21 September 1985, pp. 1–2), the *khozraschet* brigade is the ideal form of labour organisation to mobilise this self-activity and he has been consistently critical of the rate of transfer to the brigade system and the results that brigades have achieved in increasing labour productivity.

The ultimate aim is to tie work and rewards more closely together, another theme that has been continually stressed throughout the period examined in this book. It has been argued that to achieve this end it is essential that wage levelling is reduced and further differentiation in income is developed. Manevich (1985, p. 34) points out that in 1940 ITR and highly qualified workers received wages twice that of the average worker, but by 1983 the differential had been cut to approximately ten per cent. Wages have to be linked directly to results so that there is a structural dependency between wage increases and productivity increases. Breev (1986, p. 63) notes that the relationship between the total wage fund and overall returns has deteriorated considerably over the period 1970–82. According to Zaslavskaya (1986a, p. 1), unconscientious and irresponsible workers can live too well and Antosenkov (1985) confirms that the wage difference between good and bad workers can be minimal. This generates a paradoxical position where good workers see it in their interest to emulate their lax colleagues. Some sources have suggested that to overcome this, poor workers should receive incomes below the present minimum (*Pravda*, 12 April 1986, p. 2). Others have suggested that centralised wage setting should be abandoned altogether and be replaced by enterprise level wage determination by the brigades, using the KTU (Klimentov, 1984, pp. 38–51). Antosenkov (1985) argues that as bonuses are no longer an incentive but simply an accepted part of the wage, then payments in kind from the enterprise material incentive funds should be used to encourage productivity increases (as it was argued they were used in the successful phase of the Shchekino experiment). Enterprise funds would not be used to provide services for everyone, but would be used selectively for those who increase their productivity or. responsibility. The general point is that a structure of incomes which reflects work intensities more closely should develop.

These are the general intentions and objectives of the Gorbachev approach. Again, it should be stressed that in many respects they represent simply the reiteration of themes identified over the whole period from the mid-sixties. How are these aims to be achieved and what are their chances of success?

The most important mechanism for achieving these ends is via the continuation of experiments begun by Gorbachev's predecessors as well as the introduction of new experimental forms. For example, the economic experiment instituted by Andropov in enterprises and associations of five ministries in January 1984 (Aganbegyan, 1984, p. 2) and which was extended to a further twenty ministries from January 1985, has been maintained (Abalkin, 1985, pp. 22). This 'large scale economic experiment' has as its major objective the intensification of the material interest and responsibility of the enterprise (Sukhachevskii, 1984, p. 2). This was to be achieved by setting up stable economic normatives for the experimental enterprises and making individual wages and collective social provision highly dependent upon the end results of work, both with regard to quality and productivity. The experiment has had its problems, particularly with regard to unstable plans, and Gorbachev, for example, has been critical of the slow pace of dissemination of the experiment, even though approximately 30 per cent of all enterprises are now working on these lines and the ultimate intention is to generalise it by 1987. However, it has been criticised by Aganbegyan (1985a, p. 22) for not going far enough. Aganbegyan is more enthusiastic in his support for the experiment begun at Novosibirsk in 1984, where fifteen enterprises comprising 48 shops introduced full *khozraschet* throughout their whole operations, from the factory floor brigades, through all technical personnel to management cadres.

During 1984, these plants raised labour productivity by fifteen per cent (in comparison with only four per cent at comparable plants), and wages grew, because of the experiment, by six per cent (in comparison with the two per cent received elsewhere) (Aganbegyan, 1985a, p. 22). Manevich (1985, p. 35) also praises the results of the experiment begun in Leningrad engineering enterprises in July 1983 and further extended in January 1985. The aim here was to raise the quality and quantity of work carried out by technical staff and simultaneously to reduce the size of the workforce. At the end of the first eighteen months of the experiment, the workforce had been reduced by ten per cent, the volume of production had risen by over thirteen per cent and labour productivity had risen by over twenty per cent (Manevich, 1985, p. 35). As Grotseskul (1985, p. 15) notes, both the Leningrad experiment and the 'large scale economic experiment' were in many respects developed from the Shchekino experiment, the further extension of which has been explicitly supported by Gorbachev (*Pravda*, 26 February 1986, pp. 2–10). Perhaps, however, the major plank of the Gorbachev approach has remained the pressure or the further extension of the brigade system (*Pravda*, 12 April 1985, pp. 1–2). The future possibilities for these initiatives are considered in more detail in the last section.

A major new initiative begun during the Gorbachev period is the experimental initiatives at the Frunze Machine Building Association at Sumy (Moskalenko, 1986, pp. 104–08) and at *VAZ* at Togliatti (Katsura, 1985, pp. 2). The basis of this experiment is a further extension of autonomy for the management of the Association. In future, profits earned by the association will be the only source of funds for the technical re-equipping of the association's constituent enterprises and the development of social provision for the workforce. Profits will be distributed in the following proportions; 47.5 per cent will be returned to the state budget, five per cent will be paid to the appropriate ministry and the remaining 47.5 per cent will be retained by the association (Katsura, 1985, p. 2). The experimental associations were guaranteed that these proportions would be maintained for the whole plan period (remember the initial terms of the Shchekino experiment). The argument advanced for such stability was that if the enterprise management and workforce were to be encouraged to find and utilise the 'hidden' reserves, then they had to be certain that the results of such endeavours would accrue to the association (again consider the example of the Shchekino experiment). A further new element in the autonomy of the *VAZ* association is the right to sell

excess equipment which they consider obsolete, but which other
plants may find useful given the relatively advanced nature of *VAZ*,
and use the funds thus generated for purchasing new plant or for
social measures. Finally, *VAZ* will be able to retain 40 per cent of the
foreign currency earnings from the sale of its products overseas,
which account for over 30 per cent of its output (Cockburn, 1986,
p. 12). This is important because VAZ imports both plant and
components and this will enable them to expedite such imports. As
Katsura (1985, p. 2) points out, it also gives *VAZ* the possibility of
assisting its suppliers in the Soviet Union to import foreign machine
tools, as up to 25 per cent of *VAZ*'s foreign currency holdings could
be transferred to its essential suppliers who require imported components.

The incentive elements of the experiment stem from the 19.5 per
cent of the total retained profits that are transferred to collective
service provision. This is a fixed proportion and will be utilised for a
wide variety of forms of collective consumption, like consumer
services, subsidised meals, holiday facilities, health provision, sports
and cultural facilities and, of course, housing. The important point is
that the overall amount spent on these elements will be determined by
the ability of the Association to actually add to total profits, giving
the whole workforce a material stake in enterprise performance.

The desirability of the experiment, from the point of view of
management, is enhanced because of increased planning autonomy.
For the whole plan period, the number of controlling indices have
been drastically reduced. This experiment marks a continuation of the
tendency for ever further reaching experimentation. The intention is
to extend the model to a further 200 enterprises in 1987 (Abalkin,
1986). However, it should be noted that the enterprise is still heavily
constrained with regard to the options open to it. The limitations and
problems of this initiative will also be taken up in the last section.

PRACTICAL, POLITICAL AND THEORETICAL CONCLUSIONS

It has been argued throughout this book that the political economy of
the USSR is characterised by antagonistic social relations of production that produce the vicious circle of interrelated social and economic problems identified in Figure 3.1. It was suggested at the end of
Chapter 4 that the attempts by the ruling group to reform the

economic system since the mid-sixties are their response to these problems, and what they have sought are new forms of economic regulation and control that would simultaneously preserve their hegemony and enable an expansion in the socially produced surplus. This is the same problem which faces Gorbachev at present.

The experimental initiatives since the late sixties have been attempts to find new forms of control or to graft onto the basic structure of Stalinist planning new techniques for controlling the surplus extraction process. They represent a 'bottom up' approach to reform and, as the other elements of the reforms petered out, the longevity of these experiments and the manner in which they have progressed from one form to another, is a testimony to the centrality of the problems they sought to solve (Zaslavskaya, 1984, pp. 88–90). The experiments were attempts to resolve specific manifestations of the underlying antagonistic relationships by administering into existence surrogate forms of control derived ultimately from the market but not being of the market. It could be argued that the different reform initiatives imitate different elements of the law of value and attempt to fulfil similar functions. For example, the Shchekino experiment itself and the pressure for its introduction in both a 'horizontal' and 'vertical' form is an attempt to replicate the way in which the law of value operates to regulate manning levels both within the individual capitalist firm and through industries and regions. In comparison with capitalism, where this process appears as spontaneous and 'natural', in the USSR the mechanism has to be administered into existence. The same could be said of the Aksai, Dinamo and VAZ experiments discussed in Chapter 9, which were attempts to regulate the pace and intensity of work. The VAZ and Frunze experiments discussed above are similar. Their attempt to utilise the retention of profits for self-financing is reminiscent of the capitalist firm, but their inability to set prices and actually determine profitability clearly sets them apart. Therefore, as a consequence, the reforms are partial and piecemeal attempts to utilise in a technical manner some elements of the law of value, without fundamentally affecting the underlying social relations of production which are normally associated with that form of control. This explains why elements of the experimental initiatives sometimes contradict one another.

However, this raises a further question. If it is accepted that it was both impractical and impossible to return to old forms of control, that is, extra-economic force and atomisation, and that simply to raise the level of exploitation would be likely to provoke hostility, why did the ruling group not turn to the law of value as the solution to the problems they faced? Why imitate the forms without the substance?

The direct re-introduction of the law of value as the principal regulatory mechanism would appear to have been the most obvious solution for the Soviet ruling group in the mid-sixties. It could have simultaneously provided the type of unambiguous regulation that has been referred to continuously throughout this book, with the advantages of disciplining both workforce and management. Furthermore, it would have allowed the coalescence of the ruling group into a class because the re-introduction of the law of value implies the 'freeing' of labour and ultimately the formalisation of property rights. For the workforce, this would have required the sale of their labour power and for the ruling group, or at least some sections of it, ultimately real control and ownership of the means of production. However, amongst the many problems of this approach there was, and there remains, one fundamental difficulty. The re-introduction of the market would turn labour power unambiguously into a commodity and would necessitate the re-introduction of unemployment. Politically the abandonment of full employment (over-full employment) would undermine the hegemony of the ruling group and would in an immediate sense politicise factory relations. The major benefit of the atomisation of the working class was its depoliticisation and the destruction of the direct producers as a class capable of acting for itself. The re-introduction of the law of value would bring that class back into being. It would undermine the ideological legitimacy of the ruling group and sever its links with the revolutionary past. As with attempts to increase the rate of exploitation, this would be seen as a conscious decision on the part of the ruling group. Consequently, the direct return to market mechanisms was an unlikely course of action in the mid-sixties, no matter how attractive this may have appeared to some elements within the ruling group.

It is for this reason that the concept of class is adjudged to be inappropriate in the Soviet context. What exists are direct producers who produce a surplus which is extracted by a ruling group. However, the direct producers are able to exert considerable negative control over this process which is continually reproduced and this results in the instability of the ruling group. The relationship between these elements in the surplus extraction process and their composition are in a state of continual flux. In other words, there are classes in the process of 'becoming', they are not finished and formed in an unambiguous relationship to one another. The continual experimentation by the ruling group represents its attempts to find a form of exploitative relationship with the workforce that is manageable, capable of incorporating sections of the workforce and, above all, is capable of reproduction over time without continual direct administrative intervention. If the return to overt force in impossible, if direct attempts at raising the level of exploitation are likely to provoke hostility and if the law of value cannot easily be reinstated, this provides an explanation for the necessity for experimentation.

All the initiatives considered sought to influence economic relationships on a number of levels; between the direct producers and the ultimate controllers of the surplus; between the direct producers and those responsible for the supervision of the surplus extraction process; between management and the centre; between workers themselves; finally, between the individual worker and his work. The experimental initiatives could only be successful in so far as they could influence this complex of relationships and ultimately guarantee growth in the rate of surplus extraction. After twenty years of such experimentation, it should be possible to assess their past impact, consider the likely future prospects for reforms of this kind and draw some political and theoretical conclusions.

On a general level, the problems these initiatives addressed have not been resolved, nor is there any evidence to suggest that past experiments have set up a dynamic which will make the problems disappear spontaneously. On the contrary, the evidence presented in Chapters 3 and 4 and the results of the Eleventh Plan, suggest that the phenomenal forms which the antagonisms produce have deteriorated throughout the period of operation of the experimental initiatives. For example, growth continues to decline, the demographic situation becomes more acute, the problems of labour shortages grow, labour discipline indicators deteriorate, and so on. We may conclude however, that without the limited, localised successes of the experiments, these indicators would have deteriorated even further.

The continual appearance over the period of a range of experiments and their variants testifies to the necessity for change and the search for new forms of control on the part of the ruling group. The experiments may fulfil the short-term and necessary function of dealing with problems in specific sectors; the Shchekino experiment in the chemical industry, Zlobin brigades in construction and so on, but in the longer term none have been successfully generalised in an adequate form. Both the Shchekino experiment and the Brigade system have only been generalised to any extent in their weakest form. This leads to the important but obvious conclusion that in the USSR there is no mechanism that promotes spontaneous change. Localised success remains precisely that, unless administrative bodies press for its extension and even then the results are dissipated. If no spontaneous dynamic exists then further experimentation is the only form that change can take and as experimental change sets up no momentum or dynamic of its own, this implies that continual experimentation is necessary. The introduction of new experimental forms under Andropov and Gorbachev supports this view. Furthermore, the packaging of the initiatives as experiments is probably the only way to make them acceptable initially to both workforce and management, bringing prestige and publicity in return for the implementation of experimental initiatives and changing working conditions.

The failure of the experiments to achieve the desired impact can be gauged in another way. The planning reform of 1979, which, after all, encompassed elements of all the older experimental initiatives, had as its intention the stimulation of production and the provision of discipline and regulation through the sphere of economic regulation. However, Andropov's first act on coming to power was the institution of a campaign for labour, plan and production discipline referred to above. That this and the legislative changes regarding the workplace were necessary testifies to the failure of the 1979 resolution to achieve its objectives. Equally, the new experimental initiatives under Gorbachev stem from the failures or shortcomings of previous forms of experimentation. It is worth noting that alongside the calls for more complete 'economic regulation', further bureaucratic forms of regulation have also been developed. Perhaps the best example of this is the campaign for attestation or certification of workplaces (*Pravda*, 12 September 1985). Here the aim is to adjust the size of the enterprise staff complement in a manner not dissimilar to the work of the internal commissions at Shchekino.

In my view, the experimental initiatives have failed to fulfil their intended role. I believe that Rutland (1985, p. 361), for example, is wrong when he argues that these initiatives are all just examples of the 'exchange of experience of leading plants'. The search for some form of control over the workforce and the continual stress on discipline and regulation is evidence of the degree of crisis that the system faces, which will ultimately jeopardise its own reproduction. Also, I would consider that Cockburn (1986, p. 12), overstates the case when he argues, with respect to the recent *VAZ* and Frunze experiments, that with the backing of the State and Party experimental change in the USSR is 'far from being a laboratory test case for reform'. The implication that experimentation is the precursor for real change has not been borne out by the experience of the last twenty years.

This still leaves open the question of what general conclusions can be drawn from the experience of the experimental initiatives. I would argue that there are several lessons to be drawn from the experiments. The Shchekino experiment and the other earlier experimental initiatives have all followed a broadly similar pattern of development (it is perhaps more correct to identify a pattern of limited growth and decline).

Firstly, they have all been based upon localised successes in sectors of the economy or particular industries or enterprises which have been experiencing specific difficulties or perhaps have been in receipt of foreign plant.

Secondly, small scale generalisation occurred, plus adaptation of the original idea that led to the introduction of a range of variants.

Thirdly, after the initial successes party and state pressure was exerted, usually in the form of legislative changes, for the wider dissemination of the experiments.

Fourthly, resistance arose to the intention of the experiments, either in the enterprises themselves, causing further adaptation to take place, or at ministry level, causing their generalisation to be retarded.

Fifthly, where the experiments were now introduced the results were less dramatic than at the original locations.

Sixthly, the momentum slows at the original locations as the rules of the initiative change, either because of contradictory objectives at the centre or because of contradictions in the logic of the initiatives themselves.

Seventhly, complaints arise concerning the slow generalisation of the initiatives and the lack of clarity regarding responsibilities for the experiments, leading to further legislative changes. The instability of the regulations ironically further deters the acceptance of the initiatives.

Finally, the appearance is created that the experiments are being broadly disseminated, both by enterprises and ministries, but this obscures the adaptations that have taken place along the way (which in some instances destroy the logic of the experiments) and the fact that in many instances the introduction of the experimental initiatives is an illusion that has changed nothing.

Each experimental initiative has originally promised the possibility of far-reaching changes in the labour process, only to be frustrated by the external environment it is intended to transform. As long as the success of the experiment is determined by internally controllable factors the appearance of success can be maintained, but once it confronts the vagaries of Soviet industrial life, the momentum is lost both specifically and generally. Rather than transforming the system, the experiment is forced to adapt.

This pattern is easily identified from the example of Shchekino itself. It is ironic, for example, that in an article on the Shchekino experiment written in 1982 (Valavoi *et al.*, 1982, p. 3) there is a list of complaints seeking to explain the poor generalisation of the experiment which includes unstable plan targets, uncertainty about the wage fund, poor material incentives, and so on. All of these elements were central to the experiment's operation at the start in the late 1960s; their absence was continually bemoaned throughout the 1970s; they were legislated for in the series of regulatory changes in the late 1970s, noted in Chapter 8; and they were all included in the planning resolution of 1979. Nevertheless, they are all still absent and this continues to retard the dissemination of the experiment.

This raises a further question. If these conditions were present could the experiment work and if not, what conditions would be necessary?

It is ironic that the only way in which the incentive effects of the Shchekino experiment can operate is if the experiment has already been comprehensively introduced and is working well. The precondition for the implementation of the experiment is its success in raising output in Department 2 industries and forging a closer link between work and rewards as a consequence. The fact that it has proved difficult to generalise the experiment, and that it is impossible to instantaneously implement it throughout all enterprises, ministries and regions, undermines the argument that it is the incentives element that will provide the way forward. This lends further credence to the argument developed in Chapter 6.

If that analysis is correct, it was not the material incentives element that accounted for the localised success in the first instance. The basic reason for success was the increase in worker insecurity that the implementation of the experiment introduced at enterprise level. This was supplemented by the work of the internal commissions in tightening work organisation and norms. However, as has been noted, this could only have a declining effect, as the degree of worker security inevitably rose, for three reasons. The number of workers released was bound to be largest at the outset and then diminish.

Secondly, the option to move to other plants in the locality meant that it was possible to avoid the experiment. Finally, the raising of planned tasks on a ratchet basis, apart from demoralising management at the experimental enterprises, meant that they had an interest in the re-emergence of a safety factor of hoarded labour, even if it was a lower level than at the outset. Hence the experiment had its own internal limitations.

From the point of view of management, the experience of the experiment, although it may have been desirable in the first instance, became negative. In the environment of ratchet planning, plan and wage fund instability and material supply difficulties, the experiment could only be desirable if it gave advantage over other enterprises. This it did not do. If anything, it brought disadvantage in terms of the tightened internal situation and the problems of retaining workers and expanding or renewing capacity.

It is suggested, therefore, that the experiment could only succeed if it could maintain worker insecurity and provide a mechanism whereby enterprise increases in productivity could be translated into increased access to investment goods. This has implications for the workforce and for the relationship between enterprises, ministries and planners.

For the latter set of relationships, the only way to implement the experiment is to set enterprises against one another in the search for resources. In other words, the enterprises of a particular ministry would receive resources in terms of competitive tendering on the basis of past performance (and by extension a similar type of mechanism would be required to operate between ministries to enforce the intention of the experiment throughout all economic decisions). This would give direct advantage to successful enterprises and would install a mechanism whereby enterprises would be identified as failures. This would turn the implementation of the experiment into an externally coercive force upon plant management who would have to replicate the behaviour of the most successful in order to survive. Ultimately it is being suggested that some form of competitive mechanism for investment goods would be a necessary concomitant for the successful generalisation of the experiment. In a limited sense, the VAZ and Frunze experiments could be seen as a precursor to this type of change, but even this experiment is limited in scope.

From the point of view of the workforce, it would be necessary to introduce a situation whereby they could not escape the experiment. The experiment would have to be simultaneously implemented at all plants. If this were to be the case, the careful procedures adopted at

Shchekino could not be replicated elsewhere. Furthermore, the intensity of worker insecurity would have to be raised and maintained and
the differentiation of wages enhanced. Popov (1980, p. 3), for example, suggests that the experiment should be amended in the
following manner. He suggests that the enterprise freeing workers
should transfer them to some local body, the City Soviet for example.
The enterprise should also transfer from the wage fund to this body
the minimum wage for each worker, the balance of the wage fund
being retained by the enterprise for material incentives for those
remaining at the plant. The City Soviet should then be responsible for
the placement of these workers and if they cannot or will not be
placed, then the City Soviet should find them menial work and pay
them the minimum wage. Popov argues that this will have a number
of salutary effects. It will tighten the labour discipline of those who
remain employed at the enterprise, as they will not wish to be released
to this type of work. Moreover, the experience of menial work at the
minimum wage, will 'educate' those released, who in their future work
will exhibit a more disciplined approach. Popov's argument is effectively a call for the re-introduction of unemployment as a disciplining
mechanism. I would argue that this is implicit in the logic of the
Shchekino experiment and that ultimately the failure to introduce
unemployment leads to the diminishing effectiveness of the experiment.

What are the implications to be drawn from this analysis? The
antagonistic social relations of production which made the Shchekino
experiment necessary have also made it impossible for it to succeed.[3]
The further development of the Shchekino experiment could only
begin to work by acting with a degree of compulsion on both workers
and managers, and this implies the implementation of a more radical
variant with parallel reforms to supplement its operation. However,
as has been pointed out in Chapter 8, the experiment is now in its
weakest form. Ultimately it would require the re-introduction of a
competitive market for investment goods, which would act to
discipline management by providing an unambiguous mechanism for
detecting and punishing failure. Furthermore, unemployment would be
necessary to discipline the workforce. The combination of these two
elements would allow the full generalisation of the experiment and
would stop its modification and dissipation. However, if unemployment could be re-introduced, then the Shchekino experiment itself
would be redundant. As previously suggested, the likelihood of this
type of reform is remote. The widescale re-introduction of unemploy-

ment would be politically destabilising and to encourage a mechanism that unequivocally identifies enterprise failure would be resisted both by enterprise management, whose precarious position would be made more vunerable and by ministries, who are ultimately responsible. Even if the ultimate creation of a market socialist model in the USSR were in the interests of perhaps the majority of enterprise management and some sectors of the workforce (those who do not become unemployed or who have the intensity of their work increased or who occupy a lowly position in the necessarily unequal distribution of income), once it exists, the transition towards it will be resisted because potentially it is in no-one's interest. No individual manager or worker can be guaranteed that he will not be either a failure or unemployed. Therefore, it is rational to maintain the imperfect status quo than risk the uncertainties of the future. This is confirmed by Abalkin in a most unusual letter to the *Financial Times* (11 July 1986). He confirms that even with the 'large scale economic experiment', that took management only a little way along the road to greater responsibility and possible failure, there is a marked reluctance to accept responsibility. Furthermore, he points out that the rank and file recognise that if they became independent then no helping hand would be proffered from the centre. Better, therefore, to accept fewer rights but also less responsibility.

What of the possibilities for the brigade system?[4] Based upon the analysis presented in Chapter 9, this is hardly likely to be the cure-all that some Soviet sources suggest. There are doubts about the suitability of the system for all areas of production. It may well be an appropriate form for construction or agriculture, but in its full *khozraschet* form it is inappropriate for modern integrated plants. The introduction of new 'administrative' means of control, the hierarchy of brigade leaders and so on, alongside all the other internal enterprise bodies, appears as a duplication and further bureaucratic encumbrance. In times of technological change what is necessary is a form of control that simplifies rather than complicates the economic mechanism. It has been suggested by some Soviet sources (Kutyrev, 1985, pp. 42–9; Klimentov, 1984, pp. 38–51) that the brigade system should be extended to all workers, technical staff and management. If this was achieved it would presumably lead to a merging of all management and brigade functions and a simplification of internal control mechanisms, but this is clearly a long way off. The successful operation of the brigade system, like the Shchekino system before it, has its own inherent limits. For example, if brigades make drastic cuts in working time how is management to respond? The logic of the experiment is that the new time should form the basis of the new contract, but under these circumstances workers will either avoid exposing all reserves or alternatively will opt out of the system. Leading brigades, as already noted, may be used as trouble-shooters, but this can only last for a limited time. Finally, to talk of the brigade system in terms of democratisation of the workplace is simply misleading.[5] The brigade structure and its leadership should be viewed as a more comprehensive system of 'foremanship'. For example Gorbachev (*Pravda*, 12 April 1985, p. 1) has described brigade leaders as 'executives on the shop floor'. The brigade system is not a mechanism for workers' control but a means to more closely control the Soviet workforce. The ultimate logic of the brigade system is to further fragment internal factory relations, which directly contradicts the logic of the development of the productive forces.

The most recent experimental initiatives seem to be replicating the pattern experienced by earlier initiatives. The *VAZ* and Frunze experiments, for all their perceived benefits, are experiencing difficulties. Yazinskii (1986, p. 2) points out that even though the experiment has been successful at *VAZ*, transferring 65 million roubles into the fund for social and cultural needs, it has been constrained by the activities of other ministries. This applies to both supplier ministries and also to construction. Lack of components has halted the production line on a number of occasions, leading to increasing costs. The foreign exchange component of the experiment appears logical in principle but has been difficult to operate due to red tape and bureaucratic obstructions. The experiment again is being constrained by the broader environment. Just because *VAZ* has new operating criteria, this does not necessarily affect supplier ministries and so on. If incomes within *VAZ* are now heavily dependent upon performance, these external constraints will eventually erode the operation of the experiment. Finally, it has to be recognised that the degree of autonomy granted to the association was heavily constrained. For example, price formation was still outside their control and as the supply system had not been changed fundamentally, familiar problems are bound to emerge.

However, even given the relative failure of the experimental initiatives, we may expect the emergence of further new experiments with the aim of controlling Soviet labour. This may well be supported by the re-promotion of older initiatives and attempted combinations of both new and old forms. The reform initiatives will probably originate in particular problem areas like the chemical industry, construction, machine tools and robotic equipment production and so on.[6] It is also to be expected that these reform initiatives will be supplemented by further legislative changes in the area of labour laws and labour discipline. The logic of what has been developed in this book suggests that any new experiments or re-promotions of old initiatives will lead to similar cycles of growth and decline.

In conclusion, the experience of the experimental initiatives suggests that the transition to any form of market socialist model in the USSR will be extremely difficult. The experiments rather than establishing any spontaneous dynamic in this direction were resisted by both workers and enterprise management and their implementation was slowed by ministries. The experience suggests that the introduction of partial market-based forms of control will fail if the whole structure of market relations is not introduced, which in turn would be resisted by most sectors of the Soviet population. I would suggest that as long as the direct producers are excluded from control over their labour-time, and as long as production is not controlled by the needs of the direct producers, the Soviet ruling group will be faced by a crisis either of 'labour shortage' or 'labour surplus'. Labour shortage, based upon the existence of the negative control of the workforce, ultimately threatens the legitimacy and reproduction of the ruling group. Labour surplus, based upon forms of market control, may be more desirable for the ruling group, but is politically impossible to introduce. The experiments represent an attempt on the part of the ruling group to obtain the perceived benefits of elements of the law of value without introducing the social relations of production necessary for that form of control to operate. The experiments themselves are inherently unstable and contradict the logic of Soviet planning, but nevertheless provide the only way for the ruling group to introduce even limited change. The fact that they continually fail illustrates the nature of the impasse that the Soviet ruling group faces.

Appendix

The analysis presented in Part I suggests that the decline in Soviet economic growth can be explained by reference to the antagonistic nature of production relations and the absence of any unambiguous form of economic regulation. The impact of labour discipline problems has been recognised by the Soviet sources cited throughout this book, and explicitly by the Soviet leadership, but this has been disputed by western commentators (Teague, 1983, p. 23). Hanson (1983), for example, suggests that increasing labour discipline will not lead to any significant improvement in economic performance. The reason for this is that the effects of labour discipline infractions, when they emerge in surveys, appear relatively small. Hanson's argument is that it is imperfections in the planning system that lead to low shift coefficients, considerable idle-time and poor utilisation of fixed capacity. This argument requires closer examination.

Given the problems already cited with regard to mechanising production, it is particularly important that existing equipment is fully utilised, especially in Department 1 industries. The hope is that this will not only raise output, but enable the production of more mechanised equipment and lead to the freeing of manual workers, thereby easing the apparent labour shortages. The problems of the machine building industry make it desirable to be able to identify causes of idle-time and under-utilisation in that industry. The survey that Hanson cites (*Vestnik Statistiki*, 1984, No. 4, pp. 68–70) is reproduced in part in this appendix.

Table A1 identifies the percentage of non-working time for metal-working equipment in the machine building industry and the relevant shift coefficients. Five points emerge: The average shift coefficient is 1.33 (out of a maximum possible value of 3) which is well below the 1.7 deemed desirable by Soviet sources. The shift coefficient is declining over time. In the mid-seventies, shift coefficients were in the range 1.36 to 1.56, with an average of 1.41 (V. Silin and A. Sukhov, 1977, p. 98). As Bunich (1984, p. 5) has pointed out, if shift coefficients are so low, why are plans fulfilled and indeed over-fulfilled? Furthermore, the proportion of idle-time for each category of equipment is higher in auxiliary production (15.9 per cent on average) than for basic production (14.1 per cent on average), with consequent effects on shift coefficients. This supports the point made earlier with regard to problems in auxiliary production. Finally, where automatic lines are identified, shift coefficients are not appreciably better (in one instance the percentage of idle-time is below average and the shift coefficient is marginally above 1.7). Kulagin (1983, p. 105) argues that with automatic equipment and lines the shift coefficient has to approach 3 to justify the expenditures involved.

The following three tables identify the reasons for idle-time in three categories: Table A2, whole day losses; Table A3, whole shift losses; Table A4, intra-shift losses.

Hanson is formally correct to point out that losses directly attributable to infractions of labour discipline or shirking are very small; 0.1 to 0.2 per cent

Table A1 Utilisation of productive metal working equipment in enterprises of the machine building ministry
(Based on data for the 24 hours of 19/5/82)

	A*	B*	C*	D*
All metal working equipment	14.7	1.33		
In basic production	14.1	1.41	10.7	9.9
In aux. production	15.9	1.16		
Metal cutting lathes	14.5	1.32		
In basic production	14.0	1.39	10.3	9.9
In aux. production	15.6	1.17		
Of lathes in basic production				
Numerically controlled	15.3	1.41	8.9	10.2
Automatic lines	8.9	1.71	9.2	12.2
Forge pressing machines	14.8	1.40		
In basic production	14.4	1.44	12.1	10.0
In aux. production	17.5	1.13		
Automatic lines	15.4	1.61	13.9	10.9
Casting & moulding equipment	14.6	1.65		
In basic production	14.5	1.66	9.7	11.7
In aux. production	17.0	1.40		
Electrical welding equipment	15.7	1.26		
In basic production	14.7	1.34	10.5	9.5
In aux. production	18.0	1.07		

A* Non-working equipment as a % of the total.
B* Shift coefficient.
C* Intra-shift downtime as a % of the total.
D* Worked tool-hours per unit of set-up equipment in 24 hour period.

Source: *Vestnik Statistiki*, 1984, No. 4, pp. 68–70.

on Table A2; 0.2 to 0.7 per cent on Table A3; 1.1 to 2.3 per cent on Table A4. These figures are broadly comparable to those cited in Chapter 4, from Sonin and others, but it should be remembered that they argue that these under-report losses by as much as ten times.

However, leaving this last point aside, the major reason for idle-time clearly emerges on both Table A2 and Table A3, as being as a result of shortages of workers in a variety of shops; 16.1 to 26.3 per cent of the idle-time on Table A2 and 29.9 to 39.5 per cent on Table A3. Hanson correctly points out that the blame for this cannot be attributed to Soviet mothers for not producing sufficient children. However, he explains this disparity as being the consequence of inadequacies in the planning system. His failure to explain the cause of these inadequacies and his narrow conception of labour discipline

Table A2   Reasons for idle-time in basic production (%)

Quantity of Equipment Idle for 24 hours	A 100	B 100	C 100	D 100
Planned repair & modernisation	15.1	18.6	26.5	17.5
Reserves & temporarily unutilised	9.3	6.9	15.0	12.8
Superfluous equipment	3.9	2.7	2.2	3.1
Defective & unplanned repair*	10.9	14.0	15.8	12.1
Lack of productive work*	9.3	11.4	7.3	12.0
Below staff complement*	26.3	23.1	16.1	21.0
Lack of workers for administratively sanctioned reasons	6.7	4.9	3.4	5.2
Shirking*	0.2	0.1	0.1	0.2
Deficiencies in raw materials, stocks, machine parts, materials*	9.1	8.6	4.7	7.1
Deficiencies in instrumentation, technical documentation, energy sources, transport, lifting equipment etc.*	2.2	2.9	2.5	1.6
Deficiencies in computing equipment*	0.2	—	—	—
Other whole day losses*	6.8	6.8	6.4	7.4

A = Metal cutting lathes
B = Forge pressing equipment
C = Casting & moulding equipment
D = Electro-welding equipment
Source: *Vestnik Statistiki*, 1984, No. 4, pp. 68–70.

problems results in a technical explanation of a socio-economic problem. Presumably, for Hanson, these problems would be resolved if planning mechanisms were more efficient.

However, I would argue that this explanation is inadequate. As Chapter 4 sought to explain, the apparent labour shortage is the result of the contradictions of the socio-economic system and these are reproduced over time and are not the result of technical failures. If a broader perspective is taken, which sets the problems of production into the context of the antagonism between the worker and the ruling group, then a significant proportion of the idle-time can be explained as a result of labour discipline problems, either directly or indirectly.

The lines marked with an asterisk on Tables A2, A3 and A4 represent problems directly attributable to the antagonistic nature of the system. Planned repair is excluded, as it is a necessary part of any production process. Administratively sanctioned absences are also excluded, although this is more debatable. As suggested in Chapter 4, this is often a result of management recompensing workers for the poor rhythm of production, producing necessary overtime.

In the figures produced below, the first figure includes the category 'other

Table A3   Reasons for idle-time in basic production (%)

Quantity of Equipment Idle for Whole Shift	A 100	B 100	C 100	D 100
Planned repair & modernisation	7.6	9.7	11.4	9.3
Defective & unplanned repair*	9.8	11.8	14.6	10.5
Lack of production tasks*	11.9	13.0	12.9	14.5
Below staff complement*	39.5	35.5	29.9	34.2
Absence of workers with administrative sanction	8.5	7.0	6.5	6.8
Shirking*	0.3	0.2	0.7	0.2
Deficiencies in raw materials stocks, machine parts, materials*	9.1	8.7	7.9	9.0
Deficiencies in instruments, technical documentation, energy sources, transport & lifting equipment*	3.1	3.4	2.9	2.4
Other whole shift losses*	10.2	10.7	13.2	13.1

A = Metal cutting lathes
B = Forge pressing equipment
C = Casting & moulding equipment
D = Electro-welding equipment
Source: *Vestnik Statistiki*, 1984, No. 4, pp. 68–70.

causes' and this second excludes this proportion of idle-time. Without more information, nothing definite can be said about these time losses. If the totals are recalculated they read as follows:

Table A2:	A = 65%, 58.2%;	B = 66.9%, 60.1%;
	C = 52.9%, 46.5%;	D = 61.4%, 54%.
Table A3:	A = 83.9%, 73.7%;	B = 83.3%, 72.6%;
	C = 82.1%, 68.9%;	D = 83.9%, 70.8%.

A similar situation arises with Table A4, but here the only element excluded is the adjustment and resetting of equipment. Again this could be questioned on the grounds that lack of sufficient specialised equipment, and the consequent use of general purpose equipment, is a systemic failing.

Table A4:	A = 81.5%, 64%;	B = 77.3%, 60.6%;
	C = 84.4%, 71.2%;	D = 86.5%, 66.1%.

These figures suggest that the reponsibility of labour discipline infractions for idle-time are much more significant than Hanson suggests. It really depends upon how you view the nature of planning, either as a technical operation or as a reflection of the political economy of the USSR.

The original article contains two further tables which have not been reproduced here. The first considers the level of idle-time across industries and indicates that there is little variation, with an average of 14.1 per cent

Table A4   Reasons for idle-time in basic production (%)

Intra-shift Losses	A 100	B 100	C 100	D 100
Defective & unplanned repair*	16.9	16.9	26.1	14.0
Adjustment & readjustment of equipment	18.5	22.7	15.6	13.5
Deficiencies in raw materials Stocks, machine parts, etc.*	21.5	17.9	21.8	22.1
Deficiencies in instrumentation, technical documentation, energy sources, lifting & transport equipment*	7.5	7.5	9.2	10.3
Deficiencies in production tasks*	9.7	11.3	6.8	12.2
Absence of workers with administrative sanction*	6.6	5.9	5.0	5.6
Deficiencies caused by labour discipline violations*	1.8	1.1	2.3	1.9
Other intrashift losses*	17.5	16.7	13.2	20.4

A = Metal cutting lathes
B = Forge pressing equipment
C = Casting & moulding equipment
D = Electro-welding equipment
Source: *Vestnik Statistiki*, 1984, No. 4, pp. 68-70

idle-time and a shift coefficient of 1.41 (*Vestnik Statistiki*, 1984, No. 4, p. 70). The second table adds a regional dimension to this and shows significant regional variations in idle-time, (from a low of 9.8 per cent to a high of 32.6 per cent) and shift coefficients (from a high of 1.54 to a low of 0.82) (*Vestnik Statisiki*, 1984, No. 4, p. 70).

The general point to be drawn from this is that the contradictory nature of the system leads to under-utilisation of fixed capacity in this important branch of the economy. As has been suggested throughout, labour shortage and poor planning are not the causes of this but are manifestations of deeper problems.

Notes and References

Introduction

1. There is a vast literature on the economic reforms of the early sixties. For a standard Soviet account see, *Khozyaistvennaya reforms v SSSR* (1969). For a comprehensive western summary of the debates and the literature see P. R. Gregory and R. C. Stuart (1986, pp. 387–420).
2. See K. Marx (1973, pp. 100–8) for the classic exposition of the methodology of political economy.
3. For an example of the first approach see P. Binns and M. Haynes (1980, pp. 18–50). They manage to identify a tendency for the rate of profit to fall in the USSR without adequately explaining the distinctive nature of profit in the USSR. As an example of the second approach, see T. Buck (1982) where a neo-classical framework is used to analyse Soviet enterprises hence abstracting the enterprise from its unique social context. Finally, P. Corrigan, H. Ramsey and D. Sayer (1981) is a good example of the last approach.
4. P. Thompson (1984) provides an excellent introduction to this work. The contributions which I have found most useful are; H. Braverman (1974); T. Nichols and P. Armstrong (1976); CSE (ed.) (1976); A. L. Friedman (1977); T. Nichols (1980); J. S. Storey (1983).
5. A similar perspective can be found in the work of I. Wallerstein and A. G. Frank. See I. Wallerstein (1979) and any of Frank's numerous works on the International Crisis.
6. See H. H. Ticktin (1973, 1976, 1978, 1983 and 1986). See also the debates between Ticktin and Mandel (1980) and between Ticktin and Brus (1981). The other articles that have contributed most towards the development of this perspective are G. A. E. Smith (1975) and (1981); M. Cox (1975 and 1986); M. Holubenko (1975); S. Meikle (1981); R. Arnot (1981).
7. See particularly J. Berliner (1957), whose early work on the nature of the Soviet factory manager's role and position identified a number of crucial features of the system, especially the role of the 'safety factor' and D. Granick (1975, pp. 466–91), who identified the significance of the 'full employment constraint' for factory management in Eastern Europe. Also J. Kornai (1980a and 1980b) has produced a theoretical view of the significance of shortages, and specifically labour shortages (1980a, pp. 235–264) based on the Hungarian experience.

2 The Political Economy of the USSR

1. See for example, R. Conquest (1967). The journal *Workers Under Communism* appears to be of a similar perspective, making uncritical

assumptions about the 'freedoms' of workers in the west in comparison
with the 'unfreedoms' of Soviet and Eastern European workers.

2.   See for example, L. Shapiro and J. Godson (eds) (1981), which contains
both academic papers and journalistic accounts and D. Lane (ed.)
(1986). The western work I have found most useful and illuminating is
that of M. Yanovitch, particularly (1978) and (1985).

3.   It is impossible to consider fully all the various strands in this debate
which would take a separate book. The spectrum of opinion can be
summarised as follows:

(i)   The pro-Moscow Communist Parties who view the USSR as
Socialist and moving towards 'full communism'. See for example, D.
Purdy (1976).
(ii)   The Eurocommunist perspective, that the USSR is essentially
socialist but with specific problems in the political superstructure
connected with democratic rights. See Fernando Claudin (1978).
(iii)   The 'Orthodox' Trotskyist position that the USSR is a 'degenerated workers state' where the fundamental problem lies in the dislocation between a 'socialist mode of production' and a 'bourgeois mode of
distribution', necessitating a political revolution to restore the USSR to
a socialist path. See E. Mandel (1968, pp. 560–5; 1974 pp. 5–22; 1979
pp. 117–27).
(iv)   The state capitalist school, which argues that the USSR represents a new higher and more degenerate form of capitalism. See T. Cliff
(1974); C. Harman (1974); Haynes and Binns (1980). Articles from
both the 'State Capitalist' and 'Degenerated Workers' State' viewpoints are collected in *Readings on State Capitalism* (1973).
(v)   The capitalist restorationist school, which argues that capitalism
was restored with the death of Stalin. For an extreme version see Wei
Chi (1978). For a slightly more sophisticated view see C. Bettelheim
(1975) and the exchanges reprinted from *Monthly Review* in C. Bettelheim and P. Sweezy (1971).
(vi)   A variety of theorists, both western academics and East European dissidents, who either point towards a 'new class', based on the
party, the intelligentsia, the bureaucracy, the technocracy or any
combination of them; or alternatively, seek to explain the USSR by
recourse to previous social systems or modes of production, for
example, those who seek to characterise the USSR as some form of
'Asiatic mode of production' or 'Oriental Despotism'. See for example,
G. Konrad and I. Szelenyi (1979); M. Djilas (1957); M. Machover and
J. Fantham (1979); R. Bahro (1978); M. Rakovski (1978).

4.   This is precisely the problem with Nove's desire to use the *nomenklatura* as the basis of a definition of the Soviet ruling group and it derives
from this mistaken 'sociological' view of class. See for example, A.
Nove (1975; 1983a, and 1983, pp. 81–2).

5.   Ultimately all capitalist firms are competitors. Monopolisation of the
market for a product within national boundaries does not preclude
competition from overseas nor from other sectors of the domestic
economy.

6. The nationalised sector in the UK is a good illustration of the process. A combination of social-democratic government control plus strong trade unions produced an internal control over the labour process that allowed low intensity of work, high manning levels and so on. This reflected on economic performance, particularly in those sectors that competed internationally (vehicles and steel). Once the current crisis began to deepen and the social democratic government was replaced, the logic of the law of value contradicted the internal organisation of production. The result has been massive redundancies in state vehicle production, steel and latterly coal.

3 The Vicious Circle of Soviet Economic Problems

1. This argument can be reduced eventually to a question of how the commentator views the nature of economic systems. For western neo-classical economists, the Soviet planning mechanism is a series of technical relationships which facilitate the transformation of inputs into outputs. The decline in growth rates can then be explained either in terms of the unsuitability of the mechanism to deal with complex modern tasks or because of failures with respect to technological innovation, technology diffusion and so on (Gomulka, 1985, p. 27). The argument presented here accepts that complexity adds a dimension of new problems and that the 'technology gap' is growing, but neither complexity nor technology should be viewed in a vacuum. Ultimately the determining feature will be the degree to which the social relations of production facilitate the management of complexity or the introduction of new technologies.

2. The Soviet figures on output, growth and labour productivity need to be interpreted with some care. See, for example, the articles by M. Ellman, P. Wiles and A. Nove in J. Drewnowski (ed.) (1982). Ellman, for example, suggests that Soviet growth has actually come to an end. I intend to make no contribution to this debate on the interpretation of Soviet statistics, but will simply use Soviet statistics in this area to demonstrate that growth rates are declining even in Soviet terms.

3. The case of the soft drinks enterprises that failed to produce up to the rated capacity is a good example of the problems. As Poprydkin (1982, p. 2) points out, this has been due to shortages of spares for the plant, incorrect size and quality of the glass bottles (with consequent breakdowns and delays) and shortages of bottles.

5 The Shchekino Experiment

1. For the continued importance of the chemical industry for the production of fertilisers in the mid-seventies see A. Kozlov (1976, pp. 20–1) and N. Borchenko (1976, p. 28), who points out that 50 per cent of the

growth in chemical output in the early seventies was accounted for by increasing output of chemical fertilisers. For a discussion of the significance of economic reform for the chemical industry see L. Kostandov (1974, pp. 19–20).

2. It is interesting to note that Soviet sources attempt to trace the 'pedigree' of the Shchekino experiment, like most things, back to Lenin. See S. S. Novozhilov (1970, p. 7), who argues that Lenin's desire to see work and rewards linked is a precursor of the principles of the Shchekino experiment. For Lenin's argument see Lenin (1977, pp. 412–14).

3. Delamotte has pieced together from a variety of sources the approximate number of employees at Shchekino at the start of the experiment and she suggests that the number was between 7500 and 8000. This means that the original plan was to reduce the workforce by between 12.5 and 13.5 per cent. This corresponds to the estimates of Manevich, Myasnikov and others, who suggest that the level of overmanning in Soviet industry at this period was between ten and fifteen per cent. Furthermore, Delamotte's estimate is confirmed by a later source, Fil'ev (1983), who notes that over the whole period of the experiment, 1814 workers, or 23 per cent of the workforce, were released. This would put the initial workforce at 7800. It is not clear if Fil'ev's estimate includes management, therefore an assumption of a total complement of 8000 is not unreasonable. It is worth pointing out that auxiliary workers accounted for almost 80 per cent of this total. This order of figure is further confirmed by Grotseskul (1985, p. 146) who argues that the almost 2000 workers eventually released by the experiment represented 26 per cent of the workforce, which would make the workforce originally around 7700.

6 A Reappraisal of the Results of the Experiment

1. Rather than using the Russian word *bezrabotitsa*, unemployment, the Russian verb *vysvobozhdat'*, to free, release or disengage, is used continually in the literature.

2. See Rutland (1984, Section 6), who correctly argues that the experiment did not usher in unemployment. He does, however, wrongly attribute to an earlier article of mine the view that the experiment introduced the spectre of unemployment to control the working class. My argument was that this was the ultimate logic of the experiment, not that this had been achieved. See R. Arnot (1981, pp. 53–5).

3. The data in Table 5.6 yield stronger rank order correlation coefficients when productivity increases are related to changes in workforce size, rather than to increases in average wage levels. It is impossible to answer this question unequivocally, as the available information is so fragmentary, covering different time periods, expressed in different ways that are incompatible, and so on.

4. My personal experience, on the receiving end of such schemes, would

lead me to agree with the respondent cited on the back cover of T. Nichols and H. Beynon (1977): 'You move from one boring, dirty, monotonous job to another ... Somehow you're supposed to come out of it all "enriched". But I never feel enriched – I just feel knackered'. At least under capitalism the wages received do give unambiguous access to consumer goods and services. Whilst it is impossible to come to any final conclusion about the respective welfare position of the worker under capitalism (with unemployment, insecurity and crisis) and the USSR (with significant job security but shortages) there is no reason to assume that 'job enrichment' has any more meaning in the USSR than it does in the west.

7 The Attempted Generalisation of the Shchekino Experiment

1. See, for example, the debate around A. P. Butenko (1984, pp. 124–9). Butenko attempted to inject some realism into the debate concerning contradiction and antagonism in the USSR, pointing out, in a very circumspect and guarded manner, after paying lip-service to traditional formulae, that the possibility of antagonistic relations under 'socialism' should be taken seriously and studied. This avenue of debate was firmly closed by C. Chernenko (*Pravda*, 14 June 1984, p. 2) and R. Kosolapov (*Pravda*, 20 July 1984, pp. 2–3), who reasserted the contradiction-free nature of 'socialism' in the USSR.
2. A similar argument has been advanced with regard to recent productivity gains in the UK under the impact of Tory economic policies. See D. Jones (1983, p. 42).
3. Knizhnik and Levikov (1983, pp. 22–3) suggest a different interpretation of the capacity of the experiment. They suggest that the problem at Shchekino itself was that the cadres remaining at the plant became stale. Because virtually no new workers were hired for fifteen years, 'the influx of fresh forces and of new ideas stopped' (p. 22). Hence whilst they note the increase in plan assignments they ascribe the failure partially to the age of the workforce!

9 Alternative Attempts to Assert Control Over the Labour Process

1. It would be both pointless and impossible to deal with every experimental initiative cited in the Soviet press, some of which, like the variants on the Shchekino model, are either relatively short-lived or little different from the major initiatives.
2. There are some disparities between the figures provided by different authors for the dissemination of the brigade system. For example, P. Bunich (1975, pp. 67–85) cites the figure of 21 500 brigades in 1975. Furthermore, in an earlier article, V. Sevast'yanov (1973, p. 2) suggests

that there were 6000 brigades in 1973 and so on. The disparities in the figures are due to two reasons; firstly, it is not always clear what part of the year is being referred to and in this period brigades were being formed fairly rapidly; secondly, because of the problems of collecting information on the existence of brigades, the figures often only emerge retrospectively.

3.   For a dictionary of terms and descriptions of different aspects of the brigade system see *Sotsialisticheskii Trud* (1986), No. 1, pp. 124–6.

4.   This is most graphically illustrated by a cartoon in *Ekonomika i organizatsiya promyshlennogo proizvodstva* (1985), No. 8, p. 185. This shows a worker holding a gun at the back of his workmate. The shape of the gun is formed by the letters *KTU*!

10   Conclusions

1.   For a comprehensive account of the Andropov discipline campaign and a survey of press reports and comments see E. Teague (1985, pp. 12–22).

2.   As D. Slider (1985, p. 182) suggests, the effects of the reform were fairly paltry but his final conclusion has to be questioned. He argues that Andropov's statement (1983, pp. 18–20), that 'the final goal of communist self-management lies in the distant future', coupled with the introduction of the discipline campaign, reflects the unreadiness of Soviet workers to participate directly in economic management. I would argue that they are evidence of the unreadiness of the ruling group to cede any form of effective control to the workforce and the necessity to reduce their existing negative control.

3.   See also H. Norr (1986, p. 162). This article appeared after I had finished my work on the Shchekino experiment and is a meticulous survey of the experiment's fate. Whilst it does not develop from the same theoretical framework as this book, it does come to very similar conclusions concerning the overall success of the experiment. Norr suggests that the eventual fate of reform initiatives will be decided by the pressure of 'demographic realities' or by the introduction of bolder and more thorough reform.

4.   It is worth pointing out that whilst in the early seventies it was possible to find many articles dealing with the Shchekino experiment in the Soviet labour press, by the early eighties these were replaced by articles dealing with the brigade system and the other experimental initiatives.

5.   See particularly M. Yanowitch (1985, pp. 92–155) for an excellent account of the 'participatory current' in Soviet management writings and the relationship of this to the brigade form. The comment he cites from a Soviet worker and his own view of participation in brigades is worth repeating: 'the brigade system remains a facade behind which . . . "decisions, as before, are made only by the factory chiefs". While the ideas embodied in the participatory current have continued to receive a public hearing, the substance of worker participation remains largely

dormant thus far'. For an equally sceptical view see Ticktin (1986, p. 120). However, some writers, for example Teague (1986, p. 254), see possibilities for further participation in management because of the accession to power of Gorbachev, who has been critical of the fact that enterprise managers have not gone as far as the 1983 law allows. However, it can be argued that the 1983 Law, and much of the participation debate, is only about refining the mechanisms whereby workers police themselves and raise the rate of surplus extraction.

6. An example of this is the so-called 'watch system' for organising work on production sites which are a long distance from an adequate social infrastructure (Manevich, 1985a, p. 111–2). This system works by transporting a detachment of workers to the site where they live in specially constructed settlements, returning home at regular periods. This kind of migatory work organisation is very cost-effective for remote regions and has enhanced productivity.

Bibliography

ABALKIN, L., 'Perevod ekonomiki na intensivnyi put' razvitiya', *Voprosy Ekonomiki* (1982) No. 2, pp. 3–13.

——, 'Vzaimodeistvie proizvoditel'nykh sil i proizvodstvennykh otnoshenii', *Voprosy Economiki* (1985) No. 6, pp. 11–22.

——, Letter to the *Financial Times*, 12 July 1986, p. 7.

ABRAMOV, G., 'Razvitie Shchekinskogo opyta i normativnyi metod planirovaniya zarabotnoi platy', *Sotsialisticheskii Trud* (1974) No. 12, pp. 21–6.

ABSEES, Glasgow, 1970–76.

ADAM, J. (ed.), *Employment Policies in the Soviet Union and Eastern Europe*, London (1982).

AFANAS'EV, A., *Komsomol'skaya Pravda*, 22 September 1981, p. 2.

AGANBEGYAN, A., 'Na novom etape ekonomicheskogo stroitel'stva', *Ekonomika i organizatsiya promyshlennogo proizvodstva* (1985a) No. 8, pp. 3–24.

——, 'Generalnyi kurs ekonomicheskoi politiki', *Ekonomika i organizatsiya promyshlennogo proizvodstva* (1985b) No. 11, pp. 3–31.

——, *Izvestia*, 1 April 1975, p. 2; *Literaturnaya Gazeta*, 4 May 1977, p. 4; *Trud*, 17 October 1981, p. 2; *Pravda*, 24 February 1982, p. 2; *Trud*, 12 December 1982, p. 3; *Trud*, 28 August 1984, p. 2; *Trud*, 29 August 1984, p. 2; *Pravda*, 13 July 1985(c), p. 2.

AGRONOVSKII, A., *Izvestia*, 9 October 1971, p. 2; *Izvestia*, 16 July 1972, p. 1.

AGRONOVSKII, A., VUKOVICH, V., DERGACHEV, A., DROZDOV, V., NIKITIN, A. and TURBANOV, A., *Izvestia*, 26 April 1973, p. 2.

AITOV, N.,*Sovetskaya Rossiya*, 22 July 1979, p 2.

ALEKSANDROVA, E. and FEDOROVSKAYA, E., 'Mekhanizm formirovaniya i vozvysheniia potrebnostei', *Voprosy Ekonomiki* (1984) No. 1, pp. 15–26.

ALEKSEEV, N., *Pravda*, 2 June 1973, p. 2.

AMALRIK, A., *Will the Soviet Union Survive Until 1984?*, Harmondsworth (1980).

ANDRLE, V., *Managerial Power in the USSR*, London (1976).

ANDROPOV, Yu., 'Uchenie Karla Marksa i nekototorye voprosy sotsialistcheskogo stroitel'stva v SSSR', *Kommunist* (1983) No. 3, pp. 9–24.

——, *Pravda*, 23 November 1982, pp. 1–2; *Pravda*, 16 June 1983, pp. 1–2; *Pravda*, 16 March 1983, p. 2; *Pravda*, 5 July 1983, p. 2.

ANTIP'EV, A. G., 'Brigadir i ego rabota', *Sotsiologicheskie Issledovaniya* (1985) No. 3, pp. 83–7.

ANTONOV, N., *Pravda*, 23 January 1970, p. 1; *Pravda*, 29 January 1970, p. 2.

ANTOSENKOV, E., *Izvestia*, 26 April 1985.

ANTROPOV, Yu. and LYAKUTIN, V. *Sotsialisticheskaya Industriya*, 3 February 1983, p. 2.

APER'YAN, N. P., *Ekonomicheskaya Gazeta* (1983) No. 49, p. 6.

APER'YAN, V. E., *Sotsialism: Naselenie i Ekonomika*, Moscow (1983).

ARKHIPOV, N. 'Nadezhnoe sredstvo ekonomii truda', *Sotsialisticheskii Trud* (1978) No. 8, pp. 31–3.

ARMEYEV, R. and ILLARIONOV, A., *Izvestia*, 17 May 84, p. 3.

ARNOT, R., 'Soviet Labour Productivity and the Failure of the Shchekino Experiment', *Critique*, No. 15 (1981) pp. 31–57.

——, 'The Shchekino Experiment: The Problem of Control Over the Soviet Industrial Workforce', *PhD Thesis*, Glasgow University, 1985.

AZRAEL, J., *Managerial Power and Soviet Politics*, Cambridge Mass. (1966).

BABKINA, Z., 'Zanyatost' pri sotsialisme i ee burzhuaznye traktovki', *Voprosy Ekonomiki* (1983) No. 8, pp. 124–33.

BACHURIN, A. V., 'Zadacha uskoreniya rosta proizvoditel'nosti truda', *Voprosy Ekonomiki* (1978) No. 8, pp. 3–14.

——, 'Kompleksno sovershenstvovat' planirovanie, upravlenie i metody khozyaistvovaniya', *Planovoe Khozyaistvo* (1981) No. 1, pp. 14–27.

BAHRO, R., *The Alternative in Eastern Europe*, London (1978).

BAIBAKOV, A. I., *Povyshenie nauchnogo urovnia upravleniya trudom*, Moscow (1980).

BAIDERIN, V. and TURBANOV, A., *Izvestia*, 7 July 1973, p. 5.

BALASHOV, B., *Sotsialisticheskaya Industriya*, 9 January 1983, p. 2.

BANAJI, J., 'Modes of Production in a Materialist Conception of History', *Capital and Class*, No. 3 (1977) pp. 1–45.

BARAN, P., *Political Economy of Growth*, London (1957).

BARAN, P. and SWEEZY, P., *Monopoly Capital*, London (1968).

BARANENKOVA, T., 'Tekhnicheskii progress i dvizhenie kadrov v promyshlennosti', *Voprosy Ekonomiki* (1970) No. 2, pp. 51–62.

——, 'Ekonomicheskie voprosy vysvobozhdeniya rabochei sily i uluchsheniya ee ispol'zovaniya v novykh uslovyakh planirovaniya i ekonomicheskogo stimulirovaniya', in *Osnovnye problemy ratsional'nogo ispol'zovaniya trudovykh resursov v SSSR*, E. Manevich (ed.), Moscow (1971).

——, 'Rezervy ekonomii rabochei sily', *Voprosy Ekonomiki* (1980) No. 5, pp. 51–62.

——, 'Sokrashchenie tekuchesti kadrov v usloviakh intensifikatsii proizvodstva', *Voprosy Ekonomiki* (1983) No. 8, pp. 74–84.

——, 'Puti ukrepleniya trudovoi distsipliny', *Voprosy Ekonomiki* (1986) No. 5, pp. 57–67.

BARBASHOV, V. I., 'Obuchenie molodykh rabochikh i nastavnichestvo v brigade', in V. N. Shurueva (ed.), pp. 81–85.

BATKAEV, P., 'Ob ekonomicheskikh usloviyakh vnedreniya Shchekinskogo metoda', *Sotsialisticheskii Trud* (1979) No. 5, pp. 30–7.

——, 'Vazhnoe napravlenie stimulirovaniya ekonomii truda', *Sotsialisticheskii Trud* (1978) No. 7, pp. 3–9.

BATKAEV, P. and SEMIN, S., 'Shchekinskii metod v usloviyakh sovershenstvovaniya khozyaistvennogo mekhanizma', *Sotsialisticheskii Trud* (1983) No. 1, pp. 43–53.

BELKIN, V. D., 'Tovarno-denezhnaya sbalansirovannost' ee rol' i problemy obespecheniya', *Ekonomika i organizatsiya promyshlennogo proizvodstva* (1982) No. 2, pp. 74–83.

BELOTSERKOVSKY, V., 'Workers' Struggles in the USSR in the Early Sixties', *Critique*, No. 10/11 (1979) pp. 37–50.

BERGSON, A., 'The Soviet Economic Slowdown and the 1981–85 Plan', *Problems of Communism*, No. 3 (1981) pp. 24–36.

BERGSON, A. and LEVINE, H. (eds), *The Soviet Economy: Toward the Year 2000*, London (1983).

BERLINER, J., *Factory and Manager in the USSR*, Cambridge, Mass. (1957).

——, 'Marxism and the Soviet Economy', *Problems of Communism*, No. 5 (1964) pp. 1–10.

——, 'Prospects for Technological Progress', in *Soviet Economy in a New Perspective* pp. 431–49.

——, 'Managing the USSR Economy: Alternative Models', *Problems of Communism*, No. 1 (1983) pp. 40–56.

——, 'Planning and Management', in Bergson and Levine (eds), pp. 350–91.

BERRI, L. Ya. (ed.), *Planning a Socialist Economy* (two Volumes), Moscow (1977).

BETTELHEIM, C., *The Transition to the Socialist Economy*, London (1975).

BETTELHEIM, C. and SWEEZY, P., *On the Transition to Socialism*, New York (1971).

BEYNON, H., *Working For Ford*, London (1973).

BINNS, P. and HAYNES, M., 'New Theories of Eastern European Class Society', *International Socialism* No. 7 (1980), pp. 18–50.

BIRMAN, I., 'From the Achieved Level', *Soviet Studies*, Vol. 30, No. 2 (1978) pp. 153–72.

BLACKBURN, R., 'The New Capitalism', in *Ideology in Social Science*, R. Blackburn (ed.), London (1972), pp. 164–86.

BLYAKHMAN, L. and SHKARATAN, O., *Man at Work*, Moscow (1973).

BOCHARNIKOV, V., 'Shchekinskii metod v izdatel'stve', *Sotsialisticheskii Trud* (1986) No. 4, pp. 86–88.

BOGOMOLOV, G. and VANYARKIN, P., 'Sotsialisticheskoe sorevnovanie i Shchekinskii metod', *Sotsialisticheskii Trud* (1979) No. 4, pp. 39–44.

BOIKO, T. M., 'Denezhnye sberezheniya naseleniya', *Ekonomika i organizatsiya promyshlennogo proizvodstva* (1982) No. 2, pp. 131–8.

BOITER, A., 'When the Kettle Boils Over', *Problems of Communism*, No. 1 (1964) pp. 33–43.

BOLDYREV, V., *Pravda*, 26 May 72, p. 2.

BORCHENKO, N., 'Khimizatsiya – vazhneishii faktor intensifikatsii sel's-kogo khozyaistva', *Planovoe Khozyaistvo* (1976) No. 9, pp. 28–34.

BORNSTEIN, M., 'Improving the Soviet Economic Mechanism', *Soviet Studies*, Vol. 37, No. 1 (1985) pp. 1–30.

BORODIN, V. K., *Pravda*, 14 June 83, p. 3.

BRADA, J. C., 'Soviet Subsidisation of E. Europe: The Primacy of Economics Over Politics?', *Journal of Comparative Economics*, Vol. 9 (1985).

BRAVERMAN, H., *Labour and Monopoly Capital*, New York (1974).

BREEV, B., *Methods of Planning Employment in the USSR*, Moscow (1979).

——, 'Otsenka ispol'zovaniya trudovykh resursov', *Voprosy Ekonomiki* (1986) No. 4, pp. 55–65.

BREZHNEV, L. I., *Material XXV s'ezda KPSS*, Moscow (1976).

——, *Sovetskie profsoyuzi – vliyatel'naya sila nashego obshchestva*, Moscow (1977).

——, *Rech na plenume tsentral'nogo komiteta KPSS, 25 Oktyabrya 1976* Moscow (1976).

——, *Pravda*, 25 October 1976, p. 1; *Pravda*, 20 January 1977, p. 1; *Pravda*, 4 July 1978, p. 1; *Pravda*, 22 October 1980, p. 1; *Trud*, 17 March 1982, pp. 1–2.

BRIGHTON LABOUR PROCESS GROUP, 'The Capitalist Labour Process', *Capital and Class*, No. 1 (1977) pp. 3–26.

BRODERSEN, A., *The Soviet Worker*, New York (1966).

BROWN, A. and KASER, M., *The Soviet Union Since the Fall of Khrushchev*, London (1978).

BROWN, A., 'Andropov: Discipline and Reform', *Problems of Communism*, No. 1 (1983) pp. 18–31.

BROWN, E. C., *Soviet Trade Unions and Labour Relations*, Cambridge Mass. (1966).

BRUS, W., *The Market in a Socialist Economy*, London (1972).

——, *The Economics and Politics of Socialism*, London (1973).

——, 'Is Market Socialism Possible or Necessary?', *Critique* No. 14 (1981) pp. 13–41.

——, The Soviet Bloc After Brezhnev – The Economic Perspective', in W. Brus, P. Kende and Z. Mylnar (eds), *The Soviet System After Brezhnev*, No. 5.

BUCK, T., *Comparative Industrial Systems. Industry Under Capitalism, Central Planning and Self-Management*, London (1982).

BUNICH, P. G., 'Ekonomicheskoe stimulirovanie na sovremennom etape: puti sovershenstvovaniya', *Ekonomika i organizatsiya promyshlennogo proizvodstva* (1975) No. 6, pp. 67–86.

——, 'Zarabotnaya plata kak ekonomicheskii stimul', *Ekonomika i organizatsiya promyshlennogo proizvodstva* (1980) No. 7, pp. 3–17.

——, 'Ekonomicheskoe stimulirovanie vysokikh konechnykh resultatov', *Ekonomika i organizatsiya promyshlennogo proizvodstva* (1984) No. 2, pp. 3–26.

——, 'Eksperiment na distantsii', *Ekonomika i organizatsiya promyshlennogo proizvodstva* (1985) No. 2, pp. 4–16.

BURAWOY, M. *The Politics of Production*, London (1985).

BURENKOV, M., *Izvestia*, 10 January 1976, pp. 1–2.

BUTENKO, A. P., 'Eshche raz o protivorechiyakh', *Voprosy Filosofii* (1984) No. 2, pp. 124–9.

CARLO, A., 'The Socio-Economic Nature of the Soviet Union', *Telos*, Nov. (1974).

CHENTEMIROV, M., 'Puti povysheniya ekonomicheskoi effektivnosti kapital'nykh vlozhenii', *Voprosy Ekonomiki* (1980) No. 6, pp. 34–43.

CHEREDNICHENKO, K. K. and GOL'DIN, I. I., *Shchekinskii Metod*, Moscow (1978).

——, 'Shchekinskii metod: itogi i perspektivy', *Sotsialisticheskii Trud* (1976) No. 2, pp. 51–61.

CHEREVAN, V., 'Soglasovanie vosproizvodstva rabochikh mest s trudovymi resursami', *Voprosy Ekonomiki* (1982) No. 2, pp. 51–61.

——, 'Planirovanie i stimulirovanie truda v khozraschetnykh brigadakh', *Voprosy Ekonomiki* (1984) No. 2, pp. 43–54.

CHERNENKO, C., *Pravda*, 3 March 1984, pp. 1–2; *Pravda*, 14 February

1984, p. 1; *Pravda*, 14 June 1984, p. 2; *Pravda*, 23 March 1985, pp. 1–2.

CHERNICHENKO, A., *Komsomol'skaya Pravda*, 19 May 1977, p. 4; *Komsomol'skaya Pravda*, 29 April 1980, p. 2.

CHERNOV, V., *Ekonomicheskaya Gazeta*, 1980, No. 1, p. 9. *Chislennost'i sostav naseleniya SSSR*, Moscow (1984).

CHUBANOV, Y., 'Ekonomicheskie usloviya razvitiya Shchekinskogo opyta', *Sotsialisticheskii Trud* (1976), No. 2, pp. 61–5.

CLARKE, R., *Soviet Economic Facts 1917–1970*, London (1972).

CLAUDIN, F., *Eurocommunism and Socialism*, London (1978).

CLIFF, T., *Russia: A Marxist Analysis*, London (1964).

COCKBURN, A., *The Threat: Inside the Soviet Military Machine*, London (1983).

COCKBURN, P., 'A Soviet Experiment in Autonomy', *Financial Times*, 11 July 1986, p. 12.

CONQUEST, R., *Industrial Workers in the USSR*, New York (1967).

COOLEY, M., 'Contradictions of Science and Technology', in Rose and Rose (ed.), pp. 72–96.

COOPER, J., 'Western Technology and Soviet Economic Power', in *Technology Transfer and East–West Relations*, M. Schaffer (ed.), London (1985) pp. 80–110.

CORRIGAN, P., RAMSAY, H. and SAYER, D., 'Bolshevism and the USSR', *New Left Review*, No. 125 (1981), pp. 45–60.

CSE (ed.), *The Labour Process and Class Strategies*, London (1976).

Current Digest of the Soviet Press, Ohio, 1967–85.

DANILOV, L., 'Sokrashchenie ruchnogo truda – vazhnyi faktor ratsional'-nogo ispol'zovaniya trudovykh resursov', *Kommunist* (1977) No. 9, pp. 39–50.

DANILOV, L. and KOKHOVA, A., 'O stimulirovanii vysvobozhdeniya rabotnikov na predpriyatiyakh', *Planovoe Khozyaistvo* (1975) No. 3, pp. 43–50.

DANILOV, L. and KORCHAGIN, V., 'Sovershenstvovanie upravleniya trudovymi resursami', *Planovoe Khzyaistvo* (1976) No. 11, pp. 23–30.

DE SOUZA, P., 'The TPC Planning Strategy and its Role in the Development of Siberia', *University of Gothenburg Occasional Papers* (1983) No. 4.

DELAMOTTE, J., *Shchekino. Entreprise Sovietique Pilote*, Paris (1973).

DENISENKO, I., *Sotsialisticheskaya Industriya*, 28 March 1978, p. 2.

DJILAS, M., *The New Class*, London (1957).

DMITRYEV, I. N., *Ekonomicheskaya Gazeta*, 1976, No. 46, p. 6.

DREWNOWSKI, J. (ed.), *Crisis in the East European Economy*, London (1982).

DROZDOV, V., *Sotsialisticheskaya Industriya*, 17 November 1976, p. 2.

DUBOIS, P., *Sabotage*, London (1979).

DYACHENKO, V., *Sovetskaya Rossiya*, 27 August 1983, p. 2.

DYBTSYN, A., *Pravda*, 9 December 1977, p. 2.

DYKER, D., *The Soviet Economy*, London (1976).

——, 'Planning and the Worker', in Shapiro and Godson (eds); pp. 39–75.

DYMITRYEV, A. and LOPATA, P., *Pravda*, 27 September 1983, p. 3.

DYMNOV, D. and DMITRICHEV, I., *Vestnik Statistiki* (1984) No. 2, p. 68.

DZOKAEVA, T., *Literaturnaya Gazeta*, 2 April 1980, p. 14; *Literaturnaya Gazeta*, 17 February 1982, p. 11.

EGOROV, M. V., *Ekonomicheskaya Gazeta* (1980) No. 45, p. 7.

Ekonomicheskaya Gazeta (1977), No. 6, pp. 17–18; (1982), No. 20, p. 5; (1982), No. 20, p. 6; (1982), No. 27, p. 5.

ELGER, T., 'Valorisation and De-Skilling: a Critique of Braverman', *Capital and Class*, No. 7 (1979) pp. 58–100.

ELLMAN, M., *Planning Problems in the USSR*, Cambridge (1973).

——, *Socialist Planning*, Cambridge (1979).

——, 'Economic Crisis in the USSR', *Critique*, No. 12 (1979) pp. 5–13.

——, 'Against Convergence', *Cambridge Journal of Economics* (1980) Vol. 4, No. 3, pp. 199–210.

FANTHAM, J. and MACHOVER, M., *The Century of the Unexpected: a New Analysis of Soviet Type Societies*, London (1979).

FEDORENKO, N., 'Planirovanie i upravlenie: kakimi im byt'?', *Ekonomika i organizatsiya promyshlennogo proizvodstva* (1984) No. 12, pp. 3–22.

FELDBRUGGE and SIMONS (eds), *Perspectives on Soviet Law for the Eighties*, The Hague (1982).

FIL'EV, V., 'Sootnoshenie rosta proizvoditel'nosti truda i srednei zarabotnoi platy', *Voprosy Ekonomiki* (1983), No. 12, pp. 12–22.

——, 'O dal'neishem vnedrenii Shchekinskogo metoda', *Voprosy Ekonomiki* (1983) No. 2, pp. 58–68.

FRANKLIN, B., *The Essential Stalin. 1905–1952*, New York (1973).

FRIEDMAN, A. I., *Industry and Labour. Class Struggle and Monopoly Capitalism*, London (1977).

——, 'Responsible Autonomy versus Direct Control', *Capital and Class*, No. 1 (1977) pp. 43–59.

GABIDULIN, Ya., *Ekonomicheskaya Gazeta* (1975) No. 6, pp. 6–7.

——, 'Bashkirskii eksperiment v novykh usloviyakh', *Sotsialisticheskii Trud* (1977) No. 12, pp. 50–7.

GARNSEY, E., 'Capital Accumulation and the Division of Labour in the Soviet Union', *Cambridge Journal Of Economics* (1982) No. 6, pp. 15–31.

GAVIN, M. and CHERNETSKII, F., *Izvestia*, 1 November 1972, p. 3.

GAVRILOV, B. N., *Ekonomicheskaya Gazeta* (1980) No. 45, p. 6; *Ekonomicheskaya Gazeta* (1980) No. 47, p. 7.

GAVRILOV, R., 'Tempy, faktory i novye pokazateli rosta proizvoditel'nosti truda', *Voprosy Ekonomiki* (1982) No. 3, pp. 23–32.

GERASIMOV, V. and PETROV, N., *Pravda*, 27 November 1983, p. 2.

GIDDENS, A., *The Class Structure of Advanced Societies*, London (1973).

GLAZYRIN, V., NIKITINSKY, V., MAKSIMOVA, N., YARKO, A., *Soviet Employees' Rights in Law*, Moscow (1978).

GLYANTSEV, M., 'Normirovanie na urovne sovremennoi tekhniki i organizatsii truda', *Sotsialisticheskii Trud* (1981) No. 4, pp. 96–104.

——, 'Effektivnost' – glavnoe trebovanie nyneshnego etapa', *Sotsialisticheskii Trud* (1983) No. 5, pp. 64–73.

GOLOVIN, Y., ADAMCHUK, A. and SAVEL'EV, V., 'Zadaniya pyatiletki i Shchekinskii metod', *Sotsialisticheskii Trud* (1974) No. 8, pp. 45–50.

GOMBERG, Ya, and SUSHKINA, L., 'Osnovnye napravleniya different-siatsii zarabotnoi platy rabotnikov promyshlennosti', *Ekonomicheskie Nauki* (1982) No. 1, pp. 60–7.

GONCHAROV, V., *Pravda*, 1 October 1979, p. 2.

GONZAL'EZ, E., *Trud*, 15 December 1981, p. 6; *Trud*, 25 May 1982, p. 2.

GOMULKA, S., 'The Incompatability of Socialism and Rapid Innovation', in *Technology Transfer and East–West Relations*, M. Schaffer (ed.), pp. 12–31.

GOODMAN, A. and SCHLEIFER, G., 'The Soviet Labour Market in the 1980s', in *Soviet Economy in the 1980s*, pp. 323–348.

GORBACHEV, M., *Pravda*, 21 February 1985, p. 2; *Pravda*, 12 March 1985, p. 3; *Pravda*, 17 March 1985, p. 1; *Pravda*, 12 April 1985, pp. 1–2; *Pravda*, 24 April 1985, p. 1; *Pravda*, 11 June 1985, p. 1; *Pravda*, 26 February 1986, pp. 2–10; *Pravda*, 21 September 1985, pp. 1–2.

GORBUNOV, E., 'Effektivnost' sfery bytovykh uslug', *Voprosy Ekonomiki* (1974) No. 7, pp. 57–66.

GORDON, L. and KLOPOV, E., *Man After Work*, Moscow (1975).

GORLIN, A., 'Industrial Organisation: The associations', in *Soviet Economy in a New Perspective* (1976).

GORZ, A. (ed.), *The Division of Labour: the Labour Process and Class Struggle in Modern Capitalism*, Brighton (1976).

——, *Farewell to the Working Class: an essay in Post-Industrial Socialism*, London (1982).

GOSKOMTRUD SSSR, GOSPLAN SSSR, MINISTERSTVO FINANSOV SSSR i VTsSPS, 'Usloviya dalneishego vnedreniya kompleksnogo metoda sovershenstvovaniya organizatsii truda, material'nogo stimulirovaniya i planirovaniya po opytu Shchekinskogo khimicheskogo kombinata v desyatoi pyatletke', in *Ekonomicheskaya Gazeta*, No. 7 (1977) pp. 17–18.

——, 'Poryadok primeneniya Shchekinskogo metoda sovershenstvovaniya organizatsii truda, material' nogo stimulirovaniya i planirovaniya', *Sotsialisticheskii Trud* (1978) No. 7, pp. 9–11.

GREGORY, P. and STUART, R., *Soviet Economic Structure and Performance*, Third Edition, New York (1986).

——, *Comparative Economic Systems*, Boston (1980).

GRIGOR'EV, A. and KHEIFETS, L., 'Ispol'zovanie ekonomii zarabotnoi platy', *Planovoe Khozyaistvo* (1970) No. 2, pp. 55–9.

GRINKO, Yu., *Izvestia*, 26 July 1979, p. 2.

GROSSMAN, G., 'Economic Reforms: A Balance Sheet', *Problems of Communism*, No. 6 (1966).

——, 'The Economy at Middle Age', *Problems of Communism*, No. 2 (1976), pp. 18–33.

——, 'The Second Economy', *Problems of Communism*, Sept–Oct (1977), pp. 25–40.

GROTSESKUL, G. N., 'Shchekinskii metod okhvatyvaet territoriyu', *Ekonomika i organizatsiya promyshlennogo proizvodstva* (1985) No. 6, pp. 141–51.

——, *Pravda*, 8 September 1980, p. 2; *Pravda*, 14 June 1982, p. 3; *Pravda*, 18 October 1983, p. 3.

GROYS, C., 'Robots in Soviet Industry', *RL* 158/1984.
HANSON, P., 'Western Technology in the Soviet Economy', *Problems of Communism* No. 6 (1978) pp. 20–31.
——, 'Labour Discipline and Production Stoppages in the Soviet Industry', *RL* 200/1983.
HARASZTI, M., *A Worker in a Worker's State*, Harmondsworth (1977).
HARMAN, C., *Bureaucracy and Revolution in Eastern Europe*, London (1976).
HAYNES, V. and SEMYONOVA, O., *Workers Against the Gulag*, London (1979).
HEGEDUS, A., *Socialism and Bureaucracy*, London (1976).
HETHY, L. and MAKO, C., 'Work Performance, Interests, Powers and Environment', *Sociological Review Monograph* (1972) No. 17, pp. 123–50.
HOLUBENKO, M., 'The Soviet Working Class', *Critique* No. 4 (1975), pp. 5–27.
IL MANIFESTO, *Power and Opposition in Post-Revolutionary Societies*, London (1979).
ILLE, M. E. and SINOV, V. V., 'O razvitii samoupravleniya v brigadakh', *Sotsiologicheskie Issledovaniya* (1984) No. 3, pp. 59–64.
IMG PAMPHLET, *Readings on State Capitalism*, Feb (1973).
IOVCHUK, M. T. and KOGAN, L. N., *The Cultural Life of the Soviet Worker*, Moscow (1975).
IVANOV, S., 'Shchekinskii metod v desyatoi pyatiletke', *Sotsialisticheskii Trud* (1977) No. 4, pp. 7–18.
IVANOV, V. N., 'Aktual'nye voprosy sovershenstvovaniya sotsial'nogo planirovaniya', *Sotsiologicheskie Issledovaniya* (1984) No. 3, pp. 35–42.
IVANOVA, R., 'Sokrashchenie ruchnovo truda – vazhneishaya sotsial'no-ekonomicheskaya zadacha', *Voprosy Ekonomiki* (1984) No. 9, pp. 31–41.
JOINT ECONOMIC COMMITTEE OF CONGRESS OF THE UNITED STATES, *Soviet Economy in a New Perspective*, Washington (1976).
——, *Soviet Economy in the 1980's Problems and Prospects* (Two Parts), Washington (1983).
JONES, D., 'Productivity and the Thatcher Experiment', *Socialist Economic Review* (1983).
KAISER, R., *Russia The People and the Power*, London (1976).
KALAKIN, I., *Komsomol'skaya Pravda*, 16 January 1980, p. 2.
KALANDROV, I., *Trud*, 5 August 1982, p. 2.
KALESNIK, S. V. and PAVLENKO, V. F. (eds), *Soviet Union. A Geographical Survey*. Moscow (1976).
KAMENITSER, S., *The Experience of Industrial Management in the Soviet Union*, Moscow (1975).
KAMZIN, Yu., *Pravda*, 19 May 1973, p. 3.
KARPENKO, I., *Izvestia*, 28 June 1969, p. 2; *Izvestia*, 1 July 1969, p. 3; *Izvestia*, 28 January 1970, p. 3.
KARPUKHIN, D., 'O sootnoshenii rosta proizvoditel'nosti truda i zarabotnoi platy', *Planovoe Khozyaistvo* (1983) No. 10, pp. 87–92.
KATSENELINBOIGEN, A., *Studies in Soviet Economic Planning*, White Plains (1978).

KATSURA, P., *Izvestia*, 28 July 1985, p. 2.

KHACHATUROV, T., 'Aktual'nye voprosy intensifikatsii obshchestven-
nogo proizvodstva', *Planovoe Khozyaistvo* (1974) No. 6, pp. 12–19.

——, 'Intensifikatsiya proizvodstva i uskorenie ekonomicheskogo rosta',
Ekonomika i organizatsiya promyshlennogo proizvodstva (1986) No. 2,
pp. 3–16.

KHADZHINOV, L. P., *Ekonomicheskaya Gazeta* (1983) No. 46, p. 6.

KHEIFETS, L., 'Sovershenstvovanie khozyaistvennogo mekhanizma i
material'noe pooshchrenie rabotnikov', *Voprosy Ekonomiki* (1980) No. 9,
pp. 15–22.

——, 'Gosudarstvennoe regulirovanie zarabotnoi platy', *Voprosy Ekonomiki*
(1982) No. 6, pp. 33–40.

KHEIMAN, S. A., 'Proizvodstvennyi apparat mashinostroeniya i stankos-
troeniya', *Ekonomika i organizatsiya promyshlennogo proizvodstva* (1982)
No. 1, pp. 25–47.

——, 'Razvitie mashinostroeniya: organizatsionnye i strukturnye faktory',
Ekonomika i organizatsiya promyshlennogo proizvodstva (1984) No. 6,
pp. 89–112.

KHOR'KHOV, V., 'Bashkirskii eksperiment', *Sotsialisticheskii Trud* (1969)
No. 6, pp. 33–39.

Khozyaistvennaya Reforma v SSSR, Moscow (1969).

KHROMAKOV, M., *Komsomol'skaya Pravda*, 18 April 1980, p. 2.

KHROMOV, P., 'Proizvoditel'nost' truda i nakoplenie', *Voprosy Ekonomiki*
(1972) No. 8, pp. 31–40.

——, 'Proizvoditel'nost' truda i ekonomicheskii rost', *Voprosy Ekonomiki*
(1981) No. 10, pp. 15–23.

——, (ed.), *Proizvoditel'nost' truda: Vazhneisii faktor povysheniya effektivnosti proizvodstva*, Moscow (1982).

KIRSCH, J. L., *Soviet Wages. Changes in Structure and Administration Since
1956*, Mass. (1972).

KLIMENTOV, G. A., 'Chto sderzhivaet potentsial kollektivnogo truda?',
Ekonomika i organizatsiya promyshlennogo proizvodstva (1984) No. 3,
pp. 38–51.

KLIVETS, P. G., 'Usloviya vnedreniya brigadnykh metodov raboty', *Sotsiologicheskie Issledovaniya* (1983) No. 3, pp. 100–4.

KNIZHNIK, S. and LEVIKOV, A., *Is There a Labour Shortage in the
USSR?*, Moscow (1983).

KOGAN, L. N. and MERENKOV, A. V., 'Kompleksnye brigady: mneniya,
otsenki, opyt vnedreniya', *Ekonomika i organizatsiya promyshlennogo
proizvodstva* (1983), pp. 86–91.

KOLODIZH, B. N., 'Trudovaya distsiplina i tekuchest'', *Ekonomika i organizatsiya promyshlennogo proizvodstva* (1980) No. 5, pp. 126–133.

——, 'Kak vliyaet ritmichnost' proizvodstva na distsiplinu truda', *Sotsiologicheskie Issledovaniya* (1984) No. 2, pp. 42–51.

KOMOV, G., 'V Sochetanii s brigadnoi formoi organizatsii i oplaty truda',
Sotsialisticheskii Trud (1983) No. 4, pp. 17–19.

KONDRASHOV, P., *Pravda*, 16 March 1983, p. 3.

KONRAD, G. and SZELENYI, I., *Intellectuals on the Road to Class Power*,
New York (1979).

KORIAGIN, A., 'Sotsialisticheskoe vosproizvodstvo i soizmerenie zatrat truda', *Voprosy Ekonomiki* (1982) No. 7, pp. 26–36.
KORNAI, J. *Economics of Shortage* (2 Vols), Amsterdam (1980).
KOROLEV, L. P., *Trudovye resursy i ikh ispol'zovanie*, Moscow (1981).
KORUPILLO, SH., *Izvestia*, 11 July 1983, p. 6.
KOSOLAPOV, R., *Pravda*, 20 July 1984, pp. 2–3.
KOSTAKOV, V., 'Ekonomnoe ispol'zovanie truda zanyatogo naseleniya', *Planovoe Khozyaistvo* (1974) No. 7, pp. 72–7.
——, *Sovetskaya Kultura*, 4 January 1986, p. 3.
KOSTANDOV, L., 'Khimicheskaya promyshlennost' i perspektivy ee razvitiya', *Planovoe Khozyaistvo* (1974) No. 3, pp. 14–23.
——, *Izvestia*, 11 December 1975, p. 3.
KOSTIN, L. A. (ed.), *Trudovye Resursy v SSSR*, Moscow (1979).
——, 'Proizvoditel' nost' truda na sovremennom etape', *Ekonomika i organizatsiya promyshlennogo proizvodstva* (1980) No. 12, pp. 58–72.
——, *Trudovye resursy v odinnadtsatoi pyatletke*. Moscow (1981).
——, 'Reservy ispol'zovaniya', *Ekonomika i organizatsiya promyshlennogo proizvodstva* (1984) No. 1, pp. 22–38.
——, 'Sotsial'nye rezervy otrasli', *Sotsiologicheskie Issledovaniya* (1985) No. 3, pp. 3–9.
——, *Ekonomicheskaya Gazeta*, (1978) No. 35, p. 9. *Ekonomicheskaya Gazeta* (1980) No. 44, p. 18; *Pravda*, 9 September 1983, p. 2.
KOSTIN, V., *Ekonomicheskaya Gazeta* (1976) No. 36, p. 13.
KOTLYAR, A. E. 'Polnaya zanyatost' i sbalansirovannost' faktorov sotsialisticheskogo proizvodstva', *Voprosy Ekonomiki* (1983) No. 7, pp. 106–17.
——, *Pravda*, 13 May 1984, p. 2.
KOTLYAR, A. E. and TALALAI, M. I., 'Kak zakrepit' molodoye kadry', *Ekonomika i organizatsiya promyshlennogo proizvodstva* (1977) No. 4, pp. 26–43.
——, 'Puti sokrashcheniia tekuchesti kadrov', *Voprosy Ekonomiki* (1981) No. 5, pp. 33–44.
KOTOV, F., IVANOV, Y. and PROSTYAKOV, I., *The USSR Economy in 1976–1980*, Moscow (1977).
KOVALEVA, A. (ed.), *Sotsial'no-ekonomicheskie problemy narodonaseleniya*, Ashkhabad (1978).
KOZLOV, A., 'Khimicheskaya promyshlennost' – sel'skomu khozyaistvu', *Planovoe Khozyaistvo* (1976) No. 7, pp. 19–23.
KOZLOV, G. A. (ed.), *Political Economy: Socialism*, Moscow (1977).
——, (ed.), *Political Economy: Capitalism*, Moscow (1977).
KOZLOV, N., *Ekonomicheskaya Gazeta* (1980) No. 45, p. 6.
KPSS v resolyutsiyakh i resheniyakh s'ezdov, konferentsii i plenum, Vol. 10, Moscow (1972).
KRAEVA, N. M., *Rezervy povysheniya trudovoi aktivnosti naseleniya*, Moscow (1983).
KRASOVSKII, V., 'Ekonomicheskii potentsial: rezervy i otdacha', *Voprosy Ekonomiki* (1981) No. 2, pp. 88–98.
KRAWCHENKO, V., *I Chose Freedom*, London (1947).
KRISHCHEV, E. I., 'Sotsial'no-ekonomicheskaya effektovnost' brigadnogo podryada', *Sotsiologicheskie Issledovaniya* (1984) No. 3, pp. 51–8.

284   *Bibliography*

KUCHERENKO, P., *Pravda*, 21 July 1975, p. 2.

KUDRYASHOV, G., *Izvestia*, 16 December 1969, p. 3.

KUDRYATSEV, A., *Socialist Organisation of Labour*, Moscow (1978).

KULAGIN, G., 'O putiakh intensifikatsii (iz bloknota ekonomista)', *Planovoe Khozyaistvo* (1983), No. 4, pp. 101–6.

——, *Literaturnaya Gazeta*, 21 February 1979, p. 10.

KUTRYEV, B. P., 'Distsiplina truda v dinamike', *Ekonomika i organizatsiya promyshlennogo proizvodstva* (1981) No. 9, pp. 18–46.

——, 'Kak primenyat' Kollektivnyi podryad v deyatel'nosti ITR', *Sotsiologicheskie Issledovaniya* (1985) No. 3, pp. 42–49.

KUZNETSOV, N., 'Intensivnye faktory ekonomicheskogo rosta i razvitie Shchekinskogo metoda', *Sotsialisticheskii Trud* (1978) No. 8, pp. 26–30.

KUZNETSOV, O. V., 'Tekuchest' ili podvizhnost'?', *Ekonomika i organizatsiya promyshlennogo priozvodstva* (1979) No. 4, pp. 98–107.

KUZMISHCHEV, V. and ODINETS, M., *Pravda*, 17 July 1983, p. 2.

KVASKA, A. and KALINIUK, I., 'O dolgosrochnykh tendentsiiakh vosproizvodstva naseleniia', *Ekonomicheskie Nauki* (1972) No. 8, pp. 63–70.

KYUREGYAN, E. A., 'Otnoshenie k trudu i distsiplina promyshlennykh rabochikh', *Sotsiologicheskie Issledovaniya* (1983) No. 2, pp. 129–32.

LAMPERT, N. 'Job Security and the Law in the USSR', *Birmingham Conference Paper* (1984).

LANE, A., 'USSR: Private Agriculture on Centre Stage', in *Soviet Economy in the 1980s: Problems and Prospects*.

LANE, D., *Politics and Society in the USSR*, London (1978).

——, *End of Inequality? Stratification Under State Socialism*, London (1971).

——, *Socialist Industrial State*, London (1976).

—— (ed.), *Labour and Employment in the USSR*, Brighton (1986).

LANE, D. and O'DELL, F., *The Soviet Industrial Worker*, London (1978).

LANSHIN, I. A., *Ekonomicheskaya Gazeta* (1982) No. 10, p. 6.

LATIFI, O. and USANOV, V., *Pravda*, 18 June 1984, p. 2.

LATOV, A. and GOL'DIN, L., *Ekonomicheskaya Gazeta*, 12 September 1975, p. 10.

LEBANIDZE, G., *Pravda*, 18 February 1983, p. 2.

LEBEDEV, V., *Sotsialisticheskaya Industriya*, 5 July 1981, p. 2.

LENIN, V. I., *The State and Revolution*, in *Selected Works*, Moscow (1977).

——, *Collected Works*, Vols. 19, 29 (1964).

LEVIDOW, L. and YOUNG, B. (eds) *Science, Technology and the Labour Process*, London (1981).

LEVIKOV, A., *Literaturnaya Gazeta* (1978) No. 19, p. 11. *Literaturanaya Gazeta* (1978) No. 20, p. 11.

LEVIN, B. and LEVIN, M., *Sovetskaya Kultura*, 18 December 1979, p. 6. *Literaturanaya Gazeta*, 4 July 1979, p. 13.

LEVINE, M., *The Socialist Economies of the Soviet Union and Eastern Europe*, London (1974).

LIBERMAN, E., *Planning, Profits and Incentives in the USSR*, New York (1966).

LIRMAN, R. and SHEVERDIN, S., 'Piteinyi prilavok i likbez trezvosti', *Molodoi Kommunist* (1980) No. 2, pp. 64–70.

LITVINOVA, A. V., 'Mezhlichnostnye otnosheniya v brigadakh novogo-tipa', *Sotsiologicheskie Issledovaniya* (1985) No. 3, pp. 49–59.
LOMAKIN, V. and KHANT, I., 'Shchekinskii metod – pryamaya zaintere-sovannost' vypolnenii planov s men'she chislennost'yu personala', *Sot-sialisticheskii Trudd* (1979) No. 6, pp. 20–5.
LOMONOSOV, V., *Literaturnaya Gazeta*, 5 January 1977, p. 11.
LONDON, L., *Literaturnaya Gazeta*, 5 January 1977, p. 11.
MACDONALD, O., 'Workers' Opposition in Poland', *Critique*, No. 7 (1977), pp. 93–9.
MAKSIMOVA, N., 'Brigady na pereput'e', *Ekonomika i organizatsiya pro-myshlennogo proizvodstva* (1985) No. 8, pp. 151–99.
MALMYGIN, I. A., 'Sbalansirovannost' rabochikh mest i trudovykh resur-sov', *Planovoe Khozyaistvo* (1982), pp. 55–62.
——, *Sovetskaya Rossiya*, 18 September 1983, p. 2.
MANDEL, E., *Marxist Economic Theory*, London (1968).
——, 'Ten Theses on the Transition to Socialism', *Critique* No. 3 (1974), pp. 5–23.
——, 'Once Again on the Trotskyist Definition of the Social Nature of the USSR', *Critique* 12 (1979) pp. 117–27.
MANEVICH, Ye., 'Problemy vosproizvodstva rabochei sily i puti ulushche-niya ispol'zovaniya trudovykh resursov v SSSR', *Voprosy Ekonomiki* (1969) No. 10, pp. 27–51.
——, *Lenin on Work Under Socialism and Communism*, Moscow (1970).
—— (ed.), *Osnovnye problemy ratsional'nogo ispol'zovaniya trudovykh resur-sov v SSSR*, Moscow (1971).
——, 'Puti uluchsheniya ispol'zovaniya rabochei sily', *Voprosy Ekonomiki* (1973) No. 12, pp. 27–38.
——, 'Organizatsiya truda kak rezerv povysheniya ego proizvoditel'nosti', *Voprosy Ekonomiki* (1976) No. 8, pp. 117–28.
——, 'K resheniiu problemy vosproisvodstva i ispol'zovaniya', *Sotsialisti-cheskii Trud* (1977) No. 5, pp. 119–24.
——, 'Defitsit i reservy rabochei sily', *Ekonomika i organizatsiya promyshlen-nogo proizvodstva* (1978) No. 2, pp. 75–87.
——, 'Vosproizvodstvo naseleniya i ispol'zovanie trudovykh resursov', *Voprosy Ekonomiki* (1979) No. 8, pp. 38–48.
——, *Voprosy truda v SSSR*, Moscow (1980).
——, 'Ratsional'noe ispol'zovanie rabochei sily', *Voprosy Ekonomiki* (1981) No. 9, pp. 55–66.
—— (ed.), *Problemy povysheniya effektivnosti ispol'zovaniya rabochei sily v SSSR*, Moscow (1983).
——, 'Khozyaistvennyi mekhanizm i ispol'zovanie trudovykh resursov', *Ekonomika i organizatsiya promyshlennogo proizvodstva* (1985) No. 12, pp. 21–37.
——, *Labour in the USSR: Problems and Solutions*, Moscow (1985a).
MARESE, M. and VANOUS, J., *Soviet Subsidisation of Trade with E. Europe: A Soviet Perspective*, Berkeley (1983).
MARGLIN, S., *What Do Bosses Do?'*, in Gorz (ed.), pp. 13–54.
MARRIS, R., *The Theory of Managerial Capitalism*, London (1964).
MARX, K., *The Grundrisse*, London (1973).
——, *Capital*, Vols. I, II, III, London (1977).

——, 'Wage Labour and Capital', in *Marx/Engels Selected Works*, Vol. 1, London (1953).

MASLOVA, I. S., "Effektivnost' ispol'zovaniya trudovykh resursov', *Voprosy Ekonomiki* (1978) No. 8, pp. 49–59.

——, 'Sovershenstvovanie mekhanizma pereraspredeleniia rabochei sily', *Voprosy Ekonomiki* (1982) No. 7, pp. 47–58.

Materialy XXIV s'ezda KPSS, Moscow (1971).

Materialy XXV s'ezda KPSS, Moscow (1976).

MATTHEWS, M., *Soviet Sociology 1964–1975*, New York (1978).

McAULEY, M., *Labour Disputes in Soviet Russia 1957–1965*, Oxford (1969).

——, *Politics and the Soviet Union*, Harmondsworth (1977).

MEDVEDEV, T. N., *Ekonomicheskie problemy rosta naseleniya i ispol'zovaniya trudovykh resursov v SSSR*, Moscow (1978).

MEIKLE, S. 'Has Marxism a Future?', *Critique*, No. 13 (1981), pp. 103–23.

——, 'Marxism and the Necessity of Essentialism', *Critique*, No. 16 (1983) pp. 149–67.

MELENT'EV, N. R., *Pravda*, 14 June 1982, p. 3.

'Metalloobrabatyvauschee oborudovanie: tekhnicheskii uroven' i konkurentosposobnost'', *Ekonomika i organizatsiya promyshlennogo proizvodstva* (1982) No. 1, pp. 23–145.

MILUKOV, A., *Ekonomicheskaya Gazeta* (1980) No. 43, p. 10.

MIRGALEEV, A., 'Shchekinskii metod i ego perspektivy', *Voprosy Ekonomiki* (1977) No. 10, pp. 104–13.

MIRONOV, N., *Pravda*, 8 October 1981, p. 2.

MITROFANOV, A., *Sotsialisticheskaya Industriya*, 25 March 1979, p. 2.

MOKIN, A., *Sotsialisticheskaya Industriya*, 6 February 1977, p. 2.

MOLCHANOV, G., 'Shchekinskii metod i ispol'zovanie rezervov', *Sotsialisticheskii Trud* (1979) No. 2, pp. 17–20.

MOLCHANOV, A. and TITSKII, N., 'Shchekinskii metod na zheleznodorozhnom transporte', *Sotsialisticheskii Trud* (1979) No. 5, pp. 61–4.

MOROZOV, V., 'O formal'nom vnedreni brigadnogo metoda na predpriyatiyakh instrumental'noi promyshlennosti', *Sovetskie Profsoyuzy* (1982) No. 2, pp. 6–7.

MOSKALENKO, G. K. (ed.), *Labour Legislation in the USSR*, Moscow (1972).

MOSKALENKO, V. P., Khozraschetnaya zainteresovannost' v vysokikh konechnykh rezul' tatakh', *Ekonomika i organizatiya promyshlennogo proizvodstva* (1986) No. 3, pp. 99–118.

MUKACHEV, V. I. and BOROVIK, V. S., *Rabochii klass i upravlenie proizvodstvom*, Moscow (1975).

MUNTING, R., *The Economic Development of the USSR*, London (1982).

MYASNIKOV, A., *Trud*, 17 July 1979, p. 2; *Literaturnaya Gazeta*, 19 March 1980, p. 2.

NAGIBIN, N., *Literaturnaya Gazeta*, 31 August 1983, p. 13.

NAGIBIN, N. and RYAZHOKIKH, I., *Pravda*, 18 January 1975, p. 3.

Narodnoe Khozyaistvo SSSR v 1982g, Moscow (1983).

Narodnoe Khozyaistvo SSSR v 1983g, Moscow (1984).

Narodnoe Khozyaistvo SSSR v 1984g, Moscow (1985).

NASACH, V. I. and KOTELENETS, E., *V. I. Lenin i stanovlenie sotsialisti-cheskoi distsipliny truda*, Moscow (1982).
NICHOLS, T., *Capital and Labour*, Glasgow (1980).
NICHOLS, T. and ARMSTRONG, P., *Workers Divided*, Glasgow (1976).
NICHOLS, T. and BEYNON, H., *Living With Capitalism: Class Relations in the Modern Factory*, London (1977).
NIKITIN, A., *Literaturnaya Gazeta*, 21 May 1980, p. 10.
NIKITINSKII, A., *Literaturnaya Gazeta*, 24 August 1980, p. 10.
NIKITINSKY, V. and LIVSHITZ, R., *An Outline of Soviet Labour Law*, Moscow (1977).
NORR, H., 'Shchekino: Another Look', *Soviet Studies*, Vol. 38, No. 2 (1986), pp. 141–69.
NOVE, A., *An Economic History of the USSR*, Harmondsworth (1982).
——, *The Soviet Economic System* (2nd edn), London (1980).
——, *The Economics of Feasible Socialism*, London (1983).
——, 'Agriculture', in Brown and Kaser (eds), pp. 1–16.
——, 'History, Hierarchy and Nationalities', *Soviet Studies*, Vol. 21 (1969) No. 1, pp. 71–92.
——, 'Market Socialism and its Critics', *Soviet Studies*, Vol. 24 (1972) No. 1, pp. 120–38.
——, 'Is There a Ruling Class in the USSR?', *Soviet Studies*, Vol. 27 (1975) No. 4, pp. 615–38.
——, 'The Class Nature of the USSR Revisited', *Soviet Studies*, Vol. 35 (1983) pp. 298–312.
——, 'The USSR: The Reform That Never Was', in *The Reforms in the Soviet and East European Economies*, Dellin and Gross (eds) (1972).
NOVIKOV, K., 'Problemy effektivnogo ispol'zovaniya trudovykh resursov', *Kommunist* (1969) No. 13, pp. 99–108.
NOVITSKII, A., *Trud*, 29 January 1982, p. 2.
NOVOKSHONOV, P., *Izvestia*, 10 April 1975, p. 3.
NOVOZHILOV, L. V., *Pravda*, 28 January 1970, p. 1; *Ekonomicheskaya Gazeta* (1980) No. 9, p. 8.
NOVOZHILOV, S. S., 'Sovershenstvovanie sistemy material'nogo stimulirovaniya rosta proizvoditel'nosti truda', *Sotsialisticheskii Trud* (1970) No. 5, pp. 7–21.
OBLOMSKAYA, I., STARAKHOV, A., UMANETS, L., 'Sotsial'no-ekonomicheskaya odnorodnost' truda', *Voprosy Ekonomiki* (1983) No. 6, pp. 26–37.
OKHOZIN, L., *Pravda*, 26 January 1983, p. 2.
ORLOV, Ya. 'Spros naseleniia i zadachi proizvodstva i torgovli', *Voprosy Ekonomiki* (1983) No. 9, pp. 100–9.
OVRUTSKII, L. M., 'Borba s p'yanstvom i alkogolizmom: sovremennaya situatsiya i perspektiva', *Sotsiologicheskie Issledovaniya* (1985) No. 3, pp. 35–41.
PAK, Yu., *Literaturnaya Gazeta*, 9 January 1980, p.13.
PAL'CHIKOV, G., *Trud*, 13 July 1973, p. 2.
PALITSYN, V., 'Sotsial'no-psikhologicheskie rezervy rosta proiz' voditel'-nosti truda', *Sotsialisticheskii Trud* (1979) No. 8, pp. 92–8.

PANOV, YE., *Sotsialisticheskaya Industriya*, 7 March 1982, p. 3.

PARASYUK, V., *Sotsialisticheskaya Industriya*, 26 January 1983, p. 1.

PARFENOV, V., *Izvestia*, 21 July 1972, p. 1; *Pravda*, 30 June 1973, p. 2; *Pravda*, 28 May 1979, p. 5; *Pravda*, 7 April 1980, p. 2; *Pravda*, 10 August 1981, p. 2.

PARFENOV, V. and CHERKASOV, V. *Pravda*, 9 March 1977, p. 2.

PARFENOV, V. and SHVETSOV, V., *Pravda*, 28 March 1977, p. 2; *Pravda*, 29 March 1977, p. 2.

PASHUTA, N. T. and KULIKOV, G. T., *Kollektivnye formy organizatsii truda*, Moscow (1983).

PECHKUROV, E., 'Shchekinskii opyt i ekonomiya truda na morskom transporte', *Sotsialisticheskii Trud* (1981) No. 5, pp. 63–6.

PEREVEDENTSEV, V., 'Vosproizvodstvo naseleniya i sem'ya', *Sotsiologicheskie Issledovaniya* (1982) No. 2, pp. 80–7.

——, 'Migratsiya naseleniya i razvitie sel'skokhozyaistvennogo proizvodstva', *Sotsiologicheskie Issledovaniya* (1983) No. 1, pp. 54–61.

PESHEKHONOV, Yu., *Ekonomicheskaya Gazeta* (1983) No. 46, p. 15.

PLATONOV, A., and SHELYD'KO, M. 'Ministerstvo – organizator vnedreniya Shchekinskogo metoda', *Sotsialisticheskii Trud* (1978), No. 12, pp. 18–21.

PODMARKOV, V. G., ZAITSEV, A. K. and NOVIKOV, V. V., 'Problemy zavodskoi sotsiologii', *Sotsiologicheskie Issledovaniya* (1977) No. 3, pp. 162–9.

PODOROV, G. M., 'Opyt sotsiologicheskikh issledovaniya trudovoi distsipliny na predpriyatiyakh Gor'kovskoi oblasti', *Sotsiologicheskie Issledovaniya* (1976) No. 4, pp. 72–8.

PODUGOL'NIKOV, I. and SHCHERBATYKH, V., 'Organizuyushchaya rol' ministerstva', *Sotsialisticheskii Trud* (1978) No. 8, pp. 20–5.

POGOSYAN, G., 'Voprosy sovershenstvovaniya normirovaniya truda', *Planovoe Khozyaistvo* (1977) No. 4, pp. 109–14.

POKROVSKII, V., *Ekonomicheskaya Gazeta*, No. 14 (1984), p. 4.

POPOV, G., *Pravda*, 27 December 1980, p. 3.

POPRYDKIN, M., *Pravda Ukrainy*, 9 July 1982, p. 2.

PONOMAREV, L., 'Trudovoe vospitanie i kollektiv', *Sotsialisticheskii Trud* (1980) No. 1, pp. 7–16.

'Poryadok primeneniya Shchekinskogo metoda sovershenstvovaniya organisatsii truda, material'no go stimulirovaniya i planirovaniya', *Sotsialisticheskii Trud* (1978) No. 7, pp. 9–11.

Pravda, 9 October 1969, p. 1; 19 March 1973, p. 1; 27 January 1974, p. 3; 13 January 1976, p. 2; 7 March 1976, p. 1; 29 March 1977, p. 2; 30 April 1977, p. 2; 26 July, 1978, p. 1; 24 February 1981, p. 1; 5 March 1981, p. 1; 8 December 1982, p. 2; 12 November 1983, p. 1; 3 December 1983, p. 1.

PRAVDA, A., 'Is There a Soviet Working Class?', *Problems of Communism* No. 6 (1982), pp. 1–24.

PREOBRAZHENSKY, E. *The New Economics*, Oxford (1965).

Problemy ispol'zovaniya rabochei sily v uslobiyakh nauchno-tekhnicheskoi revolyutsii, Moscow (1973).

PROKHVATILOV, S., *Trud*, 1 November 1975, p. 2.

PROKOFIEV, M., *Pravda*, 7 August 1982, p. 3.
PURDY, D. 'The Soviet Union. State Capitalist or Socialist?', *Communist Party Pamphlet* (1976).
RAD'KO, *Literaturnaya Gazeta*, 16 May 1979, p. 13.
RADOV, A., *Sovetskaya Rossiya*, 19 July 1981, pp. 2–3; *Sovetskaya Rossiya*, 22 July 1981, pp. 2–3; *Sovetskaya Rossiya*, 24 July 1981, p. 2.
RAKOVSKI, M. *Towards an East European Marxism*, London (1978).
——, 'Marxism and Soviet Societies', *Capital and Class*, No. 1 (1977), pp. 83–104.
RAKOVSKY, C., 'The Five Year Plan in Crisis', *Critique*, No. 13 (1981), pp. 7–55.
RALIS, M., 'Workers' Social Perceptions', in Shapiro and Godson (eds), pp. 21–55.
RIAKUSHKIN, T. and GALETSKAYA, R., 'Dinamika i struktura naseleniia SSSR za 60 let', *Voprosy Ekonomiki* (1982) No. 9, pp. 10–19.
ROGOVSKII, N. 'Effektivnost' truda: problemy ee rosta', *Planovoe Khozyaistvo* (1976) No. 5, pp. 20–8.
——, Mekhanizatsiya ruchnogo truda – aktual'naya narodnokhozyaistvennaya zadacha', *Planovoe Khozyaistvo* (1977) No. 9, pp. 18–24.
——, "Effektivnost' truda v odinnadtsatoi pyatletke', *Voprosy Ekonomiki* (1982) No. 1, pp. 3–11.
ROSE, H. and ROSE, S. (eds), *The Political Economy of Science*, London (1976).
ROSE, M., *Industrial Behaviour*, London (1975).
RUBIN, I. I., *Essays on Marx's Theory of Value*, Detroit (1972).
RUMER, B., 'Soviet Investment Policy: Unresolved Problems', *Problems of Communism*, No. 5 (1982), pp. 53–68.
RUSANOV, E. S., *Ratsional'noe ispol'zovanie trudovykh resursov i rost proizvoditel'nosti truda*, Moscow (1983).
RUTKEVICH, M., *Sovetskaya Rossiya*, 21 August 1983, p. 3.
RUTLAND, P. 'The Shchekino Method and the Struggle to Raise Labour Productivity in Soviet Industry', *Soviet Studies*, Vol. 36, No. 3 (1984), pp. 345–365.
N. RYZHKOV, 'Nekotorye voprosy planovogo rukovodstva ekonomikoi', *Planovoe Khozyaistvo* (1982) No. 8, pp. 3–13.
RZHEVUSKII, A., *Ekonomicheskaya Gazeta* (1980) No. 46, p. 8.
SAMARTSEVA, T., *Literaturnaya Gazeta*, 24 September 1980, p. 10.
SAPOV, V., *Pravda*, 21 April 1982, p. 3.
SARNO, A. A., SLOBODSKOI, A. L., FAIBUSHEVICH, S. I., CHERKASOV, G. K., 'O nekotorykh aspektakh stanovleniya brigadnoi organizatsii truda', *Sotsiologicheskie Issledovaniya* (1983) No. 2, pp. 96–102.
SCHAPIRO, L. and GODSON, J., *The Soviet Worker. Illusions and Realities*, London (1981).
SCHROEDER, G., 'Soviet Economic Reforms at an Impasse', *Problems of Communism*, No. 4 (1971).
——, 'The Soviet Economy on a Treadmill of Reforms', in *Soviet Economy in a Time of Change*, pp. 312–336.
SCHWARZ, S., *Labour in the Soviet Union*, London (1953).
SEKACHEV, V. A., 'Praktika raspredeleniya zarabotka v usloviyakh brigad-

noi formy organizatssi i stimulirovaniya truda', in Shurueva (ed.), pp. 58–65.

SELYUNIN, V., *Sotsialisticheskaya Industriya*, 24 June 1976, p. 2; *Sotsialisticheskaya Industriya*, 2 March 78, p. 2; *Sotsialisticheskaya Industriya*, 7 June 1979, p. 2.

SEMIN, S. G. 'Novye rezervy Shchekinskogo metoda', *Ekonomika i organizatsiya promyshlennogo proizvodstva* (1976) No. 4, pp. 92–102.

SEVAST'YANOV, V. 'Trudnyi perekhod', *Kommunist* (1977), No. 7, pp. 37–46; *Pravda*, 12 December 1972, p. 2; *Pravda*, 20 May 1973, p. 2; *Pravda*, 18 December 1973, p. 2; *Pravda*, 3 April 1974, p. 2.

SEYMOUR, J., 'Why the USSR is not Capitalist', *Spartacus League Pamphlet*, New York (1977).

SHAFRANOV, O. I., *Ratsional'noe ispol'zovanie trudovykh resursov neotlozhenaia zadacha*, Moscow (1980).

SHAROV, P. 'Partiinaya organizatsiya Shchekinskogo khimkombinata', in *Bor'ba za ukreplenie distsipliny truda i sotsialisticheskogo distsiplina: opyt problemy*, Moscow (1975).

——, *Pravda*, 12 October 1969, p. 2; *Ekonomicheskaya Gazeta* (1975) No. 49, p. 10; *Ekonomicheskaya Gazeta* (1976) No. 13, p. 6.

SHILIN, I. G., *Effecktivnost' proizvodstva i material'noe stimulirovanie*, Moscow (1969).

SHIMANSKII, V., *Pravda*, 17 August 1983, p. 3.

SHIMENKOV, P., 'Ratsional'no ekonomno ispol'zovat' trudovye resursy', *Sotsialisticheskii Trud* (1981) No. 4, pp. 109–15.

SHISHKOV, Yu., 'Uchenie K. Marksa o bezrabotitse i sovremennost'', *Voprosy Ekonomiki* (1983) No. 5, pp. 37–48.

SHKARATAN, O. I., *Problemy sotsial' noi struktury rabochego klassa SSSR*, Moscow (1970).

SHKURKO, S. I., *Po primeru Shchekinskogo khimicheskogo kombinata, (stimulirovanie rosta proizvoditel'nosti truda)*, Moscow (1971).

——, Voprosy stimuliravaniya proizvoditel'nosti truda', *Planovoe khozyaistvo* (1971) No. 8, pp. 10–18.

——, *Stimulirovanie kachestva i effektivnosti proizvodstva*, Moscow (1977).

——, 'Novye formy brigadnoi organizatsii i stimulirovaniya truda', *Voprosy Ekonomiki* (1980), No. 10, pp. 26–36.

SHURUEVA, V. N. (ed.), *Brigadnaya forma organizatsii i stimulirovaniya truda*, Moscow (1983).

SIDOROV, V. A., 'Effektivnost' truda i kachestvo podgotovki rabochikh kadrov', *Ekonomika i organizatsiya promyshlennogo proizvodstva* (1981) No. 1, pp. 149–65.

SILIN, V. and SUKHOV, A., 'Rezervy effektivnosti', *Planovoe Khozyaistvo* (1977) No. 4, pp. 93–103.

——, 'Distsiplina i otvetstvennost – vazhnye usloviya dostizheniya effektivnosti', *Planovoe Khozyaistvo* (1982) No. 4, pp. 37–45.

SIMAKOV, A., *Komsomol'skaya Pravda*, 23 January 1980, p. 2.

SIMENENKO, G. K., *Ekonomicheskaya Gazeta* (1983) No. 51, p. 7.

SIMON, W. (ed.), *The Soviet Codes of Law*, The Hague (1980).

SLAVINA, S. and KOGAN, V., 'Pensioner prishel na proizvodstvo kakie usloviya nado emu sozdat'', *Sotsialisticheskii Trud* (1978) No. 10, pp. 135–9.

SLEPYKH, V., *Sotsialisticheskii Trud*, 30 November 1975, p. 3.
SLEZINGER, G., 'Reglamentatsiya truda ITR i sluzhashchikh', *Ekonomika i organizatsiya promyshlennogo proizvodstva* (1979) No. 8, pp. 79–90.
SLIDER, D., 'Reforming the Workplace: The 1983 Soviet Law on Labour Collectives', *Soviet Studies*, Vol. 37, No. 2 (1985), pp. 173–83.
Slovar' Ekonomiki i Organizatsiya Proizvodstva, Moscow (1983).
SKARUPO, Z., 'Sokrashchenie tekuchesti i ulushchenie ispol'zovaniya rabochei sily', *Planovoe Khozyaistvo* (1977) No. 6, pp. 118–25.
SMELYAKOV, N., *Trud*, 24 July 1981, p. 3.
SMIRNOV, S., *Ekonomicheskaya Gazeta* (1984), No. 14, p. 14.
SMIRNOVA, A. D. and SABO, K. (eds), *Obshchestvennaya forma truda pri sotsialisme*, Moscow (1984).
SMITH, G. A. E., 'The Political Economy of the Soviet Reforms', *Critique*, No. 4 (1975), pp. 27–43.
——, 'The Soviet Debt Problem', *Critique*, No. 7 (1976), pp. 82–8.
——, 'The Industrial Problems of Soviet Agriculture', *Critique*, No. 14 (1981), pp. 41–67.
SMITH, H., *The Russians*, London (1976).
SMYSHLYAEVA, L. 'Sovershenstvovanie vosproizvodstvennoi struktury kapital'nykh vlozhenii, *Voprosy Ekonomiki* (1983) No. 9, pp. 25–35.
SOBESLAVSKY, V. and BEAZLEY, P., *The Transfer of Technology to Socialist Countries*, Cambridge Mass. (1980).
SOBGAIDE, T., *Ekonomicheskaya Gazeta* (1977) No. 4, p. 8.
'Solidarity and the Soviet Bloc', *Workers Under Communism Symposium* (1982) No. 2, pp. 6–14.
SONIN, M. Ya., 'Effektivno ispol'zovat' trudovye resursy', *Ekonomika i organizatsiya promyshlennogo proizvodstva* (1977) No. 4, pp. 3–12.
——, 'Problemy raspredeleniya i ispol'zovaniya trudovykh resursov', *Sotsialisticheskii Trud* (1977) No. 3, pp. 65–79.
——, 'Ravnie prava, neravnye nagruzki', *Ekonomika i organizatsiya promyshlennogo proizvodstva* (1978) No. 3, pp. 5–19.
——. 'Zametki o trudovoi distsipline', *Ekonomika i organizatsiya promyshlennogo proizvodstva* (1981) No. 5, pp. 65–79.
SONIN, M. Ya. and ZHILTSOV, 'Formirovat' mobil'nye rezervy kadrov', *Ekonomika i organizatsiya promyshlennogo proizvodstva* (1974) No. 1, pp. 125–30.
SONIN, M. Ya. and STRUMILIN, S. G., 'Alkogol'nye poteri i bor'ba s nimi', *Ekonomika i organizatsiya promyshlennogo proizvodstva* (1974) No. 4, p. 36–44.
SOROKIN, G. 'Zakonomernost' sotsialisticheskie intensifikatsii', *Voprosy Ekonomiki* (1982) No. 10, pp. 108–18.
SOSIN, Yu. P., 'Faktory ukrepleniya trudovoi distsipliny', *Ekonomika i organizatsiya promyshlennogo proizvodstva* (1975) No. 5, pp. 166–73.
Sotsialisticheskaya Industriya, 19 December 1973, p. 4; 31 October 1979, p. 4; 17 May 1981, p. 4.
'Sotsiologicheskie issledovaniya – na sluzhbu stroitel'stvu kommunizma', *Sotsiologicheskie Issledovaniya* (1976) No. 2, p. 8.
SOVTSOV, Yu. and SOKOLOV, A., *Komsomol'skaya Pravda*, 13 April 1980, p. 2.
SSSR v tsifrakh v 1977 godu, Moscow (1978).

SSR v tsifrakh v 1984 godu, Moscow (1985).

STALIN, J. V., *The Economic Problems of Socialism in the USSR*, Peking (1972).

'Statisticheskie materialy o potreblenii alkogol'nykh napitov i ego posledst-viyakh', *Molodoi Kommunist* (1975) No. 9, pp. 103–5.

STOLYANOV, V., *Sotsialisticheskaya Industriya*, 13 July 1982, p. 2.

STOREY, J., *Managerial Prerogative and the Question of Control*, London (1983).

SUKHACHEVSKII, V., *Izvestia*, 2 January 1984, p. 2.

SUKHANOV, V., *Izvestia*, 6 April 1975, p. 3.

SVERDLIK, Sh. B., 'Rost sberezhenii naseleniya: prichiny i sledstviya', *Ekonomika i organizatsiya promyshlennogo proizvodstva* (1982) No. 6, pp. 115–30.

——, 'Proizvoditel'nost' truda i ego oplata', *Ekonomika i organizatsiya promyshlennogo proizvodstva* (1985) No. 4, pp. 102–17.

SVIRCHEVSKII, V. and NIKOL'SKII, D., 'Razvitie brigadnoi formy organizatsii i stimulirovaniya truda v promyshlennosti' *Vestnik Statistiki* (1984) No. 2, pp. 16–18.

SWEEZY, P. and BETTELHEIM, C., *On the Transition to Socialism*, London (1971).

TAYLOR, F. W., *The Principles of Scientific Management*, New York (1947).

TAYLOR, L. and WALTON, P., 'Industrial Sabotage: Motives and Meanings', in *Images of Deviance*, S. Cohen (ed.).

TCHITANAVA, N., *Kommunisti*, 3 September 1978, pp. 2–3.

TEAGUE, E., 'Worker Discontent in the Soviet Union', *Workers Under Communism* (1982) No. 2, pp. 22–25.

——, 'Workers' Control or Workers Controlled', *Workers Under Communism* (1983) No. 4, p. 23.

——, 'The USSR Law on Work Collectives: Workers' Control or Workers Controlled?' in Lane (ed.), pp. 239–55.

——, 'Labour Discipline and Legislation in the USSR 1979–85', *RL Supplement*, No. 2 (1985).

TECKENBERG, W., 'Labour Turnover and Job Satisfaction: Indicators of Conflict in the USSR', *Soviet Studies* Vol. 30 (1978) No. 2, pp. 193–211.

THALHEIM, K. C., 'The Balance Sheet', in *The New Economic Systems of Eastern Europe*, London (1975).

THOMPSON, P., *The Nature of Work*, London (1984).

TICKTIN, H. H., 'Towards a Political Economy of the USSR', *Critique* No. 1 (1973) pp. 20–41.

——, 'Contradictions of Soviet Society and Professor Bettelheim', *Critique* No. 6 (1976) pp. 17–44.

——, 'Class Structure and the Soviet Elite', *Critique* No. 9 (1978) pp. 37–62.

——, 'The Political Economy of the Gorbachev Era', *Critique* No. 17 (1986a), pp. 113–35.

——, 'Reply to Molyneux', *Critique* No. 19 (Forthcoming 1986b).

TIKIDZHIEV, R., 'Voprosy balansirovannosti vozproizvodsvta osonov-nykh fondov i trudovykh resursov', *Planovoe Khozyaistvo* (1981) No. 12, pp. 44–53.

TOKAREV, A., *Izvestia*, 16 December 1975, p. 2.

TOLSTIKOV, M. Ya., *Sovetskaya Estonia*, 18 September 1968, p. 2.
TRISKA, J. and GATI, C., *Blue-Collar Workers in Eastern Europe*, London (1981).
Trud, 13 July 1973, p. 2; 29 December 1982, p. 2.
TSAREV, Yu. F., 'Opyt vnedreniya brigadnogo khozyaistvennogo rascheta', in Shurueva (ed.), pp. 53–57.
TSELIKOV, A., *Trud*, 24 July 1981, p. 2.
Tsk KPSS, *Pravda*, 9 October 1968, p. 1; *Pravda*, 9 October 1969, p. 1; *Pravda*, 17 March 1985, p. 1.
——, 'O dal'neishem razvitii i povyshenii effektivnosti brigadnoi formy organizatsii i stimulirovaniya truda v promyshlennosti', *Pravda*, 4 December 1983.
TsK KPSS I SOVETA MINISTROV SSSR, 'Ob opyte raboty partinogo komiteta Shchekinskogo khimkombinata po mobilizatsii kollektiva trudyashchikhsya na uvelichenie ob'emov proizvodstva za schet rosta proizvoditel'nosti truda', in *Resheniya partii i pravitel'stva po khozyaistvennym voprosam*, Moscow (1970).
——, 'Ob uluchshenii planirovaniya i usilenii vozdeistviya khozyaistvennogo mekhanizma na povyshenie effektivnosti proizvodstva i kachestva raboty', in *Resheniya partii i pravitel'stva po khozyaistvennym voprosam*, Vol. 13, 1979–81, Moscow (1981).
TSVETKOV, B., 'Nauchno-tekhnicheskii progress i problemy vysvobozhdeniya rabochei sily v promyshlennosti', *Sotsialisticheskii Trud* (1980) No. 3, pp. 72–8.
TURBANOV, A., *Izvestia*, 5 March 1974, p. 3.
TUSHINOV, Yu., *Pravda*, 13 May 1980, p. 2.
UDOVICHENKO, Yu. N., 'Sotsiologicheskii lokator rukovoditelya', *Ekonomika i organizatsiya promyshlennogo proizvodstva* (1980) No. 10, pp. 31–7.
ULYBIN, K. A., 'Defitsit i vzaimodeistvie partnerov', *Ekonomika i organizatsiya promyshlennogo proizvodstva* (1984) No. 12, pp. 22–31.
Upravlenie narodnym khozyaistvom slovar', Moscow (1983).
USHKALOV, I., 'Effektivnost' ispol'zovaniya trudovykh resursov v stranakh-chlenakh SEV (Obzor)', *Voprosy Ekonomiki* (1977) No. 4, pp. 123–31.
VALAVOI, D., *Pravda*, 10 November 1977, p. 2; *Pravda*, 11 November 1977, p. 2; *Pravda*, 12 November 1977, p. 2.
VALAVOI, D., NIKITIN, A., SHVETSOV, V., *Pravda*, 14 June 1982, p. 3.
VARAVKA, V., *Pravda*, 11 January 1979, p. 3.
VARLAMOV, K., *Socialist Management. The Leninist Concept*, Moscow (1977).
VASIL'EVA, E. K., *The Young People of Leningrad, Work Options and Education* (1976).
VASIL'EVA, V., *Sotsialisticheskaya Industriya*, 27 September 1980, p. 2.
VASIN, M., *Pravda*, 26 April 1981, p. 2; *Pravda*, 27 April 1981, p. 2; *Pravda*, 20 April 1983, p. 2.
Vestnik Statistiki (1979), No. 2, p. 79; (1983), No. 4, p. 60; (1984), No. 1, p. 65; (1984), No. 3; (1984), No. 4, p. 66–9; (1984), No. 11, p. 36–7; (1984), No. 11, pp. 52–3; (1984), No. 12, pp. 68–9.

VOLGIN, A., *Pravda*, 28 December 1982, p. 3.
VOLGIN, A. and SIDYAKIN, K. N., 'Kak sokratit' poteri rabochego vremeni', *Sotsiologicheskie Issledovaniya* (1985) No. 4, pp. 41–7.
VOLKOV, K., *Ekonomicheskaya Gazeta*, 31 July 1983, p. 10.
VOLOVICH, G., *Izvestia*, 7 March 73, p. 2.
VON HAYEK, F., 'The Present Stage of the Debate', in *Collectivist Economic Planning*, London (1935).
VON MISES, L., 'Economic Calculation in the Socialist Commonwealth', in *Collectivist Economic Planning*, London (1935).
——, *Socialism: An Economic and Sociological Analysis*, London (1969).
VORONIN, E., 'Polnee ispol'zovat'trudovye resursy', *Planovoe Khozyaistvo* (1980) No. 9, pp. 34–43.
'Vospitanie sotsialisticheskoi distsipliny truda', *Sotsialisticheskii Trud* (1975), No. 7, pp. 11–41.
VYCHUB, G., *Sovetskaya Kultura*, 8 December 1981, p. 3.
WADEKIN, K., 'What is New About Brigades in Agriculture?', *RL* 47/1985.
WALLERSTEIN, I., *The Capitalist World Economy*, Cambridge (1979).
WANG, G. C. (ed.), *The Fundamentals of Political Economy*, White Plains (1977).
WATSON, B., 'Counterplanning on the Factory Floor', *Radical America Pamphlet*, Boston (1971).
WEI CHI, *The Soviet Union Under the New Tsars*, Peking (1978).
WILCZYNSKI, J., *The Economics of Socialism*, London (1978).
WILES, P., *Economic Institutions Compared*, London (1977).
YAFFE, D. and BULLOCKE, P., 'Inflation, Crisis and the Post-War Boom', *Revolutionary Communist* No. 3/4 (1975).
YAKUSHENKO, J., *Pravda*, 11 January 1983, p. 2.
YANHOVA, Z., *Literaturnaya Gazeta*, 5 March 1980, p. 11.
YANOWITCH, M. (ed.), *Soviet Work Attitudes. The Issue of Participation in Management*, London (1979).
——, *Work in the Soviet Union*, New York (1985).
YANOWITCH, M. and FISHER, W., *Social Stratification and Mobility in the USSR*, New York (1973).
——, *Social and Economic Inequality in the Soviet Union*, London (1977).
YAZINSKII, A., *Pravda*, 10 March 1986, p. 2.
YUNAK, I., 'Shchekinskii metod stimuliruet ratsional'noe ispol'zovanie kadrov', *Sotsialisticheskii Trud* (1984) No. 4, pp. 7–14.
ZAGAITOV, I. and POLOVINKIN, P., 'Ustoichivost sel'skohozyaistven-nogo proizvodstva', *Voprosy Ekonomiki* (1984) No. 1, pp. 75–85.
ZAIGREEV, G. G., 'O nekotorykh osobennostyakh profilaktiki p'yanstva', *Sotsiologicheskie Issledovaniya* (1983) No. 4, pp. 96–105.
ZASLAVSKAYA, T., 'The Novosibirsk Report', with an introduction by P. Hanson, in *Survey*, Vol. 28, No. 1 (1984), pp. 83–108.
——, *Sovetskaya Rossiya*, 7 January (1986a), p. 1.
——, 'Tvorcheskaya aktivnost' mass: sotsial'nye rezervy rosta', *Ekonomika i organizatsiya promyshlennogo proizvodstva* (1986b) No. 3, pp. 3–25.
ZDRAVOMYSLOV, A., *Pravda*, 23 September 1983, pp. 2–3.
ZDRAVOMYSLOV, ROZHIN and IADOV, *Man and His Work* (1970).

ZELICHONOK, M. and MILYAVSKY, I., *Pravda*, 18 October 1970, p. 2; *Pravda*, 9 March 1971, p. 2.

ZHARIKOV, V., 'Shchekinskii metod i organizatorskaya rabota na pred-priyatii', *Sotsialisticheskii Trud* (1979) No. 10, pp. 47–52.

ZLOBIN, N., *Pravda*, 15 March 1972, p. 2; *Pravda*, 23 September 1972, p. 2; *Trud*, 15 December 1981, p. 6.

ZORKAL'TSEV, V. I., 'Anatomiya defitsita. Voprosy bez otveta', *Ekono-mika i organizatsiya promyshlennogo proizvodstva*, No. 2 (1982), pp. 84–95.

ZOTOV, M., 'Intensifikatsiia investitsionnogo protsessa', *Voprosy Ekono-miki* (1984) No. 2, pp. 15–24.

ZOTOV, V., *Sotsialisticheskaya Industriya*, 5 March 1983, p. 1.

Name Index

Abalkin, L. 53, 65, 98, 248, 250, 259
Abramov, G. 162
Afanas'ev, A. 80
Aganbegyan, A. 53, 57, 179, 188, 191, 240, 243, 245–9
Agronovskii, A. 204, 206–9, 212–13
Aitov, N. 56, 77
Aleksandrova, E. and Fedorovskaya, E. 52
Alekseev, N. 238–9
Andrle, V. 114
Andropov, Yu. 31, 68–9, 71, 194, 243, 248, 254, 272–3
Antip'ev, A. G. 233
Antonov, N. 112, 118, 139, 150–1, 167, 174
Antosenkov, E. 247–8
Antropov, Yu. and Lyakutin, V. 229, 232
Aper'yan, N. 67
Aper'yan, V. 60
Armeyev, R. and Illarionov, A. 76
Arnot, R. 267, 271

Bachurin, A. 54, 160
Bahro, R. 268
Baibakov, A. 55, 166
Baiderin, V. and Turbanov, A. 208
Balashov, B. 59
Baran, P. 13
Baranenkova, T. 58, 73, 75, 77–9, 84, 89, 117, 120–1, 127–8, 166–7, 191, 217, 219, 222–3, 247
Barbashov, V. 219
Batkaev, P. 165, 181, 189, 191
Batkaev, P. and Semin, S. 188–90
Belkin, V. 51
Belotserkovsky, V. 31, 98, 101
Berliner, J. 1, 40–1, 98, 267
Berri, L. 30, 93
Beynon, H. 13
Binns, P. and Haynes, M. 134, 267
Birman, I. 38
Blackburn, R. 39
Blyakhman, L. and Shkaratan, O. 21–2, 24
Bogomolov, G. and Vanyarkin, P. 186
Boiko, T. 51

Boiter, A. 31
Boldryev, V. 118, 152–3, 160, 166, 168–9
Borchenko, N. 270
Bornstein, M. 87
Borodin, V. 186, 191
Brada, J. 32
Braverman, H. 4, 13, 16, 267
Breev, B. 93, 245, 247
Brezhnev, L. I. 31, 72, 74, 77, 165, 190, 235, 243
Brus, W. 88, 134, 267
Buck, T. 267
Bunich, P. G. 35, 86, 159, 215, 221, 241–2, 262, 272
Burawoy, M. 72
Burenkov, M. 220
Butenko, A. 271

Cherednichenko, K. K. and Gol'din, I. I. 112, 118, 140, 144, 146, 149, 154, 158–9, 162, 164, 173, 180, 186
Cherevan, V. 88
Chernenko, C. 71, 243, 271
Chernichenko, A. 88
Chernov, V. 219–20, 223, 230
Chubanov, Y. 85, 181
Cliff, T. 268
Cockburn, P. 250, 254
Cooley, M. 16
Cooper, J. 55
Corrigan, P., Ramsay, H. and Sayer, D. 267

Danilov, L. 55
Danilov, L. and Korchagin, V. 161
De Souza, P. 78
Delamotte, J. 105, 107–9, 128–9, 135–6, 149, 270
Denisenko, I. 183–4
Dmitryev, I. 211
Drewnowski, J. 269
Drozdov, V. 163
Dubois, P. 13–14, 72
Dyachenko, V. 63
Dybtsyn, A. 177
Dyker, D. 134, 194
Dymitrev, A. and Lopata, P. 62

Subject Index

Abasha experiment 194–5
absenteeism 28
  extent and effects of 75
  management complicity 75
  underreporting 75 .
Aksai plastics plant 202
  experimental initiative 238–41, 251
alcohol abuse 28, 76
  and labour productivity 28, 76
  and industrial accidents 76
  and absenteeism 76
  managerial complicity 76
Andropov discipline campaign 71, 243,
  254, 272n
  economic experiment (January
  1984) 194, 248
arrhythmic work patterns 41, 75, 79,
  264
  and labour shortage 93
Astrakhan ship repair yards 223
auxiliary sector 58, 98
  need for work norms 84

Bashkir Petro-chemical
  Association 127, 157, 169, 191–2
  in the 10th Five Year Plan 188
  variant of Shchekino
  experiment 149–52
Brezhnev
  on labour discipline 72
  on slow spread of brigades 235
brigade system of labour organisation
  auxiliary workers 219, 230
  average brigade sizes 220, 228
  brigade council 219, 224, 234
  brigade leader 219, 233
  brigade leaders' council 220, 238
  bureaucratic complexity 212, 246
  coefficient of labour participation
  (KTU) 219, 221–2, 229–32, 235,
  248, 272n
  collective disciplining
  mechanism 221, 234
  criticism of slow generalisation 235
  criticism of Zlobin brigades 204–5
  cross shift brigades 218, 227, 229
  disciplinary powers 234, 237

  extension of system to
  industry 217–37
  extent in construction 214–5, 236
  formal structure 219–20, 272n
  ideal brigade structure 227, 230–1
  instability of brigade
  conditions 212–3, 218, 231–2
  integrated brigades 220, 228
  job combination 222, 228
  Kaluga variant 209–10, 214
  khozraschet or contract brigades 203,
  207, 209, 212–6, 224, 230–1, 259
  labour discipline effects 204, 210,
  217, 223, 237
  labour productivity 203, 207, 214,
  216, 222
  leadership problems 204, 232–3, 237
  legal requirements and status 206,
  211
  machine building industry 217
  management problems 205
  material incentives 206, 216, 233–4
  number of brigades 225, 272n
  number of workers in brigades 226–7
  optimum brigade size 228
  Orel variant 210–11
  payment by final results 221
  planning from achieved level 213,
  234, 236
  problems of contract
  specification 205, 211, 216–8,
  231–2
  problems of generalisation 208–17
  problems of integration and size 218
  relations with management 220,
  233–4, 259
  resistance to 208, 233–4
  single shift brigades 219, 227
  specialist brigades 220, 228
  supply difficulties 206, 208–9, 232
  trouble-shooters 212, 260
  uneven introduction 228, 231
  Zlobin brigades in
  construction 202–8, 253
  1974 regulations 214
  1979 Planning resolution 224
  1983 regulations 237